The Art of the
French Illustrated Book
1700 to 1914

VOLUME I

(77)   Fragonard, preliminary etching for "On ne s'avise jamais de tout"

The Art of the
French Illustrated Book
1700 to 1914

VOLUME I

Gordon N. Ray

The Pierpont Morgan Library

Cornell University Press

Formal bibliographical descriptions by
THOMAS V. LANGE

Photography by
CHARLES V. PASSELA

This publication has been made possible, in part, by grants from the National Endowment for the Humanities, an agency of the United States Government.

First published 1982 by The Pierpont Morgan Library and Cornell University Press.

Published in the United Kingdom by Cornell University Press LTD, Ely House, 37 Dover Street, London WIX 4HQ.

CLOTHBOUND EDITION
International Standard Book Number 0–8014–1535–7

PAPERBOUND EDITION
International Standard Book Number 87598–078–3

Library of Congress Catalog Card Number 82–80086

Table of Contents

The Franklin Jasper Walls Lectures

FRANKLIN JASPER WALLS, who died in 1963, bequeathed his residuary estate to The Pierpont Morgan Library to establish a lecture series in the fine arts, iconography, and archaeology, with the provision that the lectures be ultimately published in book form.

Throughout his life, Mr. Walls was interested in the fine arts and in the study of art history. When the Association of Fellows of The Pierpont Morgan Library was organized in 1949, he became one of the founding members. He was particularly concerned with the Library's lecture program, and served on the Association's Lecture Committee. Without ever revealing his testamentary plans, he followed with keen attention the design and construction of the Library's new Lecture Hall, completed a few months before his death.

Dr. Ray's lectures, an interpretation of the material in this book, are the sixth series of the Franklin Jasper Walls Lectures to be published.

Preface

THESE TWO VOLUMES represent a culmination in a long series of works published by the Morgan Library concerning the art of the book. During the last decade we have been especially interested in creating a "musée du livre" which would reflect our broad interests in the book, including its illustration and binding, and our institutional strengths, which lie as much in the museum world as that of the Library. In 1976, in my Preface to Dr. Gordon Ray's study of *The Illustrator and the Book in England from 1790 to 1914*, I described our exhibition and publication program which had helped to develop this museum of the book. We have always been conscious that a detailed study of French book illustration was central to it. As Dr. Ray reconfirms here, the French tradition is without question the richest in the world. There was an early period of French dominance in the Renaissance; then from the beginning of the eighteenth century until our own time the achievement of the French has always been remarkable, and during three eras in these 214 years, superlative.

This is the most comprehensive history of French book illustration for the period it covers. Dealing in depth with albums of Romantic lithographs, it is more complete than any study in French. The fullest account in that language is now fifty years old, and there has never been any detailed general survey in English. The need and the importance of these two large volumes should therefore be immediately apparent.

All of the techniques of book illustration—except photography, which would require a separate investigation—are discussed as we go through the years 1700–1914, one or another style or medium prevailing in the various periods. "Whatever the technique," Dr. Ray explains, "French craftsmanship was usually equal or superior to that anywhere else in the world." In these two hundred years and more, painting and draftsmanship in France were often preeminent, and the list of French artists was larger and more distinguished than that for any other country. Almost all of the great painters also illustrated books. Only a very few of the artists did not: the names of Watteau, Greuze, Lancret, Natoire, Ingres, Renoir, Moreau, Seurat, and Cézanne are ones that come to mind. Most of the other masters are here, so that reading these two volumes will be for many persons a discovery of a new aspect of the mainstream of art history from 1700 to 1914.

Drawings for illustrations are often included in discussions of the books, and bindings must also be taken into account, for French collectors of the illustrated book have for the last two centuries usually demanded not only great artists and printers, but also fine papers, various states of the plates, added drawings, and special bindings. The true collector sought out the exceptional copy of a book. As Dr. Ray writes in his Introduction, "It is appropriate that *bibliophile* should be a French word, for the collectors of that country have always treasured every aspect of the ambiance of the copies that have come their way."

As in the volume *The Illustrator and the Book in England from 1790 to 1914*, more than nine-tenths of the books described here come from the collection of Dr. Ray. Once again he has written an "Introduction for Collectors" in which he explains the principles he has followed and the opportunities he has had for building this part of his library. He describes the possibilities during the last twenty-five years, and today, for forming such a collection of French illustrated books. These books, in special collectors' copies, have generally been expensive, although they have been available throughout Europe and America. There have, however, been many years when one kind or another of these illustrated books was unfashionable and hence underpriced. The story of the decline and fall and rise again of interest in the finest French books, and the special chances for buying them in the past two decades, makes fascinating reading. It is doubtful if there will again be the opportunity for a public or private collector to form such a comprehensive library. "I had the sort of run with regard to French illustrated books," Dr. Ray writes, "that the most fortunate collector can hope to experience only two or three times during his life. . . . Today the interest of collectors in illustrated books has reached a peak, extending to nearly every country, period, and technique."

The story of this collection therefore forms a chapter in the history of taste in the illustrated book. For its total scope, there is no rival for Dr. Ray's collection among private libraries, and the scholar-collector who formed it is also uniquely able to discuss and analyze the books it contains. We are most grateful and very proud to present the results of Gordon Ray's scholarship and connoisseurship, and his equally brilliant success in capturing so many outstanding books for his collection. He has devoted almost twenty-five years to building it, and several years to planning and writing these two volumes. Of course, during these years he was also a professor, and since 1960 he has been at the John Simon Guggenheim Memorial Foundation, of which he became President nearly twenty years ago. His service to universities, libraries, and bibliophilic organizations throughout this country is famous. He continues to write articles and books on many subjects, but surely these volumes form one of his most important contributions to knowledge.

We at the Morgan Library are therefore thankful to Dr. Ray, Vice-President of our Board of Trustees, for all that he has done to prepare these volumes, and we are pleased to note that his books described here will remain on deposit in the Library. Our former staff member Mr. Thomas V. Lange wrote the bibliographical descriptions; the photographs were taken at the Morgan Library by Mr. Charles V. Passela, assisted by Mr. C. Mitchell Carl. Dr. Anna Lou Ashby in particular helped with the installation of the exhibition. We are grateful to them, and to Mr. Stephen Harvard of The Stinehour Press for his masterly design of these books, and for all those at the Press and at The Meriden Gravure Company who worked with him. We are as well indebted to the following institutions, and to those persons named in connection with each, who have provided books or drawings for this publication: The Lilly Library, Indiana University, Bloomington (Mr. William R. Cagle); The Newberry Library, Chicago (Mr. James Wells); the Arents and the Spencer Collections and the Special Collections of The New York Public Library (Mr. Joseph Rankin, Dr. David H. Stam, and Mr. Walter J. Zervas); The University of Washington Libraries, Seattle (Miss Sandra Kroupa and Mr. Gary L. Menges); and to our good friends Mrs. Paul Gourary and Mr. and Mrs. Paul Mellon for the loan of books.

This exhibition and catalogue have been made possible by generous grants from the National Endowment for the Humanities, a federal agency; Schlumberger Horizons, Inc.; the Franklin Jasper Walls Fund at the Morgan Library; and gifts from two of our Trustees. We are also grateful for the support we continue to receive from The Charles Engelhard Foundation for our publications program. All public programs at the Morgan Library are supported, in part, by annual grants from the Institute of Museum Services and the New York State Council on the Arts.

CHARLES RYSKAMP
Director

Introduction for Collectors

I

THIS BOOK was written to accompany an exhibition at The Pierpont Morgan Library from April through July of 1982. From its inception it was planned to cover its subject with a fullness which lack of space would make it impossible to match in the exhibition itself. In compensation abundant illustrations have been provided. Nearly every entry has its attendant image, and multiple images display the several aspects of major books. Thus these volumes constitute the first comprehensive history in English of French book illustration from 1700 to 1914. By their inclusion of Romantic lithographic albums, indeed, they go beyond any comparable book in French.

The present work differs in several ways from *The Illustrator and the Book in England from 1790 to 1914*, which recorded a parallel exhibition at the Morgan Library in 1976. Since it was impossible to omit the French eighteenth century, arguably the greatest of all periods of illustration, it covers an additional ninety years. As the modified phrasing of its title emphasizes, it recognizes a crucial difference between the English and the French illustrated book. The English tradition for the most part has been popular and straightforward, the French often sophisticated and luxurious. A taste for such things as fine paper, special states of plates, added drawings, and particularly extra bindings has characterized French collectors since the third quarter of the eighteenth century, and this taste has often been taken into account by publishers. Where a standard copy has usually satisfied the collector of English illustrated books, the collector of French illustrated books has sought where possible to achieve an exceptional copy. It may be said, indeed, that the French illustrated book has become a province of art in its own right.

Combined with the inevitable barrier imposed by a different language, this difference in tradition has tended to make French illustrated books something of an enigma to English and American collectors. Visitors to the English exhibition told me again and again that encountering the books therein had taken them back to their childhood. French illustrated books, on the contrary, can seem exotic objects, sometimes with an ambiguous aura. For one thing, they have usually been more expensive than their English counterparts. The great eighteenth-century books, as well as collectors' copies of those of the turn of the nineteenth century, were well beyond the means of the ordinary buyer. When *livres de peintres* finally found a public after the First World War, they too became very costly. Over the last two decades, with the growing vogue of Daumier, Doré, Grandville, and the workers in color of the Belle

Epoque, there has been a bridge of sorts to general appreciation by English-speaking amateurs, but for the most part French illustrated books have appeared to be the playthings of wealthy collectors.

Another impression concerning these volumes, which today seems ludicrous as a cause for suspicion though it has so operated in the past, is their assumed impropriety. In the chapter called "Podsnappery" of *Our Mutual Friend* Dickens tells of a London businessman who dismissed foreign manners and customs of which he disapproved with the conclusive observation: "Not English!" In particular those "vagrants the Arts" were to be held strictly accountable. "The question about everything was, would it bring a blush into the cheek of the young person?" France has always seemed particularly suspect to Anglo-Saxon moralists. When I first became interested in French illustrated books as a college student fifty years ago, I discovered that my university library had sequestered many of them in a wire cage. When I began to collect them twenty-five years later, some trace of this sense of supposed licentiousness still lingered. Even today I find that mention of such books to elderly gentlemen can elicit a smirking allusion to French postcards. That French artists have indeed treated erotic themes with more freedom and effectiveness than those of any other nation will be affirmed below, but this element is nonetheless minor and occasional in the broad tradition of French illustration.

In any event, my attempt to map French book illustration for English-speaking readers was undertaken with a view to helping them surmount the barriers which I have mentioned. The effort was worth making for it is generally agreed that the French tradition is the richest in the world. Perhaps France's dominance has been most decisive in the Renaissance, the eighteenth century, and the first half of the twentieth century, but its achievement has always been high. During the 214 years here considered, there was a rhythmic alternation between periods of ordinary and exceptional accomplishment. Taking half a century to gather momentum, French illustration had its most notable surge in the third quarter of the eighteenth century. The unsettled conditions of the three decades which followed the Revolution held it back until its second flowering under the impetus of the Romantic movement between 1820 and 1850, when lithographic albums vied in interest with illustrated books. Another routine period, less readily explained by external events, extended into the middle 1880s, after which work of the most varied excellence prevailed until the First World War. Even in the two eras of lesser achievement, between 1789 and 1819 and from 1851 to 1884, there are many high points of individual accomplishment.

During these two centuries illustrators made use of several prevailing techniques. Until about 1820 they worked on metal. During the Romantic period, though steel engraving had a brief heyday, they employed lithography and wood engraving. Between 1850 and 1880 wood engraving predominated, with lithography yielding to etching as the other chief mode. The thirty years before the First World War saw the employment of all these techniques, together with photomechanical processes of reproduction, often with the introduction of color. Whatever the technique, French craftsmanship was usually equal or superior to that anywhere else in the world.

In asserting the claims of English illustrated books in my earlier volume (p. xv), I quoted Blake's defence of graphic art against painting: "he who draws best must be the best artist." The advance in standing of book illustration during the intervening six years has been such that the primacy of the image, however rendered, no longer needs specific assertion. Moreover, the list of French painters who turned their hands to books between 1700 and 1914 is long and distinguished: Coypel, Oudry, Boucher, Fragonard, Robert, Prud'hon, David, Girodet, Carle and Horace Vernet, Géricault, Bonington, Delacroix, Lami, Eugène Isabey, Daumier, Chassériau, Daubigny, Meissonier, Hugo, Manet, Redon, Tissot, Merson, Camille Pissarro, Fantin-Latour, Besnard, Forain, Toulouse-Lautrec, Denis, Bonnard, Bernard, Leheutre, Derain, Dufy, and Picasso. More than a quarter of the "100 Outstanding French Illustrated Books" listed in Appendix II have designs by such artists.

Still more productive of notable work, however, were the great career illustrators. Omitting Daumier and Denis, whose names belong here as well as above, those who met the highest standards are Gravelot, Eisen, Moreau, Grandville, Gavarni, Tony Johannot, Doré, and Lepère. Not quite at their level, with regard either to the amount or the excellence of their work, are Cochin, Choffard, Monnet, Le Barbier, Marillier, Monsiau, Charlet, Raffet, Nanteuil, Monnier, Vierge, Steinlen, and Legrand. At least thirty other fine artists of more limited achievement, like Gillot, Redouté, Gigoux, Bertall, Jacque, Lemud, Jeanniot, Grasset, Mucha, and Lunois, could readily be added to this list. No other country can offer so spectacular a roll call of illustrators.

French illustrated books as they have traditionally been collected constitute the subject surveyed in this catalogue, that is to say works of imaginative literature and other volumes the images in which have a strong aesthetic appeal. Volumes containing photographs have been omitted because quite different criteria must be applied in judging them. Though periodicals were excluded in principle, it proved necessary in practice to admit four from the Romantic period (146 to 148, 160), and five from the Belle Epoque (321, 361 to 364), since the story of how illustration developed during those eras cannot be properly told without them.

The great novelty of this survey is its inclusion of albums of Romantic lithographs, which indeed form one of the longest sections of the catalogue. Their presence is essential if the full richness and diversity of the French tradition of illustration is to be shown. They constitute a significant part of the work, in a few cases the most significant, of some of the greatest of French illustrators, namely Charlet, Daumier, Delacroix, Doré, Gavarni, Géricault, Grandville, Tony Johannot, Lami, Monnier, and Raffet. Any description of the careers and achievement of these artists which did not take account of their lithographs would have been totally inadequate.

This is a book about French illustration, not illustration in France. I have accordingly admitted Ariosto's *Orlando Furioso* of 1773 (64), even though it was printed in London by Baskerville. Doré's later books which were first published in England or the United States—*London* (251), *The Rime of the Ancient Mariner* (253), and *The Raven* (255)—could hardly be left out. Neither could the culminating work of Nanteuil's career, *Don Quijote* (213), despite its appearance in Madrid. Again Moselly's *La charrue d'érable* (394), with wood engravings after Camille Pissarro, was executed for a Parisian society of bibliophiles, though produced in London by the Eragny Press.

In the past those who do not read French have been largely cut off from information about the rich heritage of French book illustration between 1700 and 1914. Apart from exhibition catalogues, there are only two relevant books of significance, each covering a limited period. Owen Holloway's *French Rococo Book Illustration* of 1969 is a brilliantly innovative study which examines the books chiefly of the third quarter of the eighteenth century with subtle authority. Rolf Söderberg's *French Book Illustration, 1880–1905* of 1977 is a useful review of these twenty-five years, written from a perspective very different from my own. The fullest general coverage of French book illustration from the eighteenth to the twentieth centuries is to be found in David Bland's *History of Book Illustration* of 1958, where it is assigned some fifty pages, about half of which are devoted to reproductions of illustrations. *Le livre: Les plus beaux exemplaires de la Bibliothèque Nationale*, a collaborative work edited by André Lejard, was translated into English in 1947. It devotes seventeen pages of text and thirty-two of illustrations to the years 1700 to 1914.

In marked contrast is the virtual library of books and articles on the subject by the French, who have abundantly demonstrated the pride that they take in the achievement of their illustrators. Fundamental are the standard bibliographies. Henry

Cohen's *Guide de l'amateur de livres à gravures du XVIIIe siècle*, as revised and enlarged by Seymour de Ricci in 1912, is the finest of these. It is a marvel of scholarly inclusiveness. Léon Carteret's *Le trésor du bibliophile romantique et moderne, 1801–1875*, four volumes, 1924–1928, is far less comprehensive. Indeed, it largely ignores the years 1801 to 1830. In his last years Carteret provided a sequel: *Le trésor du bibliophile: Livres illustrés modernes, 1875 à 1945*, five volumes, 1946–1948.

Of the several histories of French illustrated books, the best by a considerable margin is *L'Art du livre en France des origines à nos jours* of 1931, the principal author of which was Frantz Calot. Written from the books themselves, out of a vast knowledge of the field, it is the only survey that covers the subject in much detail. Calot depended in part, as everyone must, on certain classic period studies. For the eighteenth century the essential books are the Goncourts' *L'Art au dix-huitième siècle*, three volumes, 1880–1882, and Baron Portalis' *Les dessinateurs d'illustration aux dix-huitième siècle*, two volumes, 1877. Jules Renouvier's trenchant *Histoire de l'art pendant la Révolution*, two volumes, 1862, is a valuable sequel to these works. Henri Beraldi's entertaining and encyclopedic *Les graveurs du XIXe siècle*, twelve volumes, 1885–1892, is the indispensable resource for the nineteenth century. It needs to be supplemented by Champfleury's *Les vignettes romantiques* of 1883 and Henri Bouchot's *Les livres à vignettes du XIXe siècle* of 1891 and *La lithographie* of 1895.

Complementing these books, most of which—it will be observed—were written from fifty to a hundred years ago, are hundreds of biographies, bibliographies, critical studies, monographs, exhibition catalogues, and articles, a selection from which is listed in the Bibliography. The sections of the catalogue concerning periods, movements, and artists usually identify the salient works about these subjects. Otherwise, it will not be invidious to call particular attention to the writings of Jean Adhémar, Loys Delteil, Jean Furstenberg, Pierre Gusman, Louis Réau, and Charles Saunier, as well as to the many catalogues of exhibitions at the Bibliothèque Nationale.

By studying these rich materials and above all the images of the books themselves, I have tried to provide a comprehensive and balanced view of French illustration from 1700 to 1914. The period specialists, with the exception of the genial and catholic Beraldi, didn't really aim at balance. The Goncourts disdained the baroque, Renouvier the rococo, and Baron Portalis Romantic lithography. Admirers of *livres de peintres* have sometimes seemed prepared to jettison all earlier illustration. Yet the artists of these various schools complement each other, and the total achievement of French illustration overshadows that of any single group.

No nation has treated literary classics with more consistent respect than the French. In consequence, certain books were selected for illustration again and again during the more than two centuries under consideration. Among them are *Daphnis et Chloé*, *Don Quixote*, *Gil Blas*, *Manon Lescaut*, *La nouvelle Héloïse*, *Orlando Furioso*, La Fontaine's *Fables*, and the works of Molière and Rabelais. For the eighteenth century Fénelon's *Télémaque*, La Fontaine's *Contes et nouvelles*, the plays of Racine, and Voltaire's *Candide* and *La pucelle* can be added to the list. During the Romantic period Béranger's *Chansons* and *Notre Dame de Paris* were particular favorites. There will be many opportunities in the pages which follow to compare the contrasting ways in which these texts were depicted from period to period. Indeed, there has been an effort to show how different artists realized identical subjects: for example, Oudry (5) and Grandville (191) for La Fontaine's *Fables*, Gravelot (16) and Moreau (51) for *La nouvelle Héloïse*, Moreau (50) and Jeanniot (304) for *Le misanthrope*, Prud'hon (76) and Bonnard (384) for *Daphnis et Chloé*, Tony Johannot (180) and Merson for *Notre-Dame de Paris* (298), and Tony Johannot (182), Nanteuil (213), and Vierge (297) for *Don Quixote*.

I have mentioned the tendency of English-speaking readers to associate French illustration with erotic themes. Until the general emancipation of the 1920s, French artists and writers did indeed enjoy a degree of freedom in dealing with such subjects unmatched in England or the United States. What matters, however, is the use which they made of their freedom, and here it is essential to draw an obvious distinction. When Browning wanted to suggest the prurience of the malignant monk of his "Soliloquy of the Spanish Cloister," he depicted him gloating over his

> . . . scrofulous French novel
> On grey paper with blunt type!
> Simply glance at it, you grovel
> Hand and foot in Belial's gripe.

The poet goes on to show him planning to tempt an innocent brother monk by placing the volume in his way, its pages doubled down "at the woeful sixteenth print." It must be evident that this cheap and nasty production was hardly a collector's book. Browning may have had in mind a work of the early 1790s (see below, page 138), almost the only period when books with pornographic plates were openly on sale in Paris. For the most part French erotic illustration has been at an infinitely higher level.

Indeed, the liberty enjoyed by French artists to treat such themes has operated greatly to their advantage. Working with insight, subtlety, and sophistication, they have drawn from them some of their strongest designs. This is particularly true of the eighteenth-century masters. The compositions elicited from Gravelot and Boucher by the *Decameron* (15), from Eisen (26) and Fragonard (77) by La Fontaine's *Contes et nouvelles*, from Eisen and others by Ovid's *Métamorphoses* (62), and from Monnet by *Les liaisons dangereuses* (82) and Voltaire's *Romans et contes* (35) are among their best. So too are those in Gavarni's albums depicting the Parisian world of pleasure (151 to 156). At the end of the nineteenth century Legrand and Bonnard found their most consistently rewarding subjects in similar settings.

The sophisticated tradition of the French illustrated book makes it essential to represent as many titles as possible with copies containing exceptional or unique material. It goes without saying that fine condition is a *sine qua non*. Many volumes have plates in special states. Where possible original drawings for illustrations have been included. The reader can best acquire a familiar awareness of what French collectors look for in illustrated books by considering the attractions that these things lend to the copies described below.

The most important of such added features is the binding. French publishers have usually issued their books in wrappers, leaving it to each purchaser to have them bound according to his means and taste, a gamut ranging from unadorned half-calf to sumptuous mosaic morocco with doublures. Only occasionally, as with the polychrome cloth bindings of the Romantic period, does a publisher's binding constitute collector's condition. French binding is a major subject in itself, but some conception of its changing styles and the work of its chief masters can be gained from Appendix I.

Finally, the previous ownership of the copies described has been recorded when known. It is appropriate that *bibliophile* should be a French word, for the collectors of that country have always treasured every aspect of the ambiance of the copies that have come their way. This subject is best studied in the catalogues of great auction sales, for example, those for the collections of Henri Beraldi, Raphaël Esmerian, and René Descamps-Scrive. But the Index of Provenances in this book at least suggests a preliminary approach.

II

Among the features of *The Illustrator and the Book in England from 1790 to 1914* which were found useful was a list of "100 Outstanding Illustrated Books" of the period.

Indeed, a number of libraries have employed it as a guide to acquisitions, and it has had its influence on private collectors as well. A comparable list of French illustrated books appears in Appendix II. In making my choices I again sought the help of knowledgeable scholars, collectors, and book dealers. The names of my respondents (twelve American, four Belgian, five French, and two English) are given at the end of this Introduction. The English survey was a pioneering effort in a field largely unexplored. Hence I sent those consulted only seventy-five titles and drew heavily on the suggestions I received for the remaining twenty-five. The French illustrated book, on the contrary, has been thoroughly charted. In consequence I sent my advisors 100 titles and a number of possible alternatives. With a few exceptions they recommended additions rather than deletions, and in the event I made only five substitutions.

The first title to go was Marguerite de Navarre's *Les nouvelles* (66) illustrated by Dunker and Freudeberg; here I yielded to the judgment that for all its Swiss worthiness, the book remains less than inspired. My enthusiasm for Alphonse Lemud, which had led to the inclusion of Béranger's *Oeuvres complètes* (238) of 1847, was questioned by several respondents. Examination of the ordinary edition of Zola's *Le rêve* (373), with wood engravings after Carlos Schwabe, persuaded me that it is not really a collector's book in that form. If I had seen a copy of the fine-paper issue, I might have come to a different conclusion. In the face of protestations that Georges Jeanniot was hardly a major illustrator, I reluctantly relinquished his edition of *Le misanthrope* (304). Finally, I was brought to concur with the general opinion that Louis Legrand is more suitably represented by his *Livre d'heures* (343) than by *Poèmes à l'eau-forte* (346).

In addition to *Le livre d'heures de Louis Legrand*, these books have been replaced by *La Loïe Fuller* (368), a book of striking originality; Apollinaire's *Le bestiaire* (392), with wood engravings by Dufy, the omission of which from my initial list must be ascribed to simple ignorance; Verlaine's *Sagesse* (378), illustrated by Denis, which mustered extensive support; and Richepin's *La chanson des gueux* (341), left out originally only because its drawings by Steinlen are reproduced by photomechanical process. It should be observed that all these replacements come from the years 1898 to 1911, the period which has attracted most attention from collectors in recent years and also the period concerning which judgments are least settled.

The five changes mentioned do not begin to compensate for the inevitable omission of many fine books. It is only fair to list the "also-rans" which had strong support among my respondents. Two categories among them, works of pictorial information and *livres de peintres*, are reserved for later discussion. The other titles are given below, period by period.

For the years 1700 to 1788 (twenty-one of the hundred, if one includes the *Monument du costume* (55) of 1789, the plates of which had first appeared in three *suites* between 1775 and 1783), there were three particularly praised alternatives:

> Duclos, *Acajou et Zirphile,* 1744 [Boucher]
> (24) Erasmus, *L'Eloge de la folie,* 1751 [Eisen]
> (32) Montesquieu, *Le temple de Gnide,* 1772 [Eisen]

For the period 1789 to 1819 (eight of the hundred) the absence of the following books was especially regretted:

> (95) Rousseau, *Oeuvres,* eighteen volumes, 1793–1800
>   [Monsiau and others]
> (87) Vadé, *Oeuvres poissardes,* 1796 [Monsiau]
> (80) Virgil, *Bucolica, Georgica, et Aeneis,* 1798
>   [Gérard and Girodet].

Among Romantic albums of lithographs (fourteen of the hundred) Grandville's plates for *Les métamorphoses du jour* of 1829 (132) found several advocates. Attention was claimed for *La silhouette,* four volumes, 1828–1831 (146). Three respondents would have preferred to see Daumier represented by *Les bons bourgeois* or *Les gens de justice* rather than *Les beaux jours de la vie* (168).

Regarding Romantic books illustrated with engravings on wood or metal (nineteen of the hundred), there was surprise at the omission of Balzac's *La peau de chagrin* of 1838 (225) and Sue's *Les mystères de Paris,* four volumes, 1843–1844 (233). The claims of Bertall were advanced, either for Balzac's *Petites misères de la vie conjugale* of 1845 (222) or for Brillat-Savarin's *Physiologie du gout* of 1848. Several unchosen "museums of images" with multiple illustrators had their admirers, particularly *La grande ville,* two volumes, 1842–1843 (229), with fifty-eight wood engravings after Daumier.

Disagreement concerning the period 1850–1884 (ten of the hundred) centered on Doré's works, especially those of his early career. No one questioned the inclusion of *Les contes drolatiques* (244), but the merits of two lithographic albums and three books illustrated with wood engravings were also stressed:

> (241) *Les différents publics de Paris,* 1854
> (242) Rabelais, *Oeuvres,* 1854
> (243) *Histoire . . . de la sainte Russie,* 1854

La légende du juif errant, 1856

(245) *Les folies gauloises*, 1859.

As was to be expected, the years 1885 to 1914 (twenty-eight of the hundred) produced by far the longest list of proposed substitutions. Three of these had the suffrages of several respondents:

(362) *L'Estampe moderne*, 1897–1899

(377) Dante, *Vita Nova*, 1906 [Denis]

Gerard de Nerval, *Histoire de la reine du matin*, 1909
  [Lucien Pissarro].

A number of other books garnered two votes:

(289) Theuriet, *Sous bois*, 1883 [Giacomelli]

(369) Uzanne, *Féminies*, 1896 [Rops]

(303) Constant, *Adolphe*, 1901 [Jeanniot]

(344) "Ramiro," *Faune parisienne*, 1901 [Legrand]

(312) Mérimée, *Carmen*, 1901 [Lunois]

(376) *L'Imitation de Jésus-Christ*, 1903 [Denis]

(349) Huysmans, *Le quartier Notre-Dame*, 1905 [Jouas]

(351) France, *Histoire comique*, 1905 [Chahine]

Maeterlinck, *La vie des abeilles*, 1908 [Schwabe]

(318) Barbey d'Aurevilly, *Les diaboliques*, 1910
  [Lobel-Riche]

Vaudoyer, *Album dedié à Tamar Karsavina*, 1914 [Georges Barbier]

It will be observed that most of the titles not chosen are at least included in the catalogue, usually with one or more illustrations. My reservations concerning them may be discovered in the relevant entries. See, for example, those for *La peau de chagrin* and *Les mystères de Paris*. I should also mention that considerations of balance and proportion as well as absolute merit sometimes influenced my decisions. Grandville's designs for *Les métamorphoses du jour* are in the same vein as those for the *Scènes de la vie . . . des animaux* (194), for example, while those for *Voyages de Gulliver* (192) represent another aspect of his talent.

The suggestions discussed so far relate to preferences among individual titles. More challenging are those deriving from different principles of selection. My literary and aesthetic bias did not go unreproved. Five respondents wanted to see attention paid to works of pictorial information, a phrase employed by the late Karl Kup, to "the Arts and Sciences as a counterweight to La Fontaine, Molière, and Racine."

This is another line of country from books devoted to scenery and architecture, contemporary history, and color printing, all of which have their place in the catalogue. Though there is a brief discussion of the notable eighteenth-century festival books (page 6), and Redouté's *Les roses* (89) figures in my list of 100, illustrated compilations of knowledge are indeed almost entirely missing. The actual titles proposed varied widely from respondent to respondent. Those advocated by two or more persons were:

> *Médailles sur les principaux évènements du règne de Louis legrand*, 1702
> *Cérémonies et coutumes religieuses de tous les peuples du monde*, nine volumes, 1723–1748
> > [Bernard Picart]
> Diderot and d'Alembert, *Encyclopédie ou dictionnaire raisonné des sciences, des arts et des métiers*, thirty-five volumes, 1751–1786
> Nicolas Jadelot, *Cours complet d'anatomie, peint et gravé en couleurs naturelles*, 1773
> > [Amand-Eloy Gautier d'Agoty]
> Gamelin, *Recueil d'ostéologie*, Toulouse, 1779
> Jean-Baptiste Audebert, *Histoire naturelle des singes et des makis*, 1800
> François Levaillant, *Histoire naturelle des oiseaux de paradis et des rolliers*, three volumes, 1806–1807
> *Description de l'Egypte*, twenty-three volumes, 1809–1828
> Claude-Nicolas Ledoux, *L'Architecture considerée sous le rapport de l'art, des moeurs et de la législation*, two volumes, 1804–1847
> Eugène Grasset, *La plante et ses applications ornamentales*, 1897 [Grasset]

My conscience troubles me the less about the omission of these undoubtedly impressive books because they are already widely known and highly valued by specialists in the fields to which they relate.

Finally, there was the vigorously debated issue of how many of the canonical *livres de peintres* published before the First World War (see Painters' Books) belong on a list of "100 Outstanding French Illustrated Books, 1700–1914." Concerning eight titles there was no disagreement: two illustrated by Denis (375, 378), two by Toulouse-Lautrec (380, 382), two by Bonnard (383, 384), and one each by Derain (388) and Dufy (392). Several of my respondents would have included further volumes chosen from among the following: Montorgueil's *Le café concert* and Clemenceau's *Au pied du Sinaï* (381) illustrated by Toulouse-Lautrec, *Les petites scènes familières* illustrated by Bonnard, Mirbeau's *Le jardin des supplices* (385) illustrated by Rodin, Jacob's *Saint Matorel* (390) and *Le siège de Jérusalem* (391) illustrated by Picasso, and the same author's *Les oeuvres burlesques et mystiques de Frère Matorel* (389) illustrated by Derain.

I resisted adding any of these to my list of 100, as I had earlier resisted Mallarmé's *L'Après-midi d'un faune* (278) illustrated by Manet, on the ground that this kind of book was sufficiently represented by the preferred volumes already chosen. The champions of *livres de peintres* who won the battle for these books beginning in the 1930s (see below, Painters' Books) have sometimes seen modernism as a break with the past which in effect superseded earlier art. Their success was such that for a time they established an exclusive orthodoxy. Half a century later, however, modernism is itself part of history, and its productions ought to be subjected to the same rigorous winnowing as those of every other era.

III

The narrative which follows of how the books in this catalogue were assembled, or at least the nine-tenths of them which are mine, supplements two earlier accounts of my collecting activities, the first in the *Book Collector* of Spring and Summer, 1964, and the second in the introduction to *The Illustrator and the Book in England from 1790 to 1914*. I there told of the way in which my primary interest as a collector gradually shifted in the years following 1958 from literary first editions to the formation of a "museum of the book," devoted to illustration and binding, and extending to France as well as England.

My experiences in collecting the illustrated books of these two countries have been very different. In general French books have cost a great deal more, though until the early 1970s a favorable exchange rate for the dollar kept them within range. They were also far more widely dispersed since they have always enjoyed an international public. Whereas most of my English illustrated books were acquired in England or the United States, their French counterparts came not only from these countries and from Paris, but also from a dozen other continental cities from Copenhagen to Milan. For fifteen years I found it worthwhile to visit Amsterdam, Brussels, Geneva, Zurich, Grenoble, and Lyon nearly every summer. I bought from booksellers' stocks, at auction, and even from private collectors. With so wide a market, and with indifference then prevailing among both dealers and collectors, I could expect ultimately to find a fine copy at a reasonable price of most of the titles which I sought.

Beginning in 1958, I bought sporadically over the next few years, placing more emphasis on fine bindings than on illustrations, though of course the two often went together. As related in the *Book Collector* (XIII, 179–181), I acquired a number of notable books, including most of the volumes illustrated by Denis, Lepère, and Merson. I should particularly mention Huysmans' *A rebours* (328), with Lepère's designs in a floral mosaic morocco binding by Marius Michel, which came my way in 1959, and Louis Morin's *Carnavals parisiens* (347), with all of Morin's original drawings, which I acquired in 1961.

It was not until the following year, however, that I sealed my commitment to forming a comprehensive collection of French illustrated books by the purchase of Michael Sadleir's albums of French lithographs, some 300 in number. Sadleir and I had become friends in 1946 through a common interest in first editions of Victorian novels. We soon discovered another link in Honoré Daumier. Sadleir had written a book about him in 1924, while I had become his devoted admirer by poring over Loys Delteil's ten-volume catalogue of his more than 4000 lithographs, each with its illustration, when a student of French literature at Indiana University in 1935. Regarding these compositions as a graphic supplement to Balzac's *Comédie humaine*, I made this set my first serious book purchase.

In 1962 Dudley Massey, who was entrusted with the sale of Sadleir's books after his death, offered me his lithographic albums, saying that he did so at Michael's wish. At the same time I had the prospect of acquiring a comprehensive run of Turner's *Liber Studiorum* mezzotints in their several states at a comparable price. I could not afford both, and a period of painful indecision ended only when another collector bought the Turners. I have never regretted that the choice was thus taken out of my hands.

Sadleir's collection, which had largely been formed in the 1920s, included many treasures, among them eleven albums of Daumier's lithographs, containing more than 400 plates *sur blanc*, most of Gavarni's albums and all of Doré's, as well as such outstanding individual pieces as Carle Vernet's *Cris de Paris* (121) and the four *suites* by Géricault described below (102 to 105). As a biographer and novelist, however, Sadleir had been interested above all in caricatures and other studies of manners, which he preferred in contemporary coloring. I resolved to expand his collection in two ways. I would fill the gaps in the areas to which he had devoted himself, and I would move into other areas as well.

In the former endeavor I assigned first priority to Daumier. Over the next few years my additions, which included *La caricature* (160) in 1963, raised my total of plates *sur blanc* to more than 1200. My chief ally in this campaign was the leading Parisian dealer in Daumier's graphic work, who shook his head over my refusal to acquire early proofs of single prints instead of albums. I told him that I wished to remain a book collector, a resolution to which I have continued to be faithful. I also had particular success with Henry Monnier, finding in Brussels in 1969 a large collection of his work with many impressions which he himself had colored, and Gavarni, whose albums I sought out in their uncolored state.

The other areas into which I moved included scenery and architecture, works of imaginative literature, and the Napoleonic epic. Notable acquisitions in the first included a magnificent *oeuvre* of Bonington in 1963 and the three finest series of Baron Taylor's *Voyages pittoresques . . . dans l'ancienne France* (106, 107, 109), which came to hand in 1965 and 1966; in the second, Delacroix's *Faust* (143) and *Hamlet* (145), which arrived in 1964 and 1965 respectively, as well as the first series of *L'Artiste* (147) in 1970; and in the third, a large *oeuvre* of Charlet and nearly all of Raffet's albums. These additions enabled me at least to double Sadleir's original collection.

Of all my French illustrated books, these lithographic albums would be the most difficult to duplicate. They were published initially in editions of modest size, and after the middle decades of the nineteenth century few collectors or indeed institutions made an effort to assemble them. This situation operated for some time to my advantage. In the 1960s each of the principal European dealers who concerned himself with nineteenth-century illustrated books had a shelf or two of lithographic albums. Since they were in little demand, I could count on making my choice from them every summer. When their interest and rarity began to be appreciated in the 1970s, however, such accumulations were soon exhausted, and today one must wait for the occasional appearance of significant titles at auction, where competition is apt to be keen.

The Sadleir collection led me to a ten-year campaign of acquisitions, not merely of lithographic albums but of French illustrated books in general. In effect this purchase had given me a critical mass, a resource as essential to success for an operation in book collecting as it is to an experiment in nuclear physics. Whereas my lithographs had come almost entirely from abroad, however, in the area to which I turned next, the eighteenth century, I found most salient titles at home.

For half a century after 1880 there was a wealthy and sophisticated public for such volumes in the United States. Before the War Robert Hoe and other members of the Grolier Club had collected them with ardor. Their old-world associations made them especially attractive to these gentlemen, some of whom might have stepped out of the pages of Henry James. Indeed, Carteret (1946, I, 32) relates that Hoe sometimes hesitated over a French purchase, fearing that "the book in the American setting might lose its personality." In 1920 and 1922 respectively Dr. A. S. W. Rosenbach brought the renowned Robert Schuhmann and Louis Olry-Roederer collections to this country, where another generation of rich amateurs, which included Frank Altschul, Cortlandt Field Bishop, Templeton Crocker, Mortimer Schiff, and Joseph Widener, became eager purchasers.

Yet when the Depression slowed the activities of such collectors, there turned out to be no broad interest to sustain a market in the field. For four decades these books languished on booksellers' shelves or brought derisory prices at auction. Even the occasional specialist dealer who understood these volumes did not put himself out to acquire them, since there were few customers to whom he could pass them along. As an extreme example of the naïveté which resulted from this state of apathy I may offer an anecdote concerning the manuscript of the Marquis de Pezay's poems described on page 35 below. After I acquired this simulation by pen and ink of a printed book, the dealer in question asked why he had not been able to find it in the bibliographies!

So it happened that the United States became a happy hunting ground for eighteenth-century French illustrated books during the 1960s. Indeed, supply so far exceeded demand that it was possible to pick and choose among copies. Starting at the top, I had made the Fermiers-Généraux edition of La Fontaine's *Contes et nouvelles* (26) my first big purchase in 1962, though exceptionally it was acquired in London. Among succeeding titles Philadelphia supplied one of my three variant examples of *Les métamorphoses* (62A) in 1965 and Voltaire's *Romans et contes* (35) in 1967, San Francisco the *Decameron* (15) in 1967, and New York La Fontaine's *Contes et nouvelles* illustrated by Fragonard (77) and two further copies of *Les métamorphoses* (62, 62B), all in 1968.

In what was left of the Roederer and Schuhmann collections, which had passed to Dr. Rosenbach's successor, John Fleming, I found a number of outstanding books between 1967 and 1970, among them Moreau's *Figures de l'histoire de France* (53), Gessner's *Oeuvres* (39), and Couvray's *Les amours du chevalier de Faublas* (83). Mr. Fleming also had the remains of the great portfolio of Gravelot's drawings, which had earlier contributed to the creation of exceptional copies of several notable books. Careful sifting of its seemingly miscellaneous contents enabled me to assemble the eighteen designs for Tassoni's *La secchia rapita* described on page 45 below. Monnet's compositions for *Gil Blas* (38) were acquired in Amsterdam in 1972. Most of my other drawings for eighteenth-century illustrations, including those by Eisen for Descamps' *La vie des peintres flamands*, those by Gravelot for the *Decameron*, those by Chaudet and Gérard for the Didot Racine, and those by Marillier came from a dealer in Brussels.

Far thicker on the ground during the 1960s than eighteenth-century French illustrated books were those published between 1885 and 1914. The latter had been widely admired in their heyday, but receding tides of taste left them stranded on booksellers' shelves all over the western world. Superb copies were to be found not only in France itself, Brussels, and Geneva, but also in London and the United States. Protective prices prevailed in Paris, where a market of sorts still existed, but elsewhere such books were neither understood nor valued. In this buyer's Elysium even bindings by Marius Michel commanded no particular premium.

My initial approach to the illustrated books of the Belle Epoque was tentative, not to say gingerly. Their very abundance in the marketplace made for confusion, since the account of them in Carteret's *Le trésor du bibliophile: Livres illustrés modernes, 1875 à 1945*, the standard manual, strained credulity. All of his geese seemed to be swans. His appraisals of the some 4000 titles he described soared from "interesting" and "appreciated," through "sought after," "esteemed," and "beautiful," to "great stars of the modern illustrated book." It was easier to believe, as prevailing critics of the day maintained, that there were few books that one needed to bother about and that those were largely *livres de peintres*. Only gradually did I come to see that the period was indeed rich in fine books, and that Carteret's enthusiastic characterizations, at least for the pre-1914 period, in their way made valid discriminations.

Apart from the titles illustrated by Denis, Lepère, and Steinlen already mentioned, I made only occasional purchases of books of striking visual appeal during the early and middle 1960s, among them *Les maîtres de l'affiche* (361) from a London dealer in 1964 and *L'Estampe moderne* (362) at a Brussels auction in 1967. My great leap forward with regard to the Belle Epoque came with the sale of the collection of Enrique Garcia Merou in 1968. It was rumored that New York had been the last choice for the disposal of the library of this Buenos Aires amateur, which no English or continental auction house had cared to undertake. My strategy was to entrust bids for certain exceptional books to the leading New York expert, thus removing a formidable competitor, and to employ my usual representative for a larger number of more routine volumes. Since only one major Parisian dealer was at the sale, and there was little interest among American booksellers for most of the books that Merou had collected, the prices realized were low, sometimes only a fraction of the already modest estimates.

I was successful beyond my most sanguine expectations. I obtained thirty-two books in all, either at the auction or by private treaty thereafter. I have not mentioned prices in this narrative, but the opportunities offered by the Merou sale cannot be understood without such evidence. It should suffice to note that the following eight books, each in full morocco, cost less than $1,400 in all: Doré's *Londres* on China paper (252), Quevédo's *Pablo de Ségovie* illustrated by Vierge (296), Mérimée's *Carmen* with colored lithographs by Lunois (312), Maupassant's *Le vagabond* illustrated by Steinlen (340), *Le livre d'heures de Louis Legrand* (343), Huysmans' *Le quartier Notre-Dame* colored by Jouas himself (349), Fromentin's *Dominique* with etchings by Leheutre (386), and the *Histoire des quatre fils Aymon* on Japan paper (357).

I was able to go on buying throughout the last decade in this field, despite its burgeoning popularity, by taking advantage of special situations. The veteran American collector Francis Kettaneh disposed of many of his fine French illustrated books to a New York dealer in the early 1970s. Most of those dating from the Belle Epoque surfaced in two catalogues issued by an English bookseller in the winter of 1974–1975. They moved slowly, and over the following five years I acquired a number of volumes with original drawings as well as several Marius Michel bindings. A group of handsome Belle Epoque books was offered in a Los Angeles auction sale during 1975. Since they stirred little local interest, my representative secured them virtually without competition. Among them were *Faune parisienne* illustrated by Legrand (344), *La légende dorée* illustrated by Lunois (310), and *Les dimanches parisiens* illustrated by Lepère (323A), all in incised leather bindings by Charles Meunier.

Regarding the books of the Interregnum, 1850 to 1884, not much need be said. I felt so little urgency about Doré's folios that I was almost too late to acquire them in fine copies. Manet came my way with unexpected ease. Visiting Mabel Zahn in Philadelphia in 1967, I was told that I might find something interesting in a pile of pamphlets on her desk. A third of the way down I came upon *L'Après-midi d'un faune* (278), two-thirds of the way down the much rarer *Le fleuve* (276). Both were in mint condition. I completed the trio of books illustrated by Manet with a fine copy of *Le corbeau* (277) discovered in Brussels during 1972. One further experience deserves mention. Over many years I had bought autograph letters, including some fifteen from Flaubert to Louise Colet, from the Librairie de l'Abbaye in Paris. I also managed to purchase a few books each year, though the proprietor complained that he wasn't really a bookseller and that I would eventually leave him with empty shelves. To sate my appetite he finally sent me with his shopman to the old Conard warehouse on the outskirts of the city, which had become his when he acquired the stock of that firm. It was a cavernous building, sustained by great pillars, between which were towering piles of the Conard editions of French classic authors in unfolded sheets. On the balcony were the remains of an antiquarian bookseller's stock of the 1930s, apparently unexamined since that period. This eerie experience yielded the album for the Bida Musset described below, as well as a variety of other welcome volumes.

It proved unnecessary to make a concerted effort to assemble Romantic books with engravings on wood and metal. This was the one period in France during which the best illustrations were typically produced for the great public. They were consequently to be found with ease and at modest prices, not only in Paris but also in nearly every other major city where collectors' books were sold. Even fresh examples in publishers' polychrome cloth bindings, such as Gavarni's *Oeuvres choisies* (207) and *Don Quixote* illustrated by Grandville (199), were readily available.

Of course exceptional copies of Romantic illustrated books were another matter altogether. Rarely assembled in this age of democratic bookmaking, they are to be especially treasured. Examples described below are *Les français peints par eux-mêmes* (227), which was part of the Sadleir collection, Nodier's *Journal de l'expédition des portes de fer* (235) and *Le juif errant* (206) acquired in 1965, *Paul et Virginie* (226) in 1968, and *Manon Lescaut* on China paper (183) and *Chants et chansons populaires de la France* (232) in 1969. I had good luck as well with Romantic drawings for illustrations. Those by Achille Devéria, Tony Johannot, and Henry Monnier came from the stock of Percy Muir and those by Delacroix and Nanteuil from the extra-illustrated set of Hugo's *Oeuvres* mentioned in connection with *Les travailleurs de la mer* (261).

For ten years, then, I had the sort of run with regard to French illustrated books that the most fortunate collector can hope to experience only two or three times during his life. The early 1970s saw an awakening interest in the field which gradually grew into a passion. At the same time, a decline in the exchange value of the dollar made it increasingly difficult for American collectors to buy abroad. Indeed, an invasion of European dealers sent prices sky-high in this country as well. Though I went on buying, I did so in a subdued and inconsecutive way. Some of my significant acquisitions among books of the Belle Epoque have already been mentioned. I should add to these the *Fioretti* of Maurice Denis (379) bought in Brussels during 1974 and *Renée Mauperin* with etchings by Tissot (275) bought in London during 1979. There were also occasional purchases from earlier periods: *Incroyables et merveilleuses* (80) in New York during 1977, for example, and *La Gerusalemme liberata* with Cochin's preliminary etchings (11) from the Roederer collection in 1979. My principal success during the 1970s, however, was with French Art Deco books of the 1920s and 1930s, which remained available in exceptional copies even as the supply of similar Belle Epoque books was drying up. One day I hope to make them the basis for a small sequel to this history.

Today the interest of collectors in illustrated books has reached a peak, extending to nearly every country, period, and technique. This gives me the more reason to be grateful that my years of exciting pursuit, having as their agreeable setting the great rare-book cities of the western world, have left me with a "museum" of French illustrated books which in some measure fulfills the plan which I conceived twenty years ago.

It is with profound gratitude that I acknowledge the help which I have received in writing this book. The scholars, collectors, and bookdealers who commented on my list of "100 Outstanding French Illustrated Books" were Gabriel Austin, Pierre Berès, Michael Brand, William R. Cagle, Georges Colin, John Fleming, Colin Franklin, Jean Furstenberg, Eleanor Garvey, Lucien Goldschmidt, Claude Guérin, Neil Harris, Philip Hofer, Kathleen Hunt, Marcel Lecomte, Alexandre Loewy, William Matheson, Joseph Rankin, Mme. Anne Rouzet, Leonard B. Schlosser, Florimond Tulkens, Arthur E. Vershbow, and Colonel Harry Vinckenbosch. My text was read as a whole or in part by Gabriel Austin, Eleanor Garvey, Lucien Goldschmidt, Henri Peyre, Charles Ryskamp, and G. Thomas Tanselle. Mr. Ryskamp also provided firm support during the book's preparation. Alarmed by the proportions which my manuscript was assuming, for example, I offered at one juncture to stop at 1885, only to be enjoined to press on to my planned conclusion.

As in the case of my earlier volume on English book illustration, however, my primary obligation is to Thomas V. Lange, who devoted more than a year to compiling the authoritative bibliographical descriptions of the Catalogue, and whose aid in arrangements with the Morgan Library and The Stinehour Press has been indispensable. I am also indebted to two members of the Library's staff: Dr. Anna Lou Ashby, who succeeded Mr. Lange in these liaison services and assisted with the exhibition, and Charles V. Passela, who provided the book's some 650 expert photographs.

GORDON N. RAY

December, 1981

As with the bibliographical descriptions in *The Illustrator and the Book in England*, the entries in this volume are copy-specific: the copies here described are from Dr. Ray's collection unless otherwise stated. While anomalies and obvious lacunae are noted wherever possible, considerable variation may exist in other copies. Page size is measured to the nearest ⅛ inch, with height preceding width. Titles are transcribed literally but not typographically, punctuation being added where necessary. In the collations, printed pages are counted, omitting initial and final blanks. Illustrations are counted, artists and engravers are identified, and the medium employed is noted. Printers are listed only for lithographic works, and provenance is recorded only where readily identifiable. Bibliographical references are provided to the standard works listed in the Bibliography, excluding references to *catalogues raisonnés* of prints. For their assistance I should like to thank Mr. Robert Riggs Kerr, Mr. William Kmet, Mrs. George W. Semler, and Miss Lisa Vercollone.

The Catalogue

FERVET IN INVICTO LODOICI PECTORE MAVORS,
BLANDAQVE PVRPVREO FVLGET IN ORE VENVS,
CEDITE MORTALES, SEV VI, SEV SPONTE SEQVENDV EST;
CVM SINT TOT IVNCLÆ VIRIBVS ILLECEBRÆ.

Tapisseries du Roy

Forerunners

For the purposes of this survey there is no need to describe the great French books of the Renaissance, one of the supreme periods of illustration, but some mention must be made of the baroque engravings of the seventeenth century, since they provide the point of departure for the eighteenth century. French book illustration during this era has traditionally been seen as sporadic and unexciting. Recently, however, Philip Hofer has made a case not only for its interest but also for its abundance. In the seventeenth century, he writes, there were "nearly three good French books for every English one—and more fine French books than Netherlandish, or German and Italian put together" (p. 13). But if the century can boast many imposing volumes, their illustrations are nonetheless apt to seem sparse (often limited, indeed, to a "gateway" title page), ponderous in conception, and awkward in size. They may celebrate the activities or possessions of a great man, provide a fine series of portraits, or set forth the principles of a subject like architecture or horsemanship, but they rarely offer the consecutive interpretation of a work of imaginative literature.

There was an alternative mode of smaller designs and more animated scenes, however, which looked forward to the eighteenth century. It can be traced from Jacques Callot through his most successful Italian pupil, Stefano della Bella, who also worked in France, to Sébastien Le Clerc. Most significant of all for our purposes was the Dutchman Romeyn de Hooghe. In addition to his vivid pictorial polemics, he illustrated with profusion three famous collections of short narratives, La Fontaine's *Contes et nouvelles* (1685), 70 etchings; *Les cent nouvelles nouvelles* (1701), 100 etchings; and a French translation of the *Decameron* (1697), 100 etchings. These headpieces were often reprinted, and both in their conception and dimensions they showed the way to the illustrators of the next century. To compare his *Decameron* with the edition of 1757 (15) is to discover that the artists for that celebrated work often chose the scenes which he had selected and even disposed the figures in these scenes much as he had arranged them. This is true of Gravelot in particular, but also of Boucher and

Eisen. Of course, there are modifications. Romeyn de Hooghe's designs are simplified and made harmonious. His grotesque touches are omitted, and his grosser details are suppressed. But the elegance and relative decorum of the later rococo illustrations do not disguise their frequent dependence on his vigorous baroque inventions.

REFERENCES Brun; Calot (1931); Hofer (1970); Landwehr; Lejard; Mornand (1947).

Charles Le Brun (1619–1690)

Tapisseries du Roy, ou sont répresentez les quatres élémens et les quatres saisons. Avec les devises qui les accompagnent, et leurs explications. Paris, Sébastien Mabre-Cramoisy, 1679. Contents: T.p. with unsigned engraved vignette, p. [1]–2: introduction with engraved headpiece by Le Pautre after Bailly, and engraved initial by Le Clerc, added engraved t.p. after Bailly, engraved section-title for the *Tapisseries* by Le Clerc after Bailly, p. 15–16: "L'Air," double-page engraved plate by I.G. after Le Brun, engraved section-title for the *Devises*, p. [17–24]: each *l.* with engraved central vignette, p. 35–36: "La Terre," double-page engraved plate by Le Clerc, p. [37–44]: each *l.* with engraved central vignette, p. 3–[6]: "Le Feu," double-page engraved plate by Le Clerc after Le Brun, p. [7–14]: each *l.* with engraved central vignette, p. 25–[26]: "L'Eau," double-page engraved plate after Le Brun, p. [27–34]: each *l.* with engraved central vignette, p. [45]–[50]: "Les quatres saisons, Le Printemps," double-page engraved plate after Le Brun, engraved section-title for the *Devises*, p. [51–58]: "Le Printemps," p. 59–[62]: "L'Esté," double-page engraved plate after Le Brun, p. [63–70]: each *l.* with engraved central vignette, p. 71–72: "L'Automne," double-page engraved plate by Le Clerc after Le Brun, p. [73–80], p. 81–82: "L'Hyver," with engraved tailpiece, double-page engraved plate by Le Clerc, p. [83–90]: each *l.* with engraved central vignette, 7 further double-page engraved plates, and 1 duplicate without caption. Page size: 19½ × 14¼ inches. Contemp. red morocco.

The Imprimerie du Roy, founded at the Louvre by Richelieu in 1640, set new standards for bookmaking in France. Its productions perfectly embody the Palladian classicism of the *style Louis XIV*. No book better represents the tradition thus established than this sumptuous folio, from the series of the Cabinet du Roy, illustrated with eight double-page engravings by Sébastien Le Clerc reproducing the tapestry designs of Charles Le Brun. These emblematic representations of the four elements and the four seasons are intended to show how Louis XIV brought "a new order to the Elements," and made the seasons "more beautiful and more fruitful" (p. 45). Each large plate is supplemented by four smaller "devises" developing the "mysterious" symbolism of the whole, and there are eight additional engravings. Flattery, and indeed splendor, could go no further. In the engraving of "Spring" that is shown, the château of Versailles may be seen in the background. This copy includes a second series of eight double-page engravings after Le Brun's tapestry designs by Le Clerc and others depicting great events during the reign of Louis XIV.

(15) Boccaccio, *Decameron*

First day, second tale, after Romeyn de Hooghe

Romeyn de Hooghe (1645–1708)

Les cent nouvelles nouvelles . . . qui sont moult plaisans à raconter, en toutes bonnes compagnies; par manière de joyeuseté. Cologne [i.e., Amsterdam], Pierre Gaillard, 1701. 2 v. I: [15] *l.,* 349 p. II: [12] *l.,* 325 p. Illus. after Romeyn de Hooghe: Front. by van der Gouwen, unsigned headpiece, and 45 plates engraved by Scherm (2), and unsigned (43), II: 55 plates by van Vianen (8), and unsigned (47), unsigned tailpiece. All plates have letterpress numbering. Inserted are 10 19th-century illustrations. Page size: 5⅞×3⅝ inches. Green morocco by Petit. Cohen–de Ricci 658–659; Landwehr 94.

These engravings are slightly larger than those for the *Decameron* and La Fontaine's *Contes et nouvelles,* and they have the interest of falling just within our period. In the first issue they are half-page headpieces; in this they are accorded the dignity of a full page (Landwehr, p. 94). Romeyn de Hooghe here displays his accustomed talent for devising a striking composition through which to interpret each story, and his actors perform with their usual force and decisiveness. If there is nothing subtle about their behavior, neither is there anything feeble. For these broad medieval tales, in which a bed is usually near at hand, his treatment could hardly be improved. Over the last two decades de Hooghe has achieved a place in the pantheon of outstanding illustrators, and even the numerous reissues of his illustrations for Boccaccio, La Fontaine, and *Les cent nouvelles nouvelles* are eagerly sought by collectors.

after Eisen

Fifth day, first tale, after Romeyn de Hooghe

Ninth day, second tale, after Romeyn de Hooghe

after Boucher

after Gravelot

From Baroque to Rococo (1700–1749)

The eighteenth century in France is universally recognized as one of the supreme periods of book illustration, but its time of notable achievement was concentrated between 1750 and 1780. During the first half of the century no great number of illustrated books were published, and only a few of these are of exceptional interest. Even among the artists who concerned themselves with illustration, this activity was apt to be a sideline. The contributions of painters like Boucher, Coypel, and Oudry were almost a matter of chance. There was no wide public for illustrated books, nor did the apparatus of publishers, printers, and engravers necessary to sustain substantial production as yet exist. Indeed, the two notable professional illustrators of the period, Picart and Gravelot, worked chiefly outside of France.

The Goncourts' statement that the eighteenth century was "the century of the vignette," as the seventeenth had been "the century of the frontispiece" (II, 265), again applies primarily to its third quarter. It took decades for headpieces, tailpieces, and small-scale plates to supplant frontispieces and engraved title pages as the expected adornment of books. With the death of Louis XIV, the austere formality which his regime had imposed on French life gradually disappeared. In time sheer enjoyment became an avowable motive. As the wealth which had been centered in the court was more widely distributed, there emerged a large public for all things that were unpretentiously attractive. How this change in manners and morals should be judged has always been a matter of dispute, but there can be no doubt that it eased the transition from the baroque to the rococo style, until finally "prettiness," as the Goncourts put it (I, 196), became "the soul of the age."

The eventual triumph of rococo book illustration was heralded by two series of etchings completed by engraving after Watteau: *Figures de différents caractères de paysage et d'études*, 350 prints after his drawings, 2 volumes, 1726 and 1728; and *L'oeuvre d'Antoine Watteau*, 271 prints after his paintings, 2 volumes, 1735. Jean de Jullienne was responsible for these; indeed, the second has traditionally been known as the "Recueil Jullienne." A close friend of Watteau, he had formed an extensive collection of his paintings. He determined that a record of them should be made before they passed out of his hands. Beginning in 1717, four years before Watteau's death, he brought together some of the best engravers of the time at the Gobelin factory of which he was director, and produced this great masterpiece of graphic art. Only 100 copies were assembled of the *Oeuvre*, and so keen has been the desire of collectors for its individual prints that it is now rarely found intact. At its initial appearance, however, it and the *Figures de différents caractères* provided not only a continuing inspiration but also an inexhaustible source for illustrators both in France and abroad who were working towards the new rococo style. Watteau himself had made a series of etchings of costume about 1710. Jean Furstenberg has recently demonstrated the importance of the tradition thus inaugurated of *suites* not directly connected with books by painters and illustrators.

Because of its very nature one kind of book continued to offer illustrations of baroque conception throughout the century. These were the festival books, volumes celebrating emergent occasions in the annals of the royal family. The first and most splendid was *Le sacre de Louis XV Roy de France et de Navarre, dans l'église de Reims* of 1723. This large folio with its nine double-page engravings and thirty costume plates yields nothing in magnificence to Le Brun's tributes to Louis XIV. More modest is a volume of 1775 devoted to the coronation of Louis XVI, though even it can be impressive on large paper. The series concluded with *Le sacre et couronnement de Napoléon premier* in 1806.

REFERENCES Adhémar (1963); Calot (1931); Furstenberg (1975); the Goncourts (1880); Portalis.

Bernard Picart (1673-1733)

Bernard Picart was the outstanding professional illustrator of the first third of the eighteenth century, an age during which the designs for the finest illustrated books were typically drawn by leading painters. He worked for the most part in the fading baroque tradition, but there are elements in his immense production which herald the new age. When his diverse accomplishments are finally catalogued and analyzed, his standing as a book artist will be greatly enhanced.

The son of a well-known engraver, Etienne Picart, Bernard grew up in Paris, where he was Sébastien Le Clerc's pupil. He early acquired a reputation both as artist and engraver. For a time Paris offered him full employment, but by 1712 he had removed to Amsterdam, where he became a printseller as well as a designer and engraver. During the rest of his life, with increasing help from other artists, he produced a large body of engravings for the Dutch printers. Among his earlier books may be mentioned two great folios, Boileau's *Oeuvres*, 2 volumes (1718), and his most ambitious undertaking, *Les cérémonies et coutumes religieuses de tous les peuples du monde*, 11 volumes (1723-1743). His best-known later works, to the illustration of which his pupil Dubourg contributed more than did Picart himself, are the *Métamorphoses* of Ovid, 2 volumes (1732); *Télémaque* (1734); and Rabelais' *Oeuvres*, 3 volumes (1741). All three are desirable books, though the collector should make a point of seeking out the large-paper issues of the two latter titles.

Intermingled with the stately designs, replete with allegorical and mythological trappings, that predominate in the books just listed, are others in a freer style. Picart's *Impostures innocentes ou recueil d'après divers peintres illustres* demonstrates his skill in rendering the canvases of Le Brun and other seventeenth-century masters. He was persuasive to the point of deception in his versions of Rembrandt, whose example he followed in his own etchings of humble life. The varied resources of Picart's art are displayed in an epithalamium of 1718. Before a familiar baroque gateway one sees a character-

istic allegorical composition in which a happy couple is welcomed to their garden home by angels and cupids. But through the gateway further down the plate a busy harbor is depicted with sharp realism. The design is completed by a border of cupids shooting arrows with a heart as their target. Picart's position as a transitional illustrator could not be better exampled.

REFERENCES   Portalis; Réau.

1   FRANÇOIS DE SALIGNAC DE LA MOTHE FÉNELON

Les avantures de Télémaque, fils d'Ulysse . . . Nouvelle édition, conforme au manuscrit original, et enrichie de figures en taille-douce. Amsterdam, J. Wetstein & G. Smith; Rotterdam, Jean Hofhout, 1734. [2] l., x, xiv, xxv-xxvi, 395, [1] p. Illus: Front. by Folkéma after Picart, port. by Drevet after Vivien, t.p. vignette by Tanjé after Dubourg; 24 headpieces after Dubourg by Duflos (17), Folkéma, and Tanjé (6); 21 tailpieces by: Duflos after Dubourg (11), and Schenk (10); 24 plates, after Debrie by: Folkéma, Gunst (3), and Surugue; after Dubourg by: Bernaerts (5), Folkéma (5), Gunst (5), and Surugue; by Debrie (1), and Picart (2). One of 150 copies in folio format. Page size: 14⅛×9¾ inches. Blue morocco by Thibaron-Joly. Bookplates of Robert Hoe and Templeton Crocker. Cohen–de Ricci 381–382.

This work exists in quarto and folio formats. Only the latter, which was limited to 150 copies with the text surrounded by ornamental borders, is of particular interest. At first glance even in this form the book appears to be one more example of the seventeenth century's grand style. The twenty-five plates (three by Picart, sixteen by Dubourg and six by Debrie) are stately and elaborate. The most attractive is Picart's frontispiece, in which Telemachus at the urging of Minerva renounces ignoble ease for strenuous glory. This comprehensive allegory in the high baroque manner is developed with exceptional spirit and inventiveness. Yet it should be noted that in this volume, all the formal elements of the mid-eighteenth-century French masterpieces are present. In addition to the plates and borders, the twenty-four books of Fénelon's story

B. Picart invent. et del.   Jacob Folkema Sculp. 1733

TELEMAQUE, conduit par MINERVE, & couvert de son Bouclier, renonce aux Charmes des Plaisirs, de la Volupté,
& de l'Orgueil, qui ont à leur suite l'Intemperance, l'Envie, la Trahison, & le Desespoir : & guidé par le Génie de la
véritable Gloire, il s'avance par un Chemin escarpé vers le Temple de l'Immortalité, au milieu des Vertus opposées
aux Vices qu'il laisse derrierre lui, comme la Prevoyance, le Sécret, la Fidélité, la Vérité, la Piété, la Paix, la Justice,
la Liberté, la Concorde, & la Force, toutes reconnoissables à leurs Attributs.

(1) Fénelon, *Les aventures de Télémaque*

have their headpieces and tailpieces, and further engravings appear where opportunity offers. Still missing, alas, are the charm and warmth which the rococo masters will provide.

∾ 267 engravings, many proofs, mounted or laid into a large calf album, bound by E. P. v. Bommel.

A collection of this sort is almost necessary if one is to form a comprehensive impression of the work of the prolific Picart. It would otherwise be necessary to assemble a small library of books and a portfolio of printed ephemera. Included are plates, sometimes in proof state, from all of Picart's big books. The well-known frontispiece to his *Ovid* of 1732 is here, as are engravings from *Les peintures de Charles Le Brun et Eustache Le Sueur qui sont dans l'hôtel du Chastelet* (Paris, 1711) and *La galerie de Mons. le Président Lambert représentant l'apothéose d'Hercule.* There are also a number of his "innocent impostures." Equally well represented are Picart's smaller engravings, among them frontispieces, headpieces, tailpieces, coats of arms, invitations, contributions to privately printed works, and designs celebrating the activities of the Dutch India companies. Particularly graphic is a series of twenty-two unstudied etchings of Amsterdam street life, among which may be the first sketch in history of a shoeshine.

Etchings by Picart

Philippe d'Orléans (1674–1723)

2 [LONGUS]

Les amours pastorales de Daphnis et Chloé. [Paris, Quillau], 1718. [6] *l*., 164 p. Illus: Added engraved t.p. by Audran after Coypel headpiece by Scotin, 6 small engraved initials, and 28 plates (13 folding) by Audran after Phillipe d'Orléans. Bound in at end is a grotto version of the "Petits pieds" plate, entitled "Conclusion du roman," after a design by the Comte de Caylus. Page size: 6¼×4 inches. Contemp. red morocco. Bookplates of Frederick Locker and Templeton Crocker. Cohen–de Ricci 648–651.

The reputation of this little book derives primarily from the story of how it came into being. In 1714 Prince Philippe d'Orléans made a series of drawings for the story of Daphnis and Chloe under the tutelage of Antoine Coypel, the father of Charles-Antoine Coypel. At the beginning of his Regency the drawings were engraved by Benoît Audran and published in this edition of Longus's pastoral novel. Their conception is barely at a professional level, and the draftsmanship which they display is hardly deft enough to make their small scale an asset. Yet they do tell the story in their halting way, and the background landscapes in some of the larger plates have a naïve appeal. The mildly suggestive plate of "Les petits pieds" by the Comte de Caylus, which was sometimes added to copies of the book, is

better known than any of the original illustrations. See, for example, James Gillray's adaptation in his famous caricature, "Fashionable Contrasts." Still the prestige conferred by the participation of Philippe d'Orléans made *Daphnis et Chloé* a fixture in the collections of French bibliophiles (it came to be known as "the Regent's book"), and it is often found in elaborate bindings.

REFERENCES Portalis; Réau.

2A [LONGUS]

Les amours pastorales de Daphnis et Chloé. [Paris], 1745. [5] *l*., 159, xx p. Illus: Added engraved t.p. by Audran after Coypel, unsigned t.p. vignette, 4 unsigned headpieces and 1 unsigned tailpiece; 28 plates (13 large) by Audran after Philippe d'Orléans. Bound in at end is an untitled grotto version of the "Petits pieds" plate after a design by the Comte de Caylus. The engravings are not reprints of the 1718 plates, but are entirely different engravings of the identical subjects. These re-engraved plates can be identified by the absence of an engraved page number on the plate at p. 56 (present in the original plates, and written in ink in the copied plates), and by the abbreviation "inv" on the plate at p. 19 (the original with "in"). This copy does not include the vignettes by Cochin found in some copies. Page size: 8×6⅛ inches, large-paper. Contemp. green morocco. Cohen–de Ricci 652–653.

(2) Longus, *Daphnis et Chloé*

This edition offers a small quarto format, designed to provide an improved setting for the Regent's plates. The larger engravings are included without folding, and in an *exemplaire reglé*, such as this, the hand-drawn lines mitigate what might otherwise be an excess of margin. The contemporary olive morocco binding, possibly by Padeloup, completes a sumptuous ensemble. It is reproduced in Appendix I.

Drawing of "Les petits pieds" after the Comte de Caylus

2B [LONGUS]

[Les amours pastorales de Daphnis et Chloé. Paris, 1745.] [4] *l.*, 159, xx p., lacking t.p. Illus: Added engraved t.p. by Audran after Coypel, 3 unsigned headpieces; 28 plates (13 folding) by Audran after Philippe d'Orléans. This copy is made up of the sheets of the 1745 printing (omitting the t.p.), giving the appearance of a copy of the true 1718 edition. The original plates as in the 1718 edition are used, the only such 1745 copy located. Inserted at p. 158 is a woodland version of the "Petits pieds" plate, drawn in red chalk, signed "philippus inv." Page size: 6¼×3⅞ inches, imposed as an 8vo. Contemp. black morocco. Cohen–de Ricci 652–653.

The ordinary edition of the same book. The interest of this copy derives from the presence, opposite p. 158, of a drawing in sanguine of "les petits pieds," signed "philippus inv," but after the Comte de Caylus. It appears to be contemporary, and it is certainly a sketch of verve and precision. Volumes of light literature in the eighteenth century are occasionally found, like this copy, in drab bindings of black morocco which would seem to be better suited to devotional works. In such a disguise, it is explained, they could be read in church.

Claude Gillot (1673–1722)

3 ANTOINE HOUDART DE LAMOTTE

Fables nouvelles, dédiées au Roy . . . Avec un discours sur la fable. Paris, Gregoire Dupuis, 1719. xlii p., [2] *l.*, 358 p., [1] *l.* Illus: Front. by Tardieu after Coypel, t.p. vignette by Simoneau after Vleughels, and 102 vignettes by: Gillot (55); after Gillot by: Simoneau (4), and Tardieu (2); after Coypel by: Cochin (2), and Tardieu (15); after Ranc by: Edelinck (4), and Tardieu (2); by Picart (3); 1 vignette each by Ranc, and Tardieu; 2 vignettes after Massé by Tardieu; 11 unsigned vignettes (some certainly by Gillot). Page size: 9⅝×7⅜ inches. Contemp. calf. Cohen–de Ricci 594–595.

As a painter Claude Gillot had the distinction of being the master of Watteau, but his best work came later as a designer and etcher. Among his considerable productions in this line, his vignettes for *Fables nouvelles* stand out. He contributed two-thirds of the headpieces for Houdart de la Motte's five books of twenty fables each, leaving mythological and allegorical subjects for the most part to Charles-Antoine Coypel and Bernard Picart. In contrast to their formal and posed compositions, Gillot provided unstudied glimpses of both animated nature and the ordinary human life of his time. His animals are not caricatured (except for the monkeys, where he is following his author's text), and he is particularly spirited in presenting unfamiliar creatures like elephants (v, 8) or a whale (v, 9), though his camel (iv, 14) is unconvincing.

In this truthful portrayal he had the full approval of Houdart de la Motte, who addressed him as his "brother in Apollo" (pp. 270–271). His human scenes please by their exact observation and shrewd comic touch. Against deftly sketched backgrounds one sees a disconsolate widower choosing a parrot for company in a bird shop (I, 3), an artist painting a portrait (IV, 5), Apollo prevailing over Minerva in a Greek town when he offers cures for the body and she remedies for the mind (IV, 12), and a street poet deserted by his audience when the fish market opens (V, 5).

A delight in itself, this book is also of historical importance. The brash and slapdash style of Romeyn de Hooghe has been replaced by a harmonious vision that shows existence moving at a more reasonable pace, yet with no loss of liveliness. The formula of a small-scale headpiece for each story is made more attractive by the spacious page in which the vignette is set. Indeed, it may be said that the mainstream of eighteenth-century French book illustration had its source in *Fables nouvelles*.

REFERENCES   Portalis; Réau.

(3) Houdart de la Motte, *Fables nouvelles*

(3) Houdart de la Motte, *Fables nouvelles*

Charles-Antoine Coypel (1694–1752)

Coypel came from a family of painters, and he made his own mark early, gaining admission to the Royal Academy at the age of twenty-one. A polished gentleman, he was well read and had a considerable literary gift. It was said of him, indeed, that he liked to appear as "an eminent man of letters among artists, and a distinguished artist among men of letters" (quoted by Portalis, I, 130). Certainly he had a notable understanding of comic characters and situations, as he demonstrated in his *Suite d'estampes des principaux sujets des comédies de Molière*, six engravings (1726).

His great success as an illustrator, however, came with the scenes from *Don Quixote* which he painted between 1715 and 1720. These were copied as tapestries, and through his initiative twenty-five large engravings based on them were published in 1723–1724. The reductions of these designs which appeared in 1746 assured their wide circulation. It is not too much to say that the pictorial tradition associated with Cervantes' masterpiece owes as much to Coypel as to any other artist.

REFERENCE   Portalis.

❧ Engraved plates after Coypel for *Les principales aventures de Don Quichotte* (1723–1724), bound as extra-illustration in a copy of the London, 1755, edition: 27 (of 31) engraved plates after Coypel by: Beauvais (2), C. N. Cochin (3), Magd. Hortemels Cochin (2), Haussard, Joullain (3), Lépiciér, Poilly, Ravenet (3), Silvestre, Surugues (8), and Tardieu (2), with an early proof of 1 plate by Ravenet. Sheet size of engravings: 11⅜×13½ (trimmed). Cohen–de Ricci 214–215.

Coypel's talent as a genre painter is validated in these splendid plates, which are large enough in scale to catch nearly every nuance of the canvases on which they are based. He offers a comic *Don Quixote*, his emphasis being on the farcical episodes of the novel and the ludicrous aspects of its characters. Coypel has a keen eye for the scenes best suited to his purpose, and he disposes the figures within them in a way calculated to induce a maximum of gaiety. The plate illustrating chapter 9 of Book III is one of his most astonishing successes. The Don is astride a wooden horse by the magical properties of which, he is assured, he can ride through the air to the giant Malambruno. Sancho has joined him sidesaddle, their eyes are bandaged, and excited boys suggest the perils of their adventure with firecrackers and a bellows. At the moment chosen, Don Quixote, bewildered but game, with Sancho holding on for dear life, is persuaded by a burning tow waved before his head that they have reached the region of fire in their passage through the heavens. Duennas and a pair of lovers make an amused audience, while the bust at the right offers a sardonic commentary on the scene.

4   MIGUEL DE CERVANTES DE SAAVEDRA

Les principales avantures de l'admirable Don Quichotte, représentées en figures par Coypel, Picard le Romain, et autres habiles maîtres: avec les explications des XXXI planches de cette magnifique collection . . . La Haye, Pierre de Hondt, 1746. viii, 330 p., [1] *l.* Illus: Front. and headpiece by J. von Schley; 31 plates (before numbers) after Coypel by: Fokke, Picart (12), von Schley (11), and Tanjé (3); after Le Bas by von Schley (1); after Trésmoulièrs by von Schley (1); after Boucher by Tanjé; after Trésmoulièrs by Tanjé (1). Page size: 10½×8⅞ inches. Green morocco by Reymann. Cohen–de Ricci 216–217.

One wonders how the reputation of this well-known series would have fared if the engravings of 1723–1724 from which it was copied had been generally available for comparison. Between the earlier plates and the later, the engraved surface was reduced by almost two-thirds. And this is not all. The 1724 plates are horizontally oriented, the 1746 plates vertically. Thus Coypel's figures were diminished still further to fit their drastically narrower frame, and an inch or two of vertical space in each picture came to be devoted to superfluous sky or ceiling, foreground or floor. When compared to the earlier engravings, those of 1746 can only be described as "scrowdged," to borrow Mrs. Gamp's vivid word in *Martin Chuzzlewit*. Particularly in plates with many actors, Coypel's grasp of character is seriously weakened, as the subordinate personages become puppets with doll-like faces. It is a tribute to his verve and inventiveness that the series remains attractive despite this compression of his compositions.

Cervantes, *Don Quixote*, 1723–1724

Ch. Coypel pinx.   B. Picart delin. et sculp.

Don Quichotte et Sancho, montés sur un Cheval de Bois, s'imaginent traverser les Airs, pour aller vanger Doloride.

(4) Cervantes, *Don Quixote*, 1746

Jean-Baptiste Oudry (1686–1755)

In his humble beginnings, when Oudry became a skilled engraver, it is said that he was reduced to etching rebuses for children. He then studied with the painter Largillière, who treated him as a friend as well as a pupil. His first successes were with portraits, and he was elected to the Royal Academy in 1719 as a historical painter. His work at this time is exampled in his splendid series of designs for Scarron's *Roman comique*, twenty-three of which he engraved himself. One day after Oudry had painted a hunter with his hound, Largillière told him: "Come, you will never be anything but a painter of dogs." Oudry took his master's joke seriously and eventually became the great animal painter of the age. Louis XV brought him frequently to Versailles to portray scenes of the royal hunt as well as his favorite hounds. It was after he became director of the Beauvais tapestry factory that he began to amuse himself with subjects from La Fontaine's *Fables*. He made 276 sketches in all between 1729 and 1734. Hence the book which they came to illustrate is presented here, despite the fact that it was not published until the second half of the century.

The story of how these drawings became the illustrations of the *Fables* of 1755–1759 is told in the preface to that work by its publisher, Montenault. The subjects that they presented, landscapes and animals, were those which Oudry found most congenial, and his fellow feeling for their author was such that he could be called the "La Fontaine of Painting." After the rigors of painting, these sketches were "his recreations: he composed them for his own pleasure, and in those chosen moments of imagination when an Artist grasps the idea of his subject and gives free rein to his genius." But even when the series was complete, the audience for it was limited to a few amateurs. Here engraving came to the rescue. Cochin undertook the responsibility of turning these freehand drawings into finished prints. A necessary first step was his redrawing of Oudry's originals. In his versions "one can clearly perceive that exactness of contours to which Painters never submit themselves in the heat of composition. . . . Oudry himself recognized the new merit which his work had acquired in passing through the skilled hands of his illustrious colleague." ("Avertissement," I, iv–v.) So it came about that the inscription under Cochin's frontispiece of 1752 reads: "Inventé par J. B. Oudry, terminé au burin par N. Dupuis, gravé à l'eau forte par C. N. Cochin le fils qui, d'après les originaux, a fait tous les traits, conduit et dirigé tout l'ouvrage." In effect Cochin performed much the same service for Oudry's designs that R. Catterson-Smith through his redrawing and W. H. Hooper by his engraving were to perform for the designs of Burne-Jones in the Kelmscott Chaucer.

Oudry's rendition of animals is hardly to be surpassed, but by its nature it is broad and free. In providing the detail needed by the engravers, Cochin was able to maintain Oudry's level of excellence only fitfully. With household and barnyard animals, he can be persuasive, sometimes remarkably so, as with the dogs of fable XXIX or the rabbits of fable CCIII, but as much cannot be said for the fortunately infrequent wild beasts of the *Fables*, particularly those which would not have come his way often in life. His wolves and foxes may pass, but his bears and lions are sometimes lamentable. One of the most attractive of the book's plates is that for fable LXIV. This is the piteous tale of an unwary villager who complains to the landowner of his village concerning the depredations by a cunning rabbit in his cherished garden. Visiting his home with a retinue of men, horses, and dogs, the great man does not find the rabbit, hidden under a "master cabbage," but eats his host out of house and home and ruins his garden. The design does full justice to one of La Fontaine's most carefully wrought stories, combining lively action by both beasts and men with a striking background. One can also see in this composition a sort of domestication of the royal hunt.

The appeal that La Fontaine made to Oudry was at least as much in the open-air settings of his *Fables* as in the doings of his animal actors. Indeed, it has been shown that Oudry led a cam-

LE JARDINIER ET SON SEIGNEUR . 2.*planche* . Fable LXIV.

(5) La Fontaine, *Fables*

LE MEUNIER, SON FILS ET L'ANE. A. M. D. M. Fable XLIII. 2.ᵉ *planche*.

(5) La Fontaine, *Fables*

paign to replace conventional landscape painting with the picturesque rendering of country scenes based on direct observation (see Calot, p. 122). So it came about that Oudry's best designs are often those in which the presence of animals is subordinated, sometimes, as with the frogs of fable LXV or the crayfish of fable CCXXII, presenting creatures so tiny as to be barely noticeable. In the foreground are farmyards, roads, gardens, or meadows, in the background towns, rivers, valleys, and hills, these last often of fantastic configuration. Here an engraving calls to mind a watercolor by Dürer (fable CLXXI), there a coastal scene by Claude (fable CLXXVIII). Never before had the French countryside been so comprehensively presented. Indeed, one has to go to the albums of views that marked the emergence in the latter part of the century of what Ruskin called "the landscape feeling" to find anything comparable in variety and abundance.

The fables concern human beings as well as animals, and here Cochin's sure and experienced hand enhanced Oudry's designs. Among the many notable plates in this category, the five devoted to fable XLIII stand out. In this canny tale La Fontaine is demonstrating the impossibility of trying to please everyone. A miller and his young son set out to sell their donkey at a fair. In following the advice of those they encounter on the way, the miller adopts five different arrangements for using his beast, none of which gives satisfaction. In the second plate, three merchants reproach the son for riding while his father trudges behind. (The senior Cochin did the preliminary etching from which his son made this masterly rendering of an episode from common life.) The sequence clearly belongs among the designs in which, as the publisher claimed (IV, 185) Oudry "grasped La Fontaine's intention to such a point that he appears sometimes to have enhanced the wit of the fables." The scattered mythological and allegorical plates (that for fable LXXXIX is among the best) seem studied and remote in comparison with such vigorous drawings. It may also be mentioned that the *Fables* has its share of interiors, which like those of the Boucher Molière show the decor of the 1730s (fables IX, CXXV, CCXV). In summary, the illustrations offer a world of their own, to which the reader may return again and again for delight and instruction.

With such an embarrassment of riches in the

(5) La Fontaine, *Fables*, fleuron

plates, it is not surprising that little attention has been paid to the varied and ingenious fleurons appearing at the end of each fable. These constitute almost the only significant series of wood engravings for the adornment of French books during the eighteenth century. In a concluding "Explication," indeed, the publisher notes that it was the difficulty of this unaccustomed process which led the artist, Bachelier, "to place his allegories in the genre of flowers, where one knows that he excels" (IV, 185). Explanations are offered of several of the fleurons. Of that for fable LXXVI (II, 34), the reader is informed: "A snake, symbol of prudence, hidden under flowers, forms the tailpiece— the image of the insinuating way in which moral lessons ought to be presented."

The format of these four folio volumes is luxurious. Each of the fables has its own title page and one or more plates in addition to the emblematic and floral ornaments just mentioned. Indeed, this is one of the most ambitious and successful of all illustrated books. From the time of its appearance collectors have vied with each other in commissioning sumptuous bindings for its fine-paper issues, paying careful attention to one of the best known of bibliographic points—the absence of the words "Le Léopard" on the banner of the first plate for fable CLXXII, "Le singe et le léopard"—which is supposed to ensure early impressions of the engravings.

REFERENCES Calot (1931); Martin-Réau; Réau; Portalis.

5 JEAN DE LA FONTAINE

Fables choisies, mises en vers . . . Paris, Desaint & Saillant, and Durand, 1755–1759. 4 v. I: [2] *l.*, xxx, xviii, 124 p. II: [2] *l.*, ii, 135 p. III: [2] *l.*, iv, 146 p. IV: [2] *l.*, ii, 188 p. Illus. after Oudry: I: Front. by Cochin & Dupuis, and 70 plates by: Aubert (3), Aveline (3), Baquoy (5), Cars, Chedel (3), Chenu, Chevillet, Cochin (2), Cochin & Aubert, Cochin & Beauvais, Cochin & Chenu (3), Cochin & Dupuis, Cochin & Gaillard (5), Cochin & Teucher, Fessard (2), Flipart (4), Gaillard, Galimard (2), Le Bas (3), Legrand (3), Menil, Moitte (7), Ouvrier (2), Pasquier, Pelletier, Pitre Martenasie, Rode, Sornique (2), Surugue, and Tardieu (7). II: 68 plates by: Aliamet (2), Aveline (4), Baquoy (2), Beauvarlet, Cars (2), Chedel (10), Chenu (4), Cochin & Beauvais (2), Cochin & Dupuis, Flipart, Gaillard, Legrand (3), Le Mire (2), Lempereur (4), Marvie, Marvie & Beauvais, Menil, Moitte (3), Ouvrier (4), Pasquier (3), Pitre Martinasie (6), Radigues, Riland (2), Tardieu (5), and Teucher (2). III: 68 plates by: Aveline (4), Baquoy, Cars, Chedel (7), Chenu (3), Defehrt (5), Gaillard, Lebas & Baquoy, Legrand (2), Le Mire (5), Lempereur (4), Marvie (5), Marvie & Aubert, Menil (2), Moitte (5), Ouvrier (2), Pasquier, Pitre Martinasie (3), Prévost (4), Radigues, Riland (4), Tardieu (3), and Teucher (3). IV: 69 plates by: Aliamet, Aveline (2), Beauvais, Baquoy (2), Cars (6), Chedel (12), Chenu (2), Choffard (2), Cousinet, Duret, Defehrt, Flipart, Floding, Gaillard, Gallimard, Legrand (2), Lempereur (7), Marvie, Menil, Moitte (3), Ouvrier, Pasquier, Pitre Martinasie (3), Poletnich, Prévost (6), Radigues, Riland & Beauvais, Salvador & Dupuis, Tardieu (2), and Teucher (3). Wood-engraved t.p. vignette (repeated in each volume) by Lesueur after Bachelier, 3 tailpieces, 1 headpiece; and 1 tailpiece for each fable. Inserted in v. I is the portrait of Oudry by Tardieu after Largillière, found in some copies, but not integral. Page size: 15⅞ × 10¾ inches. Contemp. stained calf, with the Gavinet arms. Cohen–de Ricci 548–550.

&• Black ink, grey wash, and china white drawing on blue paper, for La Fontaine's *Fables* (1775–1759), fable CLXXXVI. Image size: 7½ × 9½ inches; sheet size: 10¼ × 12¼ inches.
The Pierpont Morgan Library

Fable CLXXXVI tells the story of two spoiled household pets who live, like courtiers, to benefit themselves and harm others. Finding chestnuts roasting on the hearth, the monkey persuades the cat to pick them out of the fire for him to crack and eat, until the arrival of a servant ends their mischievous game. The cat's gingerly handling of its prize is caught with a deftness which goes beyond even Oudry's accustomed mastery. If the animals lose a good deal in Cochin's rendering, Oudry's sketchy background is firmly realized, and the servant at the door, no more than a shadow in the drawing, becomes a significant actor in the little drama.

(5) La Fontaine, *Fables*

Oudry, drawing for La Fontaine's *Fables*

François Boucher (1703–1770)

A precocious genius, Boucher won the grand prize of the Royal Academy in 1723 and was elected to that body eleven years later. Though soon established as a painter, he found time to design many illustrations, a métier for which he was well prepared since he had been one of the craftsmen to whom Jullienne entrusted the engraving of Watteau's *Oeuvre* and *Figures de différents caractères de paysage et d'études*. As the most successful painter of the day, he had a large part in the creation of the mid-century rococo style through his canvases and innumerable drawings. So when the Goncourts identified prettiness as "the soul of the age," they added that "it is the genius of Boucher" (I, 196). His own contribution to rococo illustration is exampled in connection with the *Decameron* of 1757 (15) and Ovid's *Métamorphoses* of 1767–1771 (62). No doubt Boucher's prominent role in this shift of taste played its part in leading Diderot to attack both the form and spirit of his work in the "Salon de 1763." It is a question here, however, of an earlier book in a different mode.

REFERENCES   Calot (1931); the Goncourts (1880); Portalis; Réau.

6   JEAN BAPTISTE POQUELIN MOLIÈRE

Oeuvres de Molière. Nouvelle édition. Paris, [Pierre Prault], 1734. 6 v. I: [3] *l.*, lxx, 300 p. II: [3] *l.*, 446 p. III: [3] *l.*, 442 p. IV: [3] *l.*, 420 p. V: [3] *l.*, 618 p. VI: [3] *l.*, 554 p. Engraved illus: Front. by Lépicié after Coypel, t.p. vignette, 14 initials and 25 head- and tailpieces by Joullain and Cars after Boucher, Blondel, and Oppenord, 4 plates by Cars after Boucher. II: T.p. vignette, 18 initials and 34 head- and tailpieces, and 6 plates by Cars after Boucher. III: T.p. vignette, 19 initials and 45 head- and tailpieces, and 6 plates by Cars after Boucher. IV: T.p. vignette, 15 initials and 29 head- and tailpieces, and 6 plates by Cars after Boucher. V: T.p. vignette, 21 initials and 39 head- and tailpieces, and 5 plates by Cars after Boucher. VI: T.p. vignette, 17 initials and 38 head- and tailpieces, and 6 plates by Cars after Boucher. Page size: 11 ¼ × 8 ½ inches. Contemp. calf. Cohen–de Ricci 712–714.

The Pierpont Morgan Library

General opinion holds that the Boucher Molière and the Oudry La Fontaine are the two masterpieces of French book illustration during the first half of the eighteenth century. As has been demonstrated by Réau, the book does for the pattern of social life under Louis XV what Moreau's *Monument du costume* (55) does for the pattern of social life under Louis XVI. Its designs make no attempt at historical reconstruction but are "systematically anachronistic." Moreover, Boucher effects a related transformation in the spirit of Molière's comedies. This is an eighteenth-century Molière. Though the plate for each of the thirty-three plays does indeed represent in a striking way the principal action, as promised in the "Avertissement" for the edition, Boucher emphasizes neither his author's comic mastery nor his moral seriousness. In his eyes Alceste, Harpagon, and Tartuffe are less interesting than the younger characters whose grace and coquetry he displays to admiration; and his best designs are usually elicited by the dramatist's least strenuous efforts. Even in illustrating Molière, Boucher was still "the painter of the Graces."

The book's format is noble, Molière's text is presented with more care than ever before, and Laurent Cars' engravings catch the spontaneity and elegance of Boucher's sketches with easy precision. Yet despite the abundance of the accompanying ornamentation (a vignette and historiated initial letter at the beginning of each act and a tailpiece at the end), it otherwise leaves much to be desired. The publisher admits that the headpieces and tailpieces have little relation to comedy, even if they are all "appropriate to the comic mode" (I, ii). And indeed, despite their fine execution, they are both conventional and repetitive. They tend to be either mythological or decorative, and frequently they are employed more than once. Boucher's own contributions, happy fantasies of impudent cupids at play, are of a higher order. His headpiece for act I of *L'amour médecin* (III, 293) even provides a lively commentary on the play. It turns up again, however, as the headpiece for act I of *Le médecin malgré lui* (IV, 3) and act I of *Le malade imaginaire* (VI, 391).

The few critics who demur to the high ranking accorded the Boucher Molière find their argument here. They regard it as inferior to the later tri-

LES PRÉCIEUSES RIDICULES

(6A) Proof before letters and artists' names for *Les précieuses ridicules*

LE MEDECIN MALGRÉ LUY

(6A) Proof before letters and artists' names for *Le médecin malgré lui*

umphs of rococo bookmaking because text, illustration, and ornament do not form a harmonious whole. For most amateurs, however, the book remains "the triumph of a genre to which one regrets that Boucher did not remain faithful still longer: the rendering of the manners of his time and their elegence" (Calot, p. 126).

6A JEAN BAPTISTE POQUELIN MOLIÈRE

A collection of 30 engraved plates for the 1734 edition of Molière's *Oeuvres*, including 14 working proofs (7 *avant lettres*) for: *L'étourdi, Le dépit amoureux, Les précieuses ridicules, Le cocu imaginaire, Le misanthrope, Le médecin malgré lui, Le sicilien, Amphitryon* (touched proof), *Le tartuffe, Monsieur de Pourceaugnac, Le bourgeois gentilhomme, Les fourberies de Scapin, Psyché,* and *Les femmes savantes.* Page size: 11½×8½ inches. Brown morocco by Riviere.

This incomplete set of plates commands attention through its seven proofs before letters and the artists' signatures, which show the achievement of Boucher and Cars at its most brilliant. The symmetric arrangement of the figures in the illustration for *Les précieuses ridicules* looks forward to the balletlike productions which Molière's farces have received in the twentieth century. The complacency of fools in their folly could not be more persuasively conveyed than in this tableau where masquerading valets dupe the ladies who have rejected their masters. Decor and costume, it will be noted, are strictly of the 1730s. For *Le médecin malgré lui,* as Réau points out, Boucher has devised a charming country scene of the kind that he had mastered as a young man by engraving Watteau's drawings.

7 PIERRE CORNEILLE

Rodogune, princesse de Parthes. Tragédie . . . [Chateau de Versailles] au Nord, 1760. [2] *l.*, 80 p. Illus: Engraved front. by Mme de Pompadour and Cochin after Boucher. Page size: 10¼×7½ inches. Contemp. red morocco. Bookplates of Robert Hoe and Cortlandt F. Bishop. Cohen–de Ricci 257–258.
    The Pierpont Morgan Library, gift of Mr. Roland L. Redmond

Another of Boucher's contributions to the illustration of the French classic drama may also be recorded here, despite its later publication date. This is the frontispiece to *Rodogune,* an all-the-

(7) Corneille, *Rodogune*

talents plate which carries the imposing legend: "Designed by F. Boucher. Etched by Mme. de Pompadour. Retouched by C. N. Cochin." Boucher's subject is the dénouement of Corneille's tangled tragedy of murder and revenge. Antiochus has just forced his mother, Cleopatra, to drink the poison she has prepared for him. Boucher depicted this moment of high stress with force and grace, but in a free, painterly way. No doubt Cochin provided the background and firm detail required for the engraving in addition to "retouching" Mme. de Pompadour's etched plate, just as Cars presumably performed a similar service before engraving Boucher's drawings for Molière.

ᴈ Two drawings by Boucher in black and white chalk on grey paper, studies for the front. of Corneille's *Rodogune* (1760). Sheet size: 11⅞×8½ inches.

    The Pierpont Morgan Library

Charles-Nicolas Cochin (1715–1790)

Cochin has a prominent place among French art-ists of the eighteenth century. His father was an engraver sufficiently well known to cause the son to adopt "Cochin fils" as his signature. Through steady application he made himself the master equally of drawing and engraving, a double ex-pertise which gave him special skill in redrawing the designs of painters for engraving, as we have seen in the case of Oudry (5) and of Boucher (7).

For a time his production of engravings was pro-digious, but eventually the widening variety of activities that accompanied success led him for the most part to forego engraving for drawing. He attained particular renown as a portraitist, estab-lishing the vogue of small-scale profile likenesses in elaborate frames. By mid-century Cochin was a powerful force in the Parisian art world, holding important positions at court and the Royal Academy. Even after he retired from his official duties, he continued to play a significant role in artistic society. An amiable bachelor, he was affectionate with his relatives and helpful to younger artists. His fragmentary autobiography shows him to have been a writer of style and wit.

With these credentials, it is understandable that critics should look with favor on Cochin's claims as an illustrator. His achievements in this line are often presented as being on a par with those of the three acknowledged rococo masters, Gravelot, Eisen, and Moreau. Without endorsing Réau's assessment that Cochin "only contributed in an accessory way to book decoration" (Martin-Réau, p. 96), one must nonetheless concede that his best achievements came early in his career and are not of the first importance. No book of which he was the principal illustrator is to be found in the list of 100 given in Appendix II, though several of those in which he collaborated are present. The most ambitious of his illustrations, indeed, were the productions of his later years, designs of high professional quality, esteemed by his contemporaries, but unmistakably task work. This congenial, responsible man was an artist whose accomplishments in general far outpaced those of that dubious bohemian Charles Eisen, yet considered specifically as an illustrator he is clearly Eisen's inferior.

Cochin's early illustrations—among which those for La Fontaine's *Contes et nouvelles* (1743), Boileau's "Le lutrin," and Lucretius' *Della natura delle cose* stand out—are marked not only by the mastery of outline and firmness of composition which never deserted him, but also by acute observation and unpretentious humor. They remain fresh and attractive today. Then came a trip to Italy between 1749 and 1751 from which Cochin returned with three volumes of notes and sketches. Brooding over these, he persuaded himself that true purity of taste was to be found in the works of Guido Reni and his contemporaries. He set forth these ideas in his *Lettre à un jeune artiste peintre* and a variety of other works assailing with sarcasm and abuse the rococo style of ornamentation, that "assassin of the straight line," wherever it had been applied. Gradually these convictions transformed his own work as an illustrator. The exquisite nicety of his earlier designs gave place to a pretentious straining after grandiose effect. (See the Goncourts, II, 341–347.)

Certainly Cochin's later illustrations embody the principles of his campaign to the point of monotony. He devoted himself to four principal enterprises: thirty-five plates to accompany Henault's *Nouvel abrégé chronologique de l'histoire de France* (63), forty-six plates for *Roland furieux*, forty-one plates for *Gerusalemme liberata*, and a number of drawings for the works of Rousseau, apparently executed between 1780 and 1782. Those for Henault's compendium differ from the rest in their overwhelming reliance on allegory. They rarely represent specific occurrences. Instead they bring together the leading figures and events of a given reign in an all-inclusive tableau of a symbolic nature. These contorted exercises in futile ingenuity were attacked by Diderot (quoted by Portalis, I, 106–107) and provoked the Goncourts to a memorable outburst of exasperation (II, 355). And indeed, if the composition is balanced and the figures correct in these plates, the ensemble is heavy and lifeless. Given its relative simplicity, "Charlemagne," reproduced on page 111 below, is a favorable example of the series.

Though Cochin lived the majority of his seventy-five years in the second half of the eighteenth century, he is better considered for the purposes of this survey with the artists of the first half. Not only was this the period of his best illustrations, but also in his later work he harks back to the lingering baroque style of the period in which he grew up. His elaborate plates for Henault and Tasso have not a little in common with the frontispieces of Bernard Picart.

REFERENCES Calot (1931); Cohen–de Ricci; the Goncourts (1880); Holloway; Jombert; Martin-Réau; Portalis; Portalis-Beraldi; Rocheblave; Stampfle.

8 NICOLAS BOILEAU-DESPRÉAUX

Oeuvres ... Nouvelle édition, avec des éclaircissemens historiques ... rédigés par M. Brossette; augmentée ... par M. de Saint-Marc. Paris, David et Durand, 1747. 5 v. I: [3] *l.*, lxxx, 488 [i.e., 494, pp. 137–138 and 433–436 repeated as *137–138 and *433–436] p. II: [5] *l.*, 492 p. III: [4] *l.*, 536 p. IV: [3] *l.*, 591, [1] p. V: xxii, 676 p. Illus: I: Front. by Daullé after Rigaud, t.p. vignette by Boucher after Eisen, 13 headpieces by Aveline after Eisen, 1 headpiece by Delafosse after Eisen, 3 headpieces by Eisen, and 9 unsigned; 2 tail-

(8) Boileau, "Le lutrin"

Della natura delle cose, libri sei. Tradotti dal latino in italiano da Alessandro Marchetti . . . Amsterdam [i.e., Paris] a spese dell'Editore, 1754. 2 v. I: [3] *l.*, 243, [1] p., incl. engraved t.p. II: [1] *l.*, [245]–543 p., incl. engraved t.p. Illus: I: Front. and engraved t.p. by Le Mire after Eisen; 4 headpieces by Gallimard after Cochin, Le Mire after Cochin (2), and Sornique after Eisen; 2 tailpieces by Aliamet, and Gallimard after Cochin; 3 plates after Cochin by: Aliamet, Le Mire, and Tardieu. II: Front. and engraved t.p. by Le Mire after Eisen; 3 headpieces after Cochin by: Baquoy, Chenu, and Flipart; 3 tailpieces by: Louise Le Daulceur after Cochin, Baquoy after Eisen, and Aliamet after Vassé; 3 plates by Sornique after Cochin (2), and Le Mire after Le Lorrain. Page size: 8⅝ × 5½ inches. Contemp. green morocco. Cohen–de Ricci 665–666.

(9) Lucretius, *Della natura delle cose*

pieces by Mathey, and 17 unsigned tailpieces. II: T.p. vignette by Boucher after Eisen, headpiece by Aveline after Eisen, headpiece by Eisen, 9 unsigned headpieces; 6 unsigned tailpieces; 6 unsigned plates (but after Cochin). III: T.p. vignette by Boucher after Eisen, headpiece by Delafosse after Eisen. IV: Unsigned t.p. vignette, unsigned headpiece. V: T.p. vignette (indistinctly signed) after Eisen. Page size: 6⅞ × 4⅝ inches. Green morocco by Charles Hering, with ticket. Cohen–de Ricci 168–170.

Though this book includes thirty-nine small headpieces and five fleurons by Eisen, it is remarkable primarily for Cochin's six spirited plates in volume two for Boileau's mock-heroic ecclesiastical satire "Le lutrin." These designs had been exhibited at the Louvre in 1742. They have all the verve of Cochin's plates for La Fontaine's *Contes et nouvelles* of 1743, and through their larger scale, crowded scenes, and occasional allegorical trappings, they point the way to his later style. In the plate for canto III an aged owl, always the harbinger of bad news, startles the drunken guardians of the lectern (*lutrin*) in the Sainte Chapelle.

This book, which seems to have been printed in some quantity, became the model for the sumptuous rococo volumes of the ensuing twenty-five years. Handsomely printed on large paper, with plates, headpieces, and tailpieces by leading artists, it is encountered more often in contemporary bindings of decorated morocco (as with this copy) than almost any other work of the time. The book belongs decisively to Cochin, though one could not be sure of this from Cohen's cloudy description (columns 665–666). He provided five of the six plates, six of the seven headpieces (that to Book

Charles-Nicolas Cochin 27

(9) Lucretius, *Della natura delle cose*

ville edition (Cohen–de Ricci 95–97). Page size: 10⅜ × 7⅞ inches. Contemp. red morocco. Cohen–de Ricci 97–98.

This ambitious book was abundantly illustrated by Cochin. Copies are often found, like this one, to which a set of the plates from the Baskerville Ariosto (64) has been added in matching frames, with elegant new designs by Moreau replacing two of Eisen's feeblest efforts. This conjunction suggests a comparison between the two series which is not to Cochin's advantage. His detailed plates are based on a conscientious study of Ariosto's text, but their literal comprehensiveness lacks the grace and charm that Moreau knew how to impart through his selective and allusive drawings. Such a comparison might be proposed, indeed, to any intending illustrator as a lesson in what to leave out.

᠁ Seven proofs of six designs by Cochin for Rousseau's *Émile*, 1780, one of which is touched and inscribed by the artist. Sheet size: 13¾ × 10⅛ inches. Marbled boards.

Touched proof for Rousseau's *Émile*, 1782

II, though unsigned, is clearly his), and three of the five tailpieces. Otherwise, only Eisen made a significant contribution. The binding of this copy is reproduced in Appendix I.

Cochin was more at home with Lucretius' philosophical poem than with the amorous classical scenes of Ovid's *Métamorphoses* (62). As in the case of Rousseau's *Émile*, he seized on the book's anecdotal moments for his illustrations. He rarely matched their consistent grace and charm in his later work.

10 LODOVICO ARIOSTO

Roland furieux, poëme héroïque, de l'Arioste. Traduction nouvelle, par M. d'Ussieux. Paris, Brunet, 1775–1783. 2 v. in 4. I: [2] *l.*, 222 p. II: [1] *l.*, [223]–488 p. III: 283 p. IV: [284]–567 p. Illus: 46 plates after Cochin by: Delaunay, Lingée, and Ponce (44). Bound in are a portrait and 46 plates from the 1773 Basker-

Drawing of "Winter"

As has been noted, one of Cochin's projects in his later years was the illustration of Rousseau's works. By 1782 this had progressed far enough for the frontispiece and a design for each of the five books of *Émile* to be engraved. Proofs of the resulting plates make up this album. Cochin's designs are all dated 1780 the date of the engraving given on the frontispiece, and the engraving for Book v is dated 1782. Nothing came of this enterprise, perhaps because the plates were found to be unsatisfactory. Not until the majestic edition of 1793–1800 in eighteen volumes (95) did twelve of Cochin's designs, including all six of these subjects, finally appear. The large quarto format of the later edition permitted the engravers to do better justice to Cochin's designs than had been achieved in the 1782 renderings. The album includes a touched proof of the engraving for Book II with instructions to the engraver in Cochin's hand. A second proof of this plate testifies that they were carried out.

Faced in *Émile* with a treatise on education, Cochin for a wonder altogether forswore allegory, creating instead five specific scenes from offhand classical allusions in Rousseau's text. In Book II one reads of a boy of good family, destined for a military career, who is led by indolence to maintain that his rank exempts him from effort. "To make of such a gentleman a light-footed Achilles,"

Rousseau continues, "the skill of Chiron himself would had hardly have sufficed." On this hint, Cochin drew, offering a little episode of his own devising.

∾ Red chalk drawing by Cochin over traces of preliminary black chalk, with added design border in black chalk. Inscribed by the artist, "L'hiver." Image size: 5⅞ × 7 inches; sheet size: 7⅜ × 8¹⁵⁄₁₆ inches.
The Pierpont Morgan Library

As Felice Stampfle has shown, the series of eight preliminary designs, of which this is a part, was executed in 1784 or a little earlier. Cochin was planning to decorate a small room of his house at Gentilly with representations of the seasons, and this drawing of winter, the largest of the group, was destined for a place above the hearth. Its masterly arrangement, precision of outline, and nice discrimination of attitudes and even of character among its personages show that Cochin's command of his art had not diminished in his old age. It is the more to be regretted that his artistic principles led him to devote his energies to conventional designs for epic poems rather than familiar studies of common life.

11 TORQUATO TASSO

La Gerusalemme liberata . . . Seconda edizione, coi rami della edizione di Monsieur. Paris, Tilliard, Didot l'aîné, & Firmin Didot [1785–1786]. 2 v. I: [2] *l.*, 331 p. II: [2] *l.*, 334 p. Illus. after Cochin: I: Front. by St. Aubin, and 20 plates by: Dambrun (3), Delaunay (2), Delignon (2), Lingée (2), Ponce, Prévost (2), Simonet, Tilliard (5), Trière, and Varin. II: 20 plates by: Dambrun (3), Delignon (2), Duclos, Lingée, Patas (2), St. Aubin, Simonet (3), Tilliard (5), and Trière (2). All plates are *avant lettres*, and with another *suite* of plates *à l'eau-forte* (39 of the 41 designs). The identification of engravers has been made from the set of illustrations in the Spencer Collection, NYPL, as the plates *avant lettres* lack that information. Limited to 200 copies. Page size: 12⅜ × 9¼ inches, uncut. The Roederer copy. ¾ green morocco. Cohen–de Ricci 977.

Like the first edition of 1784, this is a collector's book on the grand scale, luxurious in format, paper, and illustrations, and restricted to 200 copies. The Comte de Provence, who supported the edition, paid Cochin 40,000 *livres* for eighty-two drawings, half of which were engraved. Cochin did not skimp on his commission; his large plates, always well composed, are thickly populated with figures. There are battle scenes, ceremonial episodes, and occasional excursions into the suggestive (II, 328) or the marvellous (I, 94). Yet his treatment rarely rises above the pedestrian. The spirit of heroic romance was not in him, at least in the latter part of his career. This copy is exceptional in that it contains thirty-nine of the preliminary etchings and all of the engravings before letters. Something of the distinction of Cochin's original drawing survives in the etching for the first plate of canto IX (I, 274), a relatively uncrowded design in which the engraver's heavy hand has not yet deprived the actors of individuality.

(11) Tasso, *La Gerusalemme liberata*, preliminary etching

High Rococo (1750-1788)

When one thinks of eighteenth-century French book illustration, the three decades during which the rococo style was at its apogee come first to mind. There were fine books both before and after, but most of the masterpieces of the century appeared between 1750 and 1780. These were the achievements that gave rise to the Goncourts' paean to "the century of the vignette" (II, 265), and for many they constitute not merely the greatest age of French illustration but the greatest age of all illustration.

Everything conspired to make this a propitious time for beautiful and luxurious books. A large middle-class public, representing much new wealth, was avid to enjoy life in an easy, elegant way. It patronized the minor arts with enthusiasm, particularly the art of the book. Printers, artists, engravers, papermakers, and binders all found their services in increasing demand, and unlike the first half of the century, professional illustrators, not painters, were responsible for the best books. The most familiar example of what these conditions meant for fine bookmaking is the Fermiers-Généraux edition of La Fontaine's *Contes et nouvelles* (26), but its history can be paralleled by those of many other sumptuous publications. This was also the first age of sophisticated bibliophily on the grand scale, and, ever since, the book collectors of the Western world have imitated in varying degrees the practices that were then established. French bibliophiles a century later could be almost slavish in imitating their predecessors.

During this period illustration overshadowed the text, at least with regard to books of bibliophilic interest. Indeed, it was sometimes asserted that the works of poetasters like Dorat (see below, p. 52) had no right to existence except through the illustrations that adorned them. The rococo style, which had only recently achieved full dominance, offered infinite possibilities for exploration. There were two forms of engravings: the plate (*figure*), occupying the whole page and printed separately from the text, and the vignette, occupying part of the page and printed with the text. The latter included both headpiece (*en tête*) and tailpiece (*cul de lampe*). If plates remained the major focus of attention, vignettes were the more characteristic expression of the age. The varied liveliness of these abundant small illustrations exactly suited contemporary taste.

The most subtle refinements of bibliophily are displayed in the variant forms assumed by these engravings. Supplementary *suites* of vignettes, printed without text, were sometimes added to special copies, as in the editions of Voltaire's *La Henriade* (30) and La Fontaine's *Contes et nouvelles* (26) described below. But plates, unfettered by text, offered the collector his best opportunities. Furstenberg (*Das Buch als Kunstwerk*, pp. xiv–xv) lists fifteen stages through which a plate can pass between preliminary etching and finished engraving. These stages have aesthetic as well as technical significance.

Consider three states of a plate (III, 96) for Ovid's *Métamorphoses* (62). At the court of Aeneas there are two suitors for the hand of his daughter, Achelous and Hercules. When they quarrel and fight, Achelous first transforms himself into a snake, but Hercules, boasting that "conquering serpents was a feat of my infancy," defeats him easily. Achelous next becomes a bull, whereupon Hercules forces him to the ground and tears out one of his horns, which attendant nymphs turn into a cornucopia. The etching of Eisen's vigorous design, which has some engraved work, is graceful and animated; every detail is caught with clarity and precision. The gloss and richness of the plate before letters compensate to some extent for the diminished presence of these qualities. The plate with letters has a dull, brownish cast, and its lines are blurred and muddied. Comparable deterioration occurred almost inevitably whenever a copperplate engraving was printed in substantial numbers. Further examples of the superiority of etchings and plates before letters are presented below. There are etchings for La Borde's *Chansons*, (49), Ovid's *Métamorphoses* (62), La Fontaine's *Contes et nouvelles* (26), the *Contes des fées* (46), and Louvet de Couvray's *Faublas* (83). There are plates before letters for

(62B) Etching for Ovid, *Métamorphoses*

(62B) Proof before letters, Ovid, *Métamorphoses*

Molière's *Oeuvres* (6A and 50), Saint-Non's *Voyage pittoresque . . . de Naples* (34), and the *Iconologie par figures* (23).

Other variant plates were eagerly sought by collectors. A *figure refusée*, or cancelled, is a plate not finally used in the book for which it was prepared. Examples are described for the Fermiers-Généraux La Fontaine (26) and the later edition of the same text illustrated by Fragonard (77). A *figure couverte*, or covered, is a plate in which the nudity of an earlier *découverte*, or uncovered, plate is modified by retouching. Instances are provided by Fermiers-Généraux La Fontaine (26) and the *Métamorphoses* (62).

Even rarer prizes than variant states are the artist's original drawings, a subject the intricacies of which are only now beginning to be systematically studied. Since they were highly esteemed by contemporary collectors, they have survived in considerable numbers. Baron Portalis was at pains to

track down and record them, and Cohen's great manual, as revised by Seymour de Ricci, gives the location of many of them as of 1912. Original designs by several leading book artists are reproduced in this volume: Boucher, Chaudet, Cochin, Desprez, Eisen, Fragonard (from a facsimile), Gérard, Gravelot, Le Barbier, Marillier, Monnet, Monsiau, Moreau, and Oudry. It is particularly rewarding to study an engraving beside the drawing from which it was made, as may be done with Boucher for Corneille's *Rodogune* (7), with Oudry for La Fontaine's *Fables* (5), with Eisen for *Les baisers* (31), with Gravelot for *La secchia rapita* (19), with Monnet for *Gil Blas* (38), with Chaudet for Racine's *Oeuvres* (72), and with Fragonard for La Fontaine's *Contes et nouvelles* (26).

With so receptive and demanding a public, alive to all the nuances of what they did, artists and engravers alike worked with the utmost skill and devotion. The pride that they took in their accom-

(62B) Plate with letters, Ovid, *Métamorphoses*

Acheloüs se metamorphose en Taureau pour
Combattre avec Hercule, et est vaincu.

(62B) Proof of fleuron by Choffard, Ovid, *Métamorphoses*

IV. DES ESTAMPES
DES MÉTAMORPHOSES

plishments is suggested by the memorable fleuron (IV, 354) with which Choffard concluded the *Métamorphoses* (62). The proof reproduced pays tribute to the book's artists (Boucher, Le Prince, Monnet, Eisen, Moreau, and Gravelot) and to no less than eighteen engravers, pride of place being assigned to Le Mire and Augustin de Saint-Aubin. A cupid strews with crowns of flowers the medallions on which their names are inscribed, and the nature of their work is suggested by appropriate attributes: a pallet, brushes, paper, a lyre wreathed with roses, and a torch burning with eternal fire.

Finally, there was the matter of binding. Books left the printer in wrappers or leather-backed boards. Where copies chance to survive in this state, they can be very appealing. Witness the fresh paper and undisturbed gloss of the plates in Corneille's *Théâtre* (17). Books were ordinarily bound in calf with only modest decoration. In the eyes of today's collectors these copies rank more or less on a par with those

in the other usual binding, morocco of the later nineteenth century signed by recognized craftsmen. The most sought after copies, esteemed much more highly than those just described, are in contemporary morocco. If they are elaborately decorated or possess armorial bearings, interest increases in an ascending spiral. Condition, of course, is a crucial factor in appraising examples in any of these bindings.

It will be seen that judging the status of a given copy is a complex exercise. Take the three sets of Ovid's *Métamorphoses* described below (62): the first is in contemporary morocco with a distinguished provenance; the second is one of twelve copies on large paper in later nineteenth-century binding; the third is in modern morocco, but has 175 early states of the plates. Each makes its claim to the collector, but on different grounds. Or again, consider the two copies described of Dorat's *Fables nouvelles* (43). The first is in contemporary morocco,

Calligraphic manuscript of Pezay, *La nouvelle Zélis au bain*

but on small paper with routine impressions of the plates. The second is in later nineteenth-century morocco, but on large paper with brilliant impressions of the plates. It is not surprising that devoted collectors of eighteenth-century French illustrated books tend to accumulate multiple copies of salient titles.

The section which follows sets forth the leading achievements of French book illustration between 1750 and 1788. Highlights are the seventeen titles from this period, beginning with the *Decameron* of 1757 (15) and ending with Gessner's *Oeuvres* of 1786–1793 (39), included in the list of 100 outstanding French illustrated books which makes up Appendix II. Yet these are only a beginning. The overwhelming abundance of illustrated books during this period has been mentioned. Beyond the predominantly literary works covered in this survey lies a wide range of essentially docu-

mentary works which are described with succinct authority by Réau (pp. 29–34): travel books, as exampled in Saint-Non's *Voyage pittoresque . . . de Naples* (74); catalogues of collections such as the *Pierres gravées* (67); festival books, some of which are enumerated on page 6 above; and almanacs. Another sort of publication within the general purview of illustration is the independent series of prints. These are discussed at length by Furstenberg in his survey of 1975 (pp. 50–54). Several of the *suites* he mentions are described below: those for Ovid's *Métamorphoses* (62), the Tilliard *Télémaque* (36), and the Kehl Voltaire (52).

Two more manifestations of the sophisticated refinement of illustration at this time may be mentioned. One was the occasional appearance of books in which both illustrations and text are engraved, thus achieving an effect of surpassing richness. Among these are the Fessard edition of La Fontaine's *Fables* (61), La Borde's *Chansons* (49), and the Tilliard *suite* for *Télémaque* (36). The other was the extensive production of illustrated calligraphic manuscripts, some of great splendor. Perhaps the supreme example is that made to contain Fragonard's drawings for La Fontaine's *Contes et nouvelles*, the facsimile of which is described below (p. 137). Far more typical is a collection of poems after the Marquis de Pezay and others, created in 1785 as the replication of a printed book, with illustrations in the manner of Eisen.[1]

The rococo style persisted until the Revolution, but its dominance gradually declined. After 1765 the example of Moreau led to modifications, the so-called "style Louis XVI," which for a time preserved its authority. Nonetheless, attacks on the rococo and on the vignette, its chief vehicle in book illustration, became increasingly severe. Cochin deplored it as "the assassin of the straight line." Le Barbier deprecated it, and so finally did Moreau after his visit to Italy in 1785. Cazotte mocked the prevailing mania for vignettes in 1772 through the grotesque designs of his *Diable amoureux*. The Goncourts (III, 25) quote a dialogue of 1773 in which an English "Mylord" complains that "our beautiful edition of the *Baskerville Ariosto* . . . [has been] polluted by the wretched vignettes of that pitiful Eis[en]. . . . He has long infected us with his designs, but we are coming to banish him with disgrace from all our presses." Taken together with the rising vogue of neoclassicism, these stirrings hinted that the rococo could not long survive.

As it happened, its reign ended abruptly. The Revolution's repudiation of the *ancien régime* extended to illustration as to everything else. The elegance, wit, and beauty of the illustrated book were viewed as evidence of the underlying frivolity and corruption of the society of which it was a part. Voltaire's paradoxical praise of "the superfluous, a very necessary thing," was no longer persuasive. The pursuit of pleasure was discredited, "prettiness" went out of style, and decoration was regarded as trivial. The time was past when Marie Antoinette's dairy and her penchant for playing the shepherdess were seen as charming fancies. One might say that the art of the previous decades came to be epitomized in Greuze's "La cruche cassée." The suspect innocence of the girl in that painting is described by the Goncourts (II, 59) as "an innocence of Paris and the eighteenth century, a yielding innocence on the brink of its fall." It is no wonder that Thackeray, when he needed a name for a Regency lady of doubtful virtue in *Vanity Fair*, called her Mme. de la Cruchecassée.

The fortunes of eighteenth-century French book illustration have varied with posterity's view of the civilization of which it was a part. Positive disdain ceased after the Empire. Led by the Goncourts, there was an overwhelming reaction in its favor beginning in the 1850s, which lasted until new currents in life and art prevailed towards the end of the century. In our time the *livre de peintre*, which has little in common with the rococo book, has provided the norm for judgment. Now that its authority is fading in turn, eighteenth-century French illustration may at last be accorded the classic status that it deserves.

REFERENCES Calot (1931); Cohen–de Ricci; Furstenberg (1965); Furstenberg (1975); the Goncourts (1880); Holloway; Portalis; Réau.

Calligraphic manuscript of Alexandre Frédéric Jacques de Masson, marquis de Pezay: *La nouvelle Zélis au bain*, poëme en six chants . . . Edition nouvelle & unique en son genre, ornée de vignettes & culs-de lampe, le tout à la plume. Paris, scripsit et delin. A. A. Lejeune, 4 Nov. 1785. [1] *l.*, 11, [1], 12–61 p. [and:] *Nouveau recueil de poësies diverses*, tirées de meilleurs auteurs. Paris, 1785. [1] *l.*, 64, [2] p. Wash, and pen-and-ink illus: I: T.p. vignette, 6 head- and 6 tailpieces. II: Decorated t.p., and 15 tailpieces. Page size: $7\frac{5}{8} \times 5\frac{3}{8}$ inches. Bookplate of Léon Rattier. Red morocco.

1. This discussion of eighteenth-century plates and drawings for illustrations is intended merely to open the subject. The interested reader should consult Furstenberg's monographs of 1965 and 1975, and the catalogues of the collections of Henri Beraldi, René Descamps-Scrive, and Raphaël Esmerian listed in the Bibliography. All are lavishly, indeed lovingly, illustrated.

Hubert-François-Bourguignon, called Gravelot (1699-1773)

This notable illustrator was the son of a Parisian master-tailor named Bourguignon. He took the name of Gravelot, by which he is known, from his godfather. Though he departed from school at an early age, he remained a great reader throughout his life. He chose drawing and engraving as his profession, which for a time he pursued only erratically. Indeed, his early manhood was a time of idleness and dissipation, interspersed by false starts. At the age of thirty he at last embarked on serious study with the artist Restout, and in the winter of 1732–1733 he was invited to London by the engraver Claude de Bosc to help with the plates for the English edition of Picart's *Ceremonies and Religious Customs of Various Nations of the World*, seven volumes (1733–1737).

The books of Gravelot's English years have long been underestimated. Thanks to the late Hanns Hammelmann's thorough explorations, they are now better understood, and they are beginning to be ardently collected. Bringing the new French style exemplified in the work of Watteau and Gillot to the English scene, he was soon busily employed both as artist and engraver. He designed a number of significant separate prints, and he was not above such trivia as coats of arms, invitations, and trade cards; but the illustration and ornamentation of books formed his principal occupation. Hammelmann lists fifty works to which Gravelot contributed plates before he returned to France, as well as eighteen further titles published in London between 1747 and 1775. Outstanding among these are the delicate and charming engraved book *Songs of the Opera of Flora* (1737), George Bickham's celebrated *Musical Entertainer* (1738), the second series of Gay's *Fables* (1738), Richardson's *Pamela* (1742), and two editions of Shakespeare, Theobald's in eight volumes (1740), and Sir Thomas Hanmer's in six volumes (1743–1744). Gravelot's achievements made him a prominent figure in the artistic life of the metropolis. The fellow artists he saw in his Covent Garden lodgings included Hogarth and Francis Hayman. Gainsborough was his pupil, and Garrick became his lifelong friend. In 1746 he returned home, perhaps because anti-Gallican feeling in England was running high in the wake of the battle of Fontenoy.

Gravelot's reputation had preceded him to Paris, where abundant commissions came his way for the rest of his life. His two supreme achievements were the *Decameron* of 1757 and Marmontel's *Contes moraux* of 1765, but they were accompanied by a number of other works hardly less accomplished and pleasing. As in England he turned his attention to much incidental drawing and engraving, which is sampled below in an album of proofs and plates.

In his later years Gravelot's private life was not unlike Daumier's. For all the sophisticated elegance of his work, for all his considerable renown, he preferred a retired, even an obscure, existence. When at last he had attained the means to marry, he wrote to his fiancée: "We are going to be happy then, we two, through our love, in a respectable middling way, with modest wishes, a small, decent household, my pencil, my engraving tools, my books, a few friends, and please God! good health above all" (quoted by Portalis, p. 289). The echo of Horace in the phrase "une honnête médiocrité" is not casual. Gravelot had made up his mind about what he wanted from life, and he knew how to secure it. God was pleased to continue Gravelot's happiness only for a time. His wife died in 1759, and his health failed. He remarried three years before his own death in 1773.

Gravelot's way of working was highly idiosyncratic. He studied the text he was illustrating with great care, identifying the situations in the story, poem, or play which were salient in his author's mind. Then he considered how each situation could be presented in the most telling way. Here he employed "three lay figures made in London, two feet high and capable of every movement of the body, down to the fingers of both hands" (quoted by Hammelmann, p. 41, from the auction catalogue of Gravelot's effects). He had assembled a full wardrobe for these mannikins, ranging from the attire of the day to theatrical costumes and even Roman togas. Having manoeuvered and manipulated his puppets until he arrived at the disposition which best suited his purposes, he proceeded to a series of sketches in pencil and sanguine, often drawing his figures in the nude until he had caught just the movements that would reveal the essence of the scene. Only when these preliminaries were completed did he execute his finished pen drawing. It is significant, indeed, that in the letter quoted above he wrote of his pencil as essential to his well-being, not his pen or his brush. Gravelot's painstaking method, which is exampled in the drawings for *La secchia rapita* shown below, helps to account for the high level of professional accomplishment he attained in nearly all of his work.

It is generally agreed that Gravelot was at his best with scenes of contemporary life, where he approaches Moreau himself in capturing the appearance and manners of good society. This endorsement covers more ground than might at first appear, since in the *Decameron* and elsewhere he transposed both settings and costumes to the France of Louis XV. Gravelot had the good fortune to be the first illustrator of four contemporary novels which have become classics: *Pamela* in 1742, *Tom Jones* in 1750, *Manon Lescaut* in 1756, and *La nouvelle Héloïse* in 1761. Indeed, his designs appeared in the first editions of the two latter books. He contributed only two plates to *Manon Lescaut*. His interpretations of *La nouvelle Héloïse* hardly match those of Moreau (51) and Monsiau (95), though they pleased the author. Rousseau helped to determine not only the scenes to be illustrated but even the grouping of the figures. When he had examined Gravelot's first drawings, he wrote to a friend: "They will make, it seems to me, one of the most agreeable collections of prints seen for a long time past, and I don't doubt, if some success is to be hoped for the book, that they will contribute a great deal" (quoted by Portalis, pp. 278–279).

About the value of Gravelot's plates for French classical tragedy and Italian epic poetry, there is some disagreement. In disparaging his early illustrations of Shakespeare, the Goncourts (II, 272) accused him of *papillotage*. This word is untranslatable, but Tennyson's description in "The New Timon and the Poets" of Bulwer-Lytton as a dandy who shakes a lion's mane "en papillotes," that is to say in curl papers, suggests its meaning. The Goncourts believed that Gravelot trivialized Shakespeare by presenting his personages as if they were characters in an eighteenth-century light entertainment, and they contended that he returned to this unfortunate mode in his later works whenever he had to do with Greek or Roman figures, depicting, like Cochin, Eisen, and Moreau, "the men of Plutarch and the age of Tacitus" in the style of Marmontel's poetry. It is to be regretted, they concluded, that these artists did not concern themselves with "the lively images of contemporary life," rather than "monotonous and trite theatrical antiquity." As far as the other artists are concerned, it is hard to disagree with the Goncourts. With regard to Gravelot, however, a demurral must be entered. Admittedly, his illustrations for the classical tragedies of Corneille, Racine, and Voltaire do not reach the level of those for the *Contes moraux*, but they are nonetheless finely imagined, urbane, and agreeable. In fact, each of the major projects of Gravelot's later years (Corneille, Racine, Tasso, Voltaire) is a worthy addition to the roll of fine French illustrated books. Perhaps because he died before the impact of neoclassicism was fully felt, there was no disastrous anticlimax in his career as an illustrator, as there was in the careers of Cochin and Moreau.

The elegance of Gravelot's designs has been remarked by nearly every critic who has written about him, though there has been a difference of opinion as to whether it was French or English in origin. The Goncourts sought to resolve this question by claiming that "by the time he departed from England, the native elegance of his drawing, in which a memory of Watteau is reflected, had attained during his long stay a complementary finish of English elegance" (p. 273). At any rate, nearly all of Gravelot's thousands of surviving drawings possess this quality, and most of the engravings after these drawings have at least a touch of it.

Gravelot remains among the most charming, as well as the most professional, of all illustrators. Knowing both life and books, he could make almost any text interesting through his illustrations. His aspirations were not grand, but within his range he rarely failed. The list of books that follows, which does not include the great *Ovid* of 1767–1771 (62) in which he also participated, is among the longest in this survey.

REFERENCES Cohen–de Ricci; the Goncourts (1880); Hammelmann; Holloway; Portalis; Portalis-Beraldi; Réau; Salomons (1911).

12 GEORGE BICKHAM, JR.

The musical entertainer, engraved by George Bickham junr . . . London, Charles Corbett [1737–1739]. 2 v. in 1. I: [2], 100 *l*. II: [2], 100 *l*. Engraved throughout, with head- and tailpieces, vignettes, and other decoration by Bickham, including 8 plates after Gravelot. Page size: 15⅝×9⅝ inches. Contemp. calf. Cohen–de Ricci 145–146.

This engraved song-book may almost be regarded as French, since many of its headpieces were imitated from the prints in Watteau's *Oeuvre*. Gravelot's eight designs, the most attractive in the two volumes, show the rococo style already well developed.

13 JOHN GAY

Fables . . . the fifth edition. London, J. & R. Tonson and J. Watts [II: J. & P. Knapton and T. Cox], 1737–1738. 2 v. I: [7] *l.*, 194 p. II: [4] *l.*, 155 p. Illus: I: Engraved t.p. vignette (unsigned) and 51 headpieces by Van der Gucht after Kent (21), Wotton (29), and unsigned (1). II: By Scotin after Gravelot: front., t.p. vignette, and 16 plates. Page size: 7½×4¾ inches. Brown morocco by White (*remboîtage*). Cohen–de Ricci 428.

As illustrations to beast-fables Gravelot's sixteen plates for the second series of Gay's tales in verse are worthy of comparison with the plates after Oudry in La Fontaine's *Fables* (5), though they do not offer the spacious and evocative landscape backgrounds of those designs. In the engraving for fable VIII the master of the house is about to destroy an idle fly, barely visible as it sucks a peach, while a vigilant cat and faithful dog look on. Gravelot is justly praised for his mastery of small-scale illustration, but these larger plates, characteristic of his English period, make their appeal as well.

14 HENRY FIELDING

Histoire de Tom Jones, ou L'enfant trouvé, traduction de l'anglois . . . par M.D.L.P. Enrichie d'estampes dessinées par M. Gravelot. London, Jean Nourse, 1750. 4 v. in 2. I: [2] *l.*, 11, 336 p. II: [2] *l.*, 344 p. III: [2] *l.*, 282 p. IV: [2] *l.*, 341 p. Illus. after Gravelot: I: 3 plates by Chedel, and Pasquier (2). II: 5 plates after Chedel, Delafosse, Fessard, and Pasquier (2). III: 4

(13) John Gay, *Fables*

plates by Aveline, Delafosse, Fessard, and Pasquier. IV: 4 plates by Aveline, Fessard (2), and Pasquier. Page size: 6½×3¾ inches. Contemp. calf, with the arms of L. F. Du Bouchet. Cohen–de Ricci 394–395.

Gravelot's illustrations for *Tom Jones* are a modest success, better than those drawn by Moreau in his declining years (59), but inferior to the lusty designs by Rowlandson for the London edition of 1790. Gravelot captures the situations he depicts with precision, but he doesn't offer much insight into character. In examining his elegant figures, indeed, one sometimes has the uneasy feeling that they are closer to his mannikins than to life. In the plate shown (I, 189) Tom Jones has discovered Philosopher Square crouching behind a fallen rug which serves as a screen in Molly Seagrim's garret bedroom. The plates at II, 64; III, 82; and IV, 18 are dated 1749, the year in which *Tom Jones* was pub-

(14) Henry Fielding, *Histoire de Tom Jones*

lished. It would appear, therefore, that this edition preceded those which give Paris and Amsterdam as the place of publication. (See Hammelmann, p. 45.)

15 GIOVANNI BOCCACCIO

Il Decamerone . . . London [i.e., Paris, Prault], 1757. 5 v. I: [1] *l.*, xi, 292 p. II: [1] *l.*, 271 p. III: [1] *l.*, 195 p. IV: [1] *l.*, 161 [i.e., 261] p. V: [1] *l.*, 247 p. Illus: I: Engraved t.p. by Le Mire after Gravelot, port. by Lempereur after Gravelot, headpiece and 2 tailpieces by Le Mire, 3 tailpieces by Aliamet, tailpiece by Le Mire after Gravelot, 2 tailpieces by Lempereur, 23 unsigned head- and 9 unsigned tailpieces; 22 plates: after Boucher by Le Mire; after Cochin by: Flipart, and Le Mire; after Eisen by: Lempereur, Ouvrier, Pitre Martinasie, and Sornique; after Gravelot by: Aliamet (2), Flipart, Le Mire (7), Lempereur (2), Pitre Martinasie (2), and Tardieu. II: Engraved t.p. by Le Mire after Gravelot, 2 tailpieces by Aliamet after Gravelot, 13 tailpieces by Le Mire after Gravelot, 2 tailpieces by Lempereur after Gravelot, 22 unsigned head- and 2 unsigned tailpieces; 22 plates: after Boucher by: Flipart, and Le Mire; after Cochin by Lempereur; after Eisen by: Ouvrier, and Tardieu; after Gravelot by: Aliamet (2), Flipart, Le Mire (7), Lempereur (5), Ouvrier, and Pitre Martinasie. III: Engraved t.p. by Le Mire after Gravelot, tailpiece by Choffard after Gravelot, tailpiece by Fessard after Gravelot, 3 tailpieces by Fessard and St. Aubin after Gravelot, 10 tailpieces by Le Mire, 2 tailpieces by Le Mire after Gravelot, 2 tailpieces by Lempereur after Gravelot, and 22 unsigned headpieces; 22 plates after: Boucher by Aliamet; after Cochin by: Flipart, and Le Mire; after Eisen by: Aliamet, Baquoy, and Tardieu; after Gravelot by: Aliamet (3), Flipart, Le Mire, Lempereur (5), femme Lempereur, Moitte, Pasquier (2), and Pitre Martinasie. IV: Engraved t.p. by Aliamet after Gravelot, 2 tailpieces by Le Mire after Gravelot, 6 tailpieces by Le Mire, 2 tailpieces by Lempereur after Gravelot, 10 tailpieces by Pasquier after Gravelot, and 22 unsigned headpieces; 22 plates: after Boucher by Flipart; after Cochin by Flipart; after Gravelot by: Aliamet (3), Baquoy (2), Le Mire (5), Ouvrier, Pasquier (2), Pitre Martinasie (4), and Tardieu (3). V: Engraved t.p. by Aliamet after Gravelot, 4 tailpieces by Choffard after Gravelot, 5 tailpieces by Lempereur after Gravelot, 3 tailpieces by Pasquier after Gravelot, 6 tailpieces by St. Aubin after Gravelot, 22 unsigned head- and 2 unsigned tailpieces; 22 plates: after Boucher by Le Mire; after Eisen by: "N.N.," and Tardieu; after Gravelot by: Aliamet, Flipart (5), Legrand (2), Le Mire (2), Lempereur (3), Moitte, Ouvrier, and Tardieu (4). All plates with stamped paraph on verso, indicating the first printing. Page size: $7\frac{3}{4} \times 4\frac{7}{8}$ inches. Stamp of M. de Montigny; book-label of Templeton Crocker. Contemp. red morocco. Cohen–de Ricci 158–160.

Though other artists participated in its illustration, the *Decameron* belongs to Gravelot. He designed 89 of its 111 plates and all 97 of its tailpieces, the most extensive undertaking of his career as an illustrator. Boccaccio's lively tales of varied action and amorous intrigue were well suited to Gravelot's temperament. The convention by which he transposed their settings and costume to the France of his own day made it possible for him to exercise his special talent for depicting the social world around him. In composition the plates are typically more complex than those he did for *Tom Jones*, yet their smaller scale has the effect of concentrating rather than cramping his designs. This conjunction of favorable circumstances produced one of the masterpieces of the illustrated book.

Gravelot created a charmed world in the *Decameron*. For the most part his figures are young, the women graceful and pretty, the men lithe and

H. Gravelot inv.   T.IV.N.20.   Le Mire Sculp.

(15) Boccaccio, *Il decamerone*, plate and tailpiece

handsome. No one positively ugly is allowed to intrude. All levels of life are presented, from the peasant in his hovel to the King in his palace. Every variety of interior is there, from boudoirs and bedrooms to dining rooms and salons. Animated street scenes alternate with glimpses of gardens and farms, forests and river banks. The human condition has rarely been so attractively displayed. Yet all this is only a beginning. As Owen Holloway has demonstrated, Gravelot explores with unfailing subtlety the psychological implications of each situation that he selects for illustration.

Gravelot's tailpieces complete what his plates have begun. They are peopled by amusing children, who sometimes have a purely decorative function but usually play their parts in interpreting Boccaccio's text. The seventh story of the eighth day, for example, concerns a scholar's revenge on a widow. The plate shows him deceiving her into spending a July day naked atop a tower (IV, 165), while the tailpiece takes the reader back to the previous winter when he had passed a night waiting for her, naked in the snow (IV, 199). Gravelot catches the similar but contrasting scenes of humiliating exposure with his usual vividness. Elsewhere the children are content to mimic rather than advance the story. When the reader discovers them on a tomb playing at being dead, after the tragic eighth story of the fourth day (II, 241), he falls once again into the lighthearted mood which prevails throughout the *Decameron*.

When the success of the edition was established, Gravelot was asked to supplement his designs with a *suite libre*. He agreed, at sixty francs a drawing, and he promised to impart to his work "all the correctness and expression of which I am capable." He went on to inquire "to what point liveliness should be carried; for, though in this kind of composition delicacy is preferable to grossness there are people, as you know, who must have partridges and others who prefer butcher's meat." (Quoted by the Goncourts, pp. 282–283.) His patron must have specified an occasional "pièce de boucherie," for Gravelot's designs for his *Estampes galantes des contes de Boccace* are erotic indeed. Yet their grace and elegance reinforce Burke's contention in his *Reflections on the Revolution in France* that under the *ancien régime* "Vice itself lost half its evil, by losing all of its grossness."

Among the other illustrators of the *Decameron*, only Boucher made a distinctive contribution. Eisen's ten drawings seem heavy, almost coarse, in juxtaposition to Gravelot's, and the sober and formal style of Cochin's six plates clashes with Boccaccio's gay narrations. Boucher's six designs, on the other hand, have a richness of tone that fairly causes the page to glow. Illustrating some of the freest of the stories, he achieved a voluptuousness that perfectly realizes their reason for being. And he did this far more by implication than by nudity. Gravelot seems to have recognized Boucher's mastery in this line. At any rate, the specific example to which he refers in asking for instructions as to how far he should go in his *suite libre* parallels Boucher's plate for the story of Alibech and Rustico (II, 127).

French collectors have always shown a preference for the *Decameron* in their own language, but the earlier Italian text has better impressions of the illustrations. This is true even with regard to those superior copies of the French edition which contain early sets of the plates with paraphs at the reverse lower margins, attesting to their priority of printing, since the vignettes in the text are necessarily later impressions. An ideal copy, like this one, has the Italian text, is printed on Holland paper, has plates marked by paraphs, is bound in contemporary morocco, and can claim a distinguished provenance. The binding is reproduced in Appendix I.

8• Two designs for Boccaccio's *Decamerone* (1757). Pen and black ink, brown ink and wash, with traces of red chalk; one with graphite. One drawing illustrates the "IV. Journée, Nouvelle 2"; the other is for the "V. Journée, Nouvelle 6." Sheet size: 4½ × 2¼ inches.

These finished drawings in ink and wash depict the parallel climaxes of two of Boccaccio's most complicated narratives. In that for the second story of the fourth day Fra Alberto is suffering public humiliation for persuading a lady to sleep with him by pretending that he is the angel Gabriel. In that for the sixth story of the fifth day two lovers condemned for no fault of their own to be burnt at the stake are rescued at the last moment by a powerful friend. The delicate precision through which Gravelot imparts life and meaning to these miniature designs is beyond praise.

IV. Journée, Nouvelle 2.

V. Journée Nouvelle 6.

Drawings for *Il decamerone*

La honte et les remords vengent l'amour outragé.

H. Gravelot inv.   N. v. Frankendaal sc.

(16) Rousseau, *La nouvelle Héloïse*

16   JEAN JACQUES ROUSSEAU

Lettres de deux amans, habitans d'une petite ville au pied des Alpes . . . Amsterdam, Marc Michel Rey, 1761. 6 v. I: [2] *l.*, 407, [1] p. II: [2] *l.*, 319, [1] p. III: [2] *l.*, 255, [1] p. IV: [2] *l.*, 331 p. V: [2] *l.*, 311, [1] p. VI: [2] *l.*, 312 p. Illus: Each vol. with unsigned t.p. vignette, and 2 plates after Gravelot by: I: Frankeendaal; II: Frankeendaal; III: Folkema, and Frankeendaal; IV: Folkema, and Frankeendaal; V: Folkema; VI: Folkema. Bound in v. I is the same publisher's *Recueil d'estampes pour La nouvelle Héloïse, avec les sujets des mêmes estampes, tels qu'ils ont été donnés par l'éditeur,* 1761 (24 p.), and Rousseau's *Préface de La nouvelle Héloïse . . .* , Paris, Duchesne, 1761 (iv, 96 p.). Page size: 6½ × 3¾ inches. Red morocco by Riviere. See Cohen–de Ricci 904–905, these plates not seen.

The Pierpont Morgan Library

Gravelot's plates for *La nouvelle Héloïse*, to give *Lettres de deux amans* the name by which it came to be known, are charming scenes of eighteenth-century life, pretty and well composed, but they are not remarkable for insight into character. The reason may have been that Rousseau provided Gravelot with so much information that it was hardly necessary for him to study the novel's text in his customary way. Rousseau's remarks were published as *Les sujets* [*de la nouvelle Héloïse*], also in 1761, a copy of which is bound with this set. Not only did he describe the personality and appearance of each of the six principal figures of the novel, but also he set down with some minuteness the scenes which he wished to have depicted, giving each a title of his own invention. The most animated of the resulting designs (II, 294) shows Saint Preux's hasty exit from a house of ill fame, captioned: "Shame and remorse avenge outraged love." Following this conception, Gravelot shows a lady pursuing him closely, the rest of his companions looking on from above, and the coachman standing idly by. Except for Saint Preux and the lady, the figures are hardly individualized. By comparison, what Moreau did with the same scene (51) is a revelation.

17   PIERRE CORNEILLE

Théâtre . . . avec des commentaires . . . [Geneva], 1764. 12 v. I: [3] *l.*, 454 p., [2] *l.* II: [2] *l.*, 9 p., [4] *l.*, 413, [1] p., [1] *l.* III: [2] *l.*, 510 p., [1] *l.* IV: [2] *l.*, 482 p., [2] *l.* V: [2] *l.*, 429, [1] p., [1] *l.* VI: [2] *l.*, 442 p., [1] *l.* VII: [2] *l.*, 467, [1] p. VIII: [2] *l.*, 388 p., [1] *l.* IX: [2] *l.*, 443, [1] p., [1] *l.* X: [2] *l.*, 495, [1] p., [1] *l.* XI: [2] *l.*, 498 p., [1] *l.* XII: [2] *l.*, 355, [1], 47 p., [1] *l.* Illus: I: Front. by Watelet after Pierre; after Gravelot: 2 plates by Flipart, and Le Mire. II: 2 plates by Flipart, and Lempereur. III: 3 plates by Le Mire (2), and Lempereur. IV: 3 plates by Baquoy, Le Mire, and de Longueil. V: 2 plates by Le Mire. VI: 3 plates by Flipart, Le Mire, and de Longueil. VII: 3 plates by Flipart, and Le Mire (2). VIII: 3 plates by Le Mire (2), and de Longueil. IX: 3 plates by Baquoy, and Radigues (2). X: 4 plates by Le Mire (3), and Prévost. XI: 4 plates by Le Mire. XII: 2 plates by Flipart, and Le Mire. Page size: 8½ × 5⅜ inches, uncut. Contemp. ¼ pink calf. Cohen–de Ricci 255.

This famous edition was undertaken by Voltaire to provide a little fortune for Corneille's niece, who had been discovered in destitution. Having assembled an impressive list of subscribers, Voltaire secured Gravelot as his illustrator and set to work himself on a commentary for each play. By the time he had written twenty commentaries, however,

(17) Corneille, *Héraclius*

(17) Corneille, *La place royale*

Gravelot had finished only two plates. Complaining that at this rate he would die before the book appeared, Voltaire wrote in a moment of petulance that he would do without "the vain and miserable ornament of prints" (Portalis, I, 282–283). But the edition eventually appeared with Voltaire's commentaries and Gravelot's plates.

It met with general approval, and indeed Gravelot's harmonious and decorative compositions, nicely interpreting the crucial moments of the plays, are a delight to the eyes. In *Héraclius* Corneille's plot is too complex for brief summary, but the scene Gravelot has chosen (V, 101) shows the nurse Léontine defying the tyrant Phocas to decide whether Héraclius or Martian is his real son. "Guess if you can," she taunts, "and choose if you dare." Most of the other tragedies are also persuasively presented, given the conventions under

which Gravelot was working, though the Goncourts' objection to *papillotage* does come to mind when one encounters the stylish figure that the artist has made of Attila the Hun (IX, 17). Corneille's nine plays with contemporary settings elicited designs on a par with those for the *Contes moraux*. Indeed, the engravings for *La galerie du palais* (XI, 255) and *La place royale* (XII, 1), which is shown, are among Gravelot's best-known illustrations.

This copy, which came from a Dutch collection formed in the eighteenth century, is uncut and unpressed, just as it left the publisher. It has remained in a temporary casing, evidently intended to get the sheets to the final purchaser in pristine condition. The brilliance of its plates makes one wish that more eighteenth-century illustrated books had survived in such condition.

H. Gravelot invenit. — J.F. Rousseau Sculp.

LE CONNOISSEUR.

(18) Marmontel, *Contes moraux*

H. Gravelot inven. J.J. Pasquier Sculp.

L'ECOLE DES PERES.

(18) Marmontel, *Contes moraux*

18 JEAN FRANÇOIS MARMONTEL

Contes moraux . . . Paris, J. Merlin, 1765. 3 v. I: [1] *l.*, xvi p., [1] *l.*, 345 p. II: [2] *l.*, 312 p. III: [4] *l.*, 376 p. Illus: Front. by St. Aubin after Cochin, engraved t.p. by Duclos after Gravelot, and 9 plates after Gravelot by: Baquoy, de Longueil (2), Legrand, Leveau (2), Rousseau, Voyez, and unsigned (1). II: Engraved t.p. by Duclos after Gravelot, and 5 plates after Gravelot by: de Longueil (2), Le Mire (2), and Pasquier. III: Engraved t.p. by Duclos after Gravelot, and 9 plates after Gravelot by: de Longueil (5), Leveau (2), Pasquier, and Rousseau. Page size: 7¾ × 4⅞ inches. Red morocco by Chambolle-Duru. Cohen–de Ricci 686–687, first issue.

18A

Another copy, reimposed as a 12mo. Page size: 6½ × 3¾ inches. Contemp. stained calf. First issue.

Marmontel relates in his preface how he came to write these stories, the contemporary popularity of which is attested by many translations and dramatic versions. He had made a collection of little absurdities of social behavior which had gone unreproved even by Molière. Asked to contribute to a widely read periodical, the *Mercure de France*, he turned one of them into a story called "Alcibiade." Its success led to twenty-two more narratives. They first appeared in book form in 1761. To combat rampant piracy, it was decided to publish this new edition "embellished with particular care" (I, xv–xvi).

Gravelot's plates are the only embellishments of significance, and in them the artist is faithful to his author both in letter and in spirit. His plate for "Le connoisseur" (II, 327) serves as an example of how he worked. Fintac, who poses as a universal connoisseur of the arts, offers his patronage to Célicoeur, a young poet. Having fallen in love with Fintac's sprightly niece, Agathe, Célicoeur accepts him as a sponsor. The pair cannot be united, however, because of Fintac's resentment of Agathe's refusal to marry an elderly antiquary he had chosen for her. When Fintac asks Célicoeur to allow a wretched comedy he has written to be performed over Célicoeur's name, Agathe makes her lover agree to the deception. Predictably, the play is a disastrous failure, and the lovers tell Fintac that they will reveal him as its author unless they are permitted to marry.

This is the moment which Gravelot chose for his design. Agathe is excited and triumphant. Célicoeur's impetuous embrace seals the happiness he has at last achieved. Fintac, clasping the fatal manuscript of his comedy in one hand, signifies with the other his abandonment of false connoisseurship, the confusion inherent in which is attested by the litter around him, books askew, sculptures piled one on another, and a mass of miscellaneous objects including a globe and a telescope. Marmontel's little story has been dramatically presented, his mild moral effectively conveyed. Gravelot employs the same strategy in the plate for "L'école des pères" (II, 161).

Though one must read Marmontel to appreciate the psychological finesse of Gravelot's designs, the plates themselves are the important thing, not their interpretation of Marmontel's stories. Just as in the *Decameron* Gravelot is a worthy rival of Eisen in La Fontaine's *Contes et nouvelles* (26), so in the *Contes moraux* he sustains comparison with Moreau in the *Monument du costume* (55). From intrigues of gallantry in a past age, he has moved for the most part to the small crises of contemporary existence —only five of the stories are classical or oriental— and he has succeeded in presenting a whole way of life in the most charming of settings. Moreover, the larger scale of his illustrations allows him to display the elegance and urbanity of his idealized vision of society more fully than anywhere else in his work.

No doubt to achieve a wider sale, the book was published in both *de luxe* and ordinary editions.

This is a superb copy of the octavo issue on fine paper with early impressions of the plates (witnessed by the errata lists at the bottom of the contents pages). The spacious format gives full value to the engravings. The duodecimo issue, with its inferior paper and narrow margins, seems mean by comparison.

19 ALESSANDRO TASSONI

La secchia rapita, poema eroicomico . . . Paris, Lorenzo Prault & Pietro Durand, 1766. 2 v. I: [1] *l.*, cviii, 128 p. II: [1] *l.*, 239, [1] p. Illus: I: Front., t.p. vignette, 2 headpieces and 1 vignette by Le Roy after Gravelot, 4 plates after Gravelot by: Duclos, Née, Rousseau, and Pasquier; after Marillier: 3 headpieces, 2 tailpieces, and 1 vignette by Le Roy; 1 tailpiece by Le Roy after Huet. II: T.p. vignette by Le Roy after Gravelot, headpiece by Le Roy, 8 plates after Gravelot by: Duclos (2), Le Roy (2), Née, Pasquier, Rousseau, and Simonet; 6 headpieces and 3 tailpieces by Le Roy after Marillier; 1 vignette and 3 tailpieces by Le Roy after Huet; 1 headpiece by Le Roy after Quéverdo. Page size: $8\frac{5}{8} \times 5\frac{3}{8}$ inches. Contemp. stained calf. Cohen–de Ricci 980–981.

This "heroic-comic" poem tells how the citizens of Bologna and Modena waged war over a stolen bucket. In illustrating it Gravelot placed less overt emphasis on parody than Cochin did in his designs for "Le lutrin" (8), yet there are many lighthearted touches which set his plates apart from those which he did for the more imposing *Gerusalemme liberata* of 1771. Otherwise the two books follow the same pattern of illustration. For each of the twelve cantos there is a headpiece (the argument in an elaborate frame), a plate, and a tailpiece. Gravelot made the designs for the plates, but the headpieces and tailpieces were entrusted for the most part to Marillier and Huet. The most charming of the book's decorations are three full-page fleurons: by Gravelot for canto II and by Huet for canto V supplementing smaller tailpieces, and by Marillier for canto III serving itself as a tailpiece.

❧ 18 pen and black ink, and pencil drawings for plates in Tassoni's *La secchia rapita* (1766). Illustrations for cantos: I (plate—2 designs; headpiece), II (plate; tailpiece), III (plate—2 designs), IV (plate), V (plate—2 designs), VII (plate—2 designs), VIII (plate), IX (plate), X (plate), XI (plate—2 designs), XII (plate). All drawings have blackened versos and stylus marks for transfer to copperplates. Sheet and image sizes vary, but generally $5\frac{1}{4} \times 3\frac{3}{8}$ inches.

Tassoni, *La secchia rapita*, preliminary sketch for the fleuron, canto II

(19) Tassoni, *La secchia rapita*, engraving of fleuron, canto II

These eighteen drawings nicely illustrate Gravelot's method of work, since for each of cantos I, III, VII, and XI there is a preliminary sketch and a nearly finished design. The sequence shown appears early in the poem. First comes the fleuron at the end of canto II. A grim-faced Queen of Love is on her way by chariot to King Enzio of Modena. Her mission is implied by warlike attributes of weapons and armor together with the spilled wine and overturned cup of peace. In the plate at the beginning of canto III she is at Enzio's bedside, now accompanied by a cupid, urging him, as he sleeps, to come to the aid of his imperilled city. His restlessness suggests that she has made her point. There is a delicious humor in the contrast between Gravelot's formidable mythological apparatus and the homely bedroom scene—slippers negligently dis-

carded, chamberpot on the table, and bedclothes in disarray—with Enzio at its center in a most unheroic attitude.

20 JEAN BAPTISTE RACINE

Oeuvres . . . avec des commentaires, par M. Luneau de Boisjermain. Paris, Louis Cellot [v.6–7: London], 1768. 7 v. I: [4] *l.*, cxliv, 277 p. II: [2] *l.*, 443 p. III: [2] *l.*, 409 p. IV: [2] *l.*, 432 p. V: [2] *l.*, 440 p. VI: viii p., [1] *l.*, 436 p., [1] *l.* VII: vii, 399, [1] p. plus 17-p. subscribers' list. Illus: I: Port. by Gaucher after Santerre, and 2 plates after Gravelot by Flipart and Le Mire. II: 3 plates after Gravelot by Le Mire, Lempereur, and Rousseau. III: 3 plates after Gravelot by Duclos, Levasseur, and Prévost. IV: 2 plates after Gravelot by Levasseur and Simonet. V: 2 plates after Gravelot by Née. Page size: 7⅝×4⅞ inches. Contemp. stained calf. Cohen–de Ricci 847–849.

Tassoni, *La secchia rapita*, preliminary and finished sketches for canto III

Little need be said of this handsome edition, in which Gravelot did for Racine what he had done for Corneille four years earlier. It appears from the preface (I, xx) that the publishers not only sought him out to add luster to their ambitious project but also entrusted the supervision of the engravings to him. He executed his assignment with aplomb, but there are twelve plates rather than thirty-two, and only one (*Les plaideurs*, II, 163) is of a contemporary subject.

21 VOLTAIRE

[Plates for the Collection complette des **oeuvres de Mr. de Voltaire** . . . Geneva, frères Cramer, 1768–1774. 30 v.]. Illus: 7 portraits after various artists; after Gravelot: front. by Flipart, and 42 plates by: De Launay (3), Duclos (5), de Ghendt, Godefroy, Helman

(2), Levasseur (8), Leveau (2), de Longueil (2), de Lorraine (2), Masquelier, Massard (3), Née (2), Ponce, Rousseau (4), St. Aubin & Tilliard, and Simonet (4). Page size: 10 1/8 × 7 7/8 inches. Brown stained calf, with the arms of the Duke of Newcastle (*remboîtage*). Cohen–de Ricci 1041–1042.

Pleased with the eventual result of their collaboration in Corneille's *Oeuvres*, Voltaire sought Gravelot's participation in an edition of his own works. The scale chosen for his illustrations, ten for *La Henriade* and thirty-two for the plays, was larger than that employed in any other of Gravelot's major books. In sending Voltaire what he had done for *La Henriade*, indeed, Gravelot referred to his designs as "tableaux." These drawings confirm the artist's claim of showing the progression of the narrative with piquant variety (Portalis, I, 279–280), but despite their verve and animation, it is hard to feel much enthusiasm for his excursion into the territory that Cochin was making his own. Equally ambitious are the thirty-two illustrations for Voltaire's plays. Perhaps because of their size, even the designs for the comedies of modern life are deficient in Gravelot's usual charm. Nor do his carefully studied drawings for the tragedies, mostly with classical settings, equal those which he did for Corneille and Racine. One has the sense of watching actors as they declaim, rather than people as they speak. When the artist's inspiration flags, one again catches hints of Gravelot's mannikins. It is unfortunate that Voltaire thought of his epic poem and his tragedies as constituting his chief claim on posterity. In Gravelot's hands *Candide* might have been a masterpiece of illustration.

22   TORQUATO TASSO

La Gerusalemme liberata . . . Paris, Delalain, Durand, & Molini, 1771. 2 v. I: [2] *l.*, 331 p. (incl. engraved t.p. and dedication). II: [1] *l.*, 340 p. (incl. engraved t.p.). Illus. after Gravelot: I: Front. by Henriquez, t.p. vignette by Patas, engraved dedication by Le Roy, 10 head- and 7 tailpieces by Le Roy, 5 full-page vignettes by Le Roy, and 10 plates by: Baquoy, Duclos (3), Le Roy, Lingée, Née, Rousseau, and Simonet (2). II: Front. by Henriquez, t.p. vignette by Mesnil, 10 head- and 6 tailpieces by Le Roy, 4 full-page vignettes by Le Roy, tailpiece by Ponce, and 10 plates by: Duclos, Henriquez, Leveau, Lingée, Massard, Née, Patas, Ponce, Rousseau, and Simonet. Page size: 11½×8⅞ inches. Contemp. red morocco. Cohen–de Ricci 974–975.

22A

Octavo format. Page size: 9×5½ inches. Contemp. red morocco by Derome le jeune, with his ticket; binding designed by Gravelot.

This is a handsome and delightful book, particularly in the rare quarto edition where the illustrations are properly set off by ample margins. There are twenty cantos, and a plate, a headpiece, and at least one tailpiece is assigned to each. The headpieces are portraits of the principal figures in the poem with elaborate allegorical frames. The plates tell the story of Tasso's Christian heroes with fidelity and discrimination, even occasionally catching something of the poem's ambiance of

(22A) Tasso, *La Gerusalemme liberata*

mystery and romance. But it is in the tailpieces that Gravelot triumphs. There are twenty-three of them, since nine are full-page fleurons which in three instances immediately follow smaller tailpieces. "It has been thought possible to have nothing but children in them," the prospectus for the book explained (quoted by Holloway, p. 72), "who will represent either an allegory related to the canto in which they are placed, or an event mentioned either there or in the following one." Gravelot was thus enabled to present a joyous running commentary not only on Tasso's poem but sometimes on his own plates interpreting it. Without mocking chivalry, he makes it a source of sympathetic amusement. The tailpiece of canto II (1, 66) shows Goffredo and his knights receiving the Egyptian ambassadors in his tent. The folly of the indignant reproaches which lead these great personages to a declaration of war is underlined by the play-acting of the *putti*.

The *de présent* binding by Derome le jeune on the octavo edition is reproduced in Appendix I.

Iconologie par figures, ou Traité complet des allégories, emblèmes, &c. Ouvrage utile aux artistes, aux amateurs, et peuvent servir à l'éducation des jeunes personnes. Par M. M. Gravelot et Cochin. Paris, Lattré, [c. 1789], 4 v. I: [2] *l.*, xvi, 99 p. II: [2] *l.*, 112 p. III: [2] *l.*, 106 p. IV: [2] *l.*, 167 p. Illus: I: Front. by Gaucher after Delatour, engraved t.p. by Gaucher after Gravelot, port. by Gaucher after Monnet, and 45 plates after Gravelot by: Choffard (4), De Launay (3), de Ghendt (3), Le Mire (3), de Longueil, Prévost (6), Rousseau, St. Aubin, and Simonet (3); after Cochin: Aliamet, De Launay (2), de Ghendt, Ingouf, Leveau (4), Lingée (2), de Longueil, Masquelier, Massard (4), Née, St. Aubin, and Simonet (2). II: Engraved t.p. by de Ghendt after Gravelot, 48 plates after Gravelot by: Choffard, De Launay, Duclos, de Ghendt (2), Leveau, de Longueil (8), Massard (3), Prévost (2), Rousseau, St. Aubin (2), and Simonet; after Cochin: Aliamet (3), Gaucher (2), Halbou (2), Legrand (2), Leveau (5), Lingée (2), Massard (4), Nicollet (2), Ponce (2), and Simonet. III: Engraved t.p. by Legrand after Gravelot, 49 plates after Gravelot by: Baquoy (2), Choffard, Duclos (2), De Launay (3), de Ghendt (2), de Longueil (6), Le Mire, Massard (3), Prévost (6), St. Aubin, and Simonet; after Cochin: Aliamet (2), Godefroy, Goucher, Halbou, Legrand, Leveau (3), Lingée (2), Massard, Née, Ponce (3), St. Aubin, Vauvillé; and unsigned or indistinctly signed (3). IV: Engraved t.p. (unsigned) and 60 plates after Gravelot by: Baquoy, Choffard (5), De Launay (5), de Ghendt, de Longueil (2), Leveau, Massard (2), Prévost (3), and Simonet (4); after Cochin: Duflos, Gaucher (5), Godefroy (4), Legrand (2), Leveau (4), Lingée (5), Massard (2), Nicolet, Ponce (6), and Simonet; unsigned (5). Many of the plates are proofs before letters, or with scratched artists' names. Page size: $6\frac{7}{8} \times 4$ inches. Contemp. calf. Cohen–de Ricci 456–457.

Seventeen volumes of *Almanachs iconologiques* appeared between 1765 and 1781. The series is rare, however, and its plates are more readily studied as collected in the four volumes of *Iconologie par figures*. Like the *Contes moraux*, this work was issued in both octavo and duodecimo formats. Here, however, the duodecimo is to be preferred. The small plates are more in scale with the page, and some copies, like this one, contain proofs before letters with the artists' names etched rather than engraved. These impressions, according to Cohen (column 456), antedate those in the *Almanachs iconologiques* themselves.

Gravelot was responsible for the illustrations in the *Almanachs iconologiques* which appeared before his death. When Cochin succeeded him, he decided to turn the work into an iconographical treatise. The very idea of such a project calls to mind Vol-

(23) *Iconologie par figures*, proof before letters

(23) *Iconologie par figures*, proof before letters and artists' names

Petit cahier d'images pour les enfants, preliminary proof of "Blindman's buff—Shuttlecock"

taire's maxim "Tous les genres sont bons, hors le genre ennuyeux," but actually the representations of abstract conceptions in *Iconologie par figures* are delightful rather than boring. Moreover, scholarship since the Second World War has shown how fascinating the emblematic tradition in literature and art can become if it is studied in depth. Seen in this light, the *Iconologie par figures* is a rewarding as well as an elegant book.

It is arranged in the form of a dictionary. More than four hundred brief articles describing how ideas, subjects, and persons can be emblematically displayed are illustrated with 202 plates. Typical of Gravelot's work at its most pleasing are the proofs before letters of "Peinture" (IV, 7) and "Prométhée" (IV, 33). Painting is a silent art, so its representative is gagged. It should concern itself with the beautiful, so she is painting the graces. An amateur is admiring her work, and in the background a craftsman is compounding the colors she will use.

&ebar; Album of 90 engravings by or after Gravelot, many early proofs, 1 titled by the artist. Red morocco by Zaehnsdorf.

The engravings in this album, many of which are proofs, date from the years after Gravelot's return to France in 1746. They include fifty-six impressions from the *Suites des petits sujets* which J. Bacheley engraved from Gravelot's designs about 1770. In several of these series the children, who elsewhere appear in the artist's tailpieces to develop or parody the action depicted in the plates, have the stage to themselves as principal actors. The illustrations which appear in early children's books are usually primitive and dowdy. In comparison the preliminary proof of "Le colin maillard—Le jeu du volant" from the *Petit cahier d'images pour les enfants* seems a miracle of style and polish. The other prints in the album exemplify the varied work which Gravelot undertook in addition to his book illustration: invitations, address cards, advertisements, even headpieces for funeral orations. These last were apparently used again and again. At any rate, the album includes two variants of the same plate, with different coats of arms.

Charles Eisen (1720–1778)

Among the four masters of French rococo book illustration, there is most disagreement about the position which should be accorded to Eisen. Henri Cohen, who knew the detail of the subject better than anyone else, ranked him second to Moreau only because of the latter's superior range and flexibility, saying that otherwise his illustrations brought together "the maximum of grace, finish, and perfection" (p. xv). To his mind Eisen "excelled in voluptuous subjects and knew how to give an inexpressible charm to everything which makes women attractive." The Goncourts, on the other hand, thought that he had "an authentic small talent," which should not be exaggerated. For them his Flemish heaviness, his men who look like clerks on their Sunday holidays or servants in their masters' clothing, and his lifeless female figures, women of the street dressed like ladies, all testify to his inferiority to Gravelot (III, 22–23). It would almost seem that the Goncourts sought to confirm their grudging estimate of Eisen by their revelation of his unseemly private life, but at this point their argument breaks down. If an illustrator has a penchant for sensual, even licentious, themes, the fact that he is a libertine may well be to his advantage as an artist.

Charles Eisen was born in 1720, the son of François Eisen, a Belgian artist who had settled in Valenciennes early in the eighteenth century. The training which he received from his father was in the style of Flemish realism. Capable of drawing the visible world with fine precision, he came to Paris in 1741, where he studied engraving under Le Bas. His first important designs for illustration were his headpieces for Boileau's *Oeuvres* of 1747 (8).

He had need of this employment, for two years earlier an affair with an apothecary's daughter, some twelve years his senior, had led to an enforced marriage, and the couple already had two children. Henceforth he applied himself with energy both to book illustration and to the six parts of his *Oeuvre suivie*, drawings of all sorts of rococo decorative subjects. He also attempted painting in the grand manner, though few of his canvases can now be identified. His first notable success as an illustrator came with *L'Eloge de la folie* in 1751. Among the many commissions which followed were his headpiece portraits for Descamps' *La vie des peintres flamands*, his contributions to Lucretius' *Della natura delle cose* (9) and to the *Decameron* of 1757 (15), and his plates for Thomson's *Saisons*. In 1762 he achieved celebrity with the Fermiers-Généraux edition of La Fontaine's *Contes et nouvelles*. Despite his several collaborators, this is Eisen's book, just as the *Decameron* is Gravelot's.

Eisen was appointed to positions at court and even became Mme. de Pompadour's drawing master, but he didn't retain her favor for long. After remarking on his grossness, unmitigated by education or reading, the Goncourts attribute his failure to achieve a permanent place in society "to his low habits, tastes, and appetites, [and] to his way of behaving which was scandalous even for that complaisant time" (III, 19–20). Eisen's folly, if not arrogance, is shown in an anecdote which they quote from a contemporary biographical dictionary. At Mme. de Pompadour's request, he designed a costume for Louis XV in a fashion that was both simple and new. On the day when the King first wore it, he appeared at court himself, identically clad. At the age of forty-seven he left his wife and children to take up residence with his mistress. It is not surprising that he failed to be elected to the Academy.

To the less fastidious public Eisen remained a personage of importance. In the little world of rakes and dandies, there were a number of would-be poets. Beginning in 1763, the Chevalier Dorat, a retired officer of musketeers, persuaded Eisen, as the master of gallant illustration, to adorn his verse pamphlets on erotic themes, usually with a plate, a headpiece, and a tailpiece. Other poetasters like Blin de Sanmore and the Marquis de Pezay followed suit. Indeed, when Eisen contributed more designs than usual to Du Rosoi's *Les sens* in 1766, Dorat reproached him warmly (Portalis, p. 198). Thus there came into being a small library of verse epistles, stories, and comedies, which are exampled in the collection of plaquettes described below. "You are publishing too much," Grimm told their authors. "If you don't stop, we shall go on saying that you are selling us M. Eisen's pretty pictures to make acceptable your verses, which aren't pretty at all." (Quoted by the Goncourts, III, 24.) The amiable Dorat used to quote against himself some punning verses in which his reliance on Eisen's *planches* (prints) is compared to an unlucky sailor's saving himself by leaping from one *planche* (plank) to another (quoted by Portalis, p. 200). It was in part through these expensive publications that the poet exhausted his considerable fortune by the time of his death in 1780.

In 1770 this passing fashion unexpectedly gave rise to *Les baisers*, a masterpiece for which all of its presumptuous trivialities may be forgiven. In his fifty-eight plates for Ovid's *Métamorphoses* of 1767–1771 (62) and in his designs for Montesquieu's *Le temple de Gnide* of 1772, Eisen again showed his mastery of the kind of illustration that he had made his own. As much cannot be said of his plates for the Baskerville Ariosto of 1773 (64). For Voltaire's *La Henriade* of 1769–1770 and Levayer de Boutigny's *Tarsis et Zélie*, three volumes, 1774, he was called upon for different kinds of illustration and responded with professional competence. Thus he remained in full employment nearly to the end of his life.

In 1777 Eisen left Paris for Brussels, "on business" according to his wife, but probably to escape his creditors. He arrived there, a friend relates, "devoured by gout and tormented by the evils which are the consequence of libertinage and debauch" (quoted by the Goncourts, III, 27). His landlord sent word to his mistress of his death and burial early the following year. To his family he left a troubled heritage of debts and undelivered designs.

Eisen was in harmony with his age, even in his libertinage. He brought to full flower the tradition of gallant illustration initiated by Boucher. Without what Calot calls his "Flemish atavism" (p. 136), his illustrations would lack the robustness and sensuality which gives them their distinctive mark, yet the grace, delicacy, and precision with which he realized his conceptions save his work from vulgarity. He was the master of the small design, as Moreau was of the large. His penchant for light, even frivolous, subjects limited his range,

but within it he was a past master. He had a marvellous talent for pleasing.

REFERENCES Calot (1931); Cohen–de Ricci; the Goncourts (1880); Holloway; Portalis; Réau; Salomons (1914).

24 DESIDERIUS ERASMUS

L'Eloge de la folie, traduit . . . par M. Gueudeville. Nouvelle édition revûe et corrigée sur le texte de l'édition de Basle. Ornée de nouvelles figures . . . [Paris], 1751. [4] *l.*, xxiv, 222 p., [1] *l.* Illus. after Eisen: Engraved front. by Martinasie ("sous la direction de M. Le Bas"), t.p. vignette by Le Mire, headpiece by Flipart, tailpiece by Aliamet, and 13 plates by: Lafosse (2), Legrand, Le Mire (2), Le Mire and Pinssio, Pasquier, Tardieu (5), and 1 unsigned. Plates are printed in black. Page size: 9¼×7 inches (*grand papier*). ¼ brown morocco. Cohen–de Ricci 348–349, Reynaud 159–160.
The Pierpont Morgan Library

Like his headpieces for Boileau's *Oeuvres* (8), the designs in this book serve as a reminder that Eisen's development of the voluptuous style usually associated with his name came when his career as an illustrator was well advanced. Eisen's plates follow the triumphant course of Folly throughout society. He is shown in person lecturing a polite audience which includes an attentive monkey, encouraging a duel, and leading a hunt. Only the last is taken from Holbein's renowned illustrations for this work. Elsewhere the vanity of pride, avarice, gambling, and other vices is displayed. The book should be sought in the superior quarto edition, for which Eisen provided the frontispiece with a fine rococo frame. It shows Folly offering his bauble to the goddess of wisdom.

&◆ Album of 28 pen-and-ink, wash, and graphite drawings for Descamps' *La vie des peintres* . . . (1753–1764). 22 designs are portraits in vignette frames, 6 are without portraits. Sheet and image sizes vary, but generally measure 2½×3⅞ inches. Purple morocco by Pagnant.

Eisen's drawings, both in China ink and wash and in pencil, have survived in some abundance, though many are not for illustrations. It is a question here of those he did for J. B. Descamps' *La vie des peintres flamands, allemands et hollandais*, four volumes, 1753–1764. Of the plates made from these by Ficquet, the principal engraver for the project, Portalis remarks (I, 165) that there is "nothing so living, so personal, so faithful as these delicate heads of artists." This album contains eighteen finished draw-

Ch. Eisen Inv.

Ch. Eisen inv. et sec.

Gravé sous la Direction de M.r Le Bas
par P.F. Martinasie.

(24) Erasmus, *L'Eloge de la folie*

Drawing of Holbein, Descamps, *La vie des peintres flamands*

Drawing of Hendrik Goltzius, Descamps, *La vie des peintres flamands*

ings used in the work, and ten others, most of them incomplete. Eisen's pattern is a central framed portrait, with a scene, painting, or object associated with the artist on either side. Holbein, for example, is shown between his *Dance of Death* and his portrait of Sir Thomas More. Though the Goncourts preferred Eisen's "pensées," or first sketches, to his finished designs, urging that the latter had been "made stupid to accord with the intelligence and working necessities of the engraver," they granted that most of his drawings are both witty and seductive (III, 16–17). "Taking his inspiration from Boucher, . . . Eisen sets himself apart by the refinement, the delicacy of his manner, and even in calling the master to mind, he always remains himself."

25 JAMES THOMSON

Les saisons, poëme. Traduit de l'anglois de Thompson [sic]. Paris, Chaubert & Hérrisant, 1759. [5] *l.*, viii, 332 p., [2] *l.* Illus. after Eisen: Engraved t.p., 4 tail-pieces and 4 plates by Baquoy. Page size: 7 × 4½ inches, uncut. Red morocco by Gruel. Cohen–de Ricci 991.

Unimportant in itself, this small book shows Eisen approaching his characteristic manner of the 1760s. In the playful cupids of the fleuron on page 72 and the immediately following plate for "Summer," with its young man peeping from the bushes at a beautiful naked girl beside a stream, the model for his illustrations of La Fontaine's *Contes et nouvelles* is already established.

26 JEAN DE LA FONTAINE

Contes et nouvelles en vers . . . Amsterdam [i.e., Paris, Barbou], 1762. 2 v. I: xiv p., [1] *l.*, 268 p., [1] *l.*, 8 p. II: [1] *l.*, viii p., [1] *l.*, 306 p., [2] *l.*, [9]–16 p. Illus: I: Front. by Fiquet after Rigault, t.p. vignette, vignette, headpiece, and 23 tailpieces by Choffard; 39 plates after Eisen by: Aliamet (2), Baquoy, Choffard, Delafosse (2), de Longueil (7), Flipart, Le Mire (9), Lempereur, Leveau, Ouvrier, and unsigned (13). II: Front. by Fiquet after Vispré, t.p. vignette, vignette, headpiece, and 28 tailpieces by Choffard; 41 plates after Eisen by: Aliamet (2), Delafosse, de Longueil (14), Flipart, Le Mire (9), Lempereur, Leveau, and unsigned (12). The plates at I, 23 and II, 19 are in re-engraved form. Page size: 7⅛ × 4¼ inches. Contemp. green morocco. Cohen–de Ricci 558–571.

The Fermiers Généraux, an association the members of which had charge of gathering certain kinds of taxes, formed "the first financial company in the kingdom." Seeking to affirm their position, they commissioned this edition of La Fontaine's broad and spirited tales, a suitable choice for men of affairs who had recently risen to prominence and did not pretend to refined and delicate taste. They were determined that the book should be the best of its kind, and the Chevalier d'Agincourt, to whom they entrusted the project, was allowed unlimited resources. Assigning the plates to Eisen, the tailpieces to Choffard, and the engraving of their designs to Aliamet, Flipart, and de Longueil, he succeeded in giving the tax-farmers everything they desired. The Goncourts, who refer to this enterprise in their compact way as "one of the handsomest disbursements of witty and sensual money of Louis XV's reign," call the edition "the great

(26) La Fontaine, *Contes et nouvelles*

(26) La Fontaine, *Contes et nouvelles*

monument and triumph of the vignette, which dominates and crowns all the illustrations of the age" (III, 1–2).

Eisen's eighty designs for La Fontaine are the liveliest and most adroit that he ever drew. Thoroughly at home with the varied action of these lusty stories—their love passages, their intrigues, their practical jokes—he is also expert in choosing the moment in each that will best serve his purpose as an illustrator. And as with Gravelot's plates for the *Decameron* (15), the detailed meaning of his concentrated compositions is to be grasped only after prolonged examination. The world that they depict is that of the *homme moyen sensuel*, where beauty exists to satisfy desire and youth has its way over age, where cynicism is the common coin and virtue the calculated means to an end. But before the force and vitality of Eisen's scenes, normal scruples dissolve in admiration. That the innkeeper of "The cradle" (II, 29) should be deceived and baffled after the young gallants have taken their pleasure with his wife and daughter, that the nuns of "Mazet de Lamporechio" (II, 67) should have their will of a young drifter they find asleep in their garden, these episodes seem part of the nature of things in Eisen's designs.

Choffard's fifty-three tailpieces and four vignette-fleurons form a perfect complement to Eisen's plates. For all their harmonious elegance, Choffard's designs are not mere trophylike ornaments, but closely related comments on the tales that they adorn. In the plate for "The two friends" (I, 225) the gallants are shown arguing over a young girl, whose mother had been their mistress, each denying that he is her father so that he now may become her lover. The tailpiece repeats the composition with two preening birds in dispute over a third. Elsewhere the allusions are more subtle, the attributes more recondite, but the wit and point of Choffard's designs are unfailing. In the tailpiece for the last story of all, "The nightingale" (II, 306), he depicts a caged bird, thus rendering literally the metaphor on which the narrative turns, and beneath this design hangs a garlanded self-portrait.

Charles Eisen 55

The Fermiers-Généraux La Fontaine is the collector's book *par excellence*. Bibliophiles have long been attentive to the complex variants in its plates, which Cohen requires several columns to summarize. Their nature is exampled in entry 28. Since 2,000 sets of the illustrations were printed, many of which appeared with the 1762 text, the book is not rare, and it is often encountered, as is the case with this copy, in decorated bindings of contemporary morocco.

27 JEAN DE LA FONTAINE

Contes et nouvelles en vers . . . Amsterdam [Paris?], 1764. 2 v. I: x p., [1] *l.*, 214 p., [1] *l.* II: [1] *l.*, viii p., [1] *l.*, 254 p., [1] *l.* Illus: I: Front. by Macret; t.p. vignette, vignette, headpiece, and 27 tailpieces; 39 plates. II: T.p. vignette, vignette, headpiece, and 27 tailpieces; 34 plates. All illustrations are reversed copies after Eisen; scattered plates are engraved by Boilly and Milcent. Page size: 7⅞×4½ inches. Red morocco by Bedford. Cohen–de Ricci 571.

The printer Plassan explains in the prospectus cited in the next entry that this piracy succeeded because possible purchasers of the Fermiers-Généraux edition did not know how to obtain it: the title page simply reads "Amsterdam," with no mention of a publisher. The plates of the 1764 edition seem attractive enough until one compares them with Eisen's originals, of which they are reversed copies. The tailpieces, on the other hand, are greatly inferior to those of Choffard. Nonetheless, the edition is attractive.

28 JEAN DE LA FONTAINE

Contes et nouvelles en vers . . . Paris, P. Didot l'aîné, 1795. 2 v. I: viii, 256 p. II: 298 p. Illus: Extra-illustrated with over 100 plates by various artists, including the plates for the Fermiers-Généraux edition, with proof tailpieces without text. Page size: 6⅝×3¾ inches. Contemp. red morocco by Motet. Bookplates of A. Firmin-Didot and Mortimer L. Schiff; collation note by de Bure l'aîné. Cohen–de Ricci 573.

These two volumes contain a set of the illustrations for the Fermiers-Généraux *Contes et nouvelles* intended for the edition published by Plassan in 1792. In his prospectus, which is reprinted by

Cohen–de Ricci (columns 569–571), Plassan tells how 1200 of the 2,000 sets of these illustrations had come into his possession, how he had satisfied himself that they were equal in quality to those included in the edition of 1762 ("many more from the first thousand than from the second"), and how he had been able to add four plates and one tailpiece to the earlier total. In this copy both plates and tailpieces are fine, and the latter gain particular salience from being printed as proofs without text. It may be mentioned that Plassan was aware of the mixed motives of his likely customers. His puff reads in part: "The plates designed by M. Eisen present the most piquant moments of the stories without obscenity; one recognizes in some the touch of Rubens, in others that of Teniers, in most that of the Graces."

The plates in this copy are supplemented by eleven of the twenty *figures refusées*, that is to say, the original versions of plates that Eisen found wanting and replaced. Occasionally, as in the design for "The servant vindicated" (I, 47), he may have found the first version too suggestive. But for the most part his effort was to make the figures larger and the compositions bolder. "A femme avare galant escroc" (I, 81), in which La Fontaine has taken his title from a country saying, "Against a greedy woman, set a cheating gallant," may serve as an example. This tale concerns a lover who buys the favors of the wife of a money-lender. When Eisen first applied himself to its illustration, he chose the scene in which the lover tricks the wife by telling her husband that he has repaid his debt to her. The money-lender is a mere shadow, and neither the lover's triumph nor the wife's anger is conveyed with much verve. The second version, for which Eisen selected the moment before the lover's explanation, is a more complex creation. The husband's bemused preoccupation with his ledger contrasts nicely with the wife's signal of discretion and the lover's suave dissembling.

Also present in the volume are two plates for "The case of conscience" (II, 143) which may serve as examples of an occasional feature of the illustrations of the time. The first is *découverte*, or uncovered, the second covered. Cohen, who remarks that it and "The devil of Papefiguière" (II, 149) are really less common covered, lists three further plates which are much rarer in their uncovered states.

(28) La Fontaine, *Contes et nouvelles*

(28) La Fontaine, *Contes et nouvelles*

(28) La Fontaine, *Contes et nouvelles*

(28) La Fontaine, *Contes et nouvelles*

Epîtres héroïques et amoureuses. A collection, in 3 v., of 8 such texts. Page size: 7¾ × 5¼ inches. Contemp. green morocco.

I:1. [Claude Joseph Dorat]. Lettre d'Alcibiade à Glicère . . . suivie d'une lettre de Vénus à Paris, et d'une épître à la maîtresse que j'aurai. Geneva & Paris, Sébastien Jorry, 1764. 36 p. Illus. after Eisen: 3 headpieces by de Longueil (2), and Le Mire; 2 tailpieces by Aliamet, and Le Mire; 1 plate by Aliamet. Cohen–de Ricci 797.

I:2. [Claude Joseph Dorat]. Lettre du comte de Comminges à sa mère, suivie d'une lettre de Philomèle à Progné. Paris, Sébastien Jorry, 1764. 68 p. Illus. after Eisen: 2 headpieces by Aliamet, and de Longueil; 2 tailpieces by Aliamet, and de Longueil; 2 plates by de Longueil. Cohen–de Ricci 317–318.

I:3. [Jean Pierre Costard]. Lettre de Caïn après son crime, à Méhala, son épouse. Paris, Sébastien Jorry, 1765. 20 p., [1] l. Illus. after Eisen: plate by Le Mire.

II:1. Adrien Michel Hyacinthe Blin de Sainmore. Lettre de Biblis à Caunus son frère. Précédée d'une lettre à l'auteur . . . Paris, Sébastien Jorry, 1765. xii, [13]–32 p. Illus: Headpiece and tailpiece by de Longueil after Eisen; plate by Aliamet after Gravelot. Cohen–de Ricci 155.

II:2. [Claude Joseph Dorat]. Réponse de Valcour à Zéïla, précédée d'une lettre de l'auteur à une femme qu'il ne connoît pas. Paris, Sébastien Jorry, 1766. 42 p., [1] l. Illus. after Eisen: Headpiece and tailpiece by Aliamet; plate by de Longueil. Cohen–de Ricci 322.

II:3. Adrien Michel Hyacinthe Blin de Sainmore. Lettre de Gabrielle d'Etrées à Henri IV. Précédée d'une épître à M. de Voltaire et de sa réponse . . . Paris, Sébastien Jorry, 1766. x, 11–38 p., [1] l. Illus. after Eisen: Headpiece by Massard; tailpiece by Aliamet; plate by Rousseau. Cohen–de Ricci 155.

III:1. [Claude Joseph Dorat]. Lettres en vers, ou Epîtres héroïques et amoureuses. Paris, Sébastien Jorry, 1766. [2] l., viii, [9]–51 p. Illus. after Eisen: Added engraved t.p. by de Longueil; 3 headpieces by: Aliamet, and de Longueil (2); 3 tailpieces by: Aliamet (2), and de Longueil. Cohen–de Ricci 319.

III:2. [Claude Joseph Dorat]. Les tourterelles de Zelmis, poème en trois chants . . . [Paris, Sébastien Jorry, 1766] 56 p. Illus. after Eisen: Added engraved t.p., headpiece, tailpiece, and plate by de Longueil. Cohen–de Ricci 323.

As usual, these plaquettes are bound several to a volume. The eight in this collection, five by Dorat, two by Blin de Sanmore, and one by Costard, contain seven plates, twelve headpieces, and eleven tailpieces by Eisen. Each is an admitted bagatelle, a bit of evanescent badinage intended to banish boredom, as is explained in "Reflections on the Erotic Poem." This essay serves as a preface to "Les tourterelles de Zelmis," which tells how a cat steals a dove from a birdcage on a stormy night. Each little

(29) Dorat, *Les tourterelles de Zelmis*

book became a problem in physics for Eisen. How could he contrive to keep it afloat by his illustrations?

30 MARIE FRANÇOIS AROUET DE VOLTAIRE

La Henriade, nouvelle édition. Paris, la veuve Duchesne . . . [1769]–1770. 2 v. I: xi, 272 p. II: 316 p., [2] l. Illus. after Eisen: Front., engraved t.p., ten headpieces, and ten plates by de Longueil. All plates are bound in v. I, and include a *suite* of proofs of the headpieces without letterpress. Page size: 7⅛×4½ inches. Red morocco by Marius Michel. Cohen–de Ricci 1026–1027.

One does not think of Eisen as an illustrator of heroic poetry, but Voltaire was sufficiently impressed by his designs to send him a complimentary letter which the publishers were pleased to insert before the preface of this book: "I begin to believe, Sir, that La Henriade will reach posterity when I see the prints with which you have embellished it. Conception and execution do you equal honor. I am sure that the edition in which they are found will be the most sought after." The headpieces once again confirm Eisen's skill at showing much in little. They are seen at their most brilliant in the *suites* of early proofs without text, one of which is bound in this copy.

31 [CLAUDE JOSEPH DORAT]

Les baisers, précédés du Mois de Mai, poëme. La Haye & Paris, Lambert et Delalain, 1770. 119 p. Illus. after Eisen: Added engraved t.p. by Ponce, front. by de

(31) Dorat, *Les baisers*

(31) Dorat, *Les baisers*

Eisen, pen sketch for *Les baisers*

Longueil, t.p. vignette by Aliamet, 44 head- and tail-pieces by: Aliamet (4), Baquoy (5), Binet (2), De Launay (8), Lingée (2), de Longueil (6), Masquelier (4), Massard (4), Née (4), and Ponce (3); after Marillier: Massard and Ponce. Page size: 8¾ × 5⅛ inches. Red morocco by David. Cohen–de Ricci 308–311. Inserted is a sheet of pen-and-ink sketches (recto and verso) of cherubs, for the engraved t.p. of Dorat's *Les baisers* (1770). Sheet size 5¾ × 3⅜ inches.

At first glance *Les baisers* seems to be one more "trifle light as air." Complaining of the price of a louis which Dorat demanded for "this magnificent pamphlet," Grimm maintained that there was no "girl at the opera who sells her kisses so dearly" (quoted by Portalis, I, 203). But closer examination provides a different perspective. The twenty-two headpieces and twenty tailpieces with which Eisen adorned Dorat's hundred odd pages of text turn the book into a veritable paean to voluptuousness. And far from being a handicap, the small scale of the illustrations intensifies their ap-

peal. It made Eisen, the Goncourts remark (III, 22), "the man of the infinitely small feminine nude, of the duodecimo nude." This triumph of miniature art is the apotheosis of the vignette.

In the headpieces Eisen depicts his couples in various love scenes against a background of dells, alcoves, and boudoirs: a mistress gives her lover eight kisses but reserves a ninth ("La réserve"); Mars returns to Venus' couch instead of going to war when he finds a pair of lovebirds in his helmet ("La casque"). The tailpieces show cupids mimicking such scenes in ingenious ways. In a representative opening (pp. 54–55), the tailpiece displays a childish Mahomet refreshing himself from holy wars in a suitably sumptuous garden ("Hymn to the kiss"). In the headpiece opposite, Venus has descended from her swan-drawn car to gather kisses from a youth sleeping among roses who resembles her lost Adonis ("The roses").

A stop-press feature is provided by the frontis-

(31) Dorat, *Les baisers*

Car. Eisen del.   *N. le Mire Sculp.*

Une nuit que j'etois dans cet état tranquille .....

(32) Montesquieu, *Le temple de Gnide*

piece. As Grimm pointed out, this plate for "The month of May" is more than an allegorical representation of the delights of that time as described by Dorat. It is also Eisen's tribute to the Dauphin and Marie Antoinette, who were married in May of 1770. The pair join hands beside an altar, cupids hold crowns over their heads, and below overflowing cornucopias promise fruitfulness and prosperity for their reign.

Les baisers needs to be seen in its first issue on Holland paper with ample margins and early impressions of the vignettes. Such copies may be readily identified by their title pages in black and red and several errors of pagination in "Le mois de mai." Even among these, desirability varies widely according to the brilliance of the plates. This example ranks high on such a scale. Mounted in it, moreover, is a leaf with Eisen's pen drawings of cupids on each side. Among them is a preliminary sketch, or "pensée," for the book's engraved title.

32 CHARLES DE SECONDAT, BARON DE LA BRÈDE ET DE MONTESQUIEU

Le temple de Gnide, nouvelle édition, avec figures gravées par N. Le Mire . . . d'après les dessins de Ch. Eisen. Le text gravé par Droüet . . . Paris, Le Mire, 1772. [2] *l.*, vii, 104 p. Engraved throughout. Illus. by Le Mire after Eisen: Front., engraved t.p., headpiece, and 9 plates. Page size: 9½ ×6⅜ inches. Blue morocco by Joly fils. Cohen–de Ricci 726–728.

This elegant volume, in which both text and illustrations are engraved, ranks just after La Fontaine's *Contes et nouvelles*, Dorat's *Les baisers*, and Ovid's *Métamorphoses* (62) in Eisen's canon. *Le temple de Gnide* is an early work of the great political philosopher, first published in 1725, but Eisen does not fail to pay tribute to his subsequent accomplishments through an elaborate allegorical frontispiece. For the prose poem itself, which purports to be a translation from the Greek, he depicts scenes connected with life at Gnidos, where Venus reigns in her favorite temple. The plate for the fourth chant shows the narrator summoned from his travels by one of the graces, who serves as a messenger from the goddess. It is interesting to compare this design with Gravelot's rendering of a similar scene in *La secchia rapita* (19). With regard to suavity and grace Eisen never surpassed these plates.

Abbé Jean-Claude-Richard de Saint-Non (1727–1791)

It is just, as well as convenient, to consider the famous *Voyage pittoresque . . . de Naples* under its "only begetter," the Abbé de Saint-Non, rather than under the two painters to whose designs it owes much of its distinction, Jean-Honoré Fragonard and Hubert Robert. He was a sort of special providence to these artists, supporting them financially, advising them, and engraving their drawings. Moreover, he drew himself, so well on occasion that his designs have been mistaken for those of Fragonard.

Forced by his prominent and wealthy family to accept the priesthood as a suitable occupation for a younger son, Saint-Non was soon embarked on a significant career as an ecclesiastical official. Early in life, however, he had acquired a taste for music, drawing, and above all engraving, and when his career met a political check in 1753, he turned his thoughts towards the encouragement of the arts. Aided by the considerable fortune of his family, he became one of the notable amateurs of history. He demonstrated his mastery of etching in prints after Boucher, and in 1755 he published a *suite* from the designs of Le Prince.

In 1759 Saint-Non visited Italy for the first time. He was overwhelmed by the grandeur of Rome, and in February of 1760 a friend wrote: "the Abbé de Saint-Non is killing himself by sketching, engraving, and painting" (Guimbaud, p. 70). He soon became the friend and patron of Robert and Fragonard, who had been living in Rome for several years. With the former he made the obligatory tour of Naples, Vesuvius, Herculaneum, and Pompeii, and so extensive were his services to the latter, remarks Guimbaud (pp. 91–92), that Fragonard might have called himself "painter and designer in ordinary to M. the Abbé de Saint-Non,

French amateur." To gain recognition for their work, he began to engrave their drawings, eventually reproducing by etching or aquatint 150 or more after Fragonard and some fifty after Robert. He published nine *suites* between 1763 and 1774, the most important of which are the six in quarto format which concluded with *Fragments des peintures et tableaux les plus intéressants des palais et églises d'Italie* of 1774. Rare though these may be, collectors should seek them out for the quality of their impressions, which are superior to those in the *Recueil de griffonnis*. (Cohen's entry concerning these *suites* is incomplete, but Guimbaud gives full details, pp. 193–200.)

Saint-Non and Fragonard returned to France by slow stages in 1761, sightseeing and sketching along the way, with Fragonard copying many paintings by the Italian masters. Saint-Non then divided his time between Paris and the family chateau, occupying himself with etchings after the designs of his friends. Finding that this technique was not ideally suited to their work, he turned to acquatint, as it was being developed by Le Prince. The latter wrote in his manuscript treatise on engraving in the manner of watercolor: "My process has been imitated with great felicity by a skillful amateur, M. de Saint-Non, my friend" (quoted by Guimbaud, p. 134). Indeed, as Saint-Non became more experienced, he equalled Le Prince in lightness of touch, and he grew particularly expert in the procedure called "painting the shadows," which imparts luminosity to aquatint plates. Robert was pleased. "Such prints," he wrote (Guimbaud, p. 137), "are worth far more than a drawing buried in our boxes, since they are going to carry and to communicate to all lovers of Italy our most beautiful and cherished memories!"

In 1776 Benjamin de La Borde, whose *Chansons* (49) have given him a sort of fly-in-amber fame, announced plans for a major work on Switzerland and Italy. The beginning installments concerning Switzerland (finally assembled by Baron Zurlauben in three volumes between 1780 and 1783) were found to be monotonous, and in 1777 La Borde entrusted the Italian component of the enterprise to Saint-Non. Its scope was subsequently reduced to Naples and Sicily only. In his first installment, which appeared in March of 1778, he drew chiefly on his portfolio of early drawings by Fragonard and Robert, but thereafter he was under the necessity of procuring several hundred new designs. He did this through the unacknowledged agency of Baron Dominique Vivant-Denon, and soon a new group of artists (among them Desprez, Duplessis-Bertaux, Marillier, and Paris) was at work in Naples and Sicily. The enterprise progressed slowly. Saint-Non's expenses were appalling, and his detailed supervision of the project destroyed his health, but he persisted without concessions in quality until the fifth and final volume appeared in 1786.

Despite the opposition of its Secretary, Cochin, who called Saint-Non "an amateur, a half-artist, who has the misfortune to engrave badly enough, but well enough according to himself to believe he is a sort of artistic personage" (quoted by Guimbaud, p. 163), he was elected to the Academy. The other members received him cordially, however, and he had many friends in society to cheer his last years. The Revolution made his financial situation uneasy, but he died peacefully in 1791, before Fragonard fled the country and Robert was imprisoned.

Saint-Non is one of the most engaging figures in the chronicle of the French illustrated book. A small, almost frail man, he was often referred to as "little Saint-Non." Unaffected, modest, and amiable, he seemed like Fénelon in his "sweetness of soul" (Guimbaud, p. 9). His generosity was prodigal, and his loyalty proverbial. In later life, with his fortune largely dispersed, he offered to return to the now famous Fragonard the portfolios of his drawings. Saint-Non's motto (*Voyage pittoresque . . . de Naples*, i, vi) was: "What flowers are to our gardens, the arts are to life"; and the leading feature of his career was the devotion with which he served them.

REFERENCES Guimbaud; Portalis; Portalis-Beraldi; Réau.

33 JEAN-CLAUDE-RICHARD DE SAINT-NON

[**Suite de dix-neuf feuilles d'après l'antique,** consistant en figures, médaillons . . . dont plusieurs sujets sont de l'invention de Robert. Paris, La Voye, 1762]. Eighteen engraved plates, lacking t.p., by Saint-Non after Robert (in part). Page size: 12½×8¾ inches. Disbound.

Saint-Non's first significant set of etchings contains eighty-nine designs on nineteen sheets. The subjects are classical remains ("figures, medallions, low-reliefs, tripods, vases," etc.) discovered in recent excavations. Ten of the subjects are after Robert, the rest from Saint-Non's drawings, which are expert enough to have led Portalis to attribute one of them to Fragonard (Guimbaud, p. 193).

34 [JEAN-CLAUDE-RICHARD DE SAINT-NON]

Voyage pittoresque ou Description des royaumes de Naples et de Sicile . . . Paris, 1781–1786. 4 v. in 5. Collates as in Brunet and Cohen–de Ricci, many of the plates *avant lettres* or with scratched signatures. Page size: 19¾×12⅞ inches. Bookplate of Lord Northwick. Contemp. red morocco. Brunet v, 55–56; Cohen–de Ricci 928–930.

This is one of the most ambitious and successful of travel books. We have seen how Saint-Non devoted his life and fortune to bringing it to completion. The spirited designs by Desprez, Fragonard, Paris, Robert, and others, rendered by the best engravers of the time, far surpass in quality those in most collections of "views." The appeal of late eighteenth-century Italy is conveyed in all its romantic charm. Wild and rugged scenery is displayed. The passion of the age for archaeological discovery is conveyed in many plates of excavations, which are enlivened by a variety of foreground figures—the savants and diggers themselves, Saint-Non's artists recording their labors, and ordinary citizens upon their lawful occasions. When there were events of interest in the localities being visited, these too were depicted, as in the fine series of designs recording an Archbishop's arrival in Palermo (iv, 139–146).

Among these plates, a few stand out. Though the abundant decorations are of a uniformly high

» & de pierres qui, malgré un vent violent, s'éleva perpendiculairement à une
» hauteur extraordinaire, & nous annonce encore une grande fermentation
» intérieure «.

Deßiné par Robert Peintre du Roi

Gravé par Ch. Guttenberg

*Vue de la Sommité et du Cratev du Vesuve, au moment de la dernière Eruption
arrivée le 8. d'Aoû 1779. à 9. heures du soir.*

Cette formidable Gerbe de feu qui dura trois quarts d'Heure de suite, s'éleva jusqu'à une hauteur prodigieuse;

On a estimé qu'elle devoit avoir égalé celle de trois fois le Vesuve, ce qui peut revenir à 2000. Pas Géomet. ou dix mille Pieds.

VUE

(34) Engraving after Robert, *Voyage pittoresque . . . de Naples*

(34) Proof before letters after Desprez, *Voyage pittoresque . . . de Naples*

(34) Proof before letters after Saint-Non, *Voyage pittoresque . . . de Naples*

order, three may be particularly mentioned. The book begins with a magnificent full-page fleuron engraved by Choffard for the dedication to the Queen. Even more striking is Robert's depiction of Vesuvius erupting in 1779 (I, 208). Finally, there is Fragonard's stirring conception of Hercules conquering the giants (II, 149), which serves as a headpiece to the chapter on volcanoes. With regard to the plates, it is hard to choose among many superb designs by Fragonard and Robert, but the former's flair for the dramatic carries the day with his drawing of the *memento mori* encountered by fashionable sightseers at Pompeii (I, 88). Most appealing of all is a pair of plates devoted to the Temple of Isis, also at Pompeii. In the first Desprez draws it as revealed by recent excavations. Curious visitors are exploring the uncovered ruins, while an artist sketches the scene. In the second, a luminous aquatint in bister, the temple is shown as it was in 79 A.D. We are told of this plate that "the ingenious Artist, to whom we owe the greater part of these plates, has worked here as if he were himself initiated in the Mysteries and the Cult of this Egyptian Goddess. His happy and facile imagination has not only reconstructed the entire Temple for us, but he has also been pleased to represent it here during one of its most exalted Ceremonies" (I, 118). One is readily persuaded by Guimbaud (p. 202) and by the passage quoted above from the book itself, that the composition is by Saint-Non, with figures by Duplessis-Bertaux.

In this remarkable copy 329 of the engravings are before the letters, and of these 170 are also before the names of the artists. The fact that the phallus plate (II, 57) and the set of medals of Sicilian cities, repeating tailpieces in volume four, are absent (Cohen–de Ricci, column 729) hardly seems significant.

᠀ Pen and black ink, and watercolor drawing by Desprez for Saint-Non's *Voyage pittoresque . . . de Naples* (1781–1786), a view of the ruins of the temple of Juno at Metapontum, with the encampment of an archaeological expedition. Sheet size: 8⁵⁄₁₆ × 13⁷⁄₁₆ inches.

The Pierpont Morgan Library

Drawing by Desprez for *Voyage pittoresque . . . de Naples*

The last of the artists recruited by Vivant-Denon for the *Voyage pittoresque . . . de Naples* was Jean-Louis Desprez (1740–1804). This drawing of the ruins of the Doric temple at Metapontum (engraved at III, 77) shows his talent at its most spirited. The ruins are no more than a backdrop to the varied human scene which he presents. Wherever archaeologists carried out their work, a bustling little village sprang up to meet their needs. One sees why the pursuit of this science held such charms for the wealthy amateurs of the age.

JEAN-CLAUDE-RICHARD DE SAINT-NON

🙶 **Recueil de griffonis,** de vuës, paysages, fragments antiques et sujets historiques, gravés tant à l'eauforte qu'au lavis . . . d'après différents maîtres des écoles italiennes & de l école française. [Paris, 1780?] 287 plates (including title) on 153 *l.*, by Saint-Non after various artists. Page size: 19¼ × 12¾ inches. ¾ green morocco by R. Lidstone (Plymouth). Cohen–de Ricci 930–931.

This comprehensive collection of etchings and aquatints by Saint-Non after various artists differs in makeup from copy to copy. A number of Saint-Non's earlier *suites* are usually present, together with many individual prints. This copy, which has 287 plates on 153 leaves, is more inclusive than most. Particularly imposing are the six large etchings after Le Prince, with which the volume opens, and a later group of aquatints after Fragonard and Robert, most of which are also substantial in size. Even more interesting is Saint-Non's aquatint after Fragonard's copy in 1761 of a caricature by Tiepolo (p. 60). The enormous nose of this dead figure suggests a clown, the seeming weapon in the foreground a soldier. It is a mysterious and haunting design. Otherwise the claims made by the collec-

Aquatint after Tiepolo, *Recueil de griffonis*

tion are as much historical as artistic. Nowhere else are so many of what might be called aquatint incunables, dating as they do from the late 1760s and early 1770s, to be found between two covers. Guimbaud had never seen this edition; indeed he doubted its existence (pp. 205–206). Though it is undoubtedly rare, it turns up from time to time.

There is a second edition of the *Recueil de griffonnis*, with the imprint of "la veuve Lavoye," which appeared after the Revolution, probably in 1790. According to the prospectus printed by Guimbaud (pp. 174–175), it contains 296 etchings and aquatints on 158 leaves, but in fact, as in the earlier edition, the contents differ from copy to copy. The impressions of the plates are inferior.

Pierre-Philippe Choffard (1730?–1809)

Choffard was one of the most exquisite of all book artists, but he was a decorator rather than an illustrator, and his work as an engraver is overwhelmingly more abundant than his work as a designer. Though his contributions to the Fermiers-Généraux La Fontaine (26) and Ovid's *Métamorphoses* (62) are essential elements in each of these masterpieces, the very nature of his role as an ornamentist precluded him from producing a great book of his own. Indeed, his other original designs for illustration are few and far between: headpieces or tailpieces for editions of *Les saisons* in 1769 and 1775, for Imbert's *Le jugement de Paris* in 1772, and for Désormeaux's *Histoire de la maison de Bourbon* in 1779–1788; three decorations for the Abbé de Saint-Non's *Voyage pittoresque . . . de Naples* (34); and isolated engravings elsewhere. (See below, pp. 107–108.)

The date of Choffard's birth is probably 1730, though 1736 is proposed in one source. He was virtually self-educated. Having lost his father at the age of ten, he grew up in Paris, by his own admission, as "a pupil of the quays." His early artistic training came from a mapmaker and an engraver of ornaments. Throughout his career he produced a great variety of ephemeral engravings —invitations, advertisements, bookplates, and so forth—many of which are collected in the two folio volumes which were acquired by the Cabinet d'Estampes in 1812 and later catalogued by Portalis and Beraldi. His first signed engraving dates from 1749, but it was not until 1762 that his tailpieces for La Fontaine's *Contes et nouvelles* brought him to general notice. Henceforth he had his secure place in the Parisian art world, where he numbered Cochin and Moreau among his friends. He seems to have been the most modest and amiable of men. A fellow artist who appealed to him for professional help was sure of a cordial and efficient reception. When he visited friends in the country, it is related, he arrived "with a roll in his pocket for the watchdog, cookies for the puppy, candy for the children, flowers or a bottle of perfume for the lady of the house and a large tip for the servants" (quoted by Portalis, I, 85).

Choffard was among the most brilliant and productive engravers of his time, and many plates from the drawings of the great rococo illustrators are his work. His talent as a designer was not less than theirs, though he limited himself to book decoration. The magnitude of his achievement becomes apparent when one considers the restrictions under which he labored. It was his function to fill the space left by the printer at the beginning or end of a tale or chapter, to provide a decorated border for the lettering of a title or dedication. Yet one cannot but agree with Dacier (pp. 94–95) that "rarely has anyone better demonstrated that for a great artist no space is limited, no subject little." And he was not only a memorable technician, but also a man of reading and culture, who had profound imaginative resources. The characterization of his method in the *Métamorphoses* by the engraver Ponce applies equally to most of his other book designs: "Each of his subjects forms by itself a poem, in which the substance of the story is preserved as a whole and each of the incidents indicated, to the last detail, through accessories that shadow forth its elements by means of the most refined and ingenious allegories" (quoted by Renouvier, p. 326).

(26) Tailpiece for La Fontaine, *Contes et nouvelles*

The delicacy of his drawings is remarkable, even though they are often mere hints since he himself was to engrave them, which makes it the more regrettable that so few have survived.

Always devoted to his art, Choffard went on working as an engraver and occasionally as a designer after the Revolution, but the times were not propitious for this subtle and sophisticated artist. A widower with no children, he had made little preparation for his old age. Simply to earn his daily bread, he had to accept the most pedestrian commissions. Yet he found it in himself to write an authoritative *Notice historique sur l'art de la gravure* in 1804, and he was engaged on a more comprehensive treatise on the same subject when he died in 1809. His high conception of the art of engraving is witnessed by this eloquent passage from the former. "When the engraver truly feels his subject, he renders the sweet flesh tones of Venus and Adonis with the graces of the brush and the muscular forms of Mars and Milo with the energy of the chisel. He struggles to draw out the life and the passions and feelings of the soul from the original drawings before him. So the graver in his industrious hand, like the chisel, the brush, and the pen in the hands of the sculptor, the painter, and the poet, becomes the wand with which the enchanter works his magic." (Quoted by Portalis and Beraldi, I, 425.)

REFERENCES Dacier (1947); Holloway; Portalis; Portalis-Beraldi; Réau; Renouvier; Salomons (1912).

Charles Monnet (1732–1816)

Monnet was born in Paris in 1732. He studied with Restout, and after several years at the École Royale des Artistes Protégés, he had a long sojourn in Rome. For more than a decade after he came of age he tried to make his mark as a serious painter, but success eluded him. His career as an illustrator began in the middle 1760s with two of his strongest efforts: his designs for Fessard's edition of La Fontaine's *Fables* (61), to which he was the principal contributor, and those for Ovid's *Métamorphoses* (62), which were second in number only to Eisen's. From this time on he rarely lacked employment, his most ambitious undertaking being a *suite* of plates for *Télémaque*. He took the Revolution and the regimes which followed in stride, his allegorical representations of "The Triumph of the Republic" and "Bonaparte Giving Peace to Europe" meeting with the same favorable reception as had "The Coronation of Louis XVI." The fifteen large engravings of his *Description abrégée des quinze journées de la révolution* are of documentary as well as aesthetic interest.

In Voltaire's *Romans et contes* of 1778, his most attractive book, Monnet had demonstrated his mastery of erotic subjects, and during the 1790s, when such themes were in fashion, he further developed this gift in Laclos' *Les liaisons dangereuses* of 1796 (82) and Louvet de Couvray's *Aventures du chevalier de Faublas* of 1798 (83). His work during his later years is exampled in Demoustier's *Lettres à Emilie*, six volumes, 1801, one of several commissions which he received from Renouard. But his vogue was over, unlike that of another survivor, Moreau, and he gave up illustration some years before his death.

Monnet has never had his due from the critics. Laboring in the shadow of greater talents during the earlier part of his career, he came to be seen as a journeyman artist, always professional but rarely inspired. When he turned to mildly erotic illustration, he was classed with such "scabrous" designers as Binet and Borel (Réau, p. 25). Indeed, Renouvier was unkind enough to suggest that his plates for *Les liaisons dangereuses* "made it only too evident he had been more stirred by Laclos' novel than by the great events which he had witnessed"

(p. 308). Nevertheless, much of Monnet's abundant work is of high quality. If he ranks well below Moreau, Gravelot, and Eisen as an illustrator, he is not much inferior to Cochin.

REFERENCES Portalis; Réau; Renouvier.

35 MARIE FRANÇOIS AROUET DE VOLTAIRE

Romans et contes. Bouillon, aux dépens de la Société Typographique, 1778. 3 v. I: vi, 304 p. II: viii, 320 p. III: vi, 236 p. Illus: I: Front. by Cathelin after de La Tour, unsigned t.p. vignette, 5 unsigned headpieces, 15 plates after Monnet by: Châtelin, Dambrun (5), Deny (6), Thiébault (2), and Vidal. II: Front. by Dambrun after Monnet, unsigned t.p. vignette, 3 headpieces by Deny after Monnet, 2 unsigned headpieces; 19 plates after: Martini by Deny; after Monnet by: Baquoy, Dambrun (3), Deny (9), and Vidat (4); after Moreau by Deny. III: Front. by Dambrun after Monnet, unsigned t.p. vignette, indistinctly signed headpiece after Monnet, 2 unsigned headpieces; 20 plates after: Marillier by Deny (4), and Vidal; after Monnet by: Dambrun, Deny (4), Lorieux (2), Patas, and Vidat (7). The plates are before numbers. Page size: $8\frac{5}{8} \times 5\frac{1}{4}$ inches. Blue morocco by Hardy-Mennil. Bookplates of Edward George Hibbert and Clarence S. Bement. Cohen–de Ricci 1038–1039.

This book belongs to Monnet, for most of its fifty-seven plates and all of its thirteen allegorical headpieces are from his hand. In Voltaire's stories he found subjects after his own heart. Their exotic settings, their gaiety, and their frank admission of the claims of the senses enabled him to work with entire freedom. In his eight plates for *Zadig*, six for *Candide*, and seven for *Le huron, ou l'ingénu*, he surpassed himself. His designs for *Candide* are the best

(35) Voltaire, *Candide*

(35) Voltaire, *Candide*

contemporary illustrations for this masterpiece. If he gives the novel a sensual emphasis which goes beyond Voltaire's text, it is to capitalize on his special talent. His success may be judged from his depiction of the Parisian world of pleasure in Candide's supper with the Abbé Périgourdin and a hostess who calls herself the Marquise de Parolignac (II, 163). In *Le huron* Monnet shows his capacity to realize masculine as well as feminine beauty.

Since it was Monnet's custom to state rather than to suggest, objection is sometimes taken to the almost blatant nudity of some of his designs. His depiction of two girls and their monkey lovers encountered by Candide during his South American travels (II, 123) is hardly chaste, but it is certainly funny. In *Jenni* when Dona Boca-Vermeja gazes enraptured on a handsome Englishman in his bath, monstrous heretic though he may be, only to be whipped by the reverend father whose mistress she is (III, 6 and 8), Monnet goes no further than does Eisen in the Fermiers-Généraux La Fontaine (26), despite the realism and the larger scale of his plates.

Marillier was Monnet's one significant collaborator in these volumes. The sober dignity of his four fine plates for *L'homme aux quarante écus* at the end of volume three contrasts sharply with Monnet's spirited inventions. The separate pagination of this story suggests that its inclusion may have been an afterthought.

This virtually uncut copy, with plates before the numbers, shows Monnet's work at its best.

36   FRANÇOIS DE SALIGNAC DE
       LA MOTHE–FÉNELON

Les aventures de Télémaque . . . gravées d'après les desseins de Charles Monnet . . . par Jean Baptiste Tilliard. Paris, l'Auteur, 1773. [i.e., 1783]. Front. by Choffard and St. Aubin after Monnet, engraved t.p. by Montulay, 24 unsigned engraved text leaves, and 72 plates by Tilliard after Monnet. Page size: 11⅛ × 8⅛ inches. Red morocco by Riviere. Cohen–de Ricci 384.

Monnet's designs for *Télémaque* were exhibited at the Academy in 1771. They had been engraved by 1773 (Cohen, column 384), but they were not published by the engraver Jean Baptiste Tilliard for ten years. These seventy-three plates and twenty-

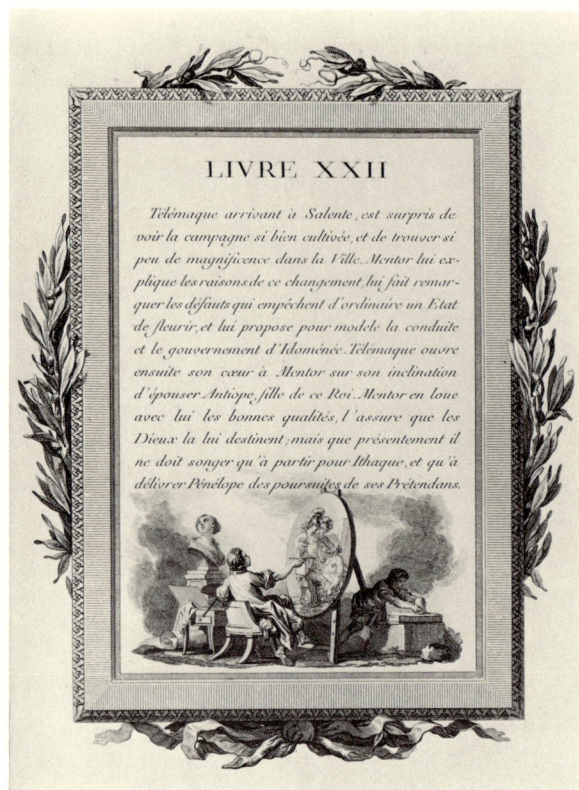

(36) Fénelon, *Les aventures de Télémaque*

four tailpieces represent Monnet's most ambitious effort as an illustrator. Imparting life to Fénelon's improving narrative was not an easy task, despite the abundance of incident it offered. Monnet was forced to subordinate his story-telling talent in order to achieve the elaborately posed compositions then deemed appropriate to classical subjects. Nonetheless, he succeeds in making Telemachus an appealing protagonist, no small achievement in itself, and he sometimes contrives to render his designs interesting as well as stately. One of his successes in Book XVII shows the encounter of Telemachus with evil monarchs in torment during the course of his journey to Hades in search of his father, Ulysses. Luckily, he had no need to strain after effect in his tailpieces. Particularly engaging is that to Book XXII in which a boy painter is at work on what can only be a scene from *Télémaque*. The summary pages with their engraved text, elegant tailpieces, and stately borders add greatly to the volume's attractiveness. This entirely engraved book was published in an edition of 200 copies.

Télémaque, en passant le Tartare,
remarque le fort qu'eprouvent les mauvais Rois.

C. Monnet inv.

J.B.Tilliard Sculp.

(36) Fénelon, *Les aventures de Télémaque*

37 FRANÇOIS DE SALIGNAC DE LA MOTHE-FÉNELON

Les aventures de Télémaque. [Paris], l'Imprimerie de Monsieur, 1785. 2 v. I: [4] *l.*, 309 p. II: 297 p., [1] *l.* Illus. I: Added engraved t.p. (for the plates, dated 1773) by Montulay, 12 unsigned text leaves, and 36 plates by Tilliard after Monnet. II: 12 unsigned text leaves, and 36 plates by Tilliard after Monnet. Inserted in v. II is the prospectus for this work, dated 1784. Page size: 14 × 10⅜ inches, uncut. Contemp. ½ red morocco. Cohen–de Ricci 384–386.

In an "avertissement" appearing after the title page of the first volume, the publishers describe the complications which delayed the appearance of this edition, which was prepared to receive Monnet's engravings. The two large quarto volumes printed by Didot on vellum paper of Annonay were worth waiting for; but though their larger page provides the plates with a more gracious setting, particularly in this uncut copy, the impressions of the plates are inferior to those in the Tilliard suite.

38 ALAIN RENÉ LE SAGE

Histoire de Gil Blas de Santillane . . . Edition ornée de figures en taille douce, gravées par les meilleurs artistes. Paris, Chaignieau aîné, l'an IX [i.e., 1801]. 8 v. I: x, 215 p. II: [2] *l.*, 231 p. III: [2] *l.*, 192 p. IV: 174 p. V:

209 p. VI: 216 p. VII: 206 p. VIII: 307 [i.e., 207], [4] p. Illus. after Monnet: I: Front. by Lingée, and 5 plates by: Bovinet, Giraud, Malapeau, and unsigned (2). II: 6 plates by: Lingée, and unsigned (5). III: 3 unsigned plates. IV: 2 unsigned plates. V: 3 unsigned plates. VI: 3 unsigned plates. VII: 2 unsigned plates. VIII: 4 unsigned plates. All plates in 2 states: before numbers, and before letters; bound in are 28 pen and black ink, and wash drawings for the plates. Page size: 5½ × 3½ inches, uncut. Red morocco by Weckesser. Cohen–de Ricci 633–634.

The twenty-eight original drawings and two states before letters of the plates make this the best possible copy of a routine book. Whoever had it assembled and bound wisely chose an uncut copy of the 18 mo (in half-sheets) edition for the text rather than the octavo edition in which the book also appeared. The smaller format provides a far more harmonious setting for Monnet's drawings, a lively series which follows with professional expertise the many turns in Le Sage's picaresque plot. They are well adapted to engraving, but the craftsmen to whom they were entrusted have hardly done them justice. In chapter 2 of Book X Gil Blas has been reunited with his parents, just in time to clasp the hand of his dying father. Altogether, this *Gil Blas* is a favorable specimen of the small books with miniature illustrations which proliferated after the Revolution.

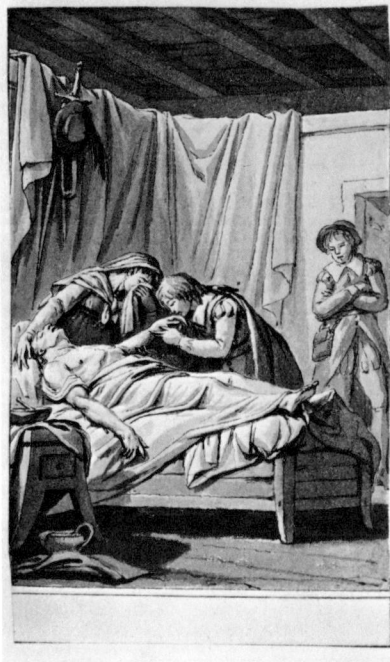

Drawing for Le Sage, *Gil Blas de Santillane*

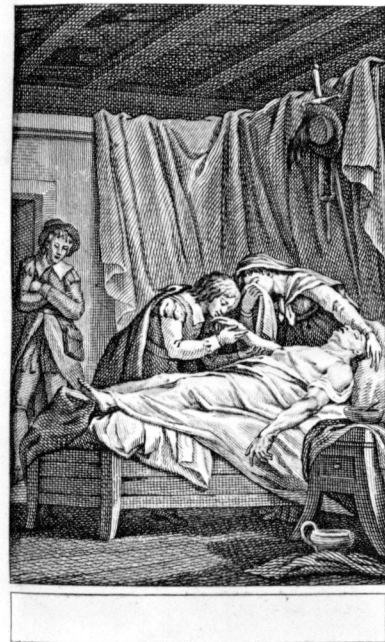

(38) Engraving for Le Sage, *Gil Blas de Santillane*

Jean-Baptiste Le Prince (1734-1781)

Born in Metz, Le Prince came to Paris early in life to study with Boucher. At the age of nineteen he married a well-to-do woman twice his age. The match was unhappy, and Le Prince soon departed for Russia to join his brothers. His talent as a painter was appreciated there, and he filled his sketchbooks with studies, but after five years the bitterness of the climate forced him to return to Paris. Diderot remarked of the paintings and drawings which he exhibited that they were "for the most part frail like the artist's health, melancholy and sweet like his character" (quoted by Portalis, 1, 352). In an epigram of the time he is referred to as "Boucher refrigerated." Le Prince turned many of his sketches into etchings, which were praised by Grimm for their documentary as well as their aesthetic value.

At length the public tired of Le Prince's Russian themes, particularly because his concentration on costume rather than substance deprived them of much variety. He made a number of designs for books, of which those for the Abbé Chappe d'Auteroche's *Voyage en Sibérie* of 1768 and Saint-Lambert's *Les saisons* of 1769 are the best. The great achievement of his life, however, was the perfecting, if not the discovery, of aquatint. A means of imitating watercolor had long been ardently desired by printmakers. Le Prince provided it in several of his *suites* through little pastoral scenes in the manner of Boucher and larger and more striking Russian studies. The process was soon imitated all over Europe. In his last years, when lung trouble had made him too weak to stand, he had his easel brought to his bedside so that he could go on painting.

REFERENCE Portalis.

• Album of various *suites* of plates by Le Prince: (1) Divers ajustements et usages de Russie, dediés à Monsieur Boucher . . . Dessinés en Russie d'après nature et gravés à l'eau forte par J. B. Le Prince. (2) 2me. suitte de divers cris de marchands de Russie. (3) IIIe. suitte de divers cris de marchands de Russie. (4) Habillements de diverses nations. (5) Suite de divers habillements des peuples du Nord. (6) IIe suitte d'habillements de diverses nations. (7) Divers habillemens des femmes de

Aquatint from *Suite de divers habillements des peuples du nord*

Moscovie. (8) IIe. suitte d'habillement des femmes de Moscovie. Illus. by Le Prince: Etched front., 8 t.p.s, and 63 plates, some with aquatint, including 20 unidentified plates. Page size: $11\frac{3}{4} \times 8\frac{5}{8}$ inches. Contemp. $\frac{1}{2}$ calf. Cohen–de Ricci 625–626; Colas 1838, 1841, 1842 (bis), 1844–1848.

There is an etching by Le Prince dated 1760, but most of his prints came between the mid-1760s and the mid-1770s. As bound in albums, they are usually encountered in one of two forms. (1) His various *suites* were assembled as they appeared to make up volumes such as the one here described. (2) In 1782, the year after his death, his *Oeuvres* were brought together in folios of varying contents which can contain as many as 163 prints on fifty-four pages. Both of these collections support the assertion on the title page of the latter that "the technique of aquatint has been developed by M. Le Prince to the highest degree of perfection." The *suites* in the earlier volumes, however, consist chiefly of etchings. In both collections the plates are largely of northern scenes, usually Russian. They vary from single figures to little episodes of common life. Expert and charming though Le Prince may be, it must be admitted that his continuing insistence on the same figures, costumes, and scenes at last becomes somewhat monotonous.

Jean-Jacques-François Le Barbier (1738–1826)

Le Barbier began to work as an illustrator when the rococo style was still dominant, but he was never at ease with it. From the first he was devoted to the antique, and indeed Portalis claims that, through his painting, his illustrations, and his writings, he was "the precursor of David" (I, 330).

Aujourd'hui je vois ma Mere
M'ordonner d'un ton sévere
De fuir avec soin Colin.

(49) La Borde, *Chansons*

Certainly his manner is cool, his composition is correct even to the point of being academic, and his care to achieve finish is extreme. No illustrator was ever less of an improviser. When neoclassicism came into vogue, he reaped his reward, his best book, Gessner's *Oeuvres*, being an early success in that style.

Le Barbier was born in Rouen, where he won prizes for drawing, but he came to Paris at an early age. For many years he was primarily a painter, and it was in this capacity that he was elected to the Academy in 1785. In both of his early important ventures in illustration, La Borde's *Chansons* (49) and Rousseau's *Oeuvres* (51), he took second place to Moreau. Thus it came about that Le Barbier's most sustained and accomplished series of illustrations, apart from that for Gessner's *Oeuvres*, has hardly received the attention it deserves. The great majority of the fifty plates in the third and fourth volumes of the *Chansons* are from his hand. Less idealized and heightened than Moreau's, they nonetheless have a grace and charm of their own. From time to time, indeed, Le Barbier creates an absorbing genre piece from La Borde's harmless verses. His plate for "The Useless Prohibition" (III, 128) would not be out of place as an illustration for Robert Burns' "Tam Glen":

> My minnie does constantly deave me,
>   And bids me beware o' young men.
> They flatter, she says, to deceive me—
>   But wha can think sae o' Tam Glen?

In a homely cottage a mother's angry reproaches move the family dog more than her demurely obstinate daughter, whose thoughts are with her lover waiting at the door. His seven plates for Rousseau's *Oeuvres* are a worthy complement to Moreau's. Indeed, the six of them which depict contemporary life are his most elaborate and convincing excursions into this territory.

In 1776 Le Barbier visited Switzerland to make the sketches on which he based his designs for Zurlauben's *Tableaux topographiques, pittoresques, physiques, historiques, politiques, moraux, littéraires de la Suisse*, 1780–1788. He came to know Gessner well, and their friendship gave rise to his illustrations for the latter's *Oeuvres*. Le Barbier played a leading part in the affairs of the Academy during the Revolution and after, working always to promote the study and emulation of classical models. Meanwhile, he continued his career as an illustrator, interpreting modern life in *Les liaisons dangereuses*; Scarron's *Roman comique*, three volumes, 1796; and the *Génie du Christianisme*; as well as classical subjects in Racine's *Oeuvres*, four volumes, 1796, and the *Idylles* of Theocritus of the same year.

The most ambitious of his later efforts was his contribution to Ovid's *Métamorphoses* (62). These forty-four designs at least bear witness to his continued mastery of composition, though the simplicity and naturalness of his drawings for Gessner have largely disappeared. Given the incapacity of the engravers for this work, it is fairer to judge Le Barbier by his drawings rather than by the plates themselves. See below, pages 153–154. He seems to have done little illustration during the last twenty years of his long life. The demanding Renouvier, who finds Le Barbier wanting in rigor and severity when compared with David, nonetheless gives him credit for "variety, inventiveness, a lively presentation, correct depiction of the nude, occasional piquant gestures, and some attractive costumes" (p. 71).

REFERENCES Portalis; Renouvier.

39 SALOMON GESSNER

Oeuvres. Paris, l'Auteur . . . [1786–1793]. 3 v. I: xii p. (incl. engraved t.p.), [1] *l.*, 215 p. II: [2] *l.* (incl. engraved t.p. by Baquoy), 182 p. III: Engraved t.p. by Baquoy, 236 p. Illus. after Le Barbier: I: Front. by Ponce, 19 tailpieces by: Alix (6), Le Barbier (3), Lépine (9), and Pauquet; unsigned headpiece, unsigned tailpieces (12); 31 plates by: Delignon, Gaucher (2), Godefroy (10), Halbou (3), de Longueil, Pauquet (2), Ponce (8), Texier, Thomas, Trière, and unsigned (1). II:

Front. by Ingouf, headpiece by Baquoy, tailpieces by: Baquoy (7), Delignon, Langlois (2), Viguet (3), and unsigned (16); 31 plates by: Baquoy (3), Delignon (2), Halbou (8), Le Beau (2), Le Villain (2), de Longueil (10), Thomas (2), and Trière (2). III: Front. by Dambrun, headpiece by Baquoy, tailpieces by Baquoy (4), unsigned headpiece, unsigned tailpieces (2); 9 plates by: Baquoy (2), Delignon, Halbou (3), de Longueil, Petit, and Thomas. Page size: $11\frac{7}{8} \times 8\frac{1}{8}$ inches. Contemp. red morocco. Bookplate of A. S. W. Rosenbach. Cohen–de Ricci 433–434.

This book represents one of the happiest of all collaborations between artist and writer. The allegorical frontispiece of volume one shows the genius of painting with brush and canvas before a large folio supported by the genius of poetry. Its title is Horace's sentence "Ut pictura poesis erit." In his dedication to the edition Le Barbier recalls that "the charm of Gessner's poems filled my imagination, and transported it to the happy centuries of the world's innocence" (I, v). He thereupon determined to make a series of paintings parallel in subject and in spirit to these works. In a letter of 1779 Gessner welcomed his proposal. He believed that pastorals should be set in ancient Greece to take advantage of its "noble simplicity" and its "mythology, which is an infinitely rich source of the most varied and gracious poetical beauties." He knew that Le Barbier could cope surpassingly well with such themes, since the artist "had formed his taste, his theory, and his art after the most beautiful remains of antiquity" (III, 321). When Gessner received the first installment of Le Barbier's designs the following year, he praised them wholeheartedly and saw his friend and himself descending together to posterity (III, 233–234).

As Gessner had foreseen, the project cost Le Barbier much "time and application." He worked on it intermittently from 1779 to 1792, and the three volumes of the *Oeuvres* appeared between 1786 and 1793. In all he composed three frontispieces, three engraved titles, seventy-two plates, four headpieces, and sixty-six tailpieces. In these the rococo style has been largely superseded, though fortunately the neoclassical chill hasn't yet set in. The scenes have animation, the figures warmth.

Most of Le Barbier's designs have the ancient world as their setting. Cupids and fawns appear occasionally, though gods and goddesses are conspicuous by their absence. Allegory is infrequent. There are many love scenes played out by the

Celui qui voulut que sa Cendre fut couverte de
si funestes images n'etait sûrement pas un Berger

Dessiné par Le Barbier
Peintre du Roi

Gravé par De Longueil
Graveur du Roi.

(39) Gessner, *Oeuvres*

(39) Gessner, *Oeuvres*

Je l'embrassai, elle se laissa aller dans mes bras,
et ses larmes recommencerent a couler sans effort.

(40) Laclos, *Les liaisons dangereuses*

shepherds and shepherdesses, but the passions that move them are subdued. Though Le Barbier was an accomplished depicter of the nude, he exercises this talent only in *Le mort d'Abel* and a few other subjects (II, 63). In contrast to the *Métamorphoses* of 1767–1771 (62), there is hardly a hint of the erotic. A few of Le Barbier's plates are almost timeless. One of these shows two shepherds coming upon a ruined arch adorned with sculptures of warlike episodes. One remarks to the other: "He who wished that his tomb might be covered with such melancholy scenes was certainly not a shepherd" (II, 57). Other designs are virtually contemporary, for example, that in which an artist, who might be Le Barbier himself, is shown sketching a villa in the neoclassical style. Certainly the caption of this plate states his own credo: "Imitate nature and follow the great masters" (II, 101).

The tailpieces often represent assemblages of rural objects or little countryside scenes. Typical in its realism is the dead wolf which decorates an idyll telling of a shepherd who had come to the aid of a boy attacked by such a beast (II, 25). In the tailpieces, as in the plates, Le Barbier's emphasis is on simplicity and naturalness. We are in a different world from the witty gallantry and sophisticated sentiment of the rococo pastoral illustrations which took their departure from the poems of Dorat or La Borde. All told, Gessner's *Oeuvres* is a work of harmonious distinction which admirably realizes the ideals of its author and illustrator.

40 CHODERLOS DE LACLOS

Les liaisons dangereuses . . . Geneva, 1792. 4 v. in 2. I: xxii, 245 [i.e., 225] p. II: 233 p. III: 225 p. IV: 250 p. Illus. after Le Barbier: I: 2 plates by Halbou, and Simonet. II: 2 plates by Thomas. III: 2 plates by Delignon. IV: 2 plates by Dambrun. Page size: $4\frac{7}{8} \times 3\frac{1}{8}$ inches. Contemp. ¼ calf. Cohen–de Ricci 234–235.

This unpretentious edition, virtually a pocket book, is now sought after for its eight small plates after Le Barbier. They show his professional competence in routine narrative illustration. If they appear pallid in comparison with the sensational designs for the edition of 1796 (82), they still represent the high points of Laclos' novel in a faithful and agreeable way. It is instructive to compare Le Barbier's treatment of Mme. de Merteuil's seduction of Cécile Volanges with Monnet's. He chooses a less provocative moment in the novel (II, 59) and develops it with relative restraint.

41 FRANÇOIS AUGUSTE RENÉ, VICOMTE DE CHATEAUBRIAND

Génie du christianisme ou Beautés de la religion chrétienne . . . Nouvelle édition, avec figures. Paris, Migneret, 1803. 4 v. I: xii, 464 p. II: [2] *l.*, 439 p. III:

[2] *l.*, 436 p. IV: 595 p. Bound at the end of v. IV is the author's *Défense du Génie du christianisme* . . . Paris, Migneret, 1803. [2] *l.*, 64 p. Illus: I: Front. by Villéry after Boichot, and 2 plates by: Delvaux after Boichot, and Dambrun after Le Barbier. II: 2 plates after Le Barbier by: Delaunay, and Delvaux. III: 2 plates by: Delvaux, and Delignon after Chaudet. IV: 2 plates after Le Barbier by: Baquoy, and Halbou. All plates are in 2 states, *avant lettres*, and published state. Printed on *papier vélin*, large-paper copy. Page size: 10⅛×7⅞ inches. Blue morocco (endpapers dated 1821).

This fine book appears to be almost unknown to collectors, though it contains the best of Le Barbier's later illustrations. It is the third edition of Chateaubriand's celebrated defense of Christianity. There is an opening dedication to First Consul Napoleon, who had supported the restoration of Catholicism as France's official religion the previous year. The dedication disappeared in later editions.

Five of the book's eight plates are after Le Barbier, and three of these are notable. The last volume offers a powerful design of a monk derided or ignored by the prisoners he seeks to console (IV, 177), but Le Barbier's triumph comes in a pair of illustrations for *René*. In this tragic tale René and his sister Amélie are all in all to each other until she discovers that she has fallen in love with him. After a period of tortured misgivings, she immures herself in a convent. In a moving plate (II, 239) Le Barbier shows the pair reunited for the last time in the haunts of their childhood. Still more evocative (II, 194) is the scene in which René contemplates by moonlight the barred window of the convent where Amélie had taken refuge. It might be called the first great Romantic illustration.

This exceptional copy is on large vellum paper, with plates both before and after the letters, in an elaborately decorated binding of blue morocco.

(41) Chateaubriand, *Génie du christianisme*

Drawing for Ovid, *Les métamorphoses*, 1806

Pierre-Clément Marillier (1740–1808)

Marillier spent the first twenty years of his life in Dijon, learning to be a painter. When he came to Paris, financial necessity forced him to turn to illustration, and he soon achieved a position in the front rank of book artists. His first notable contribution was to Desfontaines' *Les bains de Diane* of 1770. In 1773 came his masterpiece of miniature illustration, the *Fables nouvelles* of Dorat. Another success at showing much in little was a pair of volumes by Berquin, the *Idylles* of 1775 and the *Romances* of 1776. Henceforth even the works for which he was the principal illustrator are too numerous to mention, though an exception should be made in the case of *Le cabinet des fées*.

The Revolution hardly slowed the pace of Marillier's production. His outstanding accomplishment was the comprehensive illustration of *La sainte bible*, the 300 plates in which he shared with Monsiau. Like Monnet, Marillier was not behind hand in satisfying the taste of the time for erotic plates. He made a series for *La pucelle*, but his best work in this line is to be found in Louvet de Couvray's *Les amours du chevalier de Faublas* (83). He showed his capacity for allegorical decoration in the borders and portraits of *Les illustres français*, 1790–1816. In his last years he retired from the Parisian world to a comfortable life on his estate near Melun.

Marillier was among the most accomplished and abundant of eighteenth-century illustrators. His work is seen at its best in his small headpieces and tailpieces. He was a thorough professional, however, and in his extended series of plates for *Le cabinet des fées* and particularly *La sainte bible*, he maintained a high level of proficiency. Nearly all of his designs are characterized by grace, liveliness, and firmness of drawing.

REFERENCES Calot (1931); Holloway; Portalis; Réau; Renouvier.

42 GUILLAUME FRANÇOIS FOUQUES DESHAYES DESFONTAINES DE LA VALÉE

Les bains de Diane, ou, Le triomphe de l'amour. Poëme. Paris, J. P. Costard, 1770. [1] *l.*, 123, [3] p. Illus. after Marillier: Engraved t.p. by de Ghendt, 3 plates by: Massard, Ponce, and Voyez. Page size: $8\frac{1}{4} \times 5\frac{3}{8}$ inches. Red morocco by Brany. Cohen–de Ricci 295–296.

As Grimm suggested, this book might well be bound with *Les baisers* (31). The style of the two works is similar, and in both the content is a pretext for the illustrations.

43 CLAUDE JOSEPH DORAT

Fables nouvelles. La Haye et se trouve à Paris, Delalain, 1773. 2 v. in 1. I: xxii p., [1] *l.*, 176 p. II: Engraved t.p. by de Ghendt, [177]–309, [3] p. Illus. after Marillier: Front. by de Ghendt, t.p. vignette by Ponce, plate by Delaunay, 50 pairs of head- and tailpieces by: Arrivet, Baquoy, de Ghendt (11), Godefroy, Le Gouaz (8), Lebeau, Legrand, Leveau (2), Lingée, de Longueil (2), Masquelier (6), Née (11), and Ponce (4). II: Plate by Delaunay, and 49 pairs of head- and tailpieces by: Baquoy, Delaunay (2), Duflos (2), de Ghendt (6), Le Gouaz (6), Legrand (2), Leveau (3), Le Roy, de Longueil (5), Masquelier (7), Née (8), Ponce (2), Mme Ponce (2), and Simonet (2). P. 162 uncorrected. Page size: $8\frac{3}{8} \times 5\frac{3}{8}$ inches. Green morocco by Bedford. Bookplate of Lucius Wilmerding.

43A

Fables nouvelles. La Haye et se trouve à Paris, Delalain, 1773. 2 v. I: xxii p., [1] *l.*, 160 p. II: Engraved t.p. by de Ghendt, [161]–309, [3] p. Illus. after Marillier: T.p. vignette by Ponce, front. by de Ghendt, plate by Delaunay, and 99 pairs of head- and tailpieces. V. I is not the reimpression described by Cohen–de Ricci, although the page number (uncorrected in the above copy) is here corrected to read "xxii." Page 162 is in the corrected form. Some copies have the reset title: Fables ou Allégories philosophiques. Page size: $7\frac{1}{2} \times 4\frac{3}{4}$ inches. Contemp. red morocco. Cohen–de Ricci 313–316.

Dorat provided the text for the two eighteenth-century masterpieces of miniature illustration, *Les baisers* (31) and *Fables nouvelles*. There is the same profusion of small designs in each, but otherwise they are quite different. Eisen's achievement was to use Dorat's hazy and inconsequential poems as his point of departure for a memorable dream of voluptuousness. Though the *Fables* are diffuse and commonplace, they did provide Marillier with varied and substantial subjects. Moreover, love is almost entirely off the stage, and the voluptuous note of *Les baisers* is struck only occasionally (Book II, poem 1).

FABLE XXIII.

LE MERLE ET LE VER LUISANT.

PENDANT une nuit assez sombre,

Tout fier de son étoile, un jeune ver luisant

Se pavanoit dans l'épaisseur de l'ombre,

Et s'enivroit d'orgueil, en se considérant.

Sur ce globe, où chacun m'admire avec justice,

Je ne vois rien, dit-il, de comparable à moi;

Des Insectes je suis le Roi :

Eh! qui d'entr'eux pourroit entrer en lice,

Quand mon empire est si bien affermi?

Est-ce l'active Abeille, ou la sobre Fourmi?

Ces orbes éclatants qui versent la lumiere,

Pour briller empruntent mes feux;

Et l'Astre qu'adore la Terre,

N'est que le ver luisant des Cieux.

Comme il parloit, d'une branche voisine,

Un Merle fond soudain, & gobe l'Orgueilleux.

Ton éclat cause ta ruine,

Pauvre insecte!... moins lumineux,

Tu pouvois vivre, enseveli sous l'herbe :

Que je te plains d'être né si superbe!

L'obscurité t'eût rendu plus heureux.

(43) Dorat, *Fables nouvelles*

In the genial verses which Dorat wrote in praise of Marillier, his emphasis was exclusively on the artist's masterly depiction of animals. "La Fontaine has long been dead," he concluded, "but in you Oudry returns to life" (quoted by Portalis, I, 368). "The travelled mouse" (IV, ix), which shows a group of rodents disporting themselves in a larder, is a characteristically precise and spirited example of his animal headpieces. Portalis noted that in the *Fables* Marillier showed himself to be "the artist of the infinitely small" (I, 367). One almost wonders if Dorat did not foresee this talent, so much play did he make in his poems with snails, grasshoppers, flies, bees, oysters, and even a glowworm (I, xxiii). Yet people also figure prominently, both by themselves, and in company with the brute creation. Witness the village scene of "The green donkey" (II, x) and the contrasting formal garden of "The tulip and the cornflowers" (III, xviii).

The pattern of Marillier's illustration is seen at its simplest in an early fable called "The two watches" (I, vi). The headpiece shows a clockmaker's shop, in which a French dandy is listening to the proprietor's praise of a gaudy toy, while a sensible Englishman at the window carefully examines a plain but efficient instrument. The tailpiece presents two kinds of dials, a cupid holding a watch to his ear, and time's scythe. Among the most attractive of the headpieces is the river scene of "The two falcons" (I, xv), in which the quarrel-

(43) Dorat, *Fables nouvelles*

(43) Dorat, *Fables nouvelles*

(43) Dorat, *Fables nouvelles*

ling birds allow a duck, their proper prey, to escape, while their masters abuse them from the shore. As is often the case in this book, the frame is part of the picture, thus giving depth and perspective to the composition. Indeed, the river seems fairly to flow out of the design. The tailpieces, though diverse and elegant, are usually simple and straightforward in content. The slave breaking his chain in "The power of tears" (III, xiii) is a representative example.

Dorat defended the sumptuousness of the *Fables* in his opening "Avis," quoting Locke's *On Education* in support of the abundant illustrations and boasting of the book's "typographic pomp." It should be mentioned, however, that there are great differences in the *Fables* from one example to another. This large copy on Holland paper with brilliant impressions of the vignettes is much more desirable than the smaller copy described in the second entry above, despite the fact that the latter is in contemporary morocco.

44 AND 45 ARNAUD BERQUIN

Idylles [. . . second recueil]. [Paris, 1775]. 2 parts in 1 v. Engraved t.p., vi p., [1] *l.*, 55 p.; [2] *l.*, 67, [1] p. Illus: 24 plates after Marillier by: Delaunay (4), Gaucher, de Ghendt (6), Le Gouaz (6), Lebeau, Masquelier, Née, and Ponce (4). Bound with Berquin's **Romances.** Paris, Ruault, 1776. [1] *l.*, xxvi, 50 p. Illus. after Marillier: Added engraved t.p. by Ponce, 4 plates by: Delaunay (2), de Ghendt, and Ponce. (This copy, as others, lacks pp. [51–74], 2 further plates, and 6 *l.* of engraved music.) Both works printed on *papier de Hollande*, with plates before numbers. Page size: 6½×4¼ inches. Contemp. red morocco. Bookplate of Robert Hoe. Cohen–de Ricci 139–140; 141–142.

These little books constitute still another triumph of miniature illustration. For the most part Berquin's stories offered Marillier love passages or domestic scenes in the lives of shepherds and shepherdesses. Their most exciting moments come in a harmless "shipwreck" or a "favorable" storm. Altogether exceptional is "The fire" (I, I), in which a beacon lit by a shepherd maid to catch her lover's eye causes the family farmhouse to burn down. All ends happily, however, when the shepherd arrives in time to save her aged father, whose son-in-law he then proposes to become. The *Idylles* was successful enough to warrant a sequel. In the *Ro-*

(44) Berquin, *Idylles*

mances of the following year, the figures are equally elegant, but they are now city folk, who live more varied and passionate lives. The *Idylles* and *Romances* should be sought on Holland paper with the plates before the numbers, as in this copy.

45 ARNAUD BERQUIN

Romances. Paris, Ruault, 1776. [1] *l.*, xxvi, 50 p., [1] *l.*, [51]–73, [1] p. Illus. after Marillier: Added engraved t.p. by Ponce, 6 plates by: Delaunay (3), de Ghendt, Née, and Ponce; 6 *l.* engraved music. Printed on *papier de Hollande*, the plates before numbers. Page size: 6⅛×4½ inches. Brown morocco. Cohen–de Ricci 141–142.

As described in the previous entry, this book includes four stories. This is the expanded edition with six stories and two additional plates.

46

Collection d'estampes contenant **Les contes de fées** en 110 pièces, le tout gravé par M. J. de Longueil et autres, sous la direction de M. Marillier. [Paris], l'Imprimerie de Neufforge, n.d. Letterpress title. Illus: 110 plates after Marillier by: Berthet (3), Boisse, Borgnet (10), Choffard, Croutelle (2), Dambrun, Delaunay, Delignon (6), Delvaux (16), Duponchel (2), Fessard, Gaucher, de Ghendt (18), Godefroy, Halbou (4), Jonxis (4), Langlois jeune (7), Lebeau (2), Legrand, Leroy, Leveau (3), Le Villain (6), de Longueil (2), Malapeau, Mme Demonchy, Patas (7), Mlle Retor, Texier (2),

Voila du gibier qui me vient bien a propos pour traiter trois Ogres de mes amis.

(46) *Les contes de fées*

Thomas (3), and de Valnet, including 2 rejected plates by de Longueil and Delaunay. Page size: 9¾×6⅜ inches. Contemp. ¼ calf. Cohen–de Ricci 198–199.

Le cabinet des fées appeared in forty-one volumes between 1785 and 1789. It contains 120 plates in two sequences numbered 1–108 and 1–12. After its publication was concluded, there appeared this *suite* with the first sequence of 108 plates and *planches réfusées* for the first two stories concerning Bluebeard and Tom Thumb. The reason for the substitutions may have been the failure of the initial versions to achieve the style and finish to which Marillier aspired. Certainly, the second Bluebeard plate, with its giant carrying off babies to serve as the game course in the feast he proposes to give for "three ogres among my friends," is one of Marillier's most grotesque and satisfying inventions. It

(47) *La sainte bible*

(47) *La sainte bible*

must be granted, however, that in general the rococo style was not ideal for fairy tales, particularly those with classical or eastern settings which can be reduced to insipidity with dangerous ease. As in the case of the Kehl Voltaire (52), collectors may find this *suite*, which offers good impressions on large paper, easier to shelve than the forty-one volumes of *Le cabinet des fées*.

47

[298 plates for **La sainte bible** . . . Paris, 1789–1804, 12 v.]. 248 plates after Marillier by: Armond, Baquoy, Bosc, Courbe (2), Dambrun (47), Delaunay (21), De-lignon (7), Delvaux (38), Dupréel (23), Duval (7), de Ghendt (45), Giraud jeune (3), Halbou (3), Hubert (2), Hulk (8), Lebeau, Patas (6), Petit (2), Ponce (7), Trière (2), Varin, Viguet (12), and unsigned (8); 50 after Monsiau by: Baquoy (3), Dambrun (5), Delaunay (4), Delvaux, Duhamel, Dupréel (6), Duval (3), de Ghendt (2), Giraud jeune (2), Hubert, Malapeu, Patas

(9), Ponce (4), Trière, Viguet (2), and unsigned (5). Bound in at the end are: (1) the initial prospectus for the work with the distribution of plates; (2) the "Troisième supplément à la liste de Messieurs les souscripteurs" (1791); (3) the "Huitième supplément . . ." (1793); (4) the undated "Avis aux souscripteurs de la bible," announcing the publication of the 21st *livraison*. Page size: 9⅜ × 6⅛ inches. ½ green morocco by Mercier. Cohen–de Ricci 935–936.

The pertinacity with which this vast project was brought to completion between 1789 and 1804 is remarkable. Despite the vicissitudes of these fifteen hectic years, the twelve volumes were published in twenty-five numbers with their 300 plates (204 for the Old Testament and 96 for New) distributed exactly as promised by Defer de Maisonneuve in a prospectus of 1790. His only departure was the introduction of Monsiau in the place of Marillier as the illustrator of the gospels. The first 132 plates, issued in eleven numbers of twelve plates each, had

Drawings for vignettes

appeared by the end of 1792. Thereafter the volumes were published sporadically, no doubt as the conditions of the time dictated. Indeed, this is clearly a Revolutionary Bible. Marillier's fondness for voluptuous subjects, which found vent not only in "Incest of Lot's daughters" (I, 63) and "Joseph's chastity" (I, 150), but also in scenes of his own invention like "Fornication and idolatry of Israel" (II, 239), was confirmed by the taste of the day, and it is not fanciful to see an increased emphasis on violence in the designs of 1793 and 1794.

Marillier provided five-sixths of the plates for this immense undertaking and thereby joined the succession of outstanding biblical illustrators. Renouvier remarks that in his work "there was as little religion as possible, which was at the time judged to be a great merit" (p. 317). Certainly he exhibits no religious fervor. He places little emphasis on the supernatural, and he keeps the historical reconstruction of biblical settings (an obsession with some earlier illustrators) to a minimum. Once it is assumed that in a sense this is a secular Bible, however, Marillier is very persuasive. His Hebrews are a trim, fresh-faced race. They act out the conceptions of their unfailingly inventive creator with elegance and vivacity. Many sequences are both dramatic and moving, as may be demonstrated by the moonlight defeat of the Midianites in the four plates devoted to Gideon (III, 30–37) and the blinding scene in the five plates devoted to Tobit (V, 10–33).

Marillier was assisted by Monsiau in bringing this demanding assignment to completion. The latter was responsible for the forty-eight plates devoted to the gospels in volumes nine and ten. His broader style and more massive figures provide a faithful rather than a distinguished rendering of the life of Christ, but he is effective in such simple and homely episodes as the return of the prodigal son (IX, 322). See below, page 152.

Like the *Contes des fées*, the twelve volumes of *La sainte bible* take up a great deal of shelf space. This collection of the plates in fine impressions on "satined paper" for the quarto edition offers an attractive alternative way of representing the series, particularly since it is accompanied by various contemporary announcements concerning the edition.

◆ Six drawings by Marillier, pen and ink and sepia wash over graphite, for an untraced publication. Sheet size: $3\frac{1}{2} \times 3\frac{1}{2}$ inches.

These designs by Marillier were apparently intended as vignettes for a single work. The attributes they display are chiefly classical. Manuscripts entitled "Alcoran" in one design and "Système de la nature" in another suggest that religion may have been a theme of the work. At any rate, Holbach's famous treatise on materialist philosophy, published in 1770, opens out of a stricken serpent coiled round an altar.

Jean-Michel Moreau, called Moreau le Jeune (1741–1814)

Moreau was the son of a Parisian wigmaker. He came to be known as Moreau le Jeune because his brother Louis, the elder by two years, achieved a certain reputation as a landscape painter. He studied with the painter Lelorain, and when his master was appointed director of the Russian Academy of Fine Arts, Moreau accompanied him to St. Petersburg at the age of seventeen. Returning to Paris after Lelorain's death in 1759, he turned from painting to engraving and soon made himself a master of his craft. Under the tutelage of Le Bas, who paid him enough for one day's engraving to enable him to spend the rest of the week drawing, he also came to full maturity as an artist. The success of his drawings and prints was such that he was chosen to succeed Cochin as Dessinateur des Menus-Plaisirs in 1770.

Meanwhile, he was achieving fame as an illustrator. His superb fleurons for Hénault's *Abrégé chronologique de l'histoire de France* date from 1765 to 1767. His collaboration in Ovid's *Métamorphoses* of 1767–1771 (62) showed him to be the equal of the established rococo masters Boucher, Eisen, and Gravelot. It was during the 1770s, however, that he carried all before him. His masterpieces were La Borde's *Chansons* and Rousseau's *Oeuvres*, but he was also the illustrator of a fine Molière and contributed significantly to the Baskerville Ariosto (64). Nor did his pace slacken over the next decade. An exhibition of his drawings in 1780 put him above Cochin in the eyes of the public, and he was able to pick and choose among projects for illustration. Sometimes, indeed, he acted as his own publisher. His third masterpiece was the *Monument du costume* of 1789, which had its origin in a pair of *suites* published in 1777 and 1783. Also of major import were his *Figures de l'histoire de France* and the series of engravings which he published to accompany the Kehl Voltaire. Throughout the 1770s and 1780s he executed many superb individual prints, some of them in connection with his appointment at court, others in a private capacity.

Certain qualities are to be found in Moreau's designs throughout his career. His thorough command of whatever text he happened to be illustrating guaranteed him a basis of "fundamental brainwork." Moreover, his artistic seriousness ensured the technical proficiency of his compositions. "To suppress a dog's tail in the designs of Moreau," said Horace Vernet, "would be like deleting a comma from Bossuet's most beautiful period" (quoted by Renouvier, p. 314). From the middle 1760s to the middle 1780s, however, his work had even rarer merits. A keen observer of things around him, he made his plates for Molière, Rousseau, and the *Monument du costume* reflect reality as faithfully as did his separate prints of the passing scene, prints which he was careful to inscribe, "designed after nature" (the Goncourts, III, 99). When he attempted the idyllic mode, as with La Borde's *Chansons*, he was no less persuasive. Even allegory could not deaden his talent, as he showed in illustrating Ovid and *Les grâces*. Indeed, the grace and charm of his drawing during these twenty years brought about "a renaissance in the rococo style" (the Goncourts, III, 75), its culminating surge before it gave way to neoclassicism.

In 1785 Moreau went to Italy with the view of familiarizing himself with the masterpieces of classical and Renaissance art. There can be no doubt that this experience was pivotal in his development, reinforced as it was on his return by the emerging influence of Jacques-Louis David. In a passage attributed to his daughter, Mme Carle Vernet, it is claimed that "this visit unsealed his eyes, that he felt as if irradiated by a new light, that he formed the brave resolve of defending himself against the bad taste of the time, and that his manner, in changing, became both purer and more correct, his composition simpler and more elegant, and his style bolder and more noble." (The summary of Portalis, II, 444. It seems that the manuscript notice where this passage appears was actually written by Feuillet, a friend of the Vernet family. See Renouvier, pp. 308–309.) Most critics have flatly contradicted this panegyric, asserting instead that Moreau's pursuit of the furthest refinements of the classical manner made his designs increasingly cold, formal, and academic.

Moreau was an enthusiastic supporter of the Revolution. Newly elected to the Academy, he joined with David and Gérard in 1790 to advocate entire equality among its members. Even the loss of his appointments and possessions in the social upheaval of the time did not diminish his zeal, and he recorded the new order in print after print. He made do for a time as a professor of design, until at length he was accorded a small pension. Meanwhile, he continued to work as an illustrator, his chief project being the *Nouveau Testament*, five volumes, 1793–1798, which contains 113 plates.

We come now to the work of Moreau's last fifteen or twenty years, which has remained largely unexplored since the Goncourts contemptuously dismissed it. They wrote of his decadence as an illustrator, condemning particularly the series of small designs in which they found that he had descended to the level of Quéverdo or even Chasselat. And they added that "the senility of the artist seems to fall into second childhood" in his illustrations for Renouard, "delights for which bibliophiles compete with their untutored taste" (III, 119–120).

This condemnation is too sweeping. It was in 1795 that Moreau met Antoine-Augustin Renouard. He worked for him intermittently during the rest of his life. The major *suites* that thus came into being, some sold separately by Renouard, others included in the books that he published, were devoted to Boileau, Pierre and Thomas Corneille, Crébillon, Demoustier's *Lettres à Emilie*, Fénelon's *Télémaque*, Gessner, Legrand-d'Aussy's *Fabliaux ou contes*, Molière, Racine, and Voltaire. Renouard offered *suites* before letters of all of these designs. *Télémaque*, Gresset, and Voltaire could also be had as preliminary etchings. Moreau supplied other publishers with substantial series of illustrations to Fielding's *Tom Jones*, La Fontaine, Ovid, and Rousseau. There is nothing to set these apart from his work for Renouard. It is difficult to think of any other artist who illustrated the classical authors of his country on so wide a scale.

Among the several hundred designs of Moreau's last phase, there are a great many which can hardly be defended against the strictures of the Goncourts.

Certainly none approach the best work of his prime. But there are occasional oases in the desert, not merely individual plates, but whole series such as Gessner's *Oeuvres*; Demoustier's *Lettres à Emilie*, six volumes, 1809; and his twenty-nine plates for Ovid (96). One has to become accustomed to Moreau's altered style: the prevailing dryness, the stiff figures, the formal, almost diagrammatic composition. But once one learns to read this new language, there are discoveries to be made. As in the past, his designs continue to be authentic, if sometimes bizarre, interpretations of his various texts. One even comes to understand why his contemporaries remained faithful to him, why the bibliophiles of the time vied for the books which he illustrated, and why they went to the expense of having them bound by Simier and Thouvenin.

During most of his later life Moreau earned a modest living by his illustrations. We catch a glimpse of him during a visit which Mahérault, who was to be the cataloguer of his engravings, paid to his fifth-floor apartment in 1810. He was shown by the artist's wife into his study, a room lined with the books that he had illustrated and many others, all simply bound with covers of marbled paper. Moreau was seated at his table, drawing on a large sheet of paper. Beside him were his working necessities: a pencil, a crow's feather, bits of China ink and sepia, and a vessel containing the latter in solution. As his large hand moved dexterously over the composition of a ball costume, he explained to Mahérault that he was following a sketch by his son-in-law, Horace Vernet, since he himself no longer went into the world. (The Goncourts, III, 131–133.)

Moreau's last years were painful. He was afflicted by a cancerous growth on his right arm, which prevented him from drawing. A note of 1814 bears witness to his distress: "I beg M. Renouard to come to my aid, for I no longer know where to turn. I haven't a penny, I am in the greatest difficulty." (Quoted by the Goncourts, III, 130–131.) He died on November 30 of that year, not long after he had been restored to his court appointment by the returning Louis XVIII.

Moreau was a big, strong man of rough appearance and brusque speech. The Goncourts relate, indeed, that during his uncertain beginnings as an art student, his comrades called him "the Ox."

But he was also an affectionate husband and father and a faithful friend. In private company he could be witty and amusing. His wide reading and extensive observation combined with a capacious memory to make him a master of ancedote. Throughout his long life he was wholly devoted to the art by which he lived. His is the greatest name among French illustrators of the eighteenth century.

REFERENCES Adhémar (1963); Bocher; Calot (1931); the Goncourts (1880); Holloway; Mahérault; Portalis; Portalis-Beraldi; Réau; Renouvier.

Les grâces . . . Paris, Laurent Prault & Bailly, 1769. viii, 330 p., [3] *l.* Illus: Engraved front. by Simonet after Boucher, engraved t.p. by Moreau, and 5 engraved plates after Moreau by: De Launay, de Longueil, Massard (2), and Simonet. Page size: $8 \times 5\frac{1}{4}$ inches. Contemp. red morocco. Cohen–de Ricci 834–835.

In his three plates for *Les grâces* young Moreau met the challenge presented by Boucher's frontispiece for the volume. His nude ladies are less voluptuous and tempting than those of the veteran master but more graceful and engaging.

(49) Early proof of "Marley"

Mais l'ombre des Berceaux
Aigrit encor mes maux .

(49) Engraving of "Marley"

Moreau le Jeune 89

Choix de chansons mises en musique par M. de La Borde . . . ornées d'estampes par J. M. Moreau, dédiées à Madame la Dauphine. Paris, de Lormel [etc.], 1773. 4 v., engraved throughout. Illus: I: Front. (port. of de La Borde) by Masquelier after Denon, 154 p., [2] *l.* incl. t.p. vignette by Moreau, dedication by Masquelier after Moreau, and 25 plates by Moreau. II: Front. by Moreau after Denon, t.p. by Née and Masquelier after Le Bouteux, 153 p. incl. 25 plates after Le Bouteux by Masquelier (12), and Née (13). III: T.p. by Née and Masquelier after Le Barbier, 150 p., [2] *l.*, incl. 25 plates after Le Barbier by Masquelier (13) and Née (12). IV: T.p. by Née and Masquelier after Le Barbier, 150 p., [2] *l.*, incl. 25 plates by Masquelier after Le Barbier (10), Née after Le Barbier (9), Masquelier after Saint-Quentin (3), and Née after Saint-Quentin (3). Page size: 9¾×6⅛ inches. Blue morocco by Chambolle-Duru. Cohen–de Ricci 534–538.

Jean-Benjamin de La Borde was a prominent figure at court, first valet de chambre to Louis XV and Governor of the Louvre, as the dedicatory plate of his *Chansons* announces. This little hunchback pleased the king by his wit and varied accomplishments, and the royal generosity allowed him for a time to gratify his every whim. One consequence was the appearance of this book, in which his feeble songs and inept music are presented with the utmost sumptuousness. Its 100 plates and engraved text carry vanity publication to its furthest reach. That Moreau should have contrived to make the first volume of this work a masterpiece is something of a miracle, even though he ensured its perfection by engraving as well as designing the plates.

(49) Early proof of "Les plaisirs du printemps"

(49) Early proof of "La foire de Gonesse"

When he withdrew, after a disagreement with La-Borde, the magic disappeared. Given the luxuriousness of the undertaking, the remaining volumes could hardly be commonplace, and indeed the plates after Le Barbier have their decided merit (see above, p. 76), but the remaining illustrations after Le Bouteux and Saint-Quentin, are not in the same class as those by Moreau.

Moreau's problem in dealing with La Borde's vapid, not to say nebulous, songs was considerable. They are so lacking in content that they rarely offer a narrative point for illustration. His solution was to create an idealized world, extending from the countryside to the city, in which all the actors are agreeable, and every scene is entrancing. The absence of constraint from La Borde's text was thereby converted into a positive advantage. There was an obligatory series of paired shepherds and shepherdesses (I, 30), but, since they had no individuality, Moreau could content himself with making them svelte and appealing in various ways, and then go on to create detailed settings in which the range of his art could be displayed. The change of pace offered by such a scene as a country fair (I, 126) was no doubt welcome. The plates devoted to persons of quality (I, 65) allowed Moreau to come within hailing distance of reality as he contrasted the elegance of good society with the idyllic simplicity of his country folk.

ᴓ► Album containing 45 impressions of plates from La Borde's *Choix de chansons* (1773). Illus: 18 working proofs (1 touched), and 21 plates *avant lettres*. Working proofs for plates at: I: 36, 36, 65, 96, 126; II: t.p., 2, 26, 134; III: 32, 98, 122, 134; IV: t.p., 2, 26, 92, 128. *Avant lettres*: I: 6, 12, 24, 30, 42, 48, 54, 60, 72, 78, 84, 108, 114, 120, 126, 132, 138, 144, 150, II: 134; III: 20.

The Pierpont Morgan Library, The Dannie and Hettie Heineman Collection

Early states of the plates for La Borde's *Chansons* are extremely rare. They were not issued in *suites,* and the collector's only recourse has been to acquire them painfully proof by proof. This set shows how precious they can be. Even Moreau could not altogether preserve the evanescent charm of the preliminary impressions in his finished engravings. An example is provided by an etching with some engraved work of "Marley." In its final form, morning seems to have turned into dusk, making one speculate why the lady in the background needs a parasol. "Les plaisirs du printemps" and "La foire de Gonesse" are closer to their finished states, but even in those subjects the movement of the figures, their expressions, and the background details have a fine precision not altogether preserved.

50 JEAN BAPTISTE POQUELIN MOLIÈRE

Oeuvres de Molière, avec des remarques grammaticales; des avertissemens et des observations sur chaque pièce, par M. Bret. Paris, la Compagnie des Libraires Associés, 1773. 6 v. I: [2] *l.,* viii, 520 p. plus 6-p. "Prospectus" dated in type 16 and 19 August 1772. Leaves E1.8 and 2.7 in both cancelled and uncancelled states. II: [2] *l.,* 576 p. III: [2] *l.,* 551 p. IV: [2] *l.,* 560 p. V: [2] *l.,* 774 p., [1] *l.* VI: [2] *l.,* 704 p. Illus: I: Engraved front. by Cathelin after Mignard, t.p. vignette by Moreau, portrait of Molière by Ficquet after Coypel, and 4 plates by: De Launay, Duclos, Née, and Simonet after Moreau. II: Engraved plates after Moreau: t.p. vignette, 6 engraved plates by: Duclos, de Ghendt, Masquelier, Née (2), and Simonet. III: T.p. vignette and 6 plates by: Baquoy (2), Duclos, Le Bas, Née, and Leveau. IV: T.p. vignette and 6 plates by: Le Veau, Moreau, and Simonet (4). V: T.p. vignette and 5 plates by: Baquoy, Legrand, Leveau, and Née (2). VI: T.p. vignette and 6 plates by: De Launay, Duclos, de Ghendt, Helman, Leveau, and Simonet. In each volume is a *suite* of plates *avant lettres* (including t.p. vignettes) and the original pen-and-ink and watercolor drawings by Moreau for the plates. Page size: $8\frac{3}{8} \times 5\frac{1}{2}$ inches. Red morocco by Bradel. Cohen–de Ricci 716, describing this copy.

The Pierpont Morgan Library

Moreau's remarkable adaptability, his capacity for determining the kind of illustration best suited to each book he undertook, is exampled by the sharp contrast between his designs for La Borde and his exactly contemporary designs for Molière. Whereas he largely neglected La Borde's text, he packed as much of his author's meaning as possible into his illustrations for Molière. The figures in the *Chansons* are small in scale since they are only one element in Moreau's ensemble. For Molière he made them much more prominent, sometimes allowing them almost to fill his frame. Whereas beauty was uppermost in his mind with La Borde, with Molière he aimed above all at character, even approaching the grotesque for plays like *Le bourgeois gentilhomme* (V, 589) and *Le Malade imaginaire* (VI, 509). There is some loss in grace and finesse, no doubt, but in compensation Moreau achieves a firm and illuminating conception of each situation that he presents. It may also be noted that, in

(50) Drawing for *Le misanthrope*

(50) Drawing for *George Dandin*

contrast to Boucher (6), his strongest plates are usually for Molière's serious plays, rather than his lighter efforts, though he hardly falters throughout the canon.

In his design for *Le misanthrope* (IV, 3) Moreau chose the point of no return in Alceste's relationship with Célimène, the scene in which he confronts her with a letter which to his mind convicts her of faithlessness. Both Alceste's burning honesty and his extravagance, both Célimène's concern and her disdain, are conveyed in this confrontation of high comedy. Moreau is equally compelling in the farce *George Dandin*, at the opposite end of Molière's gamut. Here he selected the concluding tableau, in which the upstart peasant Dandin has been so thoroughly outmanoeuvered by his lady wife that he is forced to apologize to her, though she is in the wrong and he in the right. It is midnight, and we see by candlelight the demurely triumphant wife, her outraged parents, and Dandin kneeling before them, beaten but still rebellious, no doubt repeat-

ing inwardly: "Ah, George Dandin, you have wished this on yourself."

This celebrated copy, an *exemplaire reglé* with a *suite* of plates before the letters, contains all of Moreau's finished drawings. As usual, they are in wash. Its mosaic morocco binding by Bradel l'Aîné probably dates from about 1800. It is reproduced in Appendix I.

51

[*Suite* of plates for **Collection complète des oeuvres de J. J. Rousseau.** Londres (i.e., Bruxelles) J. L. De Boubers, 1774–1783]. Front. by St. Aubin after de La Tour and 37 engraved plates, 30 after Moreau by: Choffard, Duclos (4), Duflos, N. de Launay (6), R. de Launay (3), Le Mire (9), Leveau, Martini, Moreau, and Simonet (3); 7 after Le Barbier by: Dambrun, Halbou, Ingouf (2), Le Mire, Romanet, and Trière. Page size: 9½ × 7¼ inches. Red morocco by Zaehnsdorf. Cohen–de Ricci 908–909.

These designs were a labor of love for Moreau, who admired Rousseau and had an intimate familiarity with his books. There are thirty-five in all, including five fleurons, but the finest are the nine for *Emile* and especially the twelve for *La nouvelle Héloïse*. These last, indeed, are among the best illustrations for any novel in any language. Gravelot's plates for the first edition of the book (16) seem almost trivial in comparison. In size Moreau's designs are halfway between those for La Borde's *Chansons* and those for the *Monument du costume*. He had enough space to be circumstantial and detailed in his conceptions; indeed there is almost as much "local color" as one finds in the *Monument du costume* itself. The figures as well as the backgrounds are realized with completeness.

(51) Rousseau, *La nouvelle Héloïse*

Though all the plates are arresting, one may prefer those presenting Julie and Saint Preux in their passionate youth even to the rendering of their idyllic but more sedate later years. The series begins with a design to which Rousseau gave the title "Love's first kiss." "It is the novel itself which takes form under the artist's hand," Portalis writes (II, 432), "inspired himself by these burning pages." Three plates further on we see Saint Preux leaving some ladies of the evening, to whose apartment he had been inveigled by young officers of his acquaintance. His precipitate departure, the regretful surprise of the revelers, and the disappointment in particular of one shapely lass form a scene of great

(51) Rousseau, *La nouvelle Héloïse*

(52) Voltaire, *Candide*, the Kehl *suite*

(58) Voltaire, *Candide*, the Renouard *suite*

animation. Rousseau's works are not remarkable for humor, but despite his portentous title for this plate, "Shame and remorse revenge outraged love," one need not repress a smile.

52

Estampes destinées à orner les éditions de M. de Voltaire, dédiées à Son Altesse Royale Monseigneur le prince de Prusse, par J. M. Moreau . . . elles se vendent séparément des éditions. Paris, l'Auteur, n.d. Illus: T.p. by Beaublé, dedication, portrait by Dambrun after Moreau, 15 portraits after various artists by: Beisson, Demautort (2), Fosseyeux (5), Langlois (2), Maviez (3), and Tardieu (2), and 93 plates after Moreau by: Baquoy (4), Croutelle, Dambrun (12), Delaunay (2), Delignon (11), Duclos (7), H. Guttenberg, Halbou (9), Helman, Langlois (2), Le Mire (2), Leveau (3), Lingé (2), de Longueil (8), Masquelier, Patas, Romanet (3), Simonet (13), and Trière (10). The comte de Waldner de Freudstein copy. Page size: $8\frac{7}{8} \times 5\frac{5}{8}$ inches. Contemp. calf. Cohen–de Ricci 1042–1047.

Moreau's most ambitious project during the 1780s was his series of designs to accompany the great edition of Voltaire which had been undertaken by Beaumarchais. Produced in the printing house built at Kehl especially for this purpose, it extends to seventy volumes. The first installment of Moreau's plates appeared in 1781, the last in 1789. In July of 1782, when he had completed twenty engravings and had twenty-nine more in preparation, he wrote to Beaumarchais asking him to send to the Kehl subscribers a prospectus for his illustrations. Henceforth publisher and artist went hand in hand. When Beaumarchais changed the format of his edition from quarto to octavo, Moreau redesigned his already completed engravings for *La Henriade* and other works to fit the new format. Only because of the Revolution was Beaumarchais prevented from presenting to Catherine the Great, one of his sponsors, a splendid set of the edition

Drawing of Beaumarchais

in which Moreau's original drawings had been mounted. (Portalis, II, 439–445.)

Moreau's ninety-four plates for the Kehl Voltaire offer a conspectus of the various kinds of illustration to which he devoted himself during this period. They begin and end with Voltaire's two long poems: ten plates for *La Henriade*, and twenty-one for *La Pucelle* drawn in 1788–1789. In between are eighteen plates for Voltaire's short stories and novels and forty-one for his plays. These designs have been highly praised by Portalis and others, but for the most part they are imposing rather than agreeable. Moreau's depictions of modes and manners in the *Monument du costume* and the designs he made for his cherished Rousseau were done *con amore*. In them he could be supple and natural. But when he joined in this monumental tribute to the revered Voltaire, he worked under constraint. The figures in his compositions are stiff and posed; their attitudes are declamatory. Never were so many visages turned towards the heavens, never so many arms outstretched or upraised. Only in his illustrations for *La Pucelle* and some of the prose narratives did he relax into ease and humor. His lighter touch is exampled in the plate for the first chapter of *Candide*, in which Baron Thunder-ten-tronck banishes Candide from his castle in Westphalia after his first love-passage with Cunégonde.

The Kehl Voltaire is one of the landmarks of printing history, and it is often found in fine contemporary bindings. Yet the shelf space required for its seventy substantial volumes may well give pause to the collector of illustrated books, who can content himself instead with the series of plates which Moreau himself published.

❧ Circular pencil drawing by Moreau on vellum, a portrait of Pierre Augustin Caron de Beaumarchais, in profile. Diameter: 5 inches.

Moreau's drawing is preserved in the copy of *La folle journée* described below (68). It was engraved by Hopewood "from a design communicated by [Beaumarchais'] own family." The engraving is also present in this copy.

53

Figures de l'histoire de France, dessinées par M. Moreau le jeune, et gravées sous sa direction; avec la discours de M. l'Abbé Garnier. Paris, Moreau le jeune, 1785–1790. [8] *l.*, 65 p., [3] *l.* Prelims. include 3 different half titles, 4 different t.p.s, and [2]-p. "Préface." Bound in at the beginning are a prospectus for the *5ième livraison*, and a 4-p. "Avis pour la continuation de l'ouvrage. . . ." Illus: Engraved dedication, 4 engraved maps by Tardieu, and 161 engraved plates *avant lettres* after Moreau. Page size: 10¾×8½ inches. Red morocco by Chambolle-Duru. Cohen–de Ricci 737–738.

The complicated publishing history of this fine series of prints need not be related. Originally intended to illustrate all of French history, in the event it came down only to 1360. Even so it extends to 162 subjects drawn by Moreau between

(53) *Figures de l'histoire de France*

the 1770s and 1808. By a somewhat ruthless manoeuvre, Moreau acquired the engraved plates after the death of the originator of the enterprise, his former master Le Bas, together with a large store of prints taken from them. This set no doubt comes in part from the 2,352 proofs before letters included in his purchase.

Unlike Cochin in his allegorical designs to accompany Hénault's *Nouvelle abrégé de l'histoire de France* (63), Moreau sought out individual incidents in France's early annals, which he then depicted in as specific detail as the obscure record of those times permitted. When Portalis remarks à propos of this series that "to make beautiful paintings, it would suffice to magnify Moreau's drawings" (II, 436), he does not exaggerate. Were it not for their remote subject matter, these meticulous designs could have become as well known as Moreau's acknowledged masterpieces. Among many attractive alternatives, a few may be mentioned: the library scene of "the reestablishment of learning in the west" (49); "the extinction of Charlemagne's prosperity," which seems to prefigure the Revolution: "the birth of French poetry" (125); and "the abolition of the Order of Templars" (152). The last is one of several drawings in which Moreau achieves an eye-deceiving perspective by making the foreground of his design part of the frame.

54 JACQUES HENRI BERNARDIN DE SAINT-PIERRE

Paul et Virginie ... avec figures ... Paris, l'Imprimerie de Monsieur [i.e., Didot jeune], 1789. xxxv, 243, [1] p. Illus: 4 plates after Moreau by: Girardet, Halbou, and de Longueil (2). Printed on *papier vélin*, the plates in published states. Page size: 5 × 3 inches. Contemp. green morocco. Cohen–de Ricci 931–932.

This charming book has its place in literary collections as the first separate edition of Bernardin de Saint-Pierre's famous romance. In his preliminary notice (p. xi) the author tells how Moreau drew three of the illustrations and directed the engraving of all four "with that correctness and taste of which the combination is peculiar to his productions, above all of those for which he feels affection. He has given to each character and to each setting its proper realization; and although the size of each is small, his great talents, as usual, are displayed." Among Moreau's contributions

the fairy-tale-like plate at page 34 stands out. Here little Virginia wins the pardon of a fugitive slave from her ogreish master.

55 NICOLAS EDME RESTIF DE LA BRETONNE

Monument du costume physique et moral de la fin du dix-huitième siècle, ou Tableaux de la vie, ornés de figures dessinées & gravées par M. Moreau le jeune ... & par d'autres célèbres artistes. Neuwied sur le Rhin, Société Typographique, 1789. [1] *l.*, 36 p., [1] *l.* Illus: 26 engraved plates: 24 after Moreau by Baquoy, Baquoy and Patas, Camligue, Dambrun, De Launay, Delignon, C. Guttenberg, H. Guttenberg (2), Halbou, Helman (4), Malbeste, Martini (4), Patas, Romanet, Simonet, Thomas, and Trière; 2 unsigned plates after Freudeberg. Red morocco by Chambolle-Duru. Page size: 20½ × 14⅛ inches. Cohen–de Ricci 881.

Society under Louis XVI was persuaded that it had brought human existence to an unprecedented level of polish and refinement. There was a compelling desire to see the manners, clothes, furniture, and social ambiance of the day recorded in engravings. The climax of the artistic activity that resulted came in three series published by Prault, the royal printer. The first *Suite d'estampes pour servir à l'histoire des moeurs et de costume des français au XVIIIe siècle*, after the designs of the Swiss artist Freudeberg, had only a modest success when it appeared in 1775, but the two that followed in 1777 and 1783, after Moreau, are among the great achievements of the world's graphic art. They are described here as they were republished in 1789 with a text by Restif de la Bretonne under the title *Monument du costume*. It may be noted that the individual plates for the second *Suite* are dated 1776 and 1777. Only three plates for the third *Suite* have dates, which are 1781 and 1782.

Freudeberg's drawings had illustrated a day in the life of a fashionable young woman. The twelve plates of Moreau's continuation begin with the discovery of her pregnancy, show the attention lavished on her till her son is born, and follow her gradual resumption of her accustomed social round. The second series offers fourteen scenes (two of them by Freudeberg) centering on the amusements and daily routine of a young dandy, who is followed from morning to night, at home, at play, at the opera, and in the country.

The plates are large in scale and masterly in conception. Though they are finished to the last detail, there is a superb naturalness about them unequalled elsewhere in eighteenth-century illustration. The Goncourts have shown (III, 93–94) that Moreau's command of "local color" is to be traced in part to the exact knowledge of each subject which he acquired before he drew it. They do not attempt to explain the effortless charm which makes these scenes of high society the most convincing validation of Talleyrand's observation that no one who had not lived in France in the years before the Revolution knew how sweet life could be.

56 JEAN DE LA FONTAINE

Les amours de Psyché et de Cupidon, avec la poème d'Adonis . . . Edition ornée de figures dessinées par Moreau le jeune, et gravées sous sa direction. Paris, Didot jeune, l'An troisième [i.e., 1795]. [4] *l.*, 234 p.

(55) Restif de la Bretonne, *Monument du costume*

Illus: Engraved port. by Audouin after Rigault, 8 engraved plates after Moreau by: Dambrun (2), Duhamel, Dupréel, de Ghendt, Halbou, Petit, and Simonet; with a *suite* of the plates *à l'eau-forte*, the artist's names in dry point. Bound in is a *suite* of reduced copies by Delvaux. Page size: 11⅞ ×9 inches, uncut. ½ red morocco. Cohen–de Ricci 583.

This handsome quarto, in which the leading illustrator of the day collaborated with the leading printer, would in itself suffice to demonstrate that the making of fine books continued after the Revolution. Moreau's eight designs are as carefully conceived as those he did in the 1770s, and their engraving was executed under his direction. The scenes of interiors draw on the studies of antique remains he made during his Italian visit. In that shown (p. 166), the minions of Venus are about to

(55) Restif de la Bretonne, *Monument du costume*

Telle fut la premiere peine que Psyché souffrit.

(56) La Fontaine, *Les amours de Psyché et de Cupidon*

These designs, some of which are dated 1795, must have been among the first which Moreau drew for Renouard. Advised by "several persons of much taste" (I, vi), the publisher supplemented the small-paper edition for which they were originally intended with this large-octavo edition. For the latter format Renouard also printed copies, like this one, on vellum paper with plates both before and with the letters. Its ample margins provide an appropriate setting for Moreau's elegant depictions of Gessner's classical and biblical subjects. Just as appealing are his busy and animated designs for his author's occasional modern scenes, such as that of Idyll 29, in which Gessner entertains rustic workers on a harvest evening with tales of his travels (I, 193).

(57) Proof before letters for Gessner, *Idylles*

begin her vengeance on Psyché by destroying the beauty which has caused Cupid to fall in love with her. Elsewhere Moreau manages his mythological machinery with great suavity. Yet one cannot but regard these plates rather as accomplished academic exercises on themes set by La Fontaine than as true illustrations.

57 SALOMON GESSNER

Oeuvres . . . Paris, Antoine-Augustin Renouard, 1799. 4 v. I: xii, 319 p. II: [2] *l.*, 282 p. III: [2] *l.*, 264 p., [1] *l.* IV: [2] *l.*, 295, [1] p. Illus: 3 engraved portraits, and 48 engraved plates after Moreau by: Baquoy (3), Dambrun (2), Delvaux (7), Dupréel, de Ghendt (9), Girardet (6), Le Mire (4), Petit (4), Simonet (8), and Trière (4). All plates are in two forms, *avant* and *avec lettres*. Bound in are proofs of 3 frontispieces, 4 vignettes, 3 early states of the plates, and 6 other (rejected?) versions of the plates. Page size: 9⅜ × 6⅛ inches, uncut; unopened. One of 25 sets on *grand papier vélin*. ½ green morocco by Purgold Hering. Cohen–de Ricci 435–436; Reynaud 203–204.

58

[Deuxième suite des figures par Moreau le jeune pour les oeuvres complètes de Voltaire, 1802. Paris, Renouard, c. 1819]. Illus: 41 engraved portraits by St. Aubin, 5 portraits by various artists inserted by Renouard, and 113 plates after Moreau by: Blot (3), Coiny (3), Croutelle (2), Delvaux (7), de Ghendt (11), Girardet (3), Godefroy (3), Halbou, Ingouf, Massard, Nicollet (6), Petit (2), Ribault (2), Roger (3), Romanet (4), Simonet (43), Thomas (3), Trière (6), and Villery (9). Page size: 8⅛ × 5⅜ inches. Contemp. ¼ red morocco. Cohen–de Ricci 1047–1048; Reynaud 559.

The illustrations for Voltaire which Moreau drew for Renouard are more extensive than his earlier set (114 plates as compared with 94) and more propitiously distributed among Voltaire's various kinds of writing (32 plates as compared with 18 for the stories and novels). Otherwise they are sad examples of the falling off in his work which had occurred over an interval of some fifteen years. If anything, his style has become more emphatically declamatory, and his figures are sometimes grotesquely distorted. One cannot dismiss these elongated bodies, impossibly high waists, and small heads as simply out of drawing. The question is why Moreau wanted his people to look this way. Was he following some recondite theory that he had evolved from his studies of the antique? Did he see in such figures an elegance that is hidden from modern eyes? These drawings certainly had their vogue at the time, and they are parallelled in some ways by the designs of Horace Vernet for *Incroyables et merveilleuses* (80). It may be noted that the illustration for the first chapter of *Candide* is dated 1804; that for the same subject in the Kehl edition is dated 1787. The latter has character, life, even a touch of voluptuousness. The former is cold and stiff. Exceptionally, Moreau didn't even put himself to the trouble of rethinking his composition.

59 HENRY FIELDING

Tom Jones, ou Histoire d'un enfant trouvé . . . Traduction nouvelle et complète, ornée de douze gravures en taille-douce. Paris, Firmin Didot frères, 1833. 4 v. I: xv, 376 p. II: [2] *l.*, 411 p. III: [2] *l.*, 356 p. IV: [2] *l.*, 444 p. Illus. after Moreau: 12 engraved plates by: Simonet (3), de Villiers frères (6), and Mariage (3). All plates present in 4 forms: *à l'eau-forte, avant lettres, avant lettres* printed on *papier de chine,* and published state printed on *papier de chine.* At v. I, p. 10 is a plate by Courbe after Moreau (reversed) in 3 states; at p. 306 is a plate by Hulk after Moreau *à l'eau-forte* and *avant lettres;* at v. IV, p. 298 are plates by Hulk and Mariage after Moreau *à l'eau-forte* and *avant lettres.* Page size: 9 × 5½ inches. Red morocco by Petit. Bookplate of Francis Kettaneh. Cohen–de Ricci 395–396.

The designs for this edition must have been among Moreau's last. One is dated 1812 (I, 306), another 1813 (IV, 298). They offer painful evidence of his further decline as an illustrator. Though he studied Fielding's text with his usual care, his heavy figures, immobilized in awkward positions, are devoid of liveliness or charm. When this edition finally appeared in 1833, it must have baffled the amateurs of the day. Not for another thirty years was the thought of plates after Moreau in four states likely to give rise to excitement and rivalry among bibliophiles.

Jacques de Sève

60 JEAN BAPTISTE RACINE

Oeuvres. Paris, 1760. 3 v. I: [2] *l.*, xviii p., [3] *l.*, 414 p. II: [2] *l.*, iv, 447 p. III: [2] *l.*, iv, 412 p. Illus. after de Sève: I: Front. by Daullé, t.p. vignette by Chevillet, 5 plates by: Aliamet, Le Mire, Lempereur, Sornique, and Tardieu; 5 head- and 19 tailpieces by Baquoy. II: T.p. vignette, 5 plates by: Flipart (4) and Lempereur; 5 headpieces by Baquoy (4) and Flipart; 22 tailpieces by: Baquoy (11), Flipart (7), and Legrand (4). III: T.p. vignette by Chevillet, 2 plates by Flipart; 3 headpieces by Baquoy, and Flipart (2); 19 tailpieces by: Chevillet, Flipart (17), and Legrand. Page size: 11¼ × 8¼ inches. Contemp. red morocco. Cohen–de Ricci 846–847.

In these stately volumes Jacques de Sève did for Racine what Boucher had done for Molière. Indeed, the fact that he alone was responsible for designing the twelve plates, thirteen headpieces, and sixty tailpieces gives them a decorative unity quite unmatched in the earlier work. His figures, who belong to an angular but distinguished race, provide fitting embodiments for the decorous passions with which Racine inspires his characters. Even the cupids of the headpieces and tailpieces, often at least partially clothed, are more serious and less chubby than is usual in rococo designs.

De Sève was a painter of repute who occasionally undertook illustration, and each of his plates is in effect the engraved version of a small painting. The canvas is full, but not crowded; the figures are strikingly grouped; and the drawing is firm and correct. The crucial episodes he selects are represented with animation and psychological penetration. In *Britannicus* we are shown the poisoning scene (I, 329), which figures in the tragedy itself only through Burrhus' narration. Britannicus lies dead, the guests at Nero's banquet cry out in horror, but Narcisse hardly disguises his gratification as he snatches away the chalice he has poisoned. Nero himself sits unmoved, merely remarking that his half brother had been subject to fits in childhood.

BRITANNICUS.

T. de Seve invenit.   D. Sornique Sculpsit.

(60) Racine, *Britannicus*

(60) Racine, *Les plaideurs*

The publishers offer explanations of all the illustrations. The headpieces are said to "represent allegorically the character of the play for which they are destined" (I, xv). They are ample in size and elaborately framed with suitable attributes. Characteristic is the mock trial placed at the beginning of *Les plaideurs* (I, 249). Concerning the tailpieces the publishers promise only that they will be "analagous to the act in which they are placed." Sometimes they comment in a light-hearted way on the tragic developments of Racine's text. That for act III of *Esther*, for example, shows Ahasuerus the King of Persia, calming the fears of Esther, his Queen, the rabbit at her feet symbolizing her state of mind. Others are simply assemblages of attributes. An unusual feature is the frequent employment of tailpieces in Racine's miscellaneous writings, left unadorned in most editions of his works.

De Sève's illustrations combine with the book's imposing size and typography to make it a work of some magnificence. Though he follows the rococo style of the period, his Racine seems more akin to Oudry's La Fontaine's *Fables* (5) and Boucher's Molière (6) than to Eisen's La Fontaine's *Contes et nouvelles* (26) and Gravelot's Boccaccio (15). In any event, it is an almost faultless achievement.

Monnet, Loutherbourg, and others

61 JEAN DE LA FONTAINE

Fables choisies, mises en vers . . . Nouvelle édition gravée en taille-douce, les figures par le Sr. Fessard, le texte par le Sr. Montulay . . . Paris, Des Lauriers, 1765–1775. 6 v., engraved throughout. I: [1] *l.*, lxxi,

(60) Racine, *Esther*

100 p. II: vi, 102 p. III: iv, 95 p. IV: [3] *l.*, 134 p. V: [2] *l.*, 103 p. VI: [2] *l.*, 115 p. Illus. as in Cohen–de Ricci; second issue. Page size: 7½ × 4⅞ inches. Contemp. red morocco. Cohen–de Ricci 551–552.

This work was the creation of the engraver Fessard, who dedicated it to the Dauphin. He evidently hoped to rival the great edition illustrated by Oudry (5), and in this effort he didn't altogether fail. With regard to profusion of illustrations, indeed, he far surpassed the edition of 1755–1759. There are a plate and a headpiece for each of the 243 fables, and a tailpiece for all but seventeen. Moreover, since the text, like the designs, is engraved, the ensemble is as harmonious as it is elegant. But in the end one has to grant that the baroque style, as employed by a master like Oudry, has here prevailed over the rococo.

The choice between the two editions would be harder to make, if it were not for the fact that the Fessard *Fables* are really two books rather than one. The first three volumes, published between 1765

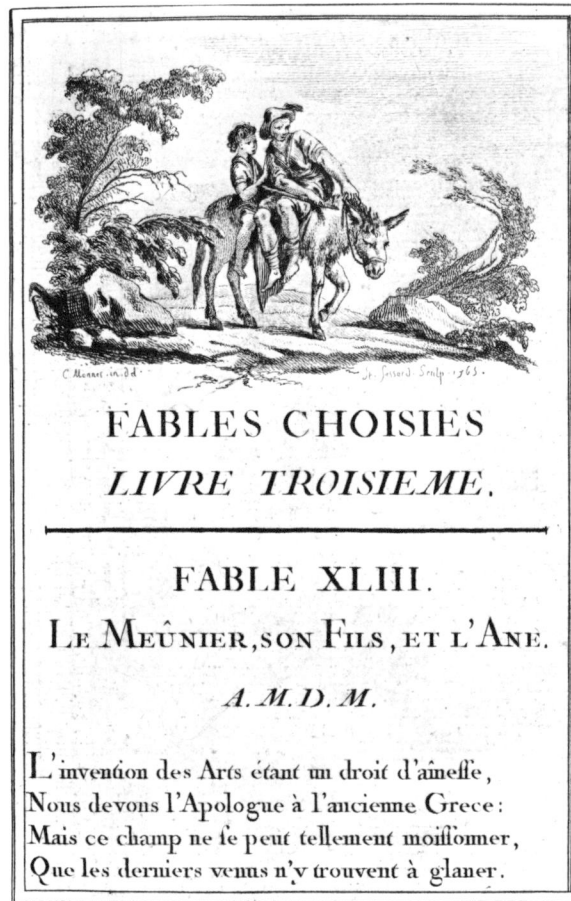

FABLES CHOISIES
LIVRE TROISIEME.

FABLE XLIII.
Le Meûnier, son Fils, et l'Ane.

A.M.D.M.

L'invention des Arts étant un droit d'aînesse,
Nous devons l'Apologue à l'ancienne Grece:
Mais ce champ ne se peut tellement moissonner,
Que les derniers venus n'y trouvent à glaner.

Le Meûnier, son Fils, &c. 5

Qu'on dise quelque chose, ou qu'on ne dise rien,
J'en veux faire à ma tête. Il le fit, & fit bien.

Quant à vous, suivez Mars, ou l'Amour, ou le Prince;
Allez, venez, courez, demeurez en province,
Prenez femme, abbaye, emploi, gouvernement:
Les gens en parleront, n'en doutez nullement.

(61) Engravings after Monnet for La Fontaine's *Fables*

(61) Engraving after Loutherbourg for La Fontaine's *Fables*

and 1767, are dominated by Monnet, who is consistently inventive and entertaining. The plates after Loutherbourg are also deft and pleasing. The second three volumes, published between 1773 and 1775, are illustrated by a variety of artists, who for the most part have little of interest to offer.

Indeed, in this book even Monnet, when compared with Oudry, seems more of a decorator than an illustrator. The plate, headpiece, and tailpiece for "The miller, his son, and the donkey" (III, 1–5) enable him to show three scenes from this fable. Pretty and graceful as they are, they don't offer anything like the insight provided by Oudry in dealing with the same story. Again Monnet's headpiece and plate for "The gardener and his master" (II, 54) are spirited enough, but they seem superficial when compared with Oudry's designs.

Though Cohen (column 551) disparages the second issue of these *Fables*, with the name Des Lauriers on the title pages, its text and illustrations are often acceptably fresh and attractive.

Various Artists

62 PUBLIUS OVIDIUS NASO

Les métamorphoses d'Ovide, en latin et en françois, de la traduction de M. l'Abbé Banier . . . Paris, Hochereau, 1767–1771. 4 v. I: [2] *l.*, xc p., [1] *l.*, 264 p. II: viii, 355 p. III: viii, 360 p. IV: viii, 367, 8 p. Illus: I: By Choffard: added engraved t.p., 2-*l.* engraved dedication, t.p. vignette, and 6 headpieces; 47 plates after: Boucher by Leveau, and St. Aubin (2); after Eisen by: Delaunay (2), de Ghendt, Le Mire (8), Leveau (4), de Longueil (2), Masquelier, Massard (2), Née, and Simonet; after Gravelot by: Binet, Leveau (2), Rousseau, and Simonet; after Le Prince by Masquelier; after Monnet by: Baquoy (2), Basan, Binet, Duclos, Le Mire, Massard, Née (2), and Rousseau; after Moreau by: Baquoy, Le Mire, Le Roy, Née, and Simonet. II: T.p. vignette by Choffard, 4 headpieces by Choffard after Monnet, 4 headpieces by Choffard, 33 plates after Boucher by: Le Mire, and St. Aubin; after Eisen by: Baquoy (2), Binet, de Ghendt (2), Le Mire, Legrand, Leveau (2), and Massard; after Monnet by: Baquoy, Delaunay (2), Le Mire, Massard (3), Née (2), Ponce, and Simonet (2); after Moreau by: Basan, Leveau, de Longueil, and Massard (2); after Parizot by Massard. III: T.p. vignette and 8 headpieces by Choffard; 37 plates after Boucher by: Le Mire (3), and Massard; after Eisen by: Baquoy, Binet (3), de Ghendt (2), Delaunay (2), Le Mire (2), Legrand, Leveau (2), Massard, Née, Ponce, and Rousseau; after Monnet by: Le Mire (3), Legrand, and Massard; after Moreau by:

Basan, Binet, Delaunay (2), Legrand (2), Leveau, Née (2), and Ponce; after St. Gois by Miger. IV: T.p. vignette and 8 headpieces by Choffard; 22 plates after Boucher by: St. Aubin & Leveau; after Eisen by: Binet (2), Massard (2), and Ponce (2); after Monnet by: Binet, Delaunay, Helman, Legrand, Leveau, de Longueil, Massard, and Ponce; after Moreau by: Delaunay, Le Mire, de Longueil, Miger, Née, and Simonet; full-page tailpiece by Choffard. Plate 13 signed by Eisen (early state), plates 135 and 138 misnumbered 134 and 137. All plates *couvertes*. Page size: 9⅞×7⅝ inches. Contemp. red morocco. Bookplate of Cortlandt F. Bishop. Cohen–de Ricci 769–772.

This is the supreme anthology of French rococo book illustration. If it has not received the detailed consideration given the *Decameron* (15), or the Fermiers-Généraux La Fontaine (26), this is no doubt because the diversity of its artists and their subjects makes the book difficult either to generalize about or to place. As is evidenced by its engraved title, the plates were at first planned to appear as a separate *suite* under the supervision of Le Mire and Basan, who chose the artists from among "the best French painters" and saw to the realization of their designs by the most adroit engravers. The plates were indeed so issued by Basan in 1770, but in the meantime they had been incorporated in an edition of the *Métamorphoses* for which the abbé Banier had provided a new translation, printed opposite Ovid's Latin text, and learned "explications" in which he sought to identify the elements of actual history in the poet's fables. Thus there came into being these four splendid volumes in which the veteran Boucher appears beside the young Moreau, with Eisen, Choffard, Monnet, and Gravelot also playing substantial roles. The result is a high point among illustrated books of the eighteenth century.

One approaches illustrations for classical fables with trepidation, anticipating the sort of allegorical machinery and drearily conventional style that in fact mark the *Métamorphoses* of 1806 (96), published in the wake of neoclassicism. But the designs of this edition quickly dispel such fears. For the most part they are as imaginative as they are elegant. Indeed, some of Choffard's headpieces tap a vein of fantasy more authentic than the eclectic style of the early twentieth century. So a panorama unrolls of "the Age of Gold," in which scenes of pleasure or exciting action are peopled with youth and beauty.

Yet there are violence and cruelty in these designs, just as in Ovid's poems. Moreau's ghastly depiction of Marsyas being flayed alive at the command of Apollo (II, 206) is an example, as is Eisen's rendering of Orpheus massacred by the Thracian bacchantes (III, 280). The transformation scenes promised by Ovid's title posed a particular problem for the illustrator. Sometimes he selects the moment before the change, as does Moreau with the assassination of Caesar (IV, 326), where there is no hint of the comet which Caesar will become; sometimes the moment after, as does Eisen with Arachne transformed by Minerva into a spider, complete with web (II, 180). The real oddities among these scenes are those in which the metamorphosis is caught halfway. There are half-a-dozen grotesque plates in which victims are shown with branches springing from their heads and shoulders. Far more successful is Moreau's rendering of Nyctimene being turned into an owl as a punishment for incest (I, 142). Her wings are graceful, and the adjustment to her head resembles a mask for a costume ball.

Eisen and Choffard must be accorded pride of place among the book's illustrators. Eisen rose effectively to the challenge presented by the fifty-eight plates for which he was responsible. The most delightful of his designs are those devoted to the seasons (I, 12), a sequence which also offers evidence of the lavish scale of the book's illustration, since all accompany a one-page fable. Diana's dismissal of the pregnant Calisto from the chaste company of her nymphs (I, 131) elicits one of Eisen's most voluptuous designs. The five plates devoted

(62B) Early proof after Moreau of "Nyctimene"

(62B) Early proof after Eisen of "Winter"

to Hercules, on the other hand, show his skill in narrative, as do shorter series concerning Perseus and Jason and Medea. In each of these the story is Eisen's preoccupation, not the realization of a sensual revery. Mention should also be made of the dazzling plate which shows Ulysses confronting Circe (IV, 187), the animation of which Eisen never surpassed. If we did not have La Fontaine's *Contes et nouvelles* (26) or Dorat's *Les baisers* (31), Eisen's varied greatness as an illustrator could still be demonstrated from his work for the *Métamorphoses*.

After Eisen it was Monnet who tugged the laboring oar. Indeed, his work for this book well examples the role he played over his long career as a sort of utility illustrator who could be counted upon to deal professionally with any subject. In the *Métamorphoses* he was typically assigned passages on which the action of the various fables turns. When he was allowed to compete with Boucher and Eisen in scenes of nudity, he proved himself more than equal to the occasion. It is hard to choose between his design for Jupiter's enjoyment of Io (I, 48), which is praised by Portalis (II, 403), and that in which the nymph Salamacis by making violent love to the uncomprehending but resisting Hermaphrodite brings about their transformation into a single being, half man, half woman (II, 34).

The *Métamorphoses* offered Moreau his first major opportunity as an illustrator, and he seized it with ready mastery. The grace and charm of his designs prefigure those he was to do for La Borde's *Chansons* (49), but it would be less easy to predict from them the authority of his plates for the *Monument de costume* (55). There is great variety in his twenty-seven illustrations, which range from the dazzling irradiation of Phaeton's visit to the Palace of the Sun (I, 96) to the sinister menace of Famine's attack on the sleeping Eresicthon (III, 64). Boucher may have had first choice among the fables, for his plates typically deal with Ovid's most familiar and pleasing subjects. Among them are his drawing of Mars and Venus (II, 17) and the matched pair in which Venus first delights in the love of Adonis (III, 240), and then despairs at his death (III, 256). Gravelot completes the roll call of major contributors of plates. Classical mythology was hardly his specialty, but his designs are unfailingly attractive. Indeed, the uncovered version of "Pan and Syrinx" (I, 56) was called "the brilliant state" by Cohen (column 771).

After Eisen's plates it was Choffard's twenty-six headpieces and three fleurons which brought most to the adornment of the *Métamorphoses*. The matter of fact "explanations of the vignettes and fleurons" which the publishers offered as a supplement to the edition hardly account for the spell which they cast. That for the headpiece to Book III (I, 188) reads: "The dragon of Cadmus, the chariot, the warriors; in the distance Acteon as a stag"; that for the headpiece to Book VII (II, 263): "Preparation of Medea's enchantments for rejuvenating Aeson; Hecate's altar, the brass vessel from which the ghost of Aeson's old age is supposed to evaporate." Working with ornaments and attributes, Choffard draws on the full resources of classical learning and allegorical tradition, and in the process he creates

(62B) Early proof after Monnet of Jupiter and Io

(62A) Choffard, headpiece to Book III

(62A) Choffard, headpiece to Book VII

images that baffle the mind while they set it dreaming. Of all the illustrations of this notable book only he took full advantage of the basic premise of Ovid's stories, that magic is inherent in the nature of things, that from time to time the supernatural may be expected to supersede the natural order.

It should be mentioned that there is a second edition of the *Métamorphoses* which can be identified by the date of 1770 (not 1771) on the title page of volume four. Though it is markedly inferior to the first, the plates are not necessarily later impressions.

REFERENCES The Goncourts (1880); Holloway; Portalis; Réau.

62A

Les métamorphoses *d'Ovide*. Large-paper copy. Paris, Leclerc, 1767–1771. Plate 13 signed by Gravelot (later state), plates 135 and 138 corrected. All plates *couvertes*.

Page size: 10½ × 8¼ inches, uncut. Red morocco by Chambolle-Duru. Bookplates of Robert Hoe and Cortlandt F. Bishop.

According to Renouard (Cohen–de Ricci, column 770), only twelve sets were printed of this magnificent large-paper issue of the *Métamorphoses*. Renouard's further advice, that these copies followed the ordinary edition on the press, cannot be correct, for the impression both of text and illustrations is uniformly fresh and fine. Moreover, the superb Holland paper has remained entirely unblemished over the years. So rare is this issue that one wonders if bibliographers have seen it in its uncut state. At any rate, none of them seems to have recorded either its dimensions (10½ by 8¼ inches as opposed to 10 by 7½ in the ordinary edition) or the fact that the first page of each of its fifteen books has a paraph on its upper outer margin giving the book's number.

Les Nymphes découvrent à Diane la, grossesse de Calisto.

(62B) Uncovered and covered proofs after Eisen of Diana and Calisto

62B

Les métamorphoses *d'Ovide*. Paris, Prault, 1767–1771. Bound in and inserted are more than 175 plates *avant lettres*, lettered in drypoint, and working proofs (some touched with graphite); plate 13 signed by Gravelot, plates 135 and 138 corrected. Page size: 10 × 7½ inches. Red morocco by Thibaron-Joly. Bookplate of Pierre van Loo.

The presence of some 175 early states of the plates makes this a notable copy of the *Métamorphoses*, though such proofs are not so rare as those for the *Chansons* of La Borde (49). Yet scarcity is the least part of their appeal. These proofs have a gloss and richness, a delicacy and finesse, which largely disappear in later impressions. It is a veritable education in the finer points of rococo book illustration to compare them in detail with the lettered states included in regularly published sets of the *Métamorphoses*. They have the same kind of aesthetic quality as the early states of exceptional prints. Proofs of Eisen's four seasons (1, 12), for example,

deserve to be collected as prints, quite as much as the renderings of the same subject by Crispin de Passe or Hollar.

The two uncovered plates of the Fermiers-Généraux La Fontaine (26) have already been noted. In keeping with its general lavishness, the *Métamorphoses* has six. Four are present in this copy: Eisen's Diana and Calisto (1, 131), Gravelot's Pan and Syrinx (1, 56), Eisen's "Perseus saving Andromeda" (11, 56), and Boucher's Cephalus and Aurora (11, 318). Indeed, there are two uncovered impressions of Pan and Syrinx. Nudity has become so commonplace in today's world that the small differences between the uncovered and covered states of Diana and Calisto may hardly seem to call for a second glance. In the collector, however, they arouse the same sort of interest as does the minuscule bibliographical point which distinguishes a first from a second edition.

Various Artists

63 CHARLES JEAN FRANÇOIS HÉNAULT

Nouvel abrégé chronologique de l'histoire de France,
contenant les événemens de notre histoire depuis Clovis
jusqu'à la mort de Louis XIV . . . Nouvelle édition
augmentée & ornée de vignettes & fleurons en taille
douce . . . Paris, Prault, 1768. 3 v. (paged continuously).
I: [4] *l.* (incl. engraved dedication), 282 p. II: [2] *l.*,
[283]–568 p. III: [569]–798 p., [36] *l.* Illus: T.p. vignette by Cochin (repeated in each volume), unsigned
engraved dedication with port. of Marie Leckzinska by
Gaucher after Nattier, 3 head- and 30 tailpieces by
Moreau, 3 initials by Chedel, and 1 unsigned full-page
vignette. Printed on *papier de Hollande.* Bound in this
copy are a series of 36 plates after Cochin, and some 200
further engraved portraits. Page size: 11 ⅛ × 8 ¼ inches.
Red morocco by Petit. Bookplate of Robert Schuhmann. Cohen–de Ricci 483–484.

This is the longest and grandest revision of President Hénault's chronicle, the first edition of which
had appeared in 1744. The rare copies on Holland
paper, like this one, are handsome indeed. There
is a dedication to the Queen, Marie Leckzinska,
with her portrait after Nattier in one of Choffard's
most elaborate frames. The young Moreau contributed thirty large-scale tailpieces of the utmost
elegance. They are stately and magnificent, rather
than familiar and delightful, but they prove him
to have been the equal of Choffard and Marillier
in this line. His tribute to Henry IV (p. 505) is even
more imposing than the full-page fleuron with
which he concludes the reign of Louis XIV (p.
762). Many copies of this edition also have bound
in a series of historical-allegorical compositions
after Cochin, drawn over many years and extending eventually to a frontispiece and thirty-five
plates. See above, page 26.

(63) Moreau, tailpiece in Henault's *Nouvel abrégé*

CHARLEMAGNE.
Roy en 768. Empereur en 800. Mort en 814.
Agé de 71 ans.

Subjugue les Saxons, est Couronné Empereur d'Occident
par le Pape Leon III: Soumet l'Allemagne et l'Italie, est
l'appuy de la Religion et le Restaurateur des Lettres et des Arts.

C.N. Cochin filius delin. 1765.   A.P.D.R.   B.L. Prevost Sculp.

(63) Cochin, plate for Hénault's *Nouvel abrégé*

Peint par J. M. Nattier en 1753.   Gravé par Ch. Gaucher en 1767.

A LA REINE.

(63) Choffard, headpiece in Hénault's *Nouvel abrégé*

Various Artists

64 LODOVICO ARIOSTO

Orlando furioso . . . Birmingham, G. Baskerville, per
P. Molini, 1773. 4 v. I: [16] *l.*, lviii, 362 p. II: [1] *l.*,
450 p. III: [1] *l.*, 446 p. IV: [1] *l.*, 446 p. Illus: I: Front.
by Fiquet after Eisen; 12 plates after: Cipriani by Bartolozzi (4); Eisen by: Delaunay, de Ghendt, de Longueil (2), Delaunay, and Massard; Moreau by: Henriquez, Delaunay, and Prévost. II: 11 plates after:
Cipriani by: Bartolozzi, and Delaunay; Cochin by Delaunay; Eisen by: de Ghendt, and Delaunay (2); Monnet by Delaunay (2); Moreau by: Delaunay (2), and
Simonet. III: 12 plates after Cipriani by: Bartolozzi
(2), and Delaunay (2); Greuze by Moreau; Monnet
by: Choffard, de Ghendt (2), and Ponce; Moreau by:
Delaunay, Duclos, and Martini. IV: 11 plates after
Cipriani by: Bartolozzi (3), and Martini; Cochin by
Delaunay (5); Moreau by: Helman, and Moreau.
Page size: 9½×5¾ inches. Contemp. red morocco.
Cohen–de Ricci 95–97; Gaskell 48.

Pietro Molini, the publisher, claimed the patronage of the "lettered" for this edition of Ariosto's

poem on the ground of the correctness of its text,
the diligence of its printer (the "notissimo Giovanni Baskerville"), and the collaboration of "the
most celebrated artists of London and Paris." Particularly in its quarto format, the edition is indeed
a fine one. Yet in comparison with the best French
books of the period, it is austere in conception and
execution. There are no ornaments, and the borders of its forty-seven plates are meager. It also has
to be granted that its plates are very uneven in
quality.

The only "artist of London" was Cipriani. Of
his fourteen plates, eleven were rendered by Bartolozzi, whose stipple technique clashes with the
line engraving employed elsewhere in the book.
Moreover, his pedestrian conceptions accord poorly
with Ariosto's airy and sophisticated text.

Among the "artists of Paris," Moreau was at the
top of his form, as might have been expected when
the most elegant of illustrators encountered the

(64) Engraving after Moreau for *Orlando Furioso*

(64) Engraving after Monnet for *Orlando Furioso*

most elegant of poets. Eleven of the plates in this edition are his, and when the entire series was reissued with more elaborate frames for inclusion in the *Roland furieux* of 1775–1783 (10), he provided two more as replacements for discarded designs by Eisen. The sense of enchantment that Moreau could lend to his interpretations is seen in the moonlit battlefield of his plate for canto XVIII with its foreground scene of suffering and sympathy. Eisen's eight plates for the most part are quite unworthy of him. As always, Monnet maintains a reliable professional level. Indeed, he rises a good deal higher when subjects particularly appeal to him, as in the scene of Bradamante at the stake (canto XXV) or of a mute shepherd at the head of his flock pointing the way to Ruggiero (canto XXXII).

Various Artists

65 [PIERRE FULCRAND DE ROSSET]

L'agriculture. Poëme . . . Paris, l'Imprimere royale, 1774. [Part I only]. [6] *l.*, lvi, 277, [1] p. Illus: Front. by Le Gouaz after Saint-Quentin, t.p. vignette by Marillier; 7 plates: after Loutherbourg by de Ghendt (3), Leveau, Lingée, and Ponce; after Saint-Quentin by Le Gouaz; headpieces by Marillier (2); headpieces after Saint-Quentin by: Hemery, Leveau, Lingée, and Ponce (2). Page size: 10 × 7½ inches. Green morocco by Chambolle-Duru. Cohen–de Ricci 899–900.

Rosset's poem is practical rather than idyllic. Instead of Amaryllis and Strephon, Saint-Quentin's first plate presents a robust laborer wearing the medal with chain of the School of Veterinary Medicine (see p. 270). The principal illustrations are by Jacques-Philippe de Loutherbourg (1740–1812),

P. G. de Loutherbourg del.

N. Ponce sculp. 1775

(65) Rosset, *L'agriculture*

XIX. NOUVELLE.

Un homme & une femme au défefpoir de ne s'être pas mariés, fe mettent en religion, l'homme à St. François, & la femme à Ste. Claire.

DU tems du marquis de Mantoue qui avoit époufé la fœur du duc de Ferrare, il y avoit chez la ducheffe une demoifelle nommée Pauline, tellement aimée d'un gentilhomme qui étoit au fervice du marquis, que tout le monde étoit furpris de l'excés de fon amour, parce qu'étant pauvre, mais bien fait de fa perfonne, & de plus fort aimé de fon maitre, il devoit s'attacher à une femme qui eût affez de bien pour tous deux : Mais il croyoit

(66) Marguerite de Navarre, *Les nouvelles*

an accomplished painter who contributed designs to an occasional book in France and later in England. His work is also to be seen in Fessard's edition of La Fontaine's *Fables* (61). Loutherbourg, who was equally proficient with landscape and with animals, devoted his six plates to haymaking, gathering grapes, cutting wood (this design has two of his famous donkeys), watering goats, and feeding chickens. Most attractive of all is the plate for the fourth chant. In the distance are sloping hills, a windmill, and an expanse of meadow; in the foreground a group of diggers and reapers go comfortably about their work. So easy, firmly modelled, and well arranged are Loutherbourg's compositions that they achieve a natural poetry quite as appealing as the magnificent confections of Moreau for the *Chansons* of La Borde (49). Saint-Quentin's two frontispieces and six headpieces for the book pale in comparison, as do even Marillier's three handsome decorations.

Sigismond Freudeberg (1745–1801) and Balthazar-Antoine Dunker (1746–1801)

66 MARGUERITE D'ANGOULÊME, QUEEN OF NAVARRE

Les nouvelles de Marguerite, reine de Navarre. Berne, Nouvelle Société Typographique, 1780–1781. 3 v. I: xlvii, 78, [81]–166, 161–275 p. II: [2] *l.*, 308 p. III: [2] *l.*, 250, [1] p. Illus: I: Front. by Eichler after Dunker; 20 headpieces by: Dunker (11), by Eichler after Dunker (3), and unsigned (6); 20 tailpieces by: Dunker (11), by Pillet after Dunker (1), and unsigned (8); 21 plates after Freudeberg by: Delaunay, C. Gutenberg (2), Halbou (3), Henriquez, Leroy (3), de Longueil (10), and Thiébault. II: Front. by Eichler after Dunker; 25 headpieces by: Dunker (17), by Eichler after Dunker (7), and unsigned; 25 tailpieces by: Dunker (19), Eichler after Dunker (3), Richter after Dunker, and unsigned (2); 25 plates after Freudeberg by: Halbou (11), Leroy (8), de Longueil (2), Thiébault (3), and unsigned. III: Front. by Eichler after Dunker; 27 headpieces by: Dunker (23), by Eichler after Dunker (2), and unsigned (2); 27 tailpieces by: Dunker (25), and unsigned (2);

27 plates after Freudeberg by: Halbou (10), Leroy (4), de Longueil (11), and Thiébault (2). Page size: 7⅝×4½ inches. Contemp. red morocco. Bookplate of Lucius Wilmerding. Cohen–de Ricci 680–681.

Though its two illustrators lived much in France, they were Swiss, and in effect this is a Swiss version of the sumptuous illustrated book of the later eighteenth century. It is obviously modelled on Gravelot's *Decameron* (15) and the Fermiers-Généraux La Fontaine (26). Indeed, it surpasses these precursors in the profusion of its designs. Sigismond Freudenberger, usually called Freudeberg, contributed seventy-one plates, and Balthazar-Antoine Dunker, seventy-two headpieces and seventy-two tailpieces. The *Heptameron*, to give Marguerite de Navarre's collection its customary name, is made up for the most part of tales of unhappy lovers and villainous friars, much moralized upon by their author. It is a sober rather than a joyous book, and appropriately enough its publishers turned for their principal illustrations to Freudeberg, whose *Suite d'estampes pour servier à l'illustration des moeurs et du costume des Français dans le dix-huitième siècle* had given him a reputation for faithful realism. (See above, p. 97.) They remark in their "Avertissement" that he was "known for this kind of agreeable design, which represents the manners and costumes of private life" (1, xx). This statement is accurate enough, but one must disagree with their further assertion that his "light hand spreads graciousness over all objects" (1, xx–xxi). In fact, the radical defect of Freudeberg's style is the heaviness of his figures and their lack of ease and movement. Dunker's headpieces hardly rise above the commonplace. The tailpieces are often quaint and amusing, sometimes merely odd. He does his best to challenge Gravelot and Choffard, and he has his successes, but he does not achieve a consistent style.

The nineteenth story will serve as an example of the kind of illustration that results. A young man and young woman, penniless though of good society, are passionately in love. Their patrons insist that they must marry for money. Vowing always to remain faithful to each other, they take holy orders instead. The moment chosen by Freudeberg for his plate (1, 251) is that in which the lady, having declared her intention, faints in her lover's arms, to the distress of her companions. Having begun their novitiate, they meet for the last time in

(66) Marguerite de Navarre, *Les nouvelles*

a chapel to confirm their resolve, and henceforth live holy lives. Dunker's headpiece is a straightforward rendering of the place of their final encounter, but his tailpiece of lovebirds in religious dress (1, 268) surely mocks the narrator's praise of their excessive devotion.

Owen Holloway, the champion of rococo illustration, finds Freudeberg's plates "thoroughly philistine" (p. 61). So they may seem in comparison with those of Gravelot or Eisen. But by 1780 the rococo era was over. If one takes Freudeberg's designs for what they are, the careful and finished renderings of dramatic episodes in the lives of characters who view life seriously, they have their solid merits. One leaves the book, not exactly with affection, but certainly with respect.

It should be mentioned that the illustrations are seen at their best in large copies, like this one, which may be identified by the presence of numbers at the bottom of most plates in volume three.

Jacques-Gabriel de Saint-Aubin (1724–1783) and others

67 LA CHAU AND LE BLOND

Descriptions des principales pierres gravées du cabinet de S.A.S. Monseigneur le duc d'Orléans . . . Paris, de La Chau & Le Blond, 1780–1784 (but dated 1785 at end of v. II). 2 v. I: [16] *l.,* 303 [i.e., 295, omitting p. 85–88 and 257–260] p. II: [2] *l.,* v, [2], 215 [i.e., 211, omitting p. 97–100], [5] p. Illus: I: Front. and t.p. vignette by Saint-Aubin, headpiece by Saint-Aubin

DRUSUS.

(67) *Les pierres gravées*

after Cochin, 45 tailpieces by Saint-Aubin, tailpiece by Saint-Aubin after Mme de Sabran, and 102 unsigned plates by Saint-Aubin. II: T.p. vignette, headpiece, 10 tailpieces, and 77 unsigned plates by Saint-Aubin. Page size: 13⅛ × 7⅞ inches. Contemp. green morocco. Cohen–de Ricci 542–543.

Though most of the illustrations described in this survey are of imaginative literature, the artists of the eighteenth century turned their attention to many other kinds of books, among them documentary works. The resulting designs are often of real merit, and they are not necessarily wanting in general interest. For this catalogue of engraved gems in the collection of the Duc d'Orléans, Jacques-Gabriel de Saint-Aubin, the older brother of Augustin, drew and engraved nearly all the plates and vignettes. With minute exactness he provided 179 representations of the gems themselves, and to these he added fifty-five tailpieces in which he set down the fancies to which these remnants of the past had given rise in his mind. After recording with dry impersonality a portrait of Tiberius in agate and onyx, for example, he offered a spirited commentary on the life of that emperor. The scene is Capri, suggested by a rocky escarpment. A bed is almost hidden by a curtain suspended from a blasted tree. The words on the

(68) Beaumarchais, *Le mariage de Figaro*

curtain suggest the secret excesses of Tiberius, as do the Spintrian medals which hang from it. Since the *Pierres gravées* was the acknowledged work of two Abbés, only the numbered side of each medal is shown clearly, not the reverse with its erotic pose. However, there are seven supplementary plates of such poses, not present in this copy, which could be added by amateurs.

Jacques-Philippe-Joseph de Saint-Quentin (1738–?)

68 PIERRE AUGUSTIN CARON DE BEAUMARCHAIS

La folle journée, ou Le mariage de Figaro, comédie en cinq actes, en prose . . . [Kehl], l'Imprimerie de la Société littéraire-typographique; Paris, Prault, 1785. 51, [1], 199, [1] p. Illus: 5 plates after Saint-Quentin by: Halbou, Liénard (3), and Lingée. Extra-illustrated with a watercolor drawing by Garnerey illustrating act I, scene ix; an autograph letter by Mme de Beaumarchais dated 27 March [1811] to M. Blin, "Chirurgien Hernière"; a pencil port. on vellum of Beaumarchais by Moreau; and 7 engravings: portrait of Beaumarchais after Moreau, portrait of Beaumarchais by Saint Aubin after Cochin, 3 portraits of Mlle Contat (1 color-printed), a portrait of Mlle Olivier, and a portrait of M. Albouy-Dazincourt. Page size: 10⅛×6½ inches, uncut. Red morocco by Gruel. Cohen–de Ricci 125–126.

Like Voltaire's *Oeuvres* (52), this edition of Beaumarchais' great comedy was printed by his Société Littéraire et Typographique at Kehl. He made it virtually an acting text through his long note on the "characters and costumes of the play" and his stage directions. Saint-Quentin seems to have tried to provide through his lively plates some record of how key scenes were actually played during early performances of *Le mariage de Figaro*. Perhaps its most exquisitely comic moment (act I, scene ix) is Count Almaviva's discovery of the amorous page, Cherubin, hidden in his wife's chamber. Cherubin's terror, the Count's anger, the Countess' embarrassment, and the priest Bazile's malign amusement are adroitly suggested.

The volume described offers a prime instance of what is called an *exemplaire truffé*, a "truffled" or "stuffed" copy. Alfred Meyer, who grangerized it, had a celebrated collection of such books. This once contained important autograph letters of Beaumarchais and Mozart (Meyer, p. 12). They are gone, alas, but Meyer's other additions, which are listed above, remain of considerable interest. Moreau's drawing of Beaumarchais is reproduced on page 96 above.

Saint-Quentin's designs were engraved a second time, though less effectively, by Malapeau and Roi.

Engraving after Guérin for Racine, *Phèdre*

Revolution to Restoration (1789–1819)

Historians for the most part have passed over the three decades after the Revolution as a "deplorable period for the art of the book" (Calot, p. 149). Yet they are by no means a wasteland between rococo and Romantic illustration. During the years immediately following both the Revolution and Waterloo, political and commercial conditions were such that few significant opportunities came the way of illustrators. On the other hand, the Directory, the Consulate, and the Empire were a time when high prosperity and great activity led to the appearance of many fine books. It is with a real sense of discovery, therefore, that the following survey is presented.

The barrenness of the early 1790s cannot be disputed. Since the displaced aristocracy and middle class were the almost exclusive patrons of fine illustrated books, the apparatus for creating them lost most of its reason for being. "Restricted to little compositions, agreeable plates," writes Renouvier (p. 306), "the dependants of publishers who sought nothing but success, [illustrators] contributed in large part to the vulgarity which tainted art even in its epic and classical intentions." There are few books of these years for which more than documentary interest can be claimed.

Neoclassicism was the prevailing style of the period, reinforced, as it was, by current political events, particularly during the Empire when admiration of Roman imperialism was general. Its chief forerunners among illustrators active before the Revolution were Cochin, Le Barbier, and Moreau. Indeed, the *style Louis XVI* associated with the last is a halfway house between the rococo and the neoclassic. Le Barbier and Moreau continued to work after the Revolution, as did such other survivors as Choffard, Marillier, and Monnet, with results that have been described in the previous section. Bouchot exaggerates when he writes (p. 10) that artists like Moreau "denied their past and became vassals of the apostle," thus immolating the rococo book "to the ashes of the virtuous Brutus," but certainly their work in what Furstenberg calls the *style Directoire-Empire* is greatly inferior to their earlier achievements.

The great new presence was Jacques-Louis David (1748–1825) who employed neoclassicism to depict the civic virtues of victorious Romans and a little later the noble simplicity of the primitive Greeks. His painting was stark, engaged, and linear, in contrast to that of the *galant* eighteenth century with its playful, curvilinear depiction of light and frivolous subjects. The Goncourts (1, 94–95) tell of the general disrepute into which rococo art fell. Those who continued to esteem it "disguised their acquisitions as folly, caprice, wanton curiosity, a collector's debauch." Watteau's masterpiece, *L'Embarquement pour Cythère*, was hung in a classroom of the Academy, where it served as a "target for the mockery and bread-crumb pellets of David's students." David and his followers had a long innings, but as early as 1808 he conceded: "In 10 years the study of the antique will be abandoned. All these gods, these heroes will be replaced by troubadours, singing under the windows of their ladies, at the foot of an old castle-tower" (quoted by Calot, p. 155). His prediction was correct.

It cannot be said that neoclassicism has left an imposing heritage in book illustration. Its chief monuments are the quartos and folios published by Pierre Didot, particularly his Virgil and Racine. Though David himself had a part in the former, the designs of Girodet most vividly realized neoclassical aspirations, with Gérard as his chief rival. Even so, there is a print after Guérin's well-known painting of 1803, *Phaedra and Hippolytus*, in which Hippolytus justifies himself to the irate Theseus after Phaedra has falsely accused him, that embodies the neoclassical style more successfully than any of Girodet's illustrations. See below, page 151. It is a pity that Didot did not add Guérin to his band of artists.

In fact, most of the outstanding illustrated books of this period are not in the neoclassical mode. *Paul et Virginie* (74) is an intensely Romantic work. Fragonard's drawings for La Fontaine's *Contes et nouvelles* (77) are survivals from the rococo age. Prud'hon's designs for Bernard's *Oeuvres* (75) and *Daphnis et Chloé* (76) are personal creations, independent of any school. And the two finest volumes of colored engravings, Horace Vernet's *Incroyables et merveilleuses* (80) and Redouté's *Les roses* (89), have no particular stylistic stamp. Among the lesser illustrated books of the time, novels, poetry, and other works reflecting the contemporary scene are usually the better for their exemption from the neoclassical chill.

These decades were hardly a great age of bibliophily, though by 1800 there was a substantial revival of the art of the book. Didot showed the way with his imposing volumes. French binders—led by the Bozerians and later Thouvenin and Simier—again rivalled the English craftsmen who had surpassed them after the Revolution. Indeed, many magnificent copies of the publications of this period have come down to posterity. A feature of the time was the conscious exploitation of the taste for early states of engravings which had grown up among bibliophiles in the later eighteenth century.

Until the 1780s such things were the occasional by-products of the illustrative process. Then *suites* of early states began to be offered for sale. An example is provided by Cochin's plates for Tasso's *Gerusalemme liberata* (11) of 1784. When publishing returned to its normal state about 1795, it became routine for *suites* of plates before letters, even of preliminary etchings, to be sold separately. For example, see the list on page 88 above of *suites* after Moreau offered by Renouard. Needless to say, the mass production of what had earlier been chance survivals greatly reduces their interest for the modern collector. The practice was much less common during the Romantic period, but from the 1860s on it again became an accepted part of the publication of fine illustrated books in France.

REFERENCES Bouchot (1891); Calot (1931); the Goncourts; Portalis; Renouvier.

The Didots and Their Illustrators

The Didots are considered here, not as great figures in the history of printing, but for the book illustrations which they published. The dynasty began in effect with François-Ambroise Didot, whose outstanding achievement was a *Collection des classiques français destinée à l'éducation du Dauphin.* Begun in 1783, and printed in various formats, the series extended eventually to thirty-two volumes, but did not include illustrations. Ambroise left these adjuncts to his sons Pierre (1761–1853), called Pierre Didot the elder, and Firmin (1764–1836). Between 1789 and 1795 the unsettled political and commercial conditions of the time made new departures unpropitious, but in the latter year *Psyché et Cupidon* illustrated by Moreau (56) initiated a series of imposing illustrated books with Pierre Didot's imprint. La Fontaine's *Contes et nouvelles* (77) with plates after Fragonard also appeared this year. Another *Psyché et Cupidon*, with plates after Gérard, was issued in 1797. Then came the four great "editions of the Louvre," so called because

Didot had been allowed to set up his presses there in the space once occupied by the Imprimerie Royale: Virgil in 1798, Horace in 1799, Racine in 1801, and La Fontaine's *Fables* in 1802. *Daphnis et Chloé* (76) had appeared in 1800, *Héro et Léandre* followed in 1801 (88), and *Paul et Virginie* in 1806. Didot also issued a number of duodecimos with miniature illustrations called the "cornflower" editions because their title pages were adorned with crowns of such posies. See below, page 150. The titles mentioned are only the highlights of his production, and the firm maintained its notable tradition in the nineteenth century, printing, among many other fine books, Baron Taylor's superb folios (106 to 109).

Apart from Prud'hon, Fragonard, and Debucourt, Didot's illustrators were chiefly of the Davidian school. It is now known that David himself made some designs for Virgil, but Girodet, Gérard, and Chaudet were the illustrators most frequently employed. Anne-Louis Girodet de Roucy-Trioson

(1767–1824) was the leader among them, and certainly his designs for Virgil and Racine are the most intense and dramatic in these works. François Gérard (1770–1837) was the busiest of the group, but also the most conventional. Only occasionally, as in his plates for Racine's *Bajazet*, does it appear why he, as well as Girodet, was described as "a romantic without knowing it" (Calot, p. 152). Antoine-Denis Chaudet (1763–1810), better remembered as a sculptor than as a painter, made his impression almost entirely through his lavish drawings for *Esther* and *Athalie*, which have not attracted the attention they deserve. Other artists who worked for Didot, like Peyron and Regnault, need only be mentioned in passing. For some time there has been great interest in David and the painters associated with him. It ought soon to extend to their illustrations.

REFERENCES   Calot (1931); George; the Goncourts; Portalis; Renouvier; Werdet.

69   JEAN DE LA FONTAINE

Les amours de Psyché et de Cupidon, suivies d'Adonis, poëme . . . Edition ornée de gravures d'après les desseins de Gérard, peintre. Paris, P. Didot l'aîné, 1797. xx, 335 p. Illus. after Gérard: Front. by Nicollet and 4 plates by: Blot, Marais, Mathieu, and Tardieu. Printed on *papier vélin*, the plates *avant lettres*. Page size: 12⅝ × 9½ inches. Green morocco by Arnaud. Bookplates of Edith Rockefeller McCormick and Léon Rattire. Cohen–de Ricci 584.

The first book illustrated for the Didots by Gérard is perhaps his most satisfactory. His four plates for *Psyché et Cupidon* and one for *Adonis* allowed him to deal with the subject that he handled best, idylls of young love. Though they conform to the neo-classic pattern, even to resembling sculptures in low-relief, they manage at the same time to be graceful, elegant, and sensuous. The artist is proudly described on the title page as "Gérard, painter." Perhaps the plate of "Psyche enraptured at the appearance of her husband" (p. 105) comes closest in feeling to the painting of *Cupid and Psyché* which brought him recognition in the Salon of 1798.

This copy is on large vellum paper with plates before the letters. Its binding by Arnaud led Edith Rockefeller McCormick to add it to her cabinet collection of books in green morocco.

(69)   Engraving after Gérard for *Les amours de Psyché et de Cupidon*

70   PUBLIUS VERGILIUS MARO

[Opera, Latin]. **Bucolica, Georgica, et Aeneis.** Paris, P. Didot "natu major," 1798. xi, 572 p. Illus: Front. by Copia after Girodet, and 22 plates after: Gérard by: Baquoy, Beisson (2), Copia (4), Delignon, Godefroy, Marais, Massard, Patas, Simonet, and Vielh; after Girodet: by Copia, Godefroy, Marais, Massard (2), and Mathieu; unsigned by Copia (2). No. 14 of 250 large-paper copies signed by Didot, of an edition of 250 copies. Page size: 18¾ × 13⅜ inches. Contemp. red morocco, "Perfectus a Jo. Cl. Bozerian." Cohen–de Ricci 1019.

The first of the great folios printed by Didot at the Louvre was an edition of the works of Virgil with twenty-four plates after Gérard and Girodet. In eight idyllic designs Gérard shows the shepherds of the *Eclogues* in varied and attractive poses. His four drawings for the *Georgics* are more elaborate and melodramatic. Both series are eclipsed, in any event, by Girodet's twelve vigorous and carefully studied plates for the *Aeneid*. Since each might have served as the basis for a characteristic painting, the

(70) Engraving after Girodet for Virgil, *Bucolica, Georgica, et Aeneis*

heavy touch of the engraver may account in part for their unequal quality as illustrations. The less crowded compositions for Books II, V, and XI stand out. The first (p. 189) shows the flight from burning Troy of Aeneas and his son, with Anchises on his shoulders.

That Gérard and Girodet made the drawings for these illustrations under David's aegis has been known from a passage in Didot's preface (p. xi). Only recently did a copy of the book with early impressions (now in the Rosenwald Collection of the Library of Congress) establish that David himself was responsible for some of the designs, his signature *à pointe* being replaced in the finished engravings by that of Gérard (*Lessing J. Rosenwald Collection*, no. 1715).

There were 251 copies of this book, this being one of 100 with plates before the letters. The elab-

orately tooled spine of its contemporary morocco binding is lettered: "Perfectus a Jo. Cl. Bozerian." See Appendix I for a plate reproducing it.

71 QUINTUS HORATIUS FLACCUS

[**Opera**, Latin]. Paris, P. Didot "natu major," 1799. viii, 404 p. Illus. after Percier: unsigned t.p. vignette, and 11 headpieces by: Coiny, Girardet (4), Portier (indistinctly signed), Racine, and unsigned (4). No. 94 of 100 large-paper copies signed by Didot, of an edition of 250 copies. Page size: 19⅛ × 13⅝ inches. Blue morocco by C. Hering. Cohen–de Ricci 499; Brunet 323.

Of Pierre Didot's great folios printed at the Louvre, this and the La Fontaine of 1802 are the least interesting. Their appeal is almost entirely typographic, since the illustrations in each case are limited to twelve agreeable headpieces after Percier. This is one of 100 copies on vellum paper, out of an edition of 250, as is attested by Didot's signature at the end of his preface.

72 JEAN BAPTISTE RACINE

Oeuvres. Paris, P. Didot l'aîné, 1801. 3 v. I: [4] *l.*, 466 p., [1] *l.* II: [2] *l.*, 500 p., [1] *l.* III: [2] *l.*, 416 p. Illus: Front. by Marais after Prud'hon; 23 plates after Chaudet by: Duval, Glairon-Mondet (2), Massard, and Vielh; after Gérard by: Duval, Lavalée, Le Villain, Romanet, and Simonet; after Girodet by: Girardet, Marais, Massard (2), and Mathieu; after Moitte by: Baquoy, Blot, Dupréel, and Duval (2); after Taunay by: Duval, Le Villain, and Prévost. II: 25 plates after Gérard by: Fischer (2), Girardet et Massard, Massard (5), and Mathieu (2); after Girodet by: Chatillon, and Massard (4); after Peyron by: Beisson, Langlois frères (2), Massard, and Ponce; after Serangeli by Massard (5). III: 8 plates after Chaudet by: Coiny, Girardet (2), Langlois, Langlois jeune, Massard (2), and Mathieu. One of 250 copies on paper, this copy not signed or numbered. Page size: 19⅝ × 14 inches, uncut. ¾ red morocco by V. Champs. Cohen–de Ricci 849–850.

Pierre Didot saw this book as the culmination of his career. He presented it to General Bonaparte, First Consul, as an achievement in the arts comparable to his in arms. In the preface we learn how the fifty-seven plates (one for each act) were begun in 1792 and executed at leisure by Didot's artists, in particular "citizens Girodet, Gérard and Chaudet, who by themselves have made two-thirds." Firmin Didot cut new characters for the work. The paper was specially manufactured by "Citizen

Montgolfier" of Annonay. Didot was thus enabled "to raise to the glory of Racine a typographical monument" which in effect was a national collaboration.

The illustrations for this edition vary greatly in quality, but all are elaborately developed and assiduously finished. Though it has been presented as the epitome in book illustration of Davidian neoclassicism, only Girodet in *Andromaque* and *Phèdre* really succeeds in the representation of classical subjects. The impossibly Roman noses of his figures (resembling the faceguards of helmets) do not prevent him from realizing the passions with a stylized elegance that enhances rather than impairs their force. In the first plate for *Andromaque* (I, 190) Orestes vainly tries to persuade King Pyrrhus of the danger of allowing Andromache's son to live, while Phoenix, Pyrrhus' tutor, looks on. In style the group seems to repeat on a larger scale the low-reliefs of the Trojan war on the wall. Gérard's uneasiness with classical tragedy is shown by his overemphatic and heavy designs, and other illustrators are even less persuasive.

(72)   Frontispiece by Prud'hon for Racine, *Oeuvres*

(72)   Engraving after Girodet for *Andromaque*

Drawing by Gérard for *Bajazet*

Drawing by Chaudet for *Esther*

CHAUDET, *INV.*   MATHIEU, *SCULP.*

ASSUERUS
VIVEZ : LE SCEPTRE D'OR QUE VOUS TEND CETTE MAIN
POUR VOUS DE MA CLÉMENCE EST UN GAGE CERTAIN.

ESTHER.   ACTE II.   SCENE VII.

(72)   Engraving after Chaudet for *Esther*

It was another story with Didot's artists when different settings released them from bondage. Taunay's vigorous seventeenth-century genre scenes for *Les plaideurs* are closer to Monsiau in *Oeuvres poissardes* (87) than to David. Gérard shows the Eastern characters of *Bajazet* with ease and force. Chaudet's series for *Esther* and for *Athalie* captures the pomp and circumstance of Eastern court life. Renouvier, who compares him to Poussin (p. 56), finds his sensibility too somber, but this is hardly a disqualification for interpreting Racine's biblical tragedies. Finest of all is Prud'hon's splendid frontispiece showing Racine "conducted to Immortality by his genius and Melpomene," a plate as harmonious as it is dignified.

ఈ Three designs for Racine's *Oeuvres* (1801):

Antoine-Denis Chaudet. Two drawings in black chalk, lead white, graphite, pen and black ink, brown and black ink, and scratchwork, for: *Esther* (III, 50), and *Athalie* (III, 132). Image size varies, but generally 10½ × 7½ inches. Titled by the artist.
François Gérard. Drawing in black chalk, lead white, graphite, pen and black ink, and watercolor, for *Bajazet* (II, 162). Image size: 10⅛ × 7¾ inches. Titled by the artist.

Apart from the designs of Girodet and Prud'hon, those by Chaudet and Gérard are the strongest of the fifty-seven made for this edition. The first of Chaudet's drawings is for the second act of *Esther* (III, 50). Incited by his High Priest, King Ahasuerus has resolved to exterminate the Jews of his kingdom, though his Queen, Esther, is herself Jewish. We see Esther in the throne room of the palace, fainting in the arms of her confidant, with another of her ladies also supporting her, even as Ahasuerus by extending his golden scepter assures her that she will be spared. The figures are statuesque yet supple, and their nobility is in keeping with the grandeur of the scene. Unfortunately the engraver has imposed upon them a rigidity which dissipates much of their humanity. Chaudet's drawing for act II of *Athalie* (III, 132) is equally impressive. It depicts the boy king Joash being interrogated by his grandmother Athaliah in the temple of Jerusalem. "Beautiful drawings of a great and serious character," which are "profoundly thought out," is the tribute of Portalis (1, 66–67).

Gérard's design is not inferior to those of Chaudet. The setting of *Bajazet* is the seraglio of Sultan Amurat in Constantinople. Roxane, the Sultan's favorite, has conceived a passion for his brother Bajazet, though she suspects that he and Atalide are in love. In the scene depicted (II, 162) Roxane has just given Atalide a letter from the Sultan ordering his brother's death. When told that the command is being executed, Atalide faints, thus confirming Roxane's suspicions. Atalide's state of shock, the concern of the slave who supports her, and Roxane's jealous rage are depicted with a restless excitement that is fairly dizzying. The vitality of this design is in marked contrast to Gérard's ponderous illustrations for Racine's classical tragedies.

73 Jean Baptiste Racine

Théâtre complet . . . orné de cinquante-sept gravures d'après les compositions de Girodet, Gérard, Chaudet, Prud'hon, Taunay, et autres. Paris, P. Didot l'aîné, 1816. 3 v. I: [2] *l.*, 332, [1] p. II: [2] *l.*, 380, [1] p. III: 387, [1] p. Illus: I: Front. by Velyn after Prud'hon; 18 plates: after Gérard by: Guyard, Massard, and Velyn (3); after Girodet by: Sisco, Velyn (4); after Moitte by: Dien, Velyn (4); after Taunay by Velyn (3). II: 20 plates: after Chaudin by Velyn (5); after Gérard by Velyn (5); after Peyron by: Dien, Velyn (4); after Serangeli by: "A.J.," Massard, and Velyn (3). III: 18 plates: after Chaudet by: Dien, Massard, and Velyn (6); after Gérard by: Croutelle & Manceau, and Velyn (4); after Girodet by Velyn (5). Page size: 8¼ × 5 inches. Contemp. green morocco by Simier.

In 1816 Didot published this three-volume octavo Racine with reductions of the fifty-seven plates in the edition of the Louvre. Typographically it is an attractive book, but the engravings are journeyman work, greatly inferior to those of 1801.

74 Jacques Henri Bernardin de Saint-Pierre

Paul et Virginie . . . Paris, P. Didot l'aîné, 1806. [2] *l.*, xcii, 194 p., [3] *l.* Illus: Front. by Ribault after Lafitte; 6 plates: after Gérard by Mecou; after Girodet by Roger; after Isabey by Pillement fils and Bovinet; after Lafitte by Bourgeois de la Richardière; after Moreau by Prot; after Prud'hon by Roger. Page size: 12½ × 9⅜ inches, uncut. Bookplate of Robert Schuhmann. ¼ green morocco by Paul Vié. Cohen–de Ricci 933.

Even though Bernardin de Saint-Pierre himself was chiefly responsible for the appearance of this book, it was printed by Didot and may appropriately appear in this section. In his preface, which is half as long as the text, he tells of the many troubles which delayed the book's completion. Wishing to celebrate the "humble pastoral" which had made

(71)   Engraving after Prud'hon for *Paul et Virginie*

(74)   Engraving after Isabey for *Paul et Virginie*

him famous, he undertook "an edition carried out by the most skillful artists of all sorts" (p. iv): printer, papermaker, designers, and engravers. Urging his friends to subscribe, he offered them a wide choice among copies: quarto or folio, plates before or after the letter and colored or uncolored, and "satined" or usual paper. It appears from the subscription list that fifty-five of them responded, most of whom selected copies like this one containing the plates with letters on unsatined paper.

He proceeds to relate how he secured the "six plates designed and engraved by the greatest masters" which enrich the book (p. i). The firmly drawn frontispiece portrait of the author and the design of Paul and Virginia in infancy (p. 15) are after the painter Louis Lafitte (1770–1828). Girodet's spirited depiction of Paul carrying Virginia across a torrent follows (p. 32). Then comes Gérard's study of the visit of M. de la Bourdonnais to Virginia's humble dwelling (p. 82), a rare genre piece by this neoclassical artist. Moreau's design of the farewell of the lovers (p. 96) is in his mannered later style, but charged with high emotion. Each is a major illustration, to which the artist has clearly devoted the greatest care. But it is in the two final plates that the series reaches its climax.

Prud'hon shows Virginia on the poop of her

foundering ship, with friends on shore lamenting her fate, and Paul risking his own life in a vain attempt to save her (p. 161). Of Virginia herself, who dominates the design, the author writes (p. xlvi): "With one hand she modestly holds down her robes, billowed out by the furious winds; in the other she grasps the portrait of her lover whom she will never see again, [as she] casts her last glances towards the heavens, her ultimate hope. Her modesty, her love, her courage, her celestial figure make this splendid design a finished masterpiece."

The final plate (p. 192), after Jean-Baptiste Isabey (1767–1855), depicts the grave of the two lovers, under symmetrical alleys of bamboos, with "their tender mothers and their faithful servants" buried on either side, and the sea in the background lit by the setting sun. Even their dog, dead of grief, is not forgotten, for his skeleton lies before their gravestone. As Bernardin de Saint-Pierre remarks (p. xlix), there is no human witness to the scene, yet the whole of the simple lives of Paul and Virginia is suggested by their surroundings. This superbly evocative drawing fittingly concludes a sequence of illustrations which were virtually a collaboration between the author and his artists, thus perfectly embodying the sensibility that gave rise to this famous romance.

Pierre-Paul Prud'hon (1758–1823)

Prud'hon was the tenth child of a Cluny stone-cutter. In a letter of 1785 he describes the painful years of neglect and suffering that followed the early death of his beloved mother: "It was very hard for me no longer to have anyone interested in my young life; yet I had to drink life to its lees. . . . I remained accordingly without money, without help, without talent; naïve, moreover, timid, trusting, without knowledge of the world, and abandoned at last even by myself." (Quoted by the Goncourts, III, 318.) But friends did come to his aid. Abbé Brisson saw to his education at the Abbey of Cluny, the treasures of which had helped him to discover his artistic vocation, and he found an understanding patron in the Baron de Joursanvault. After attending a school of painting in Dijon, he was finally enabled to seek his fortune as an artist in Paris. Meanwhile, in 1778, he had married the daughter of a Dijon notary, as a friend delicately put it, "to remedy the wrongs of love" (quoted by Dacier, p. 70). This mismatch both embittered his personal life and hindered his career.

The crucial stage in Prud'hon's artistic development was his prolonged visit to Italy, made possible by a prize which he won in 1784 at a competition in Burgundy. Encouraged like his fellow students to imitate Raphael, he found that he greatly preferred Leonardo. In a letter of the time he paid tribute to "the inimitable Leonardo da Vinci, the father, the prince, and the first of all painters." His *Last Supper* is "the first painting of the world, the masterpiece of the art," he continued. "He is my master and my hero." (Quoted by Portalis, II, 532–533.) Henceforth Prud'hon formed himself on Leonardo, in the process achieving his individual manner with its soft and graceful forms, lifelike flesh tints, and tender feeling.

After Prud'hon returned to Paris in 1789 he found little opportunity to exhibit his paintings. Living in poverty with his family, which now included three children, he accepted a number of commissions for illustrations. Among them were two from Pierre Didot which resulted in notable books, Bernard's *Oeuvres*, published in 1797, and

Longus' *Daphnis et Chloé*, published in 1800. Of less interest are the smaller designs which Prud'hon made for duodecimo editions of Lucien Bonaparte's *La tribu indienne*, two volumes, 1799; Tasso's *Aminta*, 1800; and Rousseau's *La nouvelle Héloïse*, four volumes, 1804. The first of these is a book of great rarity. He was fortunate in his engravers, relying from the beginning on his friend Louis Copia, who died in 1799, and afterwards on Barthelémy Roger, who worked with Copia and finally succeeded him. Their renderings of his illustrations and separate prints were useful in accustoming the public to his original style. Though his illustrations for Bernard's poems were highly successful, his admirer Pierre Didot assigned him only three plates in *Daphnis et Chloé* and one each in his great Racine of 1800–1801 (72) and his *Paul et Virginie* of 1806 (74). The cause of this neglect appears to have been a lack of enthusiasm on the part of David, the chief advisor of the Didots on artistic matters. Since Prud'hon's work was at odds with David's in theory and practice, it is understandable that he should have been superseded by Gérard, Girodet, and other disciples of the master. (See Portalis, II, 536–537.)

As the years passed, however, recognition finally came his way. Wealthy industrialists like the Didots bought his paintings, and he found favor in the eyes of Napoleon himself. The masterpieces of his last phase, indeed, carried all before them. After his separation in 1803 from his quarrelsome and low-bred wife, he formed an attachment with a young painter, Mlle. Mayer, with whom he lived happily for many years. Yet fate had a final shock in store for him. When the news that his wife was fatally ill reached the household in 1821, Mlle. Mayer asked if she could expect to be married. Thinking only of his earlier unhappiness as a husband, he abruptly replied, "never." The poor lady, whose irregular situation had long preyed on her mind, went away to cut her throat. (Portalis, II, 539–541.) Prud'hon died two years later.

Prud'hon's reputation is as a painter, yet the best of his illustrations are hardly inferior in con-

......quelle Scene inouie!
.... sa Phrosine etoit évanouie;

Prud'hon, inv. incidit.

(75)   Engraving by Prud'hon for Bernard, *Oeuvres*

ception to his canvasses, though with one exception they were engraved by other hands. Indeed, Delacroix said that his drawings "give better than his paintings, perhaps, a complete idea of the richness and variety of his imagination" (quoted by Dacier, p. 80). David's description of Prud'hon as "the Boucher of our age" (the Goncourts, III, 3476), which was not intended as a compliment, is appropriate enough. Both artists celebrated love and female beauty, Boucher in joyous reflections of the world around him, where he experienced so much success and pleasure; Prud'hon in visions of an antique ideal, which, at the time he conceived his illustrations, poverty and unhappiness had kept remote from realization. Indeed, the wistful languor of his designs is almost his trademark. Despite the small number of his illustrations, he must be regarded as the outstanding book artist of the turn of the century.

REFERENCES Dacier (1945); the Goncourts; Portalis; Réau; Renouvier.

75 PIERRE-JOSEPH BERNARD

Oeuvres . . . ornées de gravures d'après les desseins de Prud'hon; la dernière estampe gravée par lui-même. Paris, P. Didot l'aîné, 1797. [2] l., xi, 198 p. (Other copies examined contain 300 p., with the texts of "Castor et Pollus," and "Les surprises de l'amour.") Illus: 4 plates after Prud'hon by: Beisson (2), Copia, and Prud'hon. Page size: 12¼×9⅜ inches. Contemp. red morocco. Cohen–de Ricci 133–134.

Pierre-Joseph Bernard is remembered today, if at all, because Voltaire gave him the name "Gentil Bernard" in some verses urging him to finish *L'Art d'aimer* (pp. iii–iv). Why Pierre Didot deemed the poems of this contemporary of Dorat and La Borde worth reprinting after the Revolution is not clear. Fortunately they inspired several of Prud'hon's best designs. He took his subjects for *L'Art d'aimer* from a single verse in which Bernard sets forth the laws which a lover should follow: "choose the object" (p. 3), "stir her affections" (p. 23), and "enjoy" (p. 45). As Didot claims in the verse epistle to Prud'hon which he wrote for this edition, they are indeed wonderful realizations of the sweetness and innocence of young love. The gem of the volume, however, is the design for the second poem, *Phrosine et Mélidore* (p. 100), which Prud'hon himself engraved. Phrosine has contrived to rejoin Mélidore, at once her "lover, husband, and priest,"

and in his embrace she quickly recovers from a fainting spell. No rococo design surpasses this in voluptuousness, and Prud'hon has given his scene an air of mystery to which the artists of the previous age did not aspire. Delacroix said of this drawing that by itself it served to place its creator beside Correggio (Dacier, p. 74).

76 LONGUS

Les amours pastorales de Daphnis et de Chloé, traduites du grec . . . par Amyot. Paris, P. Didot l'aîné, 1800. viii, 200 p. Illus: 9 plates, 3 after Prud'hon by Roger; after Gérard by: Godefroy (4), Marais, and Massard. Printed on *papier vélin*, the plates *avant lettres et tablettes*; captions printed on tissues. Page size: 12¼× 9¼ inches. Red morocco by Capé. Cohen–de Ricci 656–657.

Two of Prud'hon's three designs for this book are undisputed masterpieces. In the first, "Daphnis . . . taking advantage of the occasion, insinuates his hand into Chloe's bosom, from which he withdraws the pretty grasshopper" (p. 29). In the second, "Chloe leads Daphnis to the cavern of the Nymphs . . . and . . herself washes his handsome body" (p. 38). The harmless sensuality of first love had never been so winningly conveyed, even by Prud'hon himself. The remaining six plates are after Gérard. They are accomplished exercises in the established Davidian mode, though not as fresh and unmannered as those he did for *Psyché et Cupidon*. In comparison with Prud'hon's designs, however, the figures seem rigid, the compositions posed, and the atmosphere cold.

In this vellum-paper copy the plates are before both the letters and the tablets, with captions appearing on *serpentes* (tissues protecting the plates). The intricate retrospective binding, executed in 1860 by Capé after Le Gascon, is reproduced in Appendix I. The tooling may be by the elder Marius Michel, who was Capé's chief *doreur* at the time.

76A LONGUS

[**Daphnis and Chloë,** Greek]. Loggoi poimenika to kata Daphnin kai Chloë. Paris, P. Didot "natu major," 1802. [2] l., 133 p. Illus: 9 plates after: Prud'hon by Roger (3); after Gérard by: Godefroy (4), Marais, and Massard. 7 plates are present in two forms: *avant lettres et tablettes*, and *avec tablettes*; captions printed on tissues. Inserted are 6 reduced versions of the plates, all early states *avant lettres*, and two mid-19th-century

(76A)   Proof engraving before letters after Prud'hon for Longus, *Daphnis et Chloé*

(76A)   Proof engraving before letters after Prud'hon for Longus, *Daphnis et Chloé*

plates after Prud'hon's drawings. Page size: 13¼×9⅞ inches. Red morocco by R. Wallis. Bookplate of Mortimer L. Schiff. Cohen–de Ricci 656–657; Brunet 1156.

This magnificent folio with the text in Greek is said to have been limited to 27 copies. It includes a set of the illustrations before the letters and the tablets, as well as a second set before the letters (with the exception of figures four and five by Gérard). Again the captions are printed on *serpentes*.

Jean-Honoré Fragonard (1732–1806)

77 JEAN DE LA FONTAINE

Contes et nouvelles en vers . . . Paris, P. Didot l'aîné, 1795. 2 v. I: vii, [1], 280, [2] p. II: [2] *l.*, 334 p. Illus. (states according to Wolf): 1(A), 2(A,C), 3(A,B), 4(A,C), 4A(A), 5(A,B), 6(A,B,D), 7(A,C,), 8(A), 9(A,C), 10(A,B), 11(A,B), 12(A,B), 13(A,C), 14(A,C), 15(A,C), 16(A,B), 17(A,C), 18(A,B,C), 18A(A), 19(A,D), 20(A,C,D), 22(A,D), 23(A,D), 24(A,C), 25(A,D, and D color-printed), 26(A, B?), 27(A,C), 28(A), 29(A,C), 30(A,B, and B touched with pencil), 31(B), 32(A,D), 33(A,B,C), 34(A). II: 36 (A). State B of plate 18 is noted by Wolf as a ghost; Wolf notes no color-printed plates. Page size: 12×9 inches. Red morocco by Canape et Corriez. Cohen–de Ricci 573–582.

Though Fragonard made hundreds of designs of an illustrative kind, relatively few of them found their way to publication. His drawings of the early 1760s and those of Hubert Robert yielded the outstanding plates of Saint-Non's *Voyage pittoresque . . . de Naples* (34). He also made many sketches for *Orlando Furioso*, including 137 reproduced at last as *Fragonard: Drawings for Ariosto* in 1946. In an introductory essay to this volume Agnes Mongan (p. 21) assigns these to the late 1780s. If they had been engraved, and Didot's edition of La Fontaine's *Contes et nouvelles* had been completed as planned, Fragonard would have achieved a place among French illustrators comparable to his place among French painters.

The complicated history of Fragonard's designs for the *Contes et nouvelles* can only be suggested here. (It is summarized by Edwin Wolf in an article for the *Bulletin of the New York Public Library*, March, 1949.) Fragonard's first versions were pencil sketches, possibly executed during the trip to Italy that he made with Pierre Bergeret in 1773–1774, forty-two of which are preserved in the li-

brary of a New York collector. At some later date, possibly 1780, he transferred these by rubbings to other sheets, which then served as the basis for finished drawings in sepia. Traces of pencil, indeed, can be seen beneath the wash of these designs (Beraldi, *Estampes et livres*, p. 113). Fifty-seven of them were mounted in a magnificent calligraphic manuscript of the *Contes et nouvelles*, which was bound in two volumes by Dérôme. Just before the sale at auction of the collection of Henri Beraldi in 1934 this set was acquired by the French government for the Louvre.

At least as early as 1793 (the date of a preliminary etching for his edition) Pierre Didot had decided to make Fragonard's finished drawings the leading feature of a sumptuous republication of the *Contes et nouvelles*. A prospectus, reprinted by Cohen (columns 574–575), promised eighty plates after Fragonard, issued in eight numbers of ten plates each, to adorn a text in two quarto volumes. The book duly appeared in 1795, but only two numbers of the plates were published, and in the second of these, four of them were after other artists. Seventeen further drawings, five after Fragonard, were eventually brought to various states of completion by the engravers.

Several reasons have been advanced for Didot's decision to abort the illustrations for his edition of the *Contes et nouvelles*: that they appeared in "the aftermath of the Terror" (but he continued to publish other major illustrated books); that his engravers could not cope with Fragonard's designs (but in fact they did, in some instances superbly); and that the vogue for the rococo was over (but Fragonard, like Prud'hon, was an artist of such excellence as to make a stylistic label of this kind virtually meaningless). Since Didot seems to have relied on access to the fifty-seven sepia designs described above (and all of the drawings after Fragonard actually engraved are from this collection), there is another possible explanation. In his prospectus Didot had promised eighty plates after Fragonard, presumably counting on further designs from the artist himself. When these were not forthcoming, he was under the necessity of supplementing the book's illustrations with twenty-three plates from other hands. Indeed, of the thirty-seven subjects at least partially engraved, only twenty-one are after Fragonard. But the designs by other artists (Le Barbier and Monnet are the only names of note) turned out to be greatly inferior to Fragonard's in quality and quite dissimilar in style. Faced with the prospect of a hopeless mishmash, Didot may simply have abandoned the project.

The spirit in which Fragonard worked is suggested by his pencil sketch for a frontispiece to *Orlando Furioso*: "Ariosto inspired by love and folly." Yet his affinity to La Fontaine was even closer than his affinity to the Italian master. Both were men of the world who saw society as a source of enjoyment and amusement. Both had a zest for life which made them cheerful rather than cynical. Moreover, of all La Fontaine's works, the *Contes et nouvelles* was the best suited to Fragonard, since gallantry was his way of life and the air which he breathed. His mastery of La Fontaine's text was complete. Holding every aspect of each poem in mind, he made a quick, decisive sketch of the situation which best synthesized it. When these sketches were elaborated into finished drawings, each in effect a small painting, broad and free yet precise enough to give the engraver his necessary outline, the result was a series which, considered as illustrations, surpasses his sketches for Ariosto.

Routine examples of the *Contes et nouvelles* have the first twenty plates in their finished states. They are not particularly scarce. Among the most precious prizes of the collector, however, are copies with early states of the published engravings and examples of the remaining seventeen. This copy was assembled between 1927 and 1937, as is attested by its Canape et Corriez binding (Devauchelle, III, 246). It contains none of the published states, but seventy-one of the unpublished: the first twenty engravings in two preliminary states, and thirty-one of the unpublished engravings as etchings and plates before letters. This total places it with the most distinguished examples enumerated by Cohen (columns 579–580). Given the mediocrity of the plates after other artists, perhaps a better test of the status of a copy is the number of proof states after Fragonard's designs. This has thirty-nine.

These tabulations have their significance, for several engravings after Fragonard are among the most enchanting of all illustrations, and they are seen at their best only in the preliminary etchings. Consider the following. The design for "Joconde"

(77)   Fragonard, preliminary etching for "Joconde"

(I, 22), the second of three devoted to this tale but the only one after Fragonard, shows a lover slipping under the covers to join his mistress for a night's pleasure, during which each of her two guardians will think that the other is enjoying her. The heavy slumbers of the pair, the eagerness of the girl, and the cautious deftness of the young man are caught in the etching with something approaching the grace and energy of Fragonard's drawing. Even better is the rendering of Fragonard's conception for "On ne s'avise jamais de tout" (I, 90), reproduced as the frontispiece to this volume. This trivial anecdote concerns a lover who encompasses a rendezvous with a carefully guarded wife by arranging to have her skirt soiled as she passes through the street, with the result that her duenna must depart for a fresh garment. Fragonard has illustrated it with the airiest and most animated of designs. The engraver again rose to the challenge, particularly in his brilliant preliminary etching, though one regrets his failure to include Fragonard's spirited dog. In this case, the

(77A)   Fragonard, facsimile of drawing for "On ne s'avise jamais de tout"

(77) Fragonard, engraving before letters for "On ne s'avise jamais de tout"

proof before letters is also masterly. A further triumph is the plate for "Belphégor" (I, 222), the story of a devil sent to earth for ten years to observe the condition of marriage, which accounts for the presence in Hell of most of Satan's subjects. Fragonard shows Belphégor causing consternation by exposing his shaggy leg and misshapen foot to a farmer's household, which this time includes a dog. The plate is reproduced after page 154 below as an example of printing in color. To this list of successes may be added the plates for "Pâté d'anguille" (I, 193) and "La matrone d'Ephese" (I, 211).

It must be admitted, however, that capturing Fragonard's vitality and impetus was sometimes beyond the capacity of the engravers. In the case of "Le cocu battant et content," for example, a rare *planche refusée* (I, 33) bears witness that the engraver's first attempt was so out of drawing as to make it necessary for him to begin again (I, 30), though not to much purpose. The besetting sin of the plates is the excessive detail with which Fragonard's painterly backgrounds are filled in. A detailed inventory of the objects depicted in "La coupe enchantée" (I, 135) would require pages. In their final state with the letters, moreover, the engravings often have a dark heaviness that quite destroys the grace of Fragonard's designs.

REFERENCES Beraldi (1892); *Fragonard*; Guimbaud; Portalis; Réau; Wolf.

77A JEAN DE LA FONTAINE

Contes et nouvelles en vers . . . [Facsimile of a calligraphic manuscript, with reproductions of 57 sepia drawings by Fragonard. Paris, Jacomet, 1939–1945]. 2 v. Page size: 13⅞ × 9⅞ inches; limited to 50 copies. Red morocco.

This triumph of facsimile reproduction by Jacomet, commissioned by the French government after its purchase of the original, enables the student to appreciate Fragonard's mastery almost as completely as if he had access to the original drawings in the Louvre. Didot had Fragonard's drawings engraved for the most part in their order in La Fontaine's text (only one is for volume two), and the thirty-six drawings not engraved are quite as fine as the twenty-one which were. Among the most striking is that for "Féronde" (II, 133), in

which we see Fragonard's grandiose conception of the masquerade devised by an Abbé and his novices to persuade the drugged Féronde, a mean and stupid man, that he is lying in his tomb in Purgatory, beaten and starved, to expiate the jealous suspicions aroused by the Abbé's attention to his wife. For his setting Fragonard has harked back to his designs for the *Voyage pittoresque . . . de Naples* (34). After examining these drawings, one is inclined to prefer Fragonard even to Eisen (26) as an interpreter of La Fontaine's *Contes et nouvelles*.

(77A) Fragonard, facsimile of drawing for "Féronde"

The Contemporary Scene

The three decades following 1789 were a time of political and social upheaval such as even the French nation has hardly known either before or since. The illustrated book reflects the sweeping changes of Revolution, Republic, Empire, and Restoration in several ways. Most conspicuous is the record it provides of the great events of the time. One turns first to the *Tableaux historiques de la révolution française*, published between 1791 and 1804, which documents the early years of the period with incomparable immediacy and authenticity. Also of interest is Grasset de Saint-Sauveur's *Fastes du peuple français*, 1796. Ternisien d'Haudricourt's *Fastes de la nation française* devotes most of its 168 plates to the Republic and the Empire, though earlier French history is represented as well. Its title page is dated 1807, but events as late as 1812 are illustrated.

With Napoleon's triumph the celebration of contemporary history became more grandiose. Typical folios are the *Tableaux historiques des campagnes d'Italie*, 1806, and Rouillon-Petit's *Campagnes memorables des françaises*, 1817. Elsewhere the figures of private life and their costume were depicted, often with some tincture of caricature, by various artists, among whom Carle and Horace Vernet stand out. The latter's *Incroyables et merveilleuses* of 1814, engraved by Gatine, is the great success in this line. All of these books have the further interest of showing the period as it appeared at the time, thus providing a basis for comparison with the nostalgic designs in which Charlet, Raffet, and others later celebrated the Napoleonic legend.

Meanwhile, current literature, especially the novel, was being illustrated to an unprecedented extent. The Revolution brought with it a degree of license which allowed illustrators to go far beyond Binet's designs for the stories of Restif de la Bretonne. Overt pornography was freely offered for sale in bookstores. Portalis (I, 14) tells of a respectable lady departing for the country with her children who asked a friend to purchase some improving works for their reading. One of the books which she had selected because of its title was the Marquis de Sade's *Justine, or the Misfortunes of Virtue*. Not only were his novels published in many illustrated editions between 1791 and 1800 (Cohen, columns 919–923), but older works such as Voltaire's *La pucelle* also appeared with erotic plates. Though the illustrations for Sade's works are crude daubs, two novels of amatory intrigue called forth designs of real merit, *Les liaisons dangereuses* of 1796 and *Les amours du chevalier de Faublas* of 1798. More decorous poems and stories were also illustrated as is exampled in Delille's *L'homme des champs* of 1805. There are even hints of approaching Romanticism in the plates inspired by Chateaubriand's early narratives. Particularly noteworthy in this respect are Le Barbier's designs for *René* in the third edition of the *Génie du christianisme* (41), which appeared in 1803.

REFERENCES Cohen–de Ricci; Portalis; Renouvier.

78

[Cover title:] **Tableaux de la révolution françoise,** ou Collection de quarante-huit gravures représentant les événements principaux qui ont eu lieu en France depuis . . . le 20 juin 1789. . . . Ces gravures, fruit des veilles d'une société d'artistes, seront accompagnées chacune d'un discours historique composé par une société de gens de lettres. . . . Paris, Briffault de la Charprais & Madame l'Esclapart, [1791–1796?]. vi, 396 p. Illus: 98 plates by: Berthault after Duplessis-Bertaux (4), by Berthault after Fragonard fils, by Berthault after Ozane, by Berthault after Prieur (67), by Berthault after Swebach Desfontaines (23), by Choffard after Duplessis-Bertaux, and by Swebach Desfontaines and Choffard. Page size: 18¼ × 12 inches. Contemp. calf, wrapper for the Ier *livraison* bound in. Cohen–de Ricci 969–971.

This is a book which should be obtained in two editions. It appeared in numbers consisting initially of two plates and two "historical discourses" each. Political developments eventually made the so-called "Revolutionary text" of the first eighty discourses unacceptable, and they were extensively modified in 1798. The unrevised numbers offer the best impressions of the plates, as well as the historical interest of their incendiary prose, but of

PRISE DE LA BASTILLE ,
le 14 Juillet 1789.

(78) Engraving by Prieur for *Tableaux de la révolution françoise*

course one also wants the complete edition published in three volumes in 1804, with 153 plates, 66 portrait-medallions, and 3 frontispieces (Cohen, columns 969–971). Unfortunately, collections of first issues of all 113 numbers are virtually unfindable. This copy includes the first ninety-eight discourses and plates, which carry the history of the Revolution to the latter part of 1793. Its calf binding appears to be strictly contemporary.

The early number cover which serves as title page for this volume describes the plates as "the result of the vigils of a society of artists." Their sketches were passed along to the book's illustrators, who were no doubt themselves members of the society. Two artists stand out: Jean-Louis Prieur (1732–1794) and Joseph Duplessis-Bertaux. Prieur was responsible for plates 1 to 63 and 65 to 69. Duplessis-Bertaux's major contributions, which admittedly are of greater aesthetic interest, came later, though he is represented by four plates at the end of this volume. Our concern, then, is with Prieur, a painter who took an active part in the Revolution and was guillotined by order of the Tribunal in 1794.

The interest of his designs can hardly be exaggerated. They provide a consecutive, eye-witness view of tremendous events which shook the world. As Renouvier remarks (p. 58), Prieur set down

(79)   Engraving after Carle Vernet for *Tableaux historiques des campagnes d'Italie*

with great precision "the places and the buildings which were the theatre of the most moving scenes, with the crowds which were both actors and spectators." Famous episodes pass in order: the oath of the tennis-court (1), the taking of the Bastille (16), the arrest of "Louis Capet" and "Antoinette" at Varennes (53), and the populace invading the Tuileries (62). Nor did Prieur omit moments of high drama on the margin of history: the offerings made by female artists to the National Assembly (26), the funeral of Mirabeau (50), and the triumph accorded Voltaire (55). The sequence is a surpassing achievement of pictorial journalism.

79

Tableaux historiques des compagnes d'Italie . . . Toutes les vues ont été prises sur les lieux mêmes, et les estampes sont gravées d'après des dessins originaux de Carle Vernet. Paris, Auber, 1806. [2] *l.*, 78, [77]–128 p., [1] *l.*, [129]–138, 63, [1] p. Illus: Unsigned t.p. vignette, front. by Simon after Carle Vernet, headpiece

by Roger after Duplessis-Bertaux, hand-colored map by Louvet after Dieu, 2 unsigned medallion portraits; 24 plates: 21 after Carle Vernet by Duplessis-Bertaux and: Bosq, Bovinet, Choffard, Dambrun, Daudet, De Launay (4), Delignon, Dupréel (3), Louvet, Masquelier (3), Niquet, Ponce, Saint-Aubin, and Simon; 2 after Carle Vernet by Coigny & Dambrun, and Malbeste & Niquet; after Duplessis-Bertaux by Dupréel & Duplessis-Bertaux. All plates are before letters, most are with scratched signatures; the frontispiece is in an early state. The identification of artists has been made from a copy of this title in the Spencer Collection (NYPL), which is, however, an entirely different and presumably later printing. Page size: $20\frac{1}{2} \times 13\frac{1}{2}$ inches, uncut. $\frac{3}{4}$ green morocco by "Aquarius, London." Cohen–de Ricci 971.

The engravings after Carle Vernet in this handsome folio honoring Napoleon display the major episodes of his Italian campaigns from the battle of Mondovi in 1796 to the battle of Marengo in 1800. (There was an earlier edition, before Napoleon became Emperor, called *Tableaux historiques des campagnes et révolutions d'Italie*.) It is claimed on the title page that "all the views have been taken at the places themselves." Renouvier (p. 202) found the battle scenes contrived, but he praised Vernet's several designs of the populace supporting the French army, either by revolting as at Pavia (p. 28), or by celebrating its arrival. Perhaps the best of these shows the coming of the army to Milan in 1796 (p. 24). As etched by Duplessis-Bertaux, it includes literally hundreds of figures whose activities remain lively and persuasive when studied in the smallest detail. Even more striking is the plate devoted to the crossing of the Mount Saint Bernard pass by the army in 1800 (p. 96). This remarkable demonstration of perspective was also skillfully rendered by Duplessis-Bertaux. The fineness of his work can be seen to particular advantage in this copy, in which all plates are before the letters and in some cases also before the artists' names.

80 [HORACE VERNET]

[**Incroyables et merveilleuses.** Paris, c. 1814]. 33 hand-colored engraved plates by Gatine after H. Vernet, with 2 further plates numbered 22, and 1 further plate numbered 31. Page size: 14¾ × 10 inches. ¾ blue morocco. Colas 2992; Beraldi VI, 228; XII, 221.

Under the Directory, the dandies of the day came to be called "Incroyables," because one of their favorite expressions was, "my word of honor, it's incredible" (Renouvier, p. 488). Their affected speech and bizarre dress soon became the target of caricature by writers and artists. Carle Vernet established the new style of nomenclature at the Salon of 1797 with his drawings of "Incroyables," adding the term "Merveilleuses" for their female counterparts. They were engraved at once, and widely copied and imitated. In this later album by his younger brother, Horace, the emphasis is on costume rather than caricature. The impossibly elongated torsos of the ladies, conforming to the neoclassical view of the human anatomy, have no satirical intent. See after page 154 below. Only with such figures could the styles of the day be effectively presented. Male attire required less distortion, though when Vernet dealt with English (number 26) or Russian (number 27) visitors to Paris, he allowed himself some exaggeration.

Georges-Jacques Gatine was the leading costume engraver of his time. For many years he supplied plates for the *Journal des dames*. He engraved the 115 designs which make up *Le bon genre* of 1817,

(80) Engraving after Horace Vernet for *Incroyables et merveilleuses*

a lively mélange caricaturing people and scenes of contemporary interest. He also made hundreds of plates of regional and Parisian dress. None of these remotely approaches *Incroyables et merveilleuses* in excellence, for he never again had anyone approaching Horace Vernet as his artist. Nonetheless, there is a lively demand even for his routine engravings among dealers in decorative prints.

This great record of Empire costume is rarely found complete (36 plates), with contemporary coloring, and virtually uncut, as in this copy.

81 NICOLAS EDME RESTIF DE LA BRETONNE

[Plates for **La paysanne pervertie** . . . Paris, 1784]. 6 undivided fronts. on 3 sheets, 2 fronts. on 2 sheets, and 14 undivided plates on 7 sheets after Binet by: Berthet, Giraud, Le Roy, and unsigned. Page size: 6¾ × 10⅜ inches. Brown morocco.

(81)   Engraving after Binet for Restif de la Bretonne,
La paysanne pervertie

(81)   Engraving after Binet for Restif de la Bretonne,
La paysanne pervertie

It is convenient to describe this series of plates somewhat out of chronological order, since it leads directly to the sort of illustration employed in fiction during the 1790s. Louis Binet made hundreds of designs for the novels of Restif de la Bretonne, including 120 plates for *Le paysan perverti*, four volumes, 1776, and *La paysanne pervertie*, four volumes, 1784; and no less than 283 for *Les contemporaines*, forty-two volumes, 1780–1785. Restif's stories claim attention for their realistic depiction of working-class life, if not for their melodramatic exposure of the corruption of the aristocracy. His illustrator worked under his absolute direction, and it is to Restif that the tiny feet, elongated bodies and small heads of Binet's figures must be ascribed. In Restif's mind these proportions were not only ideal for female beauty but also showed at its best the costume of the day, a subject on which he was regarded as an authority. In the twentieth century Restif's novels have attracted the particular attention of students of sexual mores. In this set of largely undivided proofs for *La paysanne pervertie* a

frontispiece of a grinning devil with Medusan curls lifting the curtain from a suggestive scene, while a giant serpent hisses below, anticipates the frontispieces of the 1796 edition of *Les liaisons dangereuses*; and an accompanying plate offers a representative study of sexual aberration.

82   [Pierre Ambroise François Choderlos de Laclos]

Les liaisons dangereuses. Lettres recueillies dans une société, et publiées pour l'instruction de quelques autres. . . . Londres [i.e., Paris], 1796. 2 v. I: 415 p. II: [2] *l.*, 398 p. Illus.: I: 6 plates after Monnet by: Godefroy, Le Mire (2), Lingée (2), and Trière; 1 plate after Fragonard fils by Bertaux et Dupréel. II: Front. by Patas after Monnet; 6 plates after Mlle. Gérard by: Baquoy, Bertaux et Dupréel, Masquelier, Paquet, Simonet, and Trière. Page size: $7\frac{1}{2} \times 4\frac{5}{8}$ inches. Contemp. pink calf by Hering. Cohen–de Ricci 235–237.

Laclos' epistolary novel offers spectacular opportunities for illustration, which are firmly grasped in this edition. Monnet's plates dominate the first volume, Mlle. Gérard's the second. Monnet's melo-dramatic frontispieces present Laclos as a severe moralist. In that for volume one, the Vicomte Valmont and the Marquise de Merteuil trample the once innocent Cécile Volanges under foot. That there may be no misunderstanding, the pair is circled by a serpent, and Valmont lifts a bland mask from his sinister face, while Cécile clutches a lamb to her bosom. In that for volume two, the tables are turned. The dying Valmont holds up one of the letters which have brought to light so much vice and cynicism, while virtue's rays blast Mme. de Merteuil, as her mask in turn falls to the ground.

The novel's epigraph is a quotation from *La nouvelle Héloïse*: "I have seen the manners of my age, and I have published these letters." Monnet's plates show how Laclos made use of his stance as a moralist to present his readers with the most daring situations. In one (I, 207) Valmont uses the naked

body of a girl whose bed he is sharing as a writing desk for a love letter to the devout Mme. de Tourvel, "even interrupting it for a complete infidelity." In another (I, 232) Mme. de Merteuil is making the most palpable advances to "the little Volanges." For almost any other novel these designs would seem overcharged, even gross, but they are wholly appropriate to Laclos' brazen, larger-than-life characters. In volume two, Mlle. Gérard's designs are less strident, but no less sensual, and it falls to her to show the admonitory punishment of Laclos' two extraordinary protagonists. In sum, these striking plates by Monnet and Mlle. Gérard form the outstanding contemporary interpretation of *Les liaisons dangereuses*. They are not likely to be superseded, however often this celebrated novel is illustrated.

This is as sound a copy as one could find: in contemporary calf signed by Hering, with binding, plates, and text equally fresh. The binding is reproduced in Appendix I.

(82)   Engraving after Monnet for Laclos, *Les liaisons dangereuses*

(82)   Engraving after Monnet for Laclos, *Les liaisons dangereuses*

Les amours du chevalier de Faublas . . . troisième édition, revue par l'auteur. Paris, l'Auteur, [1798]. 4 v. I: xvi, 244 p. II: [2] *l.*, 274 p. III: [2] *l.*, 307 p. IV: [2] *l.*, 330 p. Illus: I: 6 plates, each in 2 states: after Demarne by Choffard, and Saint-Aubin & Tilliard; after Mlle. Gérard by: Halbou, and Saint-Aubin & Tilliard; after Marillier by Courbe; after Monnet by Dupréel. II: 7 plates: after Dutertre by Le Mire (one state); the remainder in 2 states: after Marillier by: Baquoy, Courbe, Delvaux, Patas (2), and Viguet. III: 6 plates, each in 2 states: after Dutertre by Le Mire; after Mlle. Gérard by: Halbou, and Patas; after Marillier by: Dambrun, Giraud, and Patas. IV: 8 plates: after Dutertre by Delaunay (one state); the remainder in 2 states: after Demarne by Halbou; after Dutertre by Delvaux; after Mlle. Gérard by Patas; after Monsiau by: Baquoy, de Ghendt, Patas, and Trière. Bound in are 8 plates by various artists after Colin, each in 3 states. Page size: 8¼×5 inches, uncut. ½ red morocco by Koehler. Bookplate of Desbarreaux-Bernard; A. S. W. Rosenbach–Roederer copy. Cohen–de Ricci 660–661, mentioning this copy.

Apart from *Les liaisons dangereuses* of 1796, this book possesses the liveliest plates of any French novel of the period. Though other illustrators played their part, the book is dominated by Mlle. Gérard, Marillier, and Monsiau, who responded with spirit to the opportunities it offered. Young Faublas' licentious adventures could have provided the occasion for a series of suggestive designs (as is demonstrated, indeed, by Collin's overblown plates for the edition in four volumes of 1821, which have been added to this copy in three states), but the artists chose instead to concentrate on the novel's abundant episodes of action and dramatic confrontation. In the scene shown (IV, 208) Faublas is on the point of betraying his female disguise by drawing a sword to punish a captain who has affronted the company by his brutal behavior.

This may fairly be called a spectacular copy. There are impressions before the letters of all twenty-seven plates, and etchings of twenty-five. Cohen mentions only one other set with etchings. As usual, their light touch reveals nuances obscured in the finished states.

84 JACQUES DELILLE

L'homme des champs, ou Les Géorgiques françoises . . . nouvelle édition augmentée, avec figures. Paris, Levrault, Schoell, et cie., 1805. [2] *l.*, 125 p. Illus. after Catel: Front. by Haldenwang et Buchorn, head-

(83)   Preliminary etching in Couvray, *Les amours du chevalier de Faublas*

pieces by: Buchorn (2), Haldenwang et Buchorn (2), Mayer (2), and unsigned (2); 4 plates by: C. Guttenberg, H. Guttenberg, Haldenwang et Buchorn, and Mayer. Page size: 7⅞×5 inches. Contemp. polished calf. Cohen–de Ricci 279.

Catel, who provided four plates and eight headpieces for these belated pastoral poems, seems otherwise unknown to fame. Nonetheless, this book was favored by the collectors of his day, and it is often found in attractive contemporary bindings. It is a pretty volume, well designed and printed. The illustrations strike an individual note, frequented as they are for the most part by sober and sturdy men of a certain age engaged in discussion or contemplation. Indeed, some of them call to mind figures in Blake's designs of the same period. There is also a large-paper issue with the illustrations printed in color, which has five plates before the letters. See List XLV (1980) of Martin Breslauer, Inc., item 15.

85 FRANÇOIS RENÉ AUGUSTE, VICOMTE DE CHATEAUBRIAND

Atala. René. Paris, Le Normant, 1805. [2] *l.*, 46, 331 p. Illus: 6 plates after Garnier by: Saint-Aubin (3), and Choffard (3). Printed on *papier vélin*, with an extra *suite* of plates *avant lettres*. Page size: 7 1/8 × 4 1/8 inches, uncut. Brown morocco by Chambolle-Duru. Bookplate of Robert Schuhmann. Cohen–de Ricci 229; Carteret I, 161.

Atala and *René* first appeared in 1801 and 1802 respectively. These short narratives were incorpo-rated in the *Génie du christianisme* of 1802. Chateau-briand then brought them together in this book, calling *René* the "natural continuation" (p. 22) of *Atala*. The illustrations by Garnier are undistin-guished, but it is interesting to see how a contem-porary imagination conceived René as he tells his melancholy story in the American wilderness (p. 323).

The book should be sought in its rare larger format on vellum paper with the plates both before and after the letters. The dimensions of this uncut copy (180 × 105 mm.) surpass those reported by Carteret (175 × 102 mm.).

Color Printing

The later years of the century were marked by a burgeoning of books with illustrations printed in color. The troubled atmosphere of the time seems to have stimulated technical experimentation even as it dampened artistic imagination. Sergent led the way with his *Portraits des grands hommes*, the earliest plates in which are dated 1786. In 1792 Defer de Maisonneuve published Milton's *Le para-dis perdu* in two volumes with plates after Schall, and in 1793 Gessner's *La mort d'Abel* and Florian's *Galatée* with plates after Monsiau. In 1796 he issued by far the most satisfactory of these books, Vadé's *Oeuvres poissardes*, again with plates after Monsiau and printed by Didot. For the last of the series Didot called on the acknowledged master of en-graving in color, Debucourt, for illustrations to *Héro et Léandre*. All of these are handsome and imposing volumes; none can be called an artistic triumph. That achievement was reserved for Re-douté's *Les roses* of 1817–1824. It is to be regretted that there was no attempt to issue La Fontaine's *Contes et nouvelles* of 1795 (77) with the plates after Fragonard printed in color. As that for "Belphé-gor" demonstrates (I, 221), these are as beautiful as they are rare. It is reproduced after page 154 below.

REFERENCES The Goncourts; Portalis; Portalis-Be-raldi.

86 [ANTOINE-LOUIS-FRANÇOIS SERGENT-MARCEAU]

Portraits des grands hommes, femmes illustres, et su-jets mémorables de France, gravés et imprimés en couleurs. . . . Paris, Blin, [?1789–1792]. 2 v. Illus: Engraved t.p., engraved dedication by Beaublé, and 130 color-printed plates (of 192), containing the fol-lowing complete *livraisons*: A, F, H, N, P, Y, &, AA, BB, CC, UU, and XX; the following incomplete *livraisons*: B3–16; C5–6, 9–42; D3–6; EI–4; GI–10; K3–6, 5–8; LI–6, 3–4; O3,3; QI–2; lacking the following *livraisons*: I, M, EE, NN, FFF, JJJ, and OOO. Page size: 12 3/4 × 9 3/8 inches. Contemp. 1/2 calf. Cohen–de Ricci 951–952.

Antoine-François Sergent (1751–1847), who had studied engraving with Augustin de Saint-Aubin, began to concentrate his attention on engraving in color about 1786 with the first plates for this book. He did not allow his ardent and prolonged partic-ipation in the Revolution to interrupt the progress of his *Portraits des grands hommes*, though the abject flattery of Louis XVI with which it began came to seem more and more of an anomaly. The work eventually extended to forty-eight parts of four plates each. (This copy includes the first thirty-three parts.) In his dedication to the King, Pierre Blin, the publisher, promised portraits of "all the heroes of France, with the picture of their most glorious deed." The pattern which Sergent fol-lowed was established in the first two engravings:

(86) Engraving printed in color after Duplessis-Bertaux for Sergent, *Portraits des grands hommes*

87 JEAN-JOSEPH VADÉ

Oeuvres poissardes de J. J. Vadé, suivies de celles de l'Ecluse; édition tirée à 300 exemplaires, dont 100 sur grand papier; et ornée de figures imprimées en couleur. Paris, Defer de Maisonneuve, 1796. 6 p., [1] *l.*, 167 p. Illus: 4 color-printed plates by Clément after Monsiau; the lettering on pl. 2 is stencilled rather than engraved. Page size: 13¾ × 10¼ inches, uncut. Contemp. ½ red morocco. Cohen–de Ricci 1005.

The Pierpont Morgan Library

In the preface we learn how the experiences of a fiery and dissipated youth led Jean-Joseph Vadé (d. 1757) to create "a new kind of poetry" called "*poissard*." "It depicts reality, founded on truth, but it is not without its agreeable side. A picture which shows a tavern, the people dancing, soldiers drinking and smoking is not unpleasant to see. Vadé is the Teniers of poetry" (p. 5). And indeed Monsiau's four drawings of the Parisian market district, with typical figures and costumes from the contemporary scene rather than from Vadé's time, are lively and invigorating. That reproduced in color after page 154 below is the second of the series (p. 12), and presumably the one to which the preface alludes. The title page states that 300 copies of the book were printed in color. This is one of 100 on large paper.

88 [LE CHEVALIER DE QUERELLES]

Héro et Léandre, poëme nouveau en trois chants, traduit du grec . . . ornée d'un frontispice et de huit estampes en couleur, dessinées et gravées par P. L. Debucourt. . . . Paris, P. Didot l'aîné, 1801. 100 p., [1] *l.* Illus. after Debucourt: Front. (in 2 states, 1 before signatures) and 8 color-printed and hand-colored plates, all before signatures. Printed on *papier de Hollande*. Page size: 12⅝ × 9⅝ inches. Bookplates of Léon Rattier, Alain de Suzannet, and Lucien Tissot Dupont. Green morocco by Marius Michel. Cohen–de Ricci 833.

In his prime Louis-Philibert Debucourt (1755–1832) ranked as the supreme master of engravings printed in color. He was already an accomplished genre painter in 1785 when he perfected his process of printing in color with five successive coppers, which enabled him to achieve in his prints the delicacy, the suavity, and the freshness of painting itself. There ensued a series of well-known engravings in which French social life before and after the Revolution is presented with charm and vivacity. By the time he undertook to illustrate the

a portrait of Louis XVI, and an allegorical plate after Duplessis-Bertaux called the "Independence of the United States," in which this historical development is represented as largely the work of France's ineffectual monarch. His likeness surmounts those of Franklin and "Waginton" on a monument with the inscription "America and the seas, O Louis, recognize you as their liberator," while a young woman in Indian dress places her foot on the head of a spotted and compressed beast, possibly intended to represent the British lion. The portraits in the series, most of them Sergent's own work, are uniformly attractive; those of more recent "heroes" may also be authentic. The scenes, on the other hand, which are typically anecdotal rather than allegorical, are uniformly crude and inept. The proficiency of the engraving is considerable, though the coloring is bold to the point of garishness.

(88)   Engraving printed in color by Debucourt for Querelles, *Héro et Léandre*

after Pradier, decorative floral plate (in 2 forms), and 56 color-printed and hand-colored plates by: Bessin (11), Couten (3), Chapuy (21), Charlin (4), Langlois (16), and Lemaire (1). II: 59 color-printed and hand-colored plates by: Bessin (6), Chapuy (15), Charlin (5), Langlois (19), Lemaire (5), "Talbeaux" (Talbot) (4), Tilliard (2), and Victor (3). III: 54 color-printed and hand-colored plates by: Bessa (1), Bessin (5), Chapuy (6), Langlois (23), Lemaire (4), and Victor (15). One of perhaps 5 large-paper copies with the plates in two forms, printed in black on buff paper, and color-printed on white paper. Page size: 21 $\frac{3}{8}$ × 14 inches. $\frac{3}{4}$ green morocco. Nissen 1599.

The Pierpont Morgan Library

translation of *Héro et Léandre* by his friend the Chevalier Quérelles, however, ease and spirit had largely departed from his work, though its technical excellence remained. The design of Leander outracing his friends at the games (p. 35) is unintentionally comic in its rigid symmetry, while he and Hero elsewhere are as passionless as they are handsome. Only the first two plates, both of public occasions, convey something of the vitality of Debucourt's engraving "Promenade de la gallérie du Palais Royal" of 1787. Witness Hero as the priestess of Venus crowning Leander, who has just won the palm of the arts (p. 17).

This is a superb copy on large vellum paper with the plates before the letters.

Redouté was among the greatest of flower painters. Though he was born in Luxembourg, he spent most of his life in France. Before the Revolution he was employed in the Cabinet of Marie Antoinette, whom he instructed in drawing, and in 1798 Josephine Bonaparte asked him to draw the rare plants in the garden at Malmaison. Meanwhile, his fame had attracted wide patronage from amateurs. His first important book was *Les liliacées*, eight folio volumes, 1802–1816. The works which followed included *Choix des plus belles fleurs*, thirty-six parts, 1827–1832. Prosperity attended him almost to his death, when his lavish way of life was threatening him with bankruptcy.

Redouté's admitted masterpiece is *Les roses*. The 170 stipple engravings printed in color of its large folio edition command the admiration of both natural historians and artists. Working directly from the flowers themselves, he arranged his compositions to show all their significant aspects. Yet he achieved this comprehensive precision with so little sacrifice of aesthetic effect that he came to be called the "Raphael of flowers." Shown after page 154 below is the "Rosa Centifolia Bullata" (page 38), the large and shapely leaves of which rival the flower itself in beauty. This splendid copy is one of five on large paper with plates in both colored and uncolored states.

Pierre-Joseph Redouté (1759–1840)

89   PIERRE-JOSEPH REDOUTÉ

Les roses par P. J. Redouté, peintre de fleurs. . . . Avec le texte par Cl. Ant. Thory. . . . Paris, Firmin Didot, 1817–1824. 3 v. I: 156 p. II: 122 p., [2] *l.* III: 125, [1] p., [1] *l.* Illus. after Redouté: I: Front. by Gérard

89A   PIERRE-JOSEPH REDOUTÉ

Les roses, peintes par P. J. Redouté . . . décrites et classées . . . par C. A. Thory. Troisième édition, publiée sous la direction de M. Pirolle. . . . Paris, 1828–1830. V. I and II (of 3), 89 (of 183) color-printed and hand-colored plates, including 2 lithographic fronts. Page size: 9 × 5 $\frac{7}{8}$ inches. Vellum by Sangorski and Sutcliffe. Nissen 1599.

The popularity of *Les roses* was such that three octavo editions followed the original folios between 1824 and 1835. This is the second of the series. Though its plates lack the grandeur of the originals, they have an appeal of their own. Increasingly in demand by "breakers," who seek their individual prints for framing, even these later editions are gradually passing out of the reach of collectors. This incomplete copy has been bound in painted vellum by Sangorski and Sutcliffe.

The Miniature Illustrators

The unsettled political and commercial conditions prevailing after 1789 made it difficult for publishers to embark on major illustrated books. They found it easier to limit their efforts to less ambitious productions in smaller formats with miniature plates. A precedent had already been set in the edition printed by Pierre Didot of La Fontaine's *Fables*, six volumes, 1787, which contains 276 small designs by Vivier, engraved by Simon and Coiny. See number 90, below. It was confirmed by another well-known book, the *Iconologie par figures* illustrated by Cochin and Gravelot (23), for which, indeed, the plates were already available. A practice also arose of reprinting large illustrated books of the time in smaller formats with reductions of the plates. This occurred in 1797, for example, with Didot's edition of La Fontaine's *Les amours de Psyché et de Cupidon*, originally published two years earlier (56). Once established, the practice of miniature illustration proved tenacious. Though returning stability and prosperity made large-scale publications attractive once more after 1795, books with small plates continued to appear with regularity for at least another quarter of a century.

Gil Blas was particularly favored for miniature plates. Four editions appeared between 1795 and 1801, the chief of which were the earliest, with illustrations by Bornet, Charpentier, and Duplessis-Bertaux, and the last, with plates by Monnet (38). Fénelon's *Télémaque* was equally popular, with three editions in 1796 alone, and a fourth in 1797. Even Pierre Didot encouraged the vogue of these books with eight so-called "cornflower" editions, illustrated chiefly by Robert Lefèvre (1756–1800), between 1795 and 1801 (Portalis, I, 349–350). They

are exampled in *Manon Lescaut*, described below. There were also many books with miniature illustrations of such ineptness that Cohen did not find it worth his while to include them in his bibliography. Typical of these is the edition of Perrault's *Contes des fées*, included here for its original drawings.

Moreau made designs for many small plates in his last years. After his death Alexandre Desenne became illustrator in chief for the French classical authors, providing *suites* of miniature plates for Molière, Racine, Rousseau, and Voltaire. Calot claims (p. 154) that Desenne's vignettes for three books by Etienne de Jouy, *Ermite de la Chaussée d'Antin*, *L'Ermite en province*, and *Ermites en liberté*, published between 1813 and 1815, provide "the gayest and most complete picture of the Parisian life" of the time, which is not saying a great deal, given the absence of rival illustrators.

Despite its general employment, miniature illustration did not score many successes. The Goncourts were contemptuous of the run-of-the-mill artists like Chasselat and Quéverdo who specialized in this genre (III, 119), and though Portalis praised Lefèvre, its outstanding practitioner, he granted in the end that Lefèvre's was a "very minor art" (I, 350). It will suffice, then, to cite a few examples, chiefly from the early years of the fashion.

REFERENCES Calot (1931); Portalis.

90 JEAN DE LA FONTAINE

Fables . . . avec figures gravées par MM. Simon et Coigny. . . . Paris, Bossanges, Masson, & Besson, 1796. 6 v. I: [2] *l.*, 76 p. II: [2] *l.*, 75 p. III: [2] *l.*, 65 p. IV:

[2] *l.*, 106 p. V: [2] *l.*, 111 p. VI: [2] *l.*, 136 p. Illus: I: 46 plates. II: 47–96 plates. III: 97–138 plates. IV: 139–183 plates. V: 184–235 plates. VI: 236–276 plates.

Contes et nouvelles en vers . . . Paris, P. Didot l'aîné, 1795. 2 v. in 4. I: viii, 118 p. II: [2] *l.*, [119]–256 p. III: 164 p. IV: [2] *l.*, [165]–298 p. Illus: I: Headpiece by Dupréel after Rigault, 19 plates. II: 16 plates. III: 19 plates (2 in 2 states). IV: 21 plates (4 in 2 states). All plates are before letters, some with scratched signatures.

Théâtre . . . édition stéréotype d'après le procédé de Firmin Didot. Paris, P. Didot l'aîné & Firmin Didot, 1812. vi, 277 [1] p. Inserted is a 2-p. *Avertissement.*

Les amours de Psyché et de Cupidon . . . édition stéréotype . . . Paris, P. Didot l'aîné & Firmin Didot, 1803. 204 p. Illus: Front. by Delvaux after Rigault and 5 plates by Delvaux after Moreau. Page size: $6 \times 3\frac{3}{4}$ inches. Blue morocco by Thouvenin.

This set of La Fontaine is included for the *Fables* which make up its first six volumes. It is illustrated by 276 plates by Simon and Coiny after Vivier, which appeared in 1787. Vivier, who was first painter to the Prince of Bourbon, performed his exhausting task with skill, and Simon and Coiny ensured that his drawings lost nothing in the en-

graving. Oudry is omnipresent as a model, but the difference in scale between his designs and Vivier's makes the two series quite different in effect. Indeed, the simplification to which Vivier had to resort is a major factor in rendering his work animated and harmonious. The plate shown may be compared with that after Oudry of the same subject on page 17 above.

(91)   Engraving after Duplessis-Bertaux for Le Sage, *Gil Blas*

FABLE IV.
Le Jardinier et fon Seigneur.
Pl. 2ᵉ

(90)   Engraving after Vivier for La Fontaine, *Fables*

91   ALAIN RENÉ LE SAGE

Histoire de Gil Blas de Santillane . . . édition ornée de figures en taille douce, gravées par les meilleurs artistes de Paris. . . . Paris, Janet & Hubert, [1795]. 4 v. I: 398 p. II: 333 p. III: 382 p. IV: 368 p. Illus. after Hubert: I: 25 plates by: Bornet (23), and Charpentier (2). II: 25 plates by: Bornet (12), and Charpentier (13). III: 25 plates by: Bornet (6), Charpentier (15), and Duplessis-Bertaux (4). IV: 25 plates by: Bornet (9), Charpentier (13), and Duplessis-Bertaux (3). Page size: $7\frac{3}{4} \times 4\frac{7}{8}$ inches. Contemp. green morocco. Cohen–de Ricci 632.

These are the most abundant and attractive illustrations for *Gil Blas* before those by Gigoux for the edition of 1835 (214). The book's principal artists, Bornet and Charpentier, endeavored to give the reader a vivid glimpse of as many as possible of the varied episodes of Le Sage's novel. Since their emphasis is on incident rather than character, the backgrounds are developed in some detail. The plate shown (IV, 134) is one of the rare designs after Duplessis-Bertaux, which have a distinction of style beyond the reach of the book's other illustrators. It is from the history of Gil Blas' servant, Scipio.

92 Antoine François Prévost, called Prévost d'Exiles

Histoire de Manon Lescaut, et du Chevalier des Grieux. . . . Paris, P. Didot l'aîné, 1797. 2 v. I: [2] *l.*, 225 p. II: [2] *l.*, 213 p. Illus: I: 4 plates by Coiny after Lefèvre. II: 4 plates by Coiny after Lefèvre. This copy on *papier vélin*, the plates *avant lettres*. Page size: 5×2⅞ inches. Contemp. red morocco. Cohen–de Ricci 823–824.

Despite their small size, Lefèvre's eight plates for *Manon Lescaut* are as dramatic as they are inventive. They make this edition of Prévost's novel the most attractive of those published during the eighteenth century, just as it is the most desirable of Didot's "cornflower" editions. In the plate shown (II, 34) Manon is demonstrating to her elderly protector why she prefers des Grieux to him: "Make the comparison yourself, . . . for I tell you that in the eyes of your very humble servant, all the princes of Italy are not worth a lock of the hair that I am holding." This is one of 100 copies of the duodecimo edition on large vellum paper with the plates before the letters. The doublures of the contemporary morocco binding have elaborate borders, the pattern of which derives from the title-page decoration.

93 Charles Perrault

Contes des fées . . . Paris, Devaux, 1797. 2 v. in 1. I: [2] *l.*, 144 p. II: [2] *l.*, 134 p., [1] *l.* Illus: I: 8 unsigned plates. II: 2 unsigned plates. Inserted are the 10 original pen-and-ink, wash, and graphite drawings for the plates. Page size: 5⅛×3⅛ inches. Bookplates of Robert Hoe and Cortlandt F. Bishop. Contemp. stained calf.

That this selection from Perrault's tales should have gone unnoticed does not seem unreasonable

(92) Engraving after Lefèvre for Prévost, *Manon Lescaut*

Unsigned drawings for Perrault, *Contes des fées*

when one examines its ten plates. The unsigned drawings for these engravings, however, possess a naïve charm. Their delicacy and animation are best shown in "Puss in boots" (I, 23) and "Tom Thumb" (I, 116). A fresh binding of contemporary tree calf, simply but agreeably tooled, with a mosaic spine completes this attractive period ensemble.

94 JEAN RACINE

Oeuvres complètes . . . avec les notes de tous les commentateurs. Édition publiée par L. Aimé-Martin. Paris, Lefèvre, 1820. 6 v. I: [10] *l.*, clxxii, 395 p., [1] *l.* II: [2] *l.*, 515 p., [1] *l.* III: [2] *l.*, 541 p., [1] *l.* IV: [2] *l.*, 388 p V: [2] *l.*, 500 p. VI: [2] *l.*, 522 p. Illustrated and extra-illustrated with numerous series of engraved plates, including those after Moreau (in 2 states), and after Girardet and Gérard (in 3 states). Page size: $9\frac{3}{8} \times 6\frac{1}{8}$ inches, uncut. The Roederer copy. ½ bluc morocco by Simier.

Among its many added illustrations, this set of Racine's works contains twelve miniature engravings of 1818 after Desenne before the letters and on China paper. The plate shown (III, 391) depicts Phaedra's avowal of guilty love to Hippolytus, who is appalled by her passion. Desenne's figures have a distinctive cachet, but they fade to insignificance when compared to another design inspired by this play (III, 416), Duplessis-Bertaux's splendid en-

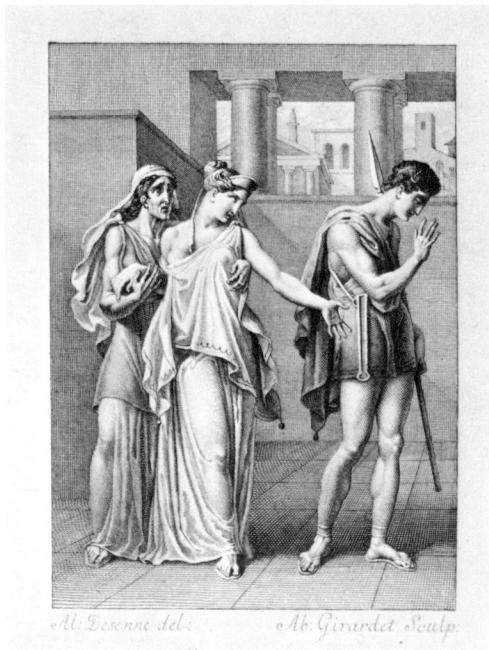

(94)   Engraving after Desenne for Racine, *Phèdre*

graving after Pierre-Narcisse Guérin (1774–1833), reproduced on page 118 above. This is Guérin's rendering of a scene from act IV as it was then played at the Théâtre-Français (Friedlander, p. 45).

Nicolas-André Monsiau (1754–1837)

Monsiau was a Parisian who attained some reputation as a painter of both classical and modern subjects. He was elected to the Academy in 1789, but though he continued to exhibit for many years, he also came to devote himself to illustration. His abundant and interesting work in this line has never received much attention. This may be attributed in part to his having been only a secondary illustrator of the major books to which he contributed, in part to his having worked in neither the rococo nor the neoclassical style, with the result that he is identified with no established school. Portalis accurately described Monsiau's qualities

when he wrote of his "*bonhomie*, observation of nature, and feeling, often lacking in his rivals, which gives to his productions something piquant and unexpected" (II, 415). Renouvier, who found his simple and natural style commonplace, is less friendly in his judgment (pp. 318–319).

Monsiau's most extensive contributions to illustration occur in *La sainte bible* of 1789–1804 (47), where he collaborated with Marillier; Rousseau's *Oeuvres* of 1793–1800, where he collaborated with Cochin; and Ovid's *Métamorphoses* of 1806, where he collaborated with Le Barbier and Moreau. Characteristic of his designs for the *Bible* is his concep-

(47) Engraving for *La sainte bible*

Drawing for Ovid's *Métamorphoses*, 1806

tion of the return of the prodigal son (IX, 322). His drawing for "The son of Agénor" in the *Métamorphoses* shows his capacity for entering into the spirit of the book he was illustrating in an inventive way. His lively design makes Ovid's monster really entertaining. Among works for which he was the sole illustrator the best known are the three which he undertook for Defer de Maisonneuve, who printed his plates in color: Florian's *Galatée* and Gessner's *La mort d'Abel* of 1793 and Vadé's *Oeuvres poissards* (87) of 1796. One of his designs for the last of these is reproduced after page 154 below. Also of interest are his six plates for Sterne's *Le voyage sentimental*, two volumes, 1797.

REFERENCES Portalis; Renouvier.

Monsiau and other artists

95 JEAN-JACQUES ROUSSEAU

Oeuvres . . . édition ornée de superbes figures d'après les tableaux et dessins de Cochin, Vincent, Regnault, et Monsiau. . . . Paris, Defer de Maisonneuve, 1793–

1800. 18 v. I: 527, [1] p. II: 600 p. III: 556 p. IV: 487 p. V: 550 p. VI: 530 p., [1] l. VII: 524 p. VIII: 484 p. IX: 604 p. X: 494 p. XI: 357 p. XII: 528 p. XIII: 518 p. XIV: [3] l., 500 p. XV: [2] l., [9]–515 p. XVI: [2] l., [9]–446 p. XVII: [2] l., 456 p. XVIII: [2] l., iv, 438 p. Illus: I: Front. by Langlois; 2 plates after Cochin by Dambrun, and Trière; 1 unsigned. II: Front. by Halbou after Cochin; 3 plates after Monsiau by: Dupréel, Patas, and Trière; 1 unsigned. III: 4 plates after Monsiau by: Dambrun, Dupréel, Le Mire, and Trière. IV: After Cochin: Front. by Le Mire; 3 plates by de Ghendt, Ponce, and Trière. V: After Cochin: 2 plates by Dambrun, and Le Mire. VI: Plate by Delaunay after Cochin. VII: 3 plates: after Cochin by Ingouf, and Lebeau; after Monsiau by de Ghendt. VIII: 10 p. engraved music, 1 folding musical table, and 3 plates; after Monsiau by de Ghendt, and Pauquet; after Regnault by Le Mire. IX: Plate by Halbou after Monsiau. X: Front. by Thomas after Cochin. XI: 13 engraved musical plates, 1 folding musical plate. XII: Front. by Trière after Cochin; 4 plates after Monsiau by: Choffard, Delvaux, Halbou, and Pauquet. XIII: 2 plates after Monsiau by Choffard, and Halbou. XVII: Engraved facsim. by Aubert. Page size: $13\frac{3}{8} \times 10$ inches. Contemp. red morocco by Bisiaux. Cohen–de Ricci 912–913.

The Pierpont Morgan Library, The Dannie and Hettie Heineman Collection

(95)   Engraving for Rousseau, *Les confessions*

Monsiau provided seventeen of the thirty-five plates for this superb edition. His drawings for *La nouvelle Héloïse* in volumes two and three are more appealing than those of Cochin for *Emile* (see above, p. 28), though they seem somewhat stiff and posed when they are compared with the supremely easy and graceful designs which Moreau provided for Rousseau's novel in the edition of 1774–1783 (51). His designs for the *Confessions* in volumes 12 and 13 are more natural, perhaps because they deal exclusively with simple and homely episodes. One of them (XII, 270) shows Rousseau star-gazing, to the astonishment and terror of passing peasants.

Monsiau and other artists

96   PUBLIUS OVIDIUS NASO

Les métamorphoses d'Ovide, traduction nouvelle avec le texte latin . . . par M. G. T. Villenave; ornée de gravures d'après les dessins de MM. Le Barbier, Monsiau, et Moreau. Paris, F. Gay and Ch. Guestard, 1806. 4 v. I: lxvii, 331 p. II: [2] *l.*, 418 p. III: 460 p.

IV: [2] *l.*, 559 p. Illus: I: Front. by Hulk after Le Barbier; 34 plates after: Le Barbier by: Baquoy, Courbe (2), Dambrun (2), Delaunay (2), Halbou (3), Hulk, Thomas (3), and Trière; after Monsiau by: Courbe (4), Dambrun, Delvaux (2), de Ghendt, Hulk (3), Langlois (2), and Malbeste; after Moreau by: Delvaux, Hulk, Langlois, and Mariage; unsigned (1). II: 30 plates after Le Barbier by: Dambrun (2), Delaunay (2), Delvaux (3), Halbou, Hulk, and Malbeste; after Monsiau by: Baquoy (2), Boisse, Choffard, Delaunay, Delvaux (2), De Villiers, Fortier, Halbou (2), and Langlois; after Moreau by: Dambrun, Delaunay (2), De Villiers, Hulk, Mariage, and Thomas; unsigned (1). III: 28 plates after: Le Barbier by: Courbe, Delaunay (2), Delvaux, Halbou (2), Hulk, Mariage, and Saint-Aubin; after Monsiau by: Baquoy, Courbe (3), Delvaux, De Villiers, Halbou, and Hulk (2); after Moreau by: Baquoy, Courbe, Dambrun, Delaunay, Delvaux (2), De Villiers, Hulk, Pigeot, and Thomas. IV: 33 plates by: Chasselat after Courbe; after Duvuvier by: Adam (2), Cazenave, Courbe (6), Delvaux (2), Heina, Mariage (2), Migueret, Manceau (2), Villery (5); after Le Barbier by: Courbe, and Hulk; after Monsiau by: Delvaux, and Mariage; after Moreau by: Courbe (2), Delvaux, and Ponce; unsigned (1). Quarto issue, the plates *avant lettres*. Page size: 10⅞ ×8¼ inches. Contemp. ¼ calf. Cohen–de Ricci 773–774.

This puzzling book was obviously intended to be an edition of some pretensions. The publishers offered a new translation, secured Didot as their printer, and promised "144 engravings, the designs for which have been entrusted to M. Le Barbier, Monsiau, and Moreau" (I, xi). Anyone unwary enough to rely on Cohen (columns 773–774) would be led to believe that the book was carried through as planned. In fact, only a part of the engravings were made from drawings by the artists named. The rest are after various journeyman illustrators. And though all volumes have 1806 on their title pages, some of the plates in volume four are dated 1820 and 1821. It is not clear why the edition foundered. The designs by Le Barbier, Monsiau, and Moreau are of high professional competence, if in an outmoded style. Perhaps the mechanical nature of the engravings made from them disappointed the public. At any rate, there was evidently a long interval between the appearance of the first three volumes and the makeshift fourth with its pompous and inept concluding illustrations. Though vastly inferior to the edition of 1767–1771 (62), this book is worth acquiring for its plates after the three original illustrators. They offer a comprehensive sampling of the work done by these masters in their later years.

Despite its utilitarian binding, this is an exceptional copy. It is in the quarto format—there was also an octavo edition—for which the illustrations were provided with substantial borders. All plates are fine impressions before the letters.

🙟 Album of 107 drawings for Ovid's **Métamorphoses** (1806), in pen and ink and sepia wash, by: Le Barbier (front. and 42 drawings), Monsiau (41 drawings), and Moreau (23 drawings). Image size: 5⅞ × 3⅝ inches; sheet size: 9 × 6¾ inches. Green morocco (*remboîtage*). From the Portalis, Roederer, and Rosenbach collections.

The Pierpont Morgan Library, gift of Mrs. George Blumenthal

The survival of this splendid album provides an opportunity of judging the work of Monsiau, Moreau, and Le Barbier by their drawings rather than by the plates made from them. They are all in sepia wash and of the same size; indeed, the artists seem to have made every effort to achieve a homogeneous series. They are also of much higher quality than could be surmised from the engraved versions.

Monsiau, who is represented by forty-one drawings, undertook most of the scenes of violent action. In his depictions of battles, rescues, and abductions he usually employs many figures distributed in small groups. Because of the restricted size of the plates, these designs are apt to seem oppressively busy and crowded. However, most of the monsters who figure in the *Métamorphoses* also came his way, and with them he worked with ingenuity and obvious pleasure.

Moreau's twenty-three designs are very unequal. Sometimes, as in his drawing of a daughter pleading with her father to be allowed to keep her virginity, he approaches his former delicacy and precision. As the series proceeds, however, his distortions become pronounced, and some of his later plates border on the grotesque. The transformation scenes in this edition are less numerous and *outré* than those in the edition of 1767–1771, but that in which Moreau shows Byblis about to be changed into a fountain (for the plate at III, 258) does startle by the abundance of water gushing from her face.

Le Barbier's forty-three drawings are by all odds the most successful of the series. In composition and draftsmanship they show little decline from his best work. He deals for the most part with Ovid's idyllic episodes. An example is his conception of the Golden Age, shown on page 80 above. But he is not at a loss with more complex scenes, such as Bacchus welcomed by the populace (for the plate at II, 42). Attempting a brutal subject like the flaying of Marsyas by Apollo (for the plate at II, 358), he characteristically chooses the moment before this operation begins, and his drawing is agreeable rather than ghastly.

Cher auteur de mes jours, disait-elle, permets que je garde toujours ma virginité.

Drawing by Moreau for *Les métamorphoses*, 1806

(77)   Engraving after Fragonard, printed in color, for La Fontaine, *Contes et nouvelles*

(87)   Engraving after Monsiau, printed in color, for Vadé, *Oeuvres poissardes*

Paris. *Merveilleuse.* N.° 18.

Chapeau de paille Garni de Crêpe. Robe de Perkale Garnie de Mousseline.

(80) Hand-colored engraving after Horace Vernet for *Incroyables et merveilleuses*

Rosa centifolia Bullata.
Rosier à feuilles de Laitue.

(89)   Engraving after Redouté, printed in color, for *Les roses*

(135)   Retouched and hand-colored lithograph by Monnier for *Galerie théâtrale*

(139)   Hand-colored lithograph by Lami and Monnier for *Voyage en Angleterre*

Romantic Lithography

Thus far nearly all the illustrations described have been engravings on copper. After the Restoration, however, this graphic tradition reached the point of total exhaustion. It was replaced by the dazzling new process of lithography, by engraving on steel, and by a vigorous revival of the old and almost forgotten technique of engraving on wood. The reign of French Romantic lithography extended from 1817 to the 1850s. It is perhaps the greatest of all schools in the history of the medium. In England, according to Charles Hullmandel (*The Art of Drawing on Stone*, 1824), lithography was "despised and abused by artists of talent." For many years there was a prejudice against it as a cheap and low process. There are many fine English books and albums with lithographic plates, but they date from the 1830s and 1840s, and the artists employed were not of the first rank. In France, on the other hand, artists were fascinated from the first by lithography. Several of the master painters of the time used it in a major way, and others employed it on occasion. It was not merely a respected but a favored medium. Only in the 1850s did it lose its status. In 1855 La Combe (p. 133) wrote regretfully of "the sort of contempt into which lithography has fallen in the artistic world," and by 1877 Portalis, the champion of eighteenth-century illustration, could speak of it with some satisfaction as a "nebulous meteor" (I, xx). In the last years of the nineteenth century lithography again became of importance, among others with the creators of *livres de peintres*, but book collectors were slow to appreciate their work, which in any event had little in common with that of their predecessors.

Histories of French illustration have included Romantic lithographs only in the rare instances in which they figure specifically in books. An example is *Faust* (143), where Delacroix's plates happen to appear in this way, though they were originally to have been published as an album by Motte. Even Calot, who has provided the most detailed survey of French Romantic book illustration, omits "albums of prints with legends, which belong more particularly to the history of graphic art" (p. 161).

Yet it really does not suffice to assign lithographic albums to the print collector, whose immediate thought on seeing one is to break it up in order to add outstanding individual plates to his collection. Moreover, the omission of lithographic albums must severely distort any survey of illustration during the Romantic period. If what Beraldi (IX, 229) calls "the great period of caricature and the print of manners" is to be displayed, it can only be through albums. The work of artists like Daumier, Gavarni, and Grandville appeared indifferently in albums and books. In what follows, indeed, the careers of Bonington, Charlet, Daumier, Delacroix, Lami, Monnier, and Raffet are inevitably presented primarily in terms of their albums rather than the books which they illustrated. The rationale for albums just outlined also justifies the inclusion of selected periodicals of the time illustrated with lithographs, not only *La caricature* (160), which has always been a recognized prize of the book collector, but also such journals as *L'Artiste* (147), *La revue des peintres* (148), and *La silhouette* (146).

Albums and books with lithographs dealt with a wide variety of subjects during their heyday of four decades. The early part of the period saw the appearance of some of the greatest of all lithographs in the albums of Géricault. Topographical and architectural lithography reached its peak during the first fifteen years of Baron Taylor's *Voyages pittoresques dans l'ancienne France* (106–109). At the same time the albums of Charlet, Bellangé, and Raffet perpetuated the Napoleonic legend. During the 1820s contemporary life was shown in unprecedented breadth and liveliness in the colored plates of artists like Lami and Monnier. French Romantic literature was stimulated and documented by lithography, most notably in Delacroix's lithographs for *Faust*. Daumier and Gavarni, both lithographers by profession, provided the culminating achievements of this notable school in their scores of albums.

It is to be regretted that space will not serve to represent the caricaturists and depictors of manners who followed in the wake of Daumier and Gavarni. Among the most attractive of the former is Amédée de Noé, known as Cham (that is, Ham, the son of Noah), of whom it was said that he had "an idea a day" for *Le charivari*. A good proportion of his thousands of lithographs were gathered into albums. His contributions to the *Album du siège* (173), in which Daumier was his collaborator, are typical of his work. Charles Philipon and, somewhat later, Alfred Darjou should also be mentioned. Among depictors of manners Edouard de Beaumont, Frédéric Bouchot, and Charles Vernier would claim attention, if they were not overshadowed by Gavarni.

Some comment should be offered concerning the vexed question of contemporary coloring. With respect to the albums of the earliest period, 1817 to 1830, there is no problem. The lithographs of Taylor's *Voyages pittoresques*, Charlet's early work, Géricault's albums, and Delacroix's *Faust* were almost never colored, nor should they have been. On the other hand, the greyish tints of albums of the passing scene during the early 1820s are improved by color, and the outline lithographs of Lami and Monnier later in the decade are incomplete without it. In the last phase of Romantic lithography, the late 1840s and the 1850s, the rich blacks of Gavarni and of the two great collections, *Les artistes contemporains* and *Les artistes anciens et modernes*, would be profaned by color.

There is room for debate, however, concerning albums of the 1830s and the earlier 1840s. With regard to Daumier, the matter was settled by Laran (p. 17) in 1929: "The plates of Daumier have no need, thank God, of any collaboration, and it is a sufficiently stupid blunder to block out their whites and overcharge their blacks with color. It was done during the artist's lifetime, but for some time past it really has been done too much. We don't want to take their living away from the wretches who practice this reprehensible trade, but it is a question of saving the last surviving masterpieces in black and white, and we wish to warn those who take pride in mounting on their wall a plate from the *Bons bourgeois* 'with contemporary coloring' that they have irremediably framed their warrant as a philistine." Five years later Laran had the satisfaction of reporting (*Bibliothèque nationale: Daumier*, p. xxiv) that "specialists are now employed, at great trouble and expense, to remove the work of colorists." With regard to Gavarni the case is not so clear. As Laran noted, lithographic albums at this time were offered by Aubert both in color and in black and white, the former commanding a premium of 100% for *Les Robert-Macaire* (161) and 50% for most other albums. The coloring was often done with brilliance and precision. It is not known what Gavarni thought of the practice; he certainly made no concessions to it in his designs. Though purists may hold out for black and white, collectors have usually preferred his albums of this period in color, and they will no doubt continue to do so.

REFERENCES Adhémar (1938); Adhémar (1944); Beraldi; Bersier; Bouchot; Curtis (1897); Laran; Man (1953); Man (1970); Twyman; Weber.

Early Lithography

As will be seen from the plate reproduced, Aloys Senefelder (1771–1834) located his invention of lithography at Munich in 1796. The process came into use in other European countries in the years that followed. A number of "lithographic incunables" have survived from this period, most of them rare and all of historic interest, but only one significant album appeared, *Specimens of Polyautography* (London, 1803). Apart from occasional designs by such artists as Blake, Baron Gros, Guérin, Ingres, and Prud'hon, these early lithographs are not of great aesthetic interest.

As far as this survey is concerned, the story begins in 1816 when the first lithographic presses were established in Paris by Comte Charles Philibert de Lasteyrie (1759–1849) and Godefroy Engelmann (1788–1839). Soon afterwards Delpech, the Gihaut brothers, Lacroix, Martinet, Motte, Villain, and others also opened lithographic printing shops. Testimony to their activity is provided by Carle Vernet's well-known lithograph of Delpech's shop and a title page of 1818 by his son Horace of one of Delpech's street hawkers. Senefelder published a French version of his treatise on lithography in 1819, as well as a supplementary album of illustrations (97). Amateur artists, many of them from good society, tried their hands at the process. In short, the vogue of lithography was assured for some years to come.

The resources of the process were admittedly somewhat limited during this early period. Yet Bersier goes too far when he states (p. 3) that "the lithographs of the Restoration are for the most part only rather pale and timid reproductions of drawings on paper." In comparison with the rich blacks at the command of Daumier and Gavarni, the prints in these early albums may indeed seem grey, but there is nothing timid about Horace Vernet's *Croquis lithographiques* (98), Carle Vernet's *Cris de Paris* (121), or J.-B. Isabey's *Caricatures de J.J.* (101), not to mention the several albums of Géricault. Moreover, the prevailing grey was often tempered by hand coloring. Though the lithographs of the time were not made for coloring, as were those of Monnier and Lami a few years later, it was a frequent resource. The soft haziness resulting from the pastel shades employed can have its distinctive appeal.

In these early years of the lithographic album, France produced many more volumes of artistic significance than any other country. Elsewhere the process was used chiefly for reproductive purposes. This sometimes happened in France as well. It is explained in the preface to Girodet's *Les amours des dieux* of 1826, for example, that these unpublished drawings had been lithographed in order to get them to the public as soon as possible after the artist's death. But for the most part, French lithographic albums of this period are original work, though of course at varying levels of achievement.

REFERENCES Adhémar (1938); Beraldi; Bersier; Bouchot; *Horace Vernet*; Man (1953); Man (1970); Twyman; Weber.

97 ALOIS SENEFELDER

Collection de plusieurs essais en dessins et gravures pour servir de supplément à l'instruction pratique de la lithographie. N.p., 1819. Lithographic t.p. and 19 litho-

graphic plates, 1 printed in black, red, and blue, 2 printed with lithotint, by: Ant. Falger (2), N. H. Jacob (2), Alois Senefelder, Clem. Senefelder, E. Stunz, and unsigned (12). Page size: $11\frac{3}{4} \times 9\frac{1}{4}$ inches, uncut. Unbound.

(97) Senefelder, *Collection de plusieurs essais . . .*

In 1818 Senefelder had finally published an authoritative manual of lithography called *Vollständiges Lehrbuch der Steindruckerey* in Munich and Vienna. A supplement of twenty plates was also issued. *L'art de la lithographie*, the French translation of his treatise, appeared the following year. This is the separately issued portfolio of illustrations which accompanied it. In plate XV Senefelder claims that "Lithography, hardly out of the cradle, is already offering remarkable results. Supported more and more by the Genius of the fine arts, it will bring forth, everything leads one to believe, some amazing achievements, and will merit a front rank among the most ingenious modern inventions." He shows how lithography can reproduce engravings on metal, engravings on wood, etchings, pen and pencil drawings, and musical scores. There are also two lithographs printed in color, a scale of the various tones within the resources of the process, and the depiction of a lithographic press. Senefelder did not fail to include two pictorial tributes to himself and his invention. The second of these (IX) was

Carle Vernet, "Delpech's shop"

especially prepared for this French portfolio. Above the lithographic press are the names of Engelmann and Lasteyrie, and the sheet being pulled from a specifically Bavarian stone has a long list of artists who have worked in the medium, headed by the two Vernets and J.-B. Isabey.

Horace Vernet (1789–1863)

98 HORACE VERNET

Croquis lithographiques [Paris], Delpech, 1818 [with other plates]. Lithographic t.p. and 46 lithographic plates by H. Vernet; printed by Delpech and Engelmann. Page size: 13 ½ × 10 inches. ½ brown morocco, original wrapper entitled "Album lithographique" bound in. Beraldi XII, p. 117.

Beraldi (XII, 210) describes Horace Vernet's work as an illustrator as an *hors d'oeuvre* in comparison with his work as a painter. This may be, but he was nonetheless responsible for several fine books. We have already encountered him as the creator

of *Incroyables et merveilleuses* (80), and we shall see him again as the illustrator of Laurent de l'Ardèche's *Histoire de Napoléon* (203). His album of 1818, supplemented in this copy by a number of slightly later plates, contains some of his most characteristic designs as a lithographer. These designs, one of which is dated 1816, launched the Napoleonic epic in lithography, thus preparing the way for Charlet. There are many animated battle scenes, but Vernet's particular talent lies in showing the humor and pathos of a soldier's daily life, foraging for food or joking with his comrades. Two well-known scenes, typical in their sentiment, are "Soldier, I weep for you," one of Napoleon's men receiving the news of the Master's defeat, and "Near a tavern," a one-legged veteran and a little girl at play, with a rustic revel in the background. These plates have the pallor that is usual in the earliest French lithographic albums. Darker and richer blacks may be found in some of the added lithographs, notably those which give Vernet's impressions of dramatic episodes in Byron's poems: *The Bride of Abydos*, *The Corsair*, *Don Juan*, and *Mazeppa*.

Carle Vernet (1758–1836), Horace Vernet, and Hippolyte Lecomte (1781–1857)

99 JEAN DE LA FONTAINE

Fables choisies . . . ornées de figures lithographiques, de MM. Carle Vernet, Horace Vernet, et Hippolyte Lecomte. Paris, Lithographié d'Engelmann, 1818[–1820]. 2 v. I: [2, 56] *l*. II: [55] *l*. Illus: I: 62 lithographic plates by: Carle Vernet (30), Horace Vernet (10), Lecomte (19), and unsigned (3). II: 59 lithographic plates by: Carle Vernet (33), Horace Vernet (9), Lecomte (15), and unsigned (2). Page size: 10¾ × 15½ inches. Bookplate of Michael Sadleir. Contemp. ½ red morocco.

For this edition, commissioned by Engelmann, Carle Vernet signed sixty-three lithographs, his son Horace nineteen, and his son-in-law Hippolyte Lecomte thirty-four. Like most family undertakings, the enterprise required some closing of ranks. Carle Vernet's designs are almost uniformly admirable, Horace Vernet's are sometimes so (see "The young widow," book VI, fable 21), and Lecomte's are often deplorable. Nonetheless, this is certainly one of the notable sequences of illustrations for the *Fables*.

To demonstrate Carle Vernet's quality as an animal illustrator, discussed by Léopold Carteret in the letter quoted below, it should suffice to reproduce his lithograph for the fable of the bitch and her mate (book II, fable 7). Seeking shelter during an approaching pregnancy, the bitch persuades her friend to lend her his hut. When he seeks to repossess it some time later, she shows her teeth. She and her litter, now grown large, will leave if he can put them out. The astonishment of the rightful owner, the lean menace of the bitch, and the snappish defiance of the smaller dogs could not have been better realized by Oudry himself.

&❧ Léopold Carteret. Autograph letter signed to [Percy Muir], dated 7 July 1948. 4 p.

At the urging of Michael Sadleir, Muir had asked Carteret why he had not included La Fontaine's *Fables choisies* in his *Trésor du bibliophile romantique et moderne, 1801–1875*. Carteret admits that he "had never seen this book illustrated by the Vernets and Lecomte," and goes on to explain that, though the Vernets are talented artists ("Lecomte is a very small illustrator"), they are "not great animal painters." Hence he concluded that the book "should be held in low esteem. The production of romantic

(98) Horace Vernet, *Croquis lithographiques*

(98) Horace Vernet, *Croquis lithographiques*

(99)   Carle Vernet, lithograph for La Fontaine, *Fables choisies*

books was so considerable that I must be excused for limiting myself."

&ewline; "Imprimerie lithographique de F. Delpech." Lithographic print by C. Vernet. Sheet size: 7¼ × 10⅛ inches (caption trimmed).

This depiction of Delpech's emporium, drawn with Carle Vernet's usual warmth and animation, bears witness to the appeal that lithography had from the first for a wide spectrum of the public. Single prints could be examined outside the shop, albums within. A boy is carrying away a lithographic stone. It dates from about 1821.

Horace Vernet

100   MARIE FRANÇOIS AROUET DE VOLTAIRE

La Henriade, poëme . . . ornée de dessins lithographiques. Paris, E. Dubois, 1825. lx, 233 p., [1] *l.* Illus: Front. and 71 lithotint portraits by various artists, full-page lithographic fleuron after Dubois, and 18 lithographic plates by H. Vernet; printed by Delpech (10, on India paper), Engelmann (1, on India paper), Mme. Formentin (2, on India paper), Langlumé (1, lithotint), and unsigned (4, 2 on India paper, 2 lithotint). Page size: 15⅝ × 10¾ inches. Contemp. red morocco. Beraldi XII, p. 171–188.

A revival of interest in Voltaire's national epic during the Empire and the Restoration led to several

(100) Horace Vernet, lithograph
for Voltaire, *La Henriade*

new editions, of which this is by all odds the most imposing. Horace Vernet executed the eighteen large lithographs commissioned by Dubois, its publisher, between 1821 and 1825, and seventy-one portraits by other hands were added. (This copy has two versions of the portrait of Queen Elizabeth I at p. 16.) Vernet's lithographs are as carefully studied as those which Delacroix drew for *Faust* (143), but they are altogether without Delacroix's Romantic afflatus. Henri IV remains dignified throughout the numerous battle scenes, and even the assassination of Coligny in the massacre of Saint Bartholomew (p. 25) is a sober affair. A curiosity is the final full-page fleuron (p. 168) after Dubois, engraved in the best eighteenth-century manner, which makes an anachronistic appearance among these early lithographs.

Jean-Baptiste Isabey (1767–1855)

101 [Jean-Baptiste Isabey]

[Cover title:] **Caricatures de J.J.** Paris, l'Auteur & Alphonse Giroux, 1818. 12 hand-colored lithographic plates; printed by C. Motte. Sheet size: 10⅛ × 13½ inches, uncut. Bookplate of Michael Sadleir. Orig. wrappers.

These twelve pseudonymous designs were the pastimes of Jean-Baptiste Isabey, a miniature painter of repute, who was the father of Eugène Isabey. Of great verve and spirit in themselves, their grotesque figures, tall or short, fat or thin, provide a link with

English caricature of the previous quarter of a century, particularly the work of Thomas Rowlandson. Isabey's situations are as gross and indelicate as his people. Indeed, "A game of whist" (plate x) is among the least *outré* of his designs. This album foreshadows what was to be the prevailing style among caricaturists of manners in the early 1820s, and plate xi anticipates Traviès' conception of M. Mayeux (see pp. 198–199 below). The series is far livelier than another set of lithographs by Isabey, to which he signed his name, the thirty plates of his *Voyage en Italie* of 1822.

(101) Jean-Baptiste Isabey, *Caricatures de J.J.*

Théodore Géricault (1791–1824)

The thirty-three years of Géricault's life sufficed to establish him as one of the greatest of French painters, as well as one of the masters of lithography. He made his first lithograph on his return from Italy in 1817, his last in 1823, not long before his death. Delteil could find only seventy-eight plates entirely from his hand. His scattered early lithographs have a variety of subjects. Like Horace Vernet, he helped his friend Charlet to give form to the Napoleonic epic with his scenes of military life. He drew portraits, and even a notable study of a boxing match (Delteil, 10). But almost from the first horses were his great artistic preoccupation; indeed two-thirds of his lithographs were to be equestrian.

Géricault went to London in 1820 to exhibit his famous "Raft of the Medusa," which achieved a success which had hardly come its way in the Paris Salon of the previous year. While there he made thirteen lithographs (including the title) printed in 1821 by Charles Hullmandel for an album entitled *Various Subjects Drawn from Life and on Stone*. According to Géricault himself (Beraldi, VII, 92), they had "an inconceivable vogue." This so-called "English Set" is his masterpiece, and one of the greatest of all lithographic works. Horses continue to predominate in these large designs, yet they also constitute a somber and powerful panorama of English working-class life, which was later to be extended by Gavarni (157) and Doré (251). Such plates as "The piper" (Delteil, 30) and "Pity the sorrows of a poor old man" (Delteil, 31) suggest that, if Géricault had lived, he might have created a human comedy as monumental as Daumier's.

Géricault's work after his return to France in 1821 is of a somewhat different character, less moving and imposing, but livelier and lighter in touch. The albums *Etudes de chevaux lithographiés* of 1822 and *Croquis lithographiques* of 1823 contain many of his works in this style. All the subjects are equestrian. His study of a horse devoured by a lion (Delteil, 67) from the latter album is the most ambitious of these lithographs. In another series of 1823, *Quatre sujets divers*, he returned to the more

spacious and solid manner of his "English Set," as is exampled in "Farm horses" (Delteil, 73).

Géricault's energy, his sense of drama, and his mastery of composition, together with the rich blacks that he knew how to elicit from his crayon, have placed his lithographs among the great prizes of the print collector. His "English Set" is now even further out of the reach of the amateur of illustrated books than are the major albums of Daumier. Though his lesser albums can still be found, they will probably not be available for long.

REFERENCES Beraldi; Curtis; Delteil—*Géricault*.

102 THÉODORE GÉRICAULT

[Cover title:] **Etudes de chevaux lithographiés** . . . Paris, Gihaut, 1822. 12 lithographic plates by Géricault; printed by Engelmann. Delteil 46–57, second states (no. 48 in first state).

103 THÉODORE GÉRICAULT

[Cover title:] **Croquis lithographiques.** Paris, Gihaut, 1823. 10 lithographic plates by Géricault; printed by Engelmann and Villain. Delteil 58–67, second states (the wrapper unrecorded).

104 JOSEPH VOLMAR

[Cover title:] **Chevaux d'après Géricault** par Volmar. [Paris], Gihaut, 1823. 4 lithographic plates by Volmar after Géricault; printed by Villain. Delteil Appendix, 3–6.

105 THÉODORE GÉRICAULT

[Cover title:] **Quatre sujets divers.** Paris, Mme. Hulin, 1823. 4 lithographic plates by Géricault; printed by Engelmann. Delteil 73–75, second states. Page size: $10\frac{1}{8} \times 13\frac{1}{2}$ inches. Bookplate of Michael Sadleir. Four albums bound together in contemp. (publisher's?) brown cloth.

(102)   Géricault, *Croquis lithographiques*

(105)   Géricault, *Quatre sujets divers*

Baron Taylor and the Picturesque

During his prodigious career of ninety years, Baron Isidore Taylor (1789–1879), born of English parents in Brussels, was a professional soldier, a diplomat, a governmental administrator, a dramatist, a writer, an artist, and a collector. His great object in life, however, was to celebrate the scenery and the medieval architecture of his adopted country in *Voyages pittoresques et romantiques dans l'ancienne France*, a work which appeared in nineteen large-folio volumes between 1820 and 1878. Taylor conceived this almost Napoleonic dream in 1810, but he realized that engraving the required illustrations would be impossibly laborious and expensive. He returned to his project in 1818 after lithography had emerged as an artistic medium. Believing that the new process "should be for the arts of drawing what typography had been for literature" (preface to *Dauphiné*, 1854), he obtained financial support from the government and put a band of painters to work, with such success that he was able to publish the first volume of *Ancienne Normandie* two years later.

The plates of the *Voyages pittoresques* are largely of landscape and buildings, the latter predominating in the later volumes. They have a certain family likeness, imposed by their topographical-architectural subjects and their similarity of format. The plates were printed on China paper and mounted. There are also many vignettes on the paper of the edition itself, and in *Languedoc* and *Picardie* an abundance of massive ornamental and pictorial borders. The major artists involved significantly in the undertaking were Bonington and Eugène Isabey (1803–1886), but over 150 are represented in all. In the first nine volumes, our particular concern, the chief designers were Adrien Dauzats (1804–1868), the most frequent contributor by a wide margin; Louis Bichebois (1801–1850), Nicolas Chapuy (1790–1858), Alexandre Fragonard (1780–1850), his son Théophile Fragonard (1806–1876), Louis Haghe (1806–1885), James Duffield Harding (1797–1863), and Léon Sabatier (d. 1887). It may be noted that Louis-Jacques-Mandé Daguerre made lithographs for the first five volumes, before he turned his attention to photography.

Taylor's intention had been to cover the whole of France in his survey, but in the event he was able to describe only nine provinces. The pace of the edition slowed as the years went by. His time was pre-empted by other work; and there were complaints about the heavy subsidy which the publication required. Though ten volumes had appeared by 1837, the remaining nine took forty-one years, and the last of these, the third volume of *Normandie*, was illustrated with lithographs made decades earlier. After *Languedoc* the plates are not numbered, but the total has been estimated as between 2,700 and 3,000 (Twyman, p. 231).

The spirit in which the *Voyages pittoresques* was undertaken is set forth in Charles Nodier's eloquent preface to the first volume. Speaking for Taylor and Cailleux as well as for himself, the "last travellers among the ruins of old France" (p. 8), he begins by suggesting what imagination can read into the plates which will follow. "It is not as scholars that we wander through France, but as travellers curious about its interesting aspects and eager for noble memories" (p. 4). Even local legends are worthy of their notice. Since they seek the picturesque and Romantic, scenery is an object as well as architectural remains. Particular attention will be given to ruins that are about to disappear and to scenes with moving historical associations. Nodier goes on to explain why they have turned to lithography to accomplish their purpose. The process is still regarded with scepticism, but it offers many advantages. "Freer, more original, and more rapid than the graver, the bold crayon of the lithographer seems to have been invented to fix once for all the free, original, and rapid inspirations of the traveller who wishes to account to himself for his responses" (p. 10). Given the eminence of artists who are collaborating, the *Voyages pittoresques* will be the means by which lithography will develop, thus furnishing its advocates with "the most powerful, the most irrefutable of their arguments" (p. 11).

Taylor's title promises that his travels will be not only picturesque but Romantic. The picturesque mode had established itself in the later eighteenth century, and he was thus far returning to a familiar kind of illustration after its neglect during decades of neoclassical dominance. The word *Romantic* promised something less familiar as far as views were concerned, an emphasis on buildings rather than landscape, and in particular on the architectural remains of the Middle Ages: churches, castles, indeed Gothic ruins of all descriptions. Adhémar (pp. 269–272) has shown how the imagination of Hugo, Balzac, and other authors was stirred by these images. Their use of medieval settings in their writings had a powerful influence in turn on artists. For example, the Languedoc volumes of the *Voyages pittoresques* may be regarded as the counterpart in lithography of Hugo's exactly contemporary *Notre-Dame de Paris*. Their hundreds of borders are filled with ornaments and vignettes after the fashion of medieval manuscripts. Indeed, Célestin Nanteuil's lithographed frames are as compellingly Romantic as his etchings and wood engravings.

The *Voyages pittoresques* was sent to its subscribers in parts, each volume typically requiring years to achieve completion. The number of copies printed, as recorded by Adhémar, declined as the series progressed: *Normandie*, 600; *Franche Comté*, 500; *Auvergne*, 500; *Languedoc*, 350; *Picardie*, 350; *Bretagne*, 300; *Dauphiné*, 300. The set is now almost unfindable complete, but fortunately its interest for the collector of illustrated books lies chiefly in the volumes through *Languedoc*, and to a lesser degree *Picardie*, which still appear from time to time. They are well worth seeking out, for Taylor's work, given both the quality and the quantity of its plates, may fairly be called the greatest of all publications illustrated with lithographs.

As Jean Adhémar remarks in his survey of topographical and architectural albums of Romantic lithographs, the *Voyages pittoresques* were "at once the model and the best example" of these publications (p. 191). He lists 746 albums which appeared between 1817 and 1854. Taken together they provide a vast anthology of views. The bulk of them are concerned with the scenery and buildings of old France, the first now transformed almost beyond recognition, the second often entirely destroyed. In the remaining albums French lithographers extended their attention to many other countries. With four exceptions the *Voyages pittoresques* must stand for this immense production in our survey: an *oeuvre* of Bonington, Pernot's *Vues pitto-*

resques dans l'Ecosse, Croquis par divers artistes, and Milbert's *Itinéraire pittoresque du fleuve Hudson*; but mention may at least be made of two other albums of exceptional interest: Chapuy's *Vues pittoresques des cathédrales,* 1823–1831, and A. Regnier's *Habitations des personnages les plus célèbres de France,* 1831–1834. Examples of topographical-architectural lithographs also abound in *L'Artiste* (147) and *La revue des peintres* (148).

REFERENCES Adhémar (1938); Beraldi; Bouchot; Curtis (1897); Twyman.

106 CHARLES NODIER

Voyages pittoresques et romantiques dans l'ancienne France, par MM. Ch. Nodier, J. Taylor, et Alph. Cailleux. [*Ancienne Normandie*]. Paris, P. Didot l'aîné, 1820[-1825] 2 v. I: [5] *l.,* 131 p., [5] *l.* II: 190 p., [2] *l.* Lithographic illus: Added t.p. vignette, t.p. vignette, numerous tailpieces, 82 plates, and numerous outline *croquis* by Baron Taylor. II: Plates 82–182 [i.e., 232], 2 *bis* plates, and many outline *croquis* by Baron Taylor. Many plates with lithotint, printed on *chine appliqué.* Page size: 20¾ × 13¾ inches. Contemp. calf. Beraldi XII, p. 91–93.

(106) Lithograph by Daguerre after Taylor for *Ancienne Normandie*

(106) Lithograph by Bonington for *Ancienne Normandie*

Among all the volumes in the *Voyages pittoresques* the 388 lithographs of *Ancienne Normandie* offer the freshest and most varied designs. A number of the earlier plates by Taylor are in two states, and the many tinted lithographs make one regret that this resource was soon abandoned. Baron Atthalin, the elder Fragonard, and Louis Villeneuve (1796–1842) are the illustrators most generally employed, and they have responded with rich and harmonious conceptions. There are lively vignettes in which the artist has given his fancy play without documentary restraint, among them Géricault's study of William the Conqueror lying in state at the Abbey of Saint-Georges de Bocherville (II, 45) and Horace Vernet's sketch of the Princess Marguerite strangled for adultery at the Château Gaillard (II, 125). But the triumphs of *Ancienne Normandie* are the five lithographs by Bonington. Nothing could be more remote from the usual architectural print than these brilliant renderings of human activity. They culminate in two designs which are among the masterpieces of all lithography. In the background of the first are two splendid houses in the ornate Italian taste of the fifteenth century ("Rue du gros horloge, Rouen," plate 173), in the background of the second is a powerful yet graceful tower built in 1417 during the English occupation ("Tour du gros-horloge, Evreux," plate 226). In the foreground of each townspeople of 1824 are going about their routine affairs. This contrast of extraordinary past and commonplace present is what the *Voyages pittoresques* is all about.

107 CHARLES NODIER

Voyages pittoresques et romantiques dans l'ancienne France, par MM. Ch. Nodier, J. Taylor, et Alph. de Cailleux. [*Franche-Comté*]. Paris, P. Didot l'aîné, 1825. [4] *l.*, 222 p. Lithographic illus: Front., t.p. vignette, numerous tailpieces, and 148 plates. The plates are printed on *chine appliqué*. Page size: 21¼ × 13¾ inches, uncut. Contemp. ½ red morocco. Beraldi XII, p. 93–94.

After describing the success of "the immense exploration of France during the Middle Ages" (p. 1) that he and his associates have undertaken, Nodier speaks with some disdain of their numerous imitators. Conceding that Franche-Comté can hardly compare with Normandy in architectural remains and historical associations, he urges that it is nonetheless rich in natural beauty, particularly in the Jura. And indeed the views of mountain scenery are what one chiefly recalls from this volume. The artists most in evidence are still Baron Atthalin, the elder Fragonard, and Villeneuve, but its best plates come from the English collaborators. Bonington is represented by ten lithographs (five made from drawings by others), which for the most part are inferior to those in *Ancienne Normandie*. This rural province did not offer the dazzling buildings and scenes of busy life that inspired his earlier masterpieces. Harding's designs, smaller in scale than is customary in the *Voyages pittoresques*, are among the finest of all lithographic landscapes. He rarely matched the delicacy and compositional mastery of such plates as "Gorge du Mont Terrible" (plate 129) in his later work. Louis Haghe and Samuel Prout (here invariably called "Proust") also make their appearance. There is a curious vignette by Ingres (p. 13), one of the nine lithographs of his career, of "the four magistrates who governed Besançon, when it was a free city" (p. 208).

108 CHARLES NODIER

Voyages pittoresques et romantiques dans l'ancienne France, par MM. Ch. Nodier, J. Taylor, et Alph. de Cailleux, [*Auvergne*]. Paris, P. Didot l'aîné, 1829[–1833]. Vol. 1 only (of 2). 4, 9, 133 p. Illus: Front., t.p. vignette, large initials, and 134 (of 272) plates. The plates are printed on *chine appliqué*. Page size: 21½ × 14¼ inches, uncut. Unbound. Beraldi XII, p. 94–97.

Like Franche-Comté, as Nodier points out, Auvergne is a province in which scenery takes precedence over antiquities. The wild grandeur of its mountains is relieved by the pastoral grace of its valleys. Yet it is not lacking in castles and old churches. The artists who best took advantage of these opportunities in the first volume of *Auvergne* were Eugène Isabey, the son of Jean-Baptiste Isabey, Dauzats, Sabatier, and Harding. Isabey's contributions rank with Bonington's in *Ancienne Normandie* as the finest in the *Voyages pittoresques*. Beraldi saw in his plates "the picturesque pushed to the extreme, more of *chic* than of truth" (XII, 96), but

(107) Lithograph by Harding for *Franche-Comté*

(108) Lithograph by Eugène Isabey for *Auvergne*

this is surely a perverse judgment. Isabey's ability to make his compositions dramatic through selection and contrast is his greatest asset after his suave and opulent manner of drawing. In any event, his eleven lithographs in this volume are among his more restrained productions. The chief set piece, indeed, is the "Abside extérieure de l'église Saint Nectaire" (plate 108), which few people would wish less personal and original. This was the first volume of the *Voyages pittoresques* in which Dauzats had a major role. His bold, free, open lithographs, unusually large in scale, brought a breath of fresh air to a work in which the plates of the older artists were coming to seem too studied and careful. Sabatier makes his impression in much the same manner with a series of sweeping panoramas, and Harding's designs are scarcely inferior to those which he made for *Franche-Comté*. There is a vignette of Vercingetorix by Delacroix which is sometimes overlooked because it is signed "Lacroix."

109   CHARLES NODIER

Voyages pittoresques et romantiques dans l'ancienne France, par MM. Ch. Nodier, J. Taylor, et Alph. de Cailleux. [*Le Languedoc*]. Paris, Firmin Didot frères, 1833[–1837]. 2 v. in 4. Illus: Lithographic vignettes, borders, tailpieces, and 591 plates. Plates are printed on *chine appliqué*. Page size: 21 1/8 × 13 3/4 inches, uncut. Contemp. 1/4 green morocco. Beraldi XII, p. 97–99.

After *Ancienne Normandie*, *Languedoc* is perhaps the most impressive of the sections of the *Voyages pittoresques*. Its plates are of generally high quality, with Dauzats as the dominant artist. Sabatier, Harding, and another Englishman, Thomas Shotter Boys (1803–1874), also make contributions of importance. But the great novelty of the work, a renewal of inspiration indeed for the whole project, lies in the elaborate borders provided for its almost 800 pages of text. Though these frames are sometimes repeated, the continuing inventiveness required for their design must have been even more demanding than for the creation of the plates themselves. The architectural-restorer Eugène Viollet-le-Duc provided the majority of these adornments, and he was aided by Théophile Fragonard and others. Yet it remained for Célestin Nanteuil to make them unforgettable in the chapters on Mois-

sac and to a lesser extent Narbonne. The final page of the former, with its vignette of the struggle of angel and devil for the soul of a dying Christian (volume one, part one), is characteristic in its combination of passionate feeling and luxuriant abundance.

Jacques-Gérard Milbert (1766–1840)

110

Itinéraire pittoresque du fleuve Hudson et des parties latérales de l'Amérique du Nord, d'après les dessins originaux pris sur les lieux, par J. Milbert . . . et lithographiés par Adam, Bichebois, Deroy, Dupressoir, Jacottet, Joly, Sabatier, Tirpenne et Villeneuve . . . Paris, Henry Gaugain, 1828–1829. Text v. I (of two). Illus: 53 lithographic plates after Milbert (52) by: Arnout (2), Bichebois (3), Bichebois & Adam (9), Deroy (8), Deroy & Adam, Dupressoir & Adam (4), Jacottet & Adam (2), Joly (2), Sabatier (5), Sabatier & Adam (6), Sabatier & Bichebois & Adam, Tirpenne, Tirpenne & Adam (3), Villeneuve (2), and Villeneuve & Adam (2); after J. R. Smith by Dupressoir & Adam; plate 51 unsigned and uncaptioned. Printed by Ardit (6, 12, 33), Bove (1–5, 7–11, 13–24, 27, 43), Gaugain (25, 26, 28–32, 34–42, 44–50, 52–53). Bound in at end is the lithographic map by Toquet; all plates are printed on *chine appliqué*. Page size (plates): 13 1/4 × 16 1/4 inches. Publisher's 1/4 purple cloth. Sabin 48916.

The painter Milbert set out for the United States in 1815 as a correspondent of the Museum of Natural History in Paris. He remained for seven years, sending back to France almost 8000 specimens of American flora and fauna. He also brought home many sketches from which fifty-two lithographs for his book were made by such artists as Adam, Bichebois, Sabatier, and Villeneuve. For the most part they are views of the Hudson river and the towns along its course, though other northeastern states receive some attention. The powerful influence of the *Voyages pittoresques* on French topographical lithography is everywhere evident in these plates. Indeed, their scenic panoramas, falls, rapids, and striking rock formations are so relentlessly picturesque that the eye welcomes occasional city views like that of Church Street in New York City (plate 3) or the house of the first Dutch governor in Albany (plate 14). It is clear, however, that the three views of Niagara Falls (plates 34 to 36) were the successes of the series. Milbert's sec-

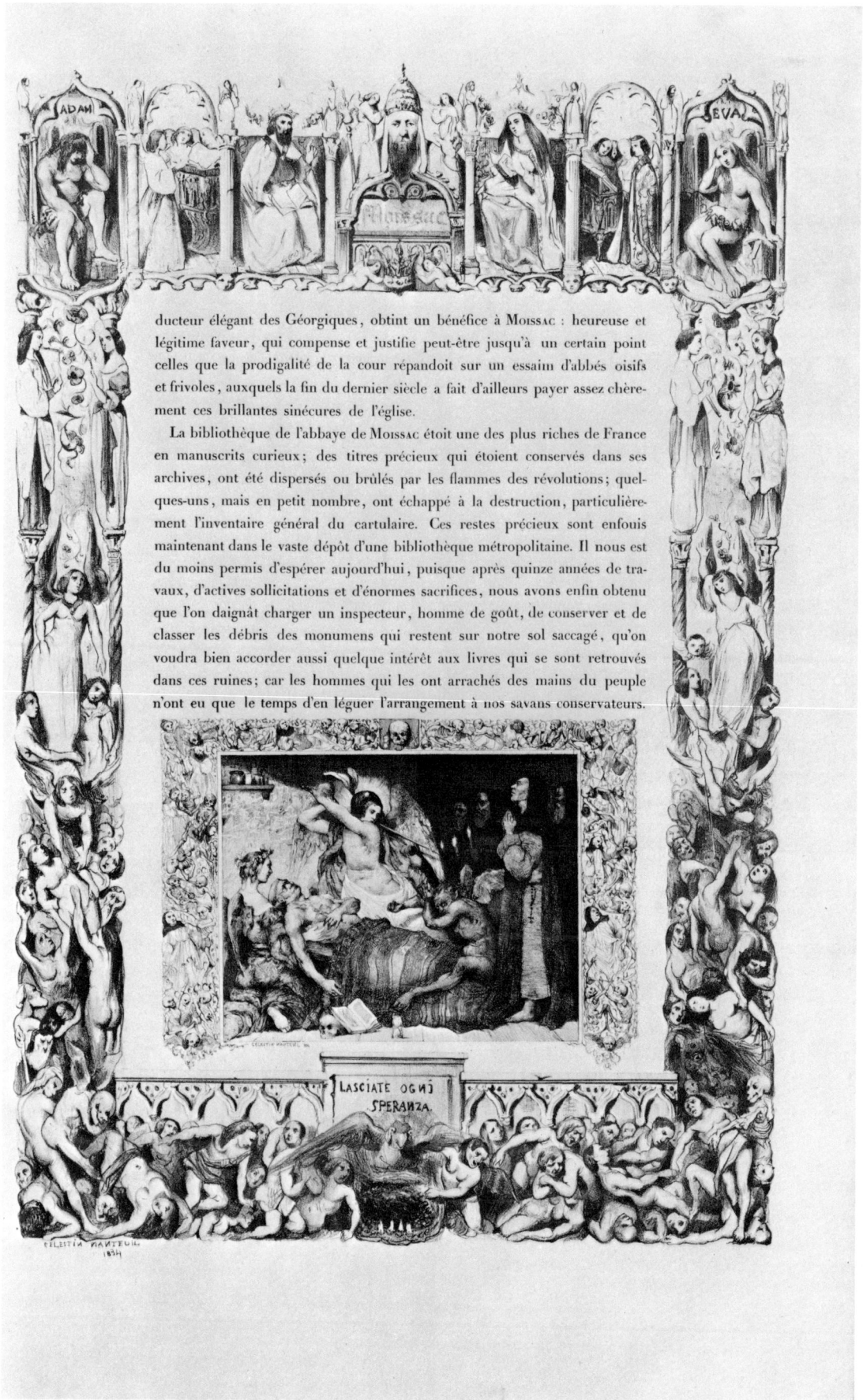

ducteur élégant des Géorgiques, obtint un bénéfice à MOISSAC : heureuse et
légitime faveur, qui compense et justifie peut-être jusqu'à un certain point
celles que la prodigalité de la cour répandoit sur un essaim d'abbés oisifs
et frivoles, auxquels la fin du dernier siècle a fait d'ailleurs payer assez chère-
ment ces brillantes sinécures de l'église.

La bibliothèque de l'abbaye de MOISSAC étoit une des plus riches de France
en manuscrits curieux ; des titres précieux qui étoient conservés dans ses
archives, ont été dispersés ou brûlés par les flammes des révolutions ; quel-
ques-uns, mais en petit nombre, ont échappé à la destruction, particulière-
ment l'inventaire général du cartulaire. Ces restes précieux sont enfouis
maintenant dans le vaste dépôt d'une bibliothèque métropolitaine. Il nous est
du moins permis d'espérer aujourd'hui, puisque après quinze années de tra-
vaux, d'actives sollicitations et d'énormes sacrifices, nous avons enfin obtenu
que l'on daignât charger un inspecteur, homme de goût, de conserver et de
classer les débris des monumens qui restent sur notre sol saccagé, qu'on
voudra bien accorder aussi quelque intérêt aux livres qui se sont retrouvés
dans ces ruines ; car les hommes qui les ont arrachés des mains du peuple
n'ont eu que le temps d'en léguer l'arrangement à nos savans conservateurs.

(109)   Border by Nanteuil for *Languedoc*

(110)   Lithograph by Milbert for *Itinéraire pittoresque du fleuve Hudson*

ond American publication in 1829, *Amérique septentrionale: Vues des chutes du Niagara*, extended his coverage of this marvel of nature in a spectacular way.

Eugène Isabey, Alexandre Decamps (1803–1860), and others

111

[Croquis par divers artistes. Paris, Rittner, 1830]. 62 (of 72) lithographic plates by: Bellangé (4), Charlet (4), Decamps (20), Gavarni, Isabey (10), Lamy (4), Lepoittevin (6), Mozin (8), Roqueplan (2), Tassaert, and Tirpenne (2); printed by: Bichebois aîné (2), Frey, Lemercier (55), and Villain (4). Page size: 10¼ × 14⅛ inches. Contemp. green cloth.

This uncommon album of unpretentious sketches, the quick responses of artists to little scenes that caught their fancy, has two claims to attention. It marks the first phase in the lithographic career of Eugène Isabey. He was primarily a painter, but between 1830 and 1833 he concentrated on lithography, making sixty-two of the 109 plates assigned to him by Atherton Curtis. Three works contain the majority of these lithographs: *Croquis par divers artistes* with thirteen, Taylor's *Auvergne* (108) with seventeen, and his masterpiece, *Six marines* of 1833. Thus even the ten plates in this incomplete copy of *Croquis par divers artistes* (Curtis, nos. 10 to 19, with first states of 15 and 17) have their interest. The album contains as well twenty lithographs by Alexandre Decamps, another early master of landscape lithography, whose influence on the development of its style was second only to that of Bonington (Adhémar, p. 254). Also represented are Bellangé, Charlet, Gavarni, and Lami.

Richard Parkes Bonington (1802-1828)

Bonington was born near Nottingham in 1802. His father was a teacher of drawing. Involvement in the lacemaking business caused the family to move to Calais in 1817 and to Paris in 1820. Bonington learned watercolor painting from Louis Francia and afterwards entered the studio of Baron Gros. He first began to exhibit in 1822, and he died of tuberculosis six years later. Though his artistic career was so short, he can hardly be called an "inheritor of unfulfilled renown," since he made a lasting mark both as a painter and a lithographer. His best epitaph is to be found in what Sir Thomas Lawrence wrote to a friend on the day of his funeral: "Alas! for Bonington! your presage has been fatally verified. The last duties have been paid to him this day. Except in the case of Mr. Harlowe, I have never known in my own time the early death of talent so promising and so rapidly and obviously improving. If I may judge from the later direction of his studies and from remembrance of a morning's conversation, his mind seemed expanding every way, and ripening into full maturity of taste and elevated judgment, with that generous ambition which makes confinement to lesser departments in the arts painfully irksome and annoying." (Quoted on the title page of Harding's *Series of Subjects from the Works of the late R. P. Bonington*.)

The "lesser departments in the arts" to which Lawrence referred included lithography. Atherton Curtis lists only sixty plates by Bonington, of which about a third are from the designs of other artists. Nonetheless, his importance in the development of lithography can hardly be overstated. Of his plates for *Ancienne Normandie* (106) Adhémar writes (p. 253) that they "set the themes which will be those of picturesque landscape to its end, . . . and above all created the style which will make it possible to render them." Delacroix learned much from him when they worked together in 1825–1826, and Eugène Isabey was his avowed disciple.

Bonington's first lithographs appeared in an album called *Restes et fragmens d'architecture du moyen âge*. There ensued his superb plates for *Ancienne Normandie* and *Franche-Comté* (107) in Taylor's *Voy-*

ages pittoresques. After this beginning, the remainder of his lithographs are something of an anticlimax, which perhaps explains why he told Lawrence that the medium had become "irksome and annoying" to him. Nevertheless, his designs for *Vues pittoresques de l'Écosse* and *Contes du gay sçavoir* are by no means negligible. Bonington's career as a lithographer was short but splendid.

REFERENCES Adhémar (1938); Beraldi; Bouchot; Curtis—*Bonington*; Musée Jacquemart-André.

❧ Richard Parkes Bonington. An *oeuvre* of 94 engraved and lithographic plates by and after Bonington, formed by J. Carpenter. Page size: 21 ¼ × 14 ½ inches. Bookplate of Napoléon III. Contemp. ¾ brown morocco.

This truly remarkable collection of ninety-four plates by and after Bonington was put together by J. Carpenter, the Pall Mall publisher who issued Harding's *Series of Subjects from the Works of the late R. P. Bonington* in 1830. There is a descriptive entry on its final page copied from a note by "S.A.I. le Prince Napoléon," who purchased the album from Carpenter, it would appear in June of 1849. The collection includes twenty-six lithographs by Bonington, among them "La petite Normandie" and thirteen of his "Scotch sketches." His one completed etching, "Bologna," is present in two early states. These things can be found elsewhere, however, and it is the sixty-eight remaining plates which make the album unique. They represent Carpenter's exhaustive effort to bring together all contemporary lithographs and engravings after Bonington, most of them English in origin, to supplement Harding's *Series of Subjects*. Particularly impressive are four mezzotint engravings by S. W. Reynolds and eight large aquatints of coast and river scenes, chiefly in Normandy.

112 RICHARD PARKES BONINGTON

[Restes et fragmens d']Architecture du moyen âge. [Paris, 1824]. Lithographic t.p. and 9 lithographic plates by Bonington, printed by Feillet. All but the final plate printed on yellow paper. Bound in the *oeuvre*, page size varies. Beraldi XII, p. 159.

EGLISE ST SAUVEUR.

(112)   Bonington, *Restes et fragmens d'architecture du moyen âge*

Bonington's first lithographs were issued on several kinds of paper: white, China, and colored. Except for one plate which appeared belatedly in 1827, this set is on yellow paper. Such uniformity is rare. The album is customarily called "La petite Normandie" to distinguish it from Bonington's larger plates in *Ancienne Normandie* (106). As will be seen from the lithograph of "Eglise Saint Sauveur," a Gothic church sheltering a lively marketplace, he has already established his characteristic way of approaching a subject. Other plates in the series, "La tour du marché" in Bergues with its medieval tower and "Maison grande rue Saint-Pierre" in Caen with its rich residential façades, are studies on a smaller scale for what were to be Bonington's two finest plates in *Ancienne Normandie*.

113 Amédée Pichot

Vues pittoresques de l'Ecosse, dessinées d'après nature par F. A. Pernot; lithographiées par Bonington, David, Deroi . . . etc.; ornées de douze vignettes d'après les dessins de Delaroche jeune et Eugène Lami; avec un texte explicatif extrait en grande partie des ouvrages de Sir Walter Scott, par Am. Pichot. Paris, Charles Gosselin et Lami–Denozan, 1826. [2] *l.*, viii, 127 p. Illus: T.p. vignette by Lami, 12 vignettes by: Bonington (2), Lami (7), Lami after Delaroche (2), and Lami and Sabatier (1); 60 lithographic plates by: Bichebois (4), Bonington (11), David (8), Deroy (9), Enfantin, Francia, Golain (2), Jacottet (9), Joly (4), Sabatier (7), and Villeneuve (4); printed by Villain. Page size: 13⅛ × 9¾ inches. Contemp. ½ brown morocco; portions of original wrappers bound in.

(113)   Pichot, *Vues pittoresques de l'Ecosse*

Bonington contributed eleven plates to this volume based on the designs of F.-A. Pernot, as well as two vignettes that he had himself composed. Curtis thinks it likely that he treated his models with some freedom, putting "a good deal of his own in them." It is known, indeed, that Pernot found his lithographs "too romantic." The vignettes, both scenes from Scott's novels, are remarkable for their dramatic force, as is shown in his drawing of the duel between Francis Obaldistone and his villainous cousin Rashleigh from *Rob Roy* (p. 115). In 1828 Colnaghi published *Scotch Sketches drawn on stone by the late R. P. Bonington*, comprising his thirteen contributions to the *Vues pittoresques*, with captions in English. India proofs of these are present in the *oeuvre* described above.

It should be mentioned that the *Vues pittoresques* offers a very favorable example of the depiction of foreign scenery by French lithographers. Harding, Sabatier, and Villeneuve were among the artists who joined Bonington in rendering Pernot's designs for the plates, while Eugène Lami drew all but one of the ten remaining vignettes. The latter series is among the most spirited and engaging of all illustrations of Scott's fiction.

113A

Another copy, as above, but with all illustrations hand-colored; lacking the section title (pp. 1–2). Page size: 12½ × 9¼ inches. Contemp. (publisher's?) ¾ brown morocco.

Careful contemporary coloring, in which the blues of sky and water and the greens of forest and meadow predominate, decidedly enhances the appeal of the plates in this copy. The vignettes, on the other hand, are obviously to be preferred in black and white.

114 Joseph Adolphe Ferdinand Langlé

Les contes du gay sçavoir. Ballades, Fabliaux et traditions du moyen âge . . . ornés de vignettes et fleurons, imités des manuscrits originaux par Bonington et Monnier. Paris, Firmin Didot pour Lami Denozan, 1828. [4] *l.*, cxlvi, 48 p. Illus: Lithographic t.p. and 10 lithographic vignettes by Bonington (6) and Monnier (4). The vignettes are printed on thin paper and pasted in place. Woodcut initials are colored; vignettes are plain. Bound in are 82 leaves of manuscript fables. Page size: $8 \times 4\frac{7}{8}$ inches. Contemp. blue morocco. Brunet II, 819.

(114) Langlé, *Les contes du gay sçavoir*

Bonington's seven lithographs for this medieval miscellany, printed in Gothic type with historiated initial letters, were made with pen rather than crayon and printed on China paper. They are intentionally primitive in conception. The title page supports Bouchot's contention (p. 91) that Bonington may be commenting ironically on the *Hours of Simon Vostre*. Henry Monnier's four lithographs are in the same spirit. This copy, which is in a pretty *plaque* binding of the period, has eighty-two manuscript leaves of further medieval narratives.

115 RICHARD PARKES BONINGTON

A series of subjects from the works of the late R. P. Bonington, drawn on stone by J. D. Harding . . . London, J. Carpenter, [1830]. Lithographic portrait, t.p., and 20 lithographic plates by Harding after Bonington; printed by Hullmandel. Plates are printed on *chine appliqué* except "Maternal solicitude" and "Church of St. Sauveur," which are lithotints. The captions and imprints on all plates except "Church of St. Sauveur" and "French coast" are masked in printing, leaving only the names of Harding and Bonington. Bound in the *oeuvre*, page size varies.

This album made up of a portrait, a pictorial title page, and nineteen plates, which are represented in the *oeuvre* described above by proofs of Carpenter's selection, is doubly significant. It preserves some of Bonington's most attractive sketches of town and country life, and it shows an important phase in Harding's development. The plates are smaller and more tentative than those Harding did for the Taylor's *Voyages pittoresques* (107), but hardly less appealing.

The Napoleonic Epic

The coming of lithography to France coincided with the fall of the Empire. The Bourbons had returned to the throne, but there existed among the French people a nostalgia for the years of France's greatness. Beginning in 1817 the separate prints of Horace Vernet and Charlet established the Napoleonic tradition in lithography, which the albums of Charlet and Bellangé and their many imitators confirmed during the 1820s and early 1830s. For the most part theirs was an anecdotal art, sometimes charged with emotion, sometimes broadly farcical, but always popular in its appeal. Raffet's albums of the 1830s, which appeared side by side with those of Charlet and Bellangé, were for a time in the same vein, but they gradually achieved a heroic quality which aroused the admiration of connoisseurs who were indifferent to the designs of his predecessors. His later Russian and Roman albums, quiet and truthful studies of the contemporary scene, seemed marvels of fidelity to life until photography in effect superseded them.

On the whole, sceptics have prevailed in their estimates of the Napoleonic legend preserved in these prints. It takes an effort of the historical imagination to understand that "singular epoch which retraced on the walls of the Restoration the great deeds of the first Empire," and which, "confounding by the strangest of illusions chauvinism with liberty, created an opposition by celebrating Napoleon's veteran soldiers" (Charles Blanc, quoted by Adeline, p. iv). Yet the achievement of these "painters of the people," Horace Vernet, Charlet, Bellangé, and Raffet, "who gave their whole existence to the present century and to the Fatherland" (Francis Wey, quoted by Beraldi, II, 5), was a considerable one. Decisively rejecting neoclassicism, they recorded, chiefly through their lithographs, the great events of their time and the impact of these events on ordinary lives.

A later phase in the cultivation of the Napoleonic epic by these artists came with the books of the 1830s and 1840s which they illustrated with engravings on wood or metal: Horace Vernet in Laurent de l'Ardèche's *Histoire de l'empereur Napoléon* (203), Charlet in Las Cases' *Mémorial de Sainte-Hélène* (205), Bellangé in the *Napoléon en Egypte* of Barthélémy and Méry of 1842, and Raffet in the 1835 edition of the same work, Norvins' *Histoire de Napoléon* (202), and the *Musée de la révolution* (201). Taken together, these albums and books played a significant role in enabling Napoleon to hold in thrall the imaginations of his contemporaries after his downfall and in preparing the way for the Second Empire.

REFERENCES Adeline; Baudelaire; Beraldi; Bouchot; Curtis (1897); Giacomelli; La Combe—*Charlet.*

Nicolas-Toussaint Charlet (1792–1845)

Charlet was born in Paris in 1792. When he was very young, his soldier-father died on active duty. His mother, a fanatical patriot, used the great public ceremonies of the time to help make up to her son for the household's poverty. At school he manifested a precocious talent for drawing; and after he lost his position as a petty bureaucrat, he spent the years 1817–1820 at the atelier of Baron Gros, where Bonington, Bellangé, and Lami were among his fellow students. Though Gros was a thoroughgoing advocate of neoclassicism—he used to tell his pupils: "It is not I who speaks to you, it is

David, David, and always David" (La Combe, p. 11)—, he recognized Charlet's idiosyncratic gift and urged him to go his own way.

Charlet's first lithograph dates from 1817. During the next five years he made over 200 designs for Lasteyrie, Delpech, Motte, and other lithographic printers. These early lithographs were published in small numbers and cannot have had wide circulation (La Combe, p. 16), yet their fame gradually spread, and today they are the only part of Charlet's work that is generally known. La Combe, who was himself a hero of the Napoleonic wars, thought that "the soldier of Horace Vernet . . . was a conventional soldier, an actor dressed as a soldier, a soldier of Scribe if you prefer; designed, clothed, *manipulated* with finesse, but lacking in character and truth" (p. 15). Charlet, he maintained, showed Napoleon's warriors as they really were. Concerning the best of Charlet's early lithographs, this verdict would appear to be just. "Bonaparte, General in Chief of the army of Italy" (La Combe, no. 18), a large and magnificent plate of great rarity, epitomizes Charlet's conception of Napoleon, which was to impose itself on most later artists. "Alms" (La Combe, no. 87) shows a formidable and bemedalled grenadier, coming to the assistance of an old beggar and his two boys. Gros remarked of this plate "I would like to have done that" (La Combe, p. 222). Among the other lithographs by which Charlet impressed his vision of Napoleon's army unforgettably on the French mind are "The Grenadier of Waterloo," his most famous design; "Two grenadiers of Waterloo"; "Siege of Saint-Jean-d'Acre"; and a pair of stalwart warriors from the French Light Infantry, "Rifleman" and "Skirmisher," in which, so Beraldi contended (IV, 102), Charlet "condensed, without suspecting it, all of the Grande-Armée."

In 1822 Charlet entrusted his lithographs to the brothers Gihaut, who were henceforth to be his publishers. Between 1822 and 1837 they offered at least one album from his hand each year. Indeed, the title page of his *Album lithographique* of 1828 is a joking allusion to the abundant productivity of himself, Bellangé, and other lithographers. It shows these artists in the pillory, about to be consumed by flames from burning albums piled beneath them. The legend reads: "The public has obtained justice! The rascals will make no more albums." The more than 400 lithographs in these albums are mostly genre pieces, quite different from those of Charlet's first phase. Most are still about soldiers, but he has now come, like Horace Vernet before him, to manipulate his puppets to achieve effects of comedy and irony, sentiment and pathos. Charlet's children, another specialty, have been described by the unfriendly Baudelaire (p. 997) as "dear little angels who will make such pretty soldiers, who love old veterans so much, and who play at war with wooden swords." Baudelaire found them too good to be true. The accuracy of this appraisal may be tested by "The little French army" (La Combe, no. 509), from the *Recueil de croquis à l'usage des petits enfants* of 1822, Charlet's first album. He was as sympathetic to the working populace as to his soldiers, but the dominant bourgeoisie he usually treated with scorn. Witness "He has refused to recognize an old comrade" (La Combe, no. 536) from *Croquis lithographiques* of 1824, in which a failed artist, painting a sign, is ignored by a prosperous former colleague of the atelier. On occasion Charlet returns to his earlier manner. In *Souvenirs de l'armée du nord* of 1833, an album concerned with the campaign in Holland, one encounters "Soldiers of the infernal company" (La Combe, no. 810), a lithograph in the "black manner" which is charged with energy and drama.

The Gihaut connection, together with his happy marriage in 1824, brought some measure of prosperity and order into Charlet's life. The sale of his lithographs and his drawings resolved his financial problems. He once told La Combe (p. 28) that he would never see him again if his friend paid 500 francs for one of his drawings. When La Combe protested that this was his usual price, Charlet replied: "Oh! that is different. I sell them to the English and exhibit patriotism." He had a pleasant studio, where he showed great kindness to pupils from whom he would accept no fees. He had many friends, predominantly artists, amateurs, and army officers. Among them were Bellangé and the unhappy and difficult Géricault, whom he had accompanied to London in 1820. He also saw much of the working class, a principal source of inspiration for him. La Combe (p. 25) tells how he would spend evenings drinking with soldiers in cabarets, "in order to make their popular vitality spurt forth."

After 1837 Charlet's production of lithographs be-

"Alms"

Recueil de croquis à l'usage des petits enfants

"Bonaparte, General in Chief of the army of Italy"

Croquis lithographiques of 1824

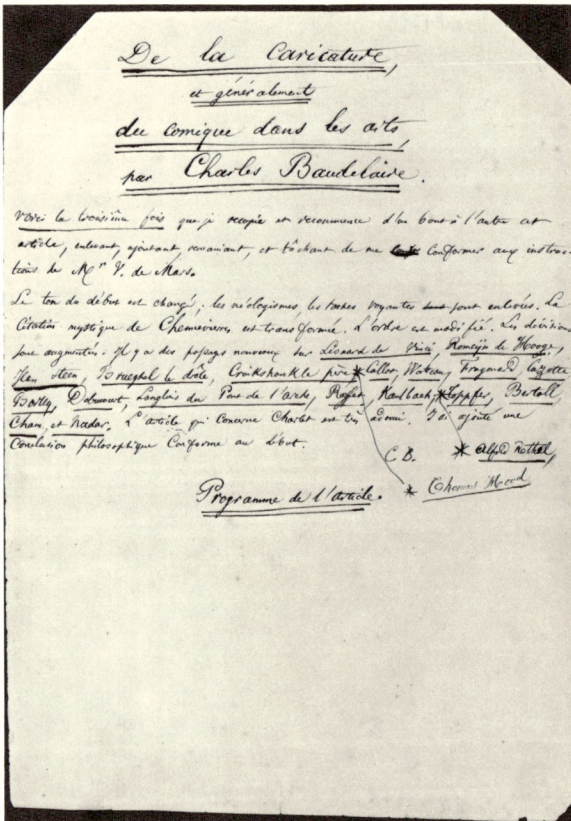

Souvenirs de l'armée du nord

Baudelaire, summary of his essay on caricature

came sporadic. He had joined the National Guard, in which he became a high officer. He devoted himself more and more to painting. In 1836, indeed, he had aspired to Carle Vernet's place at the Academy but was rejected because "he had only made little things" (La Combe, p. 100). He was named a professor at the École Polytechnique. He accepted an extraordinarily demanding commission for drawings to illustrate Las Cases' *Mémorial de Saint-Hélène* (205). He also composed lithographic albums from time to time, the most ambitious among them being the *Vie civile, politique, et militaire du caporal Valentin*, the fifty lithographs of which occupied him from 1838 to 1842. Why he was not encouraged to do more in this line is suggested by a passage from the unused preface to that work. Referring to the early albums of Gavarni, who had become the most successful lithographer of the period, Charlet wrote: "I hear a jester saying to the public: Don't buy this book of sketches; once again it is a soldier-laborer, old rubbish, a veteran complainer who comes to rake the ground with his Old-Guard saber; it is detestable, we don't want any more of that. What we require is young women at their toilette, agreeable and frivolous subjects, pleasantries, gauze, flowers, love-affairs. A corporal! What is there picturesque and airy about a corporal?" (Quoted by La Combe, p. 118.) If Charlet was out of style, he remained unrepentant.

Charlet's politics are an inescapable part of his work. His lithographs prepared the way both for the Revolution of 1830 and the Second Empire. For the most part his message is implied in his prints, but he spoke more directly in a forgotten album of 1840 called *Croquis à la manière noire, sujets philosophiques, populaires, moraux, politiques, critiques, civils, religieux, et militaires*, which he dedicated to Béranger. These eighteen lithographs are overtly Bonapartist. An old soldier tells a young man: "If I had signed the treaties of 1815! I would cut off my fist." He celebrates the people and the army against the middle class. Everywhere the sturdy and honest laborer is contrasted with the effete and venal bourgeois. One design, which shows soldiers and laborers joining ranks, has the legend: "To arms, citizens! Form your battalions!"

Most of Charlet's critics have allowed his politics to affect, if not to determine, their judgment of his artistic merit. So Bouchot and La Combe are cordial, while Beraldi and Atherton Curtis are cool. Curtis even brought himself to prefer Charlet's genre studies to his heroic early lithographs. But the prime example of ideological predetermination is provided by Baudelaire's notable essay of 1857–1858 on French caricaturists (*Oeuvres*, pp. 996–999). After a perfunctory mention of Charlet's reputation as one of "the glories of France," he goes on to denounce him at length as a slave of the people. Baudelaire's conclusion is that Charlet will shortly be forgotten, along with Horace Vernet and Béranger, "his cousins-german in ignorance and stupidity." Against this judgment may be put Delacroix's words after the appearance of La Combe's catalogue: "Charlet is of the lineage of those immortal mockers who attack the absurd and the vicious more surely than the preachers of virtue. . . . I don't hesitate to place him, with respect to the depiction of characters, beside Molière and La Fontaine." (Quoted by Beraldi, IV, 113.)

Charlet's last years were painful in the extreme, yet he remained cheerful and active. Finding it impossible to paint, he began once more, to *crayon-ailler*, as he put it to La Combe (p. 185), "a military gallery since 92." The lithographs which he completed appeared in 1853, eight years after his death, as *L'Empereur et la garde impériale*. So he ended his career, as he began it, by celebrating Napoleon and his army.

REFERENCES Baudelaire; Beraldi; Bouchot; Curtis (1897); La Combe.

ᴕ Charles Baudelaire. De la caricature, et généralement du comique dans les arts. . . . Autograph manuscript signed, undated. 1 page. Sheet size: $10\frac{3}{4} \times 7\frac{7}{8}$ inches.

On the cover of Baudelaire's *Salon de 1845* a book entitled *De la caricature* was announced as "appearing shortly." In the event his famous essay finally achieved publication in several overlapping and reworked articles between 1855 and 1858. This summary was written about 1855 for the *Revue des deux mondes*, where the essay in fact did not appear. The summary is printed in Baudelaire's *Oeuvres*, p. 1696. One notes his comment that "the article on Charlet has been made much milder."

ᴕ An *oeuvre* of 496 lithographic plates bound in 5 volumes, some prints on *chine appliqué*, a few with lithotint. Page size: $13\frac{1}{2} \times 10\frac{1}{4}$ inches. Contemp. $\frac{1}{2}$ purple calf.

Charlet's vast popularity has been mentioned. His admirers formed collections of his plates, which they bound together as *oeuvres* (collected works) of this sort. These five volumes contain 496 lithographs out of the 1089 listed by La Combe. The notable plates of Charlet's first period are well represented, as are the separate lithographs of his later years. Twenty-six of his albums are present, most of them complete, including all of those to which reference is made above.

Proof lithograph by Bellangé with marginal sketches

Hippolyte Bellangé (1800-1866)

Hippolyte Bellangé was primarily a historical painter, yet in his early career he drew 488 lithographs. He and Charlet studied together at the studio of Baron Gros, and for some time he followed his friend's lead by supporting himself through albums of lithographs, publishing at least one a year between 1823 and 1835. From 1836 to 1853 he was Conservator of the Rouen Museum, a post which allowed him to devote himself with considerable success to painting. Later in life he returned to lithography with a series of large plates on the Crimean War.

There is little to say about Bellangé's life and character, both of which were models of prudence and simplicity. It was not for him to mingle with soldiers and workers in search of inspiration or to try through his designs to bring about the reform of his country along Bonapartist lines. His lithographs have the usual subjects of the time: scenes in the margin of military life (he rarely attempted combat), amiable glimpses of the bourgeois and the populace, and studies of children at play. All are composed with a painter's eye. His command of the lithographic crayon is masterly. There are engaging touches of quiet humor. These plates may give rise to a smile or a sigh, but they rarely evoke a more profound response. One senses a lack of final commitment, as if Bellangé wanted to be worthy of his hire, yet was eager to get back to what really interested him, his painting.

REFERENCES   Adeline; Beraldi.

☙ Hippolyte Bellangé. An *oeuvre* of 130 lithographic plates, mostly printed on *chine appliqué*; printed by Villain. Page size: 16 × 10⅝ inches. Contemp. ¾ brown morocco.

This fine collection includes Bellangé's first seven *Albums*, several series of *Croquis*, including an album for 1828, and a number of separate plates. Particularly notable are five large lithographs at the end, two of which are early proofs of characteristic military subjects before the artist's marginal sketches were effaced from the stone.

Auguste Raffet (1804-1860)

In his own time Raffet's public was far smaller than Charlet's. A quiet worker, wholly devoted to his meticulous art, he had little of his master's flamboyant appeal. Reading the appraisals that appeared after his death, one senses a general feeling that he had not been accorded the recognition that was his due. In the years that followed, his work inspired passionate devotion among connoisseurs, who took Giacomelli's fine catalogue of 1862 as their bible. Indeed, Beraldi made the startling assertion that Raffet's was "the greatest name of the century in original prints," adding that "this still isn't enough to say. One of the greatest names of French art." (XI, 65.) Atherton Curtis (p. 116) thought that in his combination of intellectual range and technical mastery he was the equal of any lithographer. Bouchot called him "the Moreau le jeune of lithography" (p. 181). Today Raffet's albums of lithographs and the books with illustrations after him (see Romantic Engraving) are regarded with respect and admiration, but they hardly arouse the enthusiasm that greets the work of Daumier, Grandville, and Doré.

Raffet was a Parisian who like Charlet had early in life lost his father, a former soldier turned postal employee. He worked as a craftsman in wood and later porcelain during the day to support his mother and sisters, while attending drawing school in the evening. A turning point in his career was his admission to Charlet's atelier in 1824. He remained there for five years, learning lithography and eventually producing albums of his own. Then he studied with Baron Gros in the hope of becoming a historical painter, but this dream vanished when he failed in the competition for the Rome Prize in 1831.

Raffet's lithographs during these early years were primarily his way of earning a living, and few of these more than 200 plates are of lasting interest. His battle scenes, drawings of uniforms, genre pieces, sketches of children at play, and the rest conform to the tradition created by Horace Vernet, Charlet, and Bellangé without adding anything very novel to it. Only after the Gihaut brothers became his publishers in 1830 did his personal style begin to emerge. He started slowly in the eight albums which he did for them over the next seven years, but that for 1832 contains five of his most animated episodes of military history, together with the first of those scenes of imperial camaraderie by which he made the Napoleonic tradition so humorously appealing. In the remaining five albums Raffet moved from strength to strength. He also

(116) Raffet, *Album lithographique*, 1833

did some interesting work for *La caricature* (147) and *L'Artiste* (160).

Meanwhile, he had embarked on a career of pictorial journalism, which in the eyes of his contemporaries carried him to an even higher level of achievement than his lithographs of French history. His first album of this kind was the *Siège de la citadelle d'Anvers*, twenty-four lithographs, 1833. This was followed by the *Retraite et prise de Constantine* and much later by the *Expédition et siège de Rome*. Ethnographic rather than military emphasis marked still another folio, the *Voyage dans la Russie méridionale et la Crimée*. By the end of his career, as Beraldi has shown in his section on "Raffet, Historical Painter" (VII, 114–149), he had created a comprehensive and detailed panorama of French military annals from the 1790s to 1859.

It is undeniable that Raffet's Russian and Roman albums lack the popular appeal of his earlier work. He suppressed the dash and drama of his Napoleonic designs as he refined and chastened his conceptions. His aim was to be as true as possible to reality, and no expense of effort was too great to ensure that every detail in his plates was accurate and natural. At the same time, his mastery of composition and his command of the lithographic medium were unimpaired. It is understandable, then, that admirers once contended that his later work redeemed lithography from triviality, bringing it to its "synthetic phase, the end result of all the talents, of all the efforts of our national scale school" (Bouchot, p. 178).

The honors that came Raffet's way in later years did not change his modest character or his retired way of life. He continued to work at his lithographs and occasional paintings until his death in 1860.

REFERENCES Beraldi; Bouchot; Curtis (1897); Giacomelli.

116 DENIS AUGUSTE MARIE RAFFET

Albums lithographiques . . . Paris, Gihaut frères, 1830–1837. 8 v. Each v. with lithographic t.p. and 12 lithographic plates by Raffet; printed by Gihaut frères. Page size: 10½ × 14⅞ inches. ¾ red morocco.

These eight albums, which in effect are one, remain Raffet's outstanding achievement. They have

(116A)   Raffet, *Album lithographique,* 1836

many kinds of interest, but their great theme is France's military epic from the Republic to Waterloo, with Napoleon as the dominant presence. Sometimes he is center stage as in "The eye of the master" (1833, no. 8), sometimes in the remote background as in "Attention! The Emperor has his eye on us," but always he provides the focus of the scene. Moreover, he is "The man of the people," the comrade as well as the leader of his soldiers. In one design he grasps a soldier's hand as he clambers up a river bank; in another a grenadier offers him a potato, as he walks through his camp one night, with the words: "My Emperor, it is the most cooked." The solidarity that he thus established with his men is movingly conveyed in "They grumbled, but they always followed him" (1836, no. 11). When compared with these scores of masterly studies, the glimpses which Vernet, Bellangé, and even Charlet had offered of Napoleon and his soldiers seem occasional and anecdotal.

By a stroke of genius Raffet conceived, as his final plate, "The nocturnal review" (1837, no. 12), which brings together the varied aspects of his imperial saga. Raffet found his subject in a ballad of this title by Sedlitz, an obscure German poet.

The scenario there proposed is a general rising from their graves of Napoleon and his legions for a midnight review on the Champs-Elysées. When the drums begin to beat, the words "Sainte-Hélène" resound along the Seine. Raffet changed this reflection on the vanity of human wishes to a requiem for France's glorious past. His midnight tableau, illuminated by a half hidden moon, shows squadrons of Napoleon's cavalry circling the emperor, who is in the middle distance. Only the men and horses in the foreground are drawn firmly in black; Napoleon and the rest of his soldiers are shown indistinctly in luminous grey. This eerie composition has an element of mystery to which Raffet hardly aspired elsewhere in his work, except in "Le reveil" of 1848, another lithograph inspired by Sedlitz's ballad.

116A   DENIS AUGUSTE MARIE RAFFET

An *oeuvre* of 57 plates from various volumes of Raffet's *Albums lithographiques,* 1830–1837. 1830: plates 3, 4, 10, 11. 1831: 2, 6, 7, 10. 1832: 1, 2, 4–8. 1833: 1, 2, 4–6, 8, 10–12. 1834: 1, 2, 4, 8–12. 1835: 1, 2, 6, 8–12. 1836: 3, 3, 4, 5, 7–9, 11. 1837: Title, 1–3, 6–8, 10, 11. All are

(116)   Raffet, *Album lithographique*, 1837

hand-colored lithographic plates heightened with gum arabic; printed by Gihaut frères. Page size: $10\frac{1}{8} \times 13\frac{3}{4}$ inches. $\frac{1}{2}$ green morocco by Bernasconi.

These albums appeared in three forms: (1) on white paper with colored or uncolored plates, (2) on China paper, (3) on colored paper. Raffet must obviously have been aware that some copies would be hand-colored and touched with gum (*gommées*), but whether this consideration affected his manner of drawing is not clear. At any rate, the plates in this copy, which is from the library of the Duc d'Orléans, the older son of Louis Philippe, are surpassingly attractive. Since the cover design is an early proof from the *Album* for 1837, it may be that they were not of the published issue but specially colored. Certainly they bear witness to particular care and finesse in planning and execution. The dreary setting of "They grumbled, but they always followed him," for example, is rein-

forced by the suave blues and browns which have been added; even the gum seems justified by the glinting reflections from the wet ground and the soldiers' uniforms that it contributes. Again in the "Last charge of the Red Lancers, at Waterloo," the clarity of the design is much enhanced by its coloring. Raffet in his way was as masterly a lithographer as Daumier, but cries of protest need not be raised against the addition of color to his plates.

117   DENIS AUGUSTE MARIE RAFFET

Retraite de Constantine. Six sujets . . . Paris, Gihaut frères, [1837]. Hand-colored lithographic t.p. vignette and six hand-colored lithographic plates printed on *chine appliqué*, heightened with gum arabic; printed by Gihaut frères.

Prise de Constantine. Douze sujets . . . Paris, Gihaut frères, [1837]. Hand-colored lithographic t.p. vignette and 12 hand-colored lithographic plates printed on *chine appliqué*, heightened with gum arabic; printed by Gihaut frères. Page size: 18 × 12⅜ inches. Bookplate of Michael Sadleir. ¾ blue cloth.

As with his *Albums* of 1830–1837, this record of the French war with Abd el-Kader in Algeria was published in three forms: on white paper, colored or uncolored; on China paper; and on colored paper. Exceptionally, this copy has colored and gummed plates on China paper. The engagements depicted took place in November of 1836 and October of 1837. Raffet's lithographs, imagined scenes based on what he had learned from those who had been in Algeria, were executed in 1837 and 1838. In his albums dealing with current military operations, Raffet came gradually to put the Napoleonic legend behind him and to show the modern French soldier as he actually was. In this series he is only a modest distance along his way. The two illustrated titles are entirely in his earlier manner. In that for the somber *Retraite*, a French veteran shakes his fist defiantly at the Arabs, saying, "We'll recapture [Constantine] in the spring." That for the victorious *Prise* shows another French soldier standing among the city's ruins; Raffet's comment is: "They have kept their word." The plates vary between swirling battle scenes in the manner of his Napoleonic compositions and more sober and studied designs of quieter moments in the campaign which look forward to his Russian and Roman albums. It is not until later that Paul de Saint Victor's

comparison (quoted by Giacomelli, p. xxxiv) finds its application: "Charlet was the cynical veteran in painting battles; Raffet was the young and enthusiastic officer."

119 ANATOLE NIKOLAEVICH DEMIDOFF, PRINCIPE DI SAN DONATO

[Album of plates for:] **Voyage dans la Russie méridionale & la Crimée** . . . exécuté en 1837, sous la direction de M. Anatole de Demidoff, par Mm. de Sainson, Le Play, Huot, Léveillé, de Nordmann, Rousseau, et du Ponceau . . . Paris, Gihaut frères, [1838–1848]. Lithographic t.p. with lithographic plate-list on verso, 64 p. Illus: 100 lithographic plates by Raffet printed on *chine appliqué*; printed by Auguste Bry. Page size: 21 ⅛ × 14 inches. Bookplate of the 6th Duke of Portland. ¾ purple morocco by Proudfoot.

In 1837 Prince Demidoff appointed Raffet staff artist for an expedition through Hungary to southern Russia, returning by way of Constantinople. This "numerous group of travellers, friends of knowledge and still more of travelling" (p. 3), was on the road from 2 July to 10 November, when Raffet returned to Paris with many sketches. He told the Gihaut brothers that he was "burning to execute them" as lithographs (Bouchot, p. 174), but his pursuit of perfection delayed the appearance of Prince Demidoff's book for ten years.

The aspect of the countries and people visited by Demidoff, not to mention the nature of their manners and customs, was largely unfamiliar to the Europeans of that day. Raffet placed these things before them in such a way, Jules Janin observed

(119) Demidoff, *Voyage dans la Russie méridionale et la Crimée*

(quoted by Giacomelli, p. xxix), as to capture the interest of "the military expert and the engineer, the captain and the simply curious like ourselves." The wild scenery and exotic architecture of the region are displayed; cities and villages alternate with rivers, plains, and mountains. Hungarian, Tartar, and gypsy life is shown with a vivid command of "local color." The grandiose military colony of Czar Nicholas at Vosnessensk appears in all its glory, even as the vast Russian army is passed in review. And there are many portraits, the most striking of which is that of the Czar (no. 56), the most engaging that of Raffet himself (no. 94) in the uniform of the expedition with his sketchbooks under his arm.

It is invidious to choose among many outstanding plates. As representative as any is the group of "Jewish traders and merchants" (no. 30) observed at Odessa, the metropolis of southern Russia. They are shown in animated discussion outside a favored café. All are dressed in long robes with broad-brimmed hats, even the children who have joined their fathers on the way home from school.

120 [Denis Auguste Marie Raffet]

Souvenirs d'Italie. Expédition de Rome [Siège de Rome. 1849]. Paris, Gihaut, [1859]. Lithographic t.p. and 36 lithographic plates (incl. 2 section titles) by Raffet; printed by Auguste Bry. Plates are on *chine appliqué*; section titles, and plates 9 and 16 printed with lithotint. Page size: 22 × 14¾ inches. ¾ red morocco by Pagnant.

This fine album is in two parts. The first eight plates, entitled *Expédition de Rome, 1849*, show the landing of the French army at Civita Vecchia and its approach to Rome in April. The remaining thirty-six, entitled *Siège de Rome, 1849*, show the conquest of the city in June. Four of the latter were not drawn on stone by Raffet himself, though they are from his designs. The artist made his lithographs from sketches taken on the spot at a later date (one of which is reproduced in the album), but as usual he took his time in developing these sketches into finished drawings. "Batterie No. 9" (plate 26) depicts a scene of 20 June 1849; it was finally lithographed on 15 February 1859. Most of Raffet's plates present military operations: some are of whole battlefields, but the bulk are smaller in scope, detailed and precise enough to serve as the basis for a lecture on tactics. The remaining plates are devoted to groups of French soldiers, austere young professionals who seem to belong to a different race from the comradely veterans to whom Charlet and even Raffet himself had accustomed the public thirty years earlier. "Batterie No. 9" combines the two kinds of designs. In this superb composition the battery is making a breach in the walls of an enemy bastion according to established procedure, yet each gunner is an individual, natural and at ease. Curtis (p. 133) relates on the authority of Raffet's son that with regard to the plates of smaller groups "nearly all the figures were drawn from the nude before being placed upon the stone, and where this was not done he made use of the draped model. In some cases he even went so far as to make a study of the whole composition, with all the figures nude." Looking at this lithograph with modern eyes, accustomed to seeing everything as the camera shows it, we may not realize how remarkable an achievement in truthful art it seemed to Raffet's contemporaries.

(120)   Raffet, *Siège de Rome*

The Passing Scene Presented in Color

The 1820s saw the appearance of many albums recording the ordinary life of the day, some in a straight-forward way, others with an element of caricature. In the earlier part of the decade albums thus assembled had plates of a greyish hue, which almost require color to bring them to life. Sometimes the ink from the lithographer's crayon clashes with the added coloring, and the resulting print is simply muddy, but for the most part a soft pastel effect is achieved which can be very agreeable. This is true of the albums of Carle Vernet, Marlet, Chalon, Bacler d'Albe, and Thomas described below. These volumes have considerable documentary value, and their fresh and unaffected representation of the people and scenes of the time gives them a degree of charm.

Pigal and Victor Adam also used crayon, with coloring often added, but the interest of their lithographs is of a different kind. They are representative of a more numerous group of designers in whose work caricature predominates, though they were less given to exaggeration than the painter Louis-Léopold Boilly (1761–1845), a survivor from the eighteenth century known for groups of massed heads called *grimaces*. Beraldi dismisses these caricaturists as *amuseurs*, who dealt in "easy jokes" which are "without value as art" (XI, 171–173). Champfleury thought that their common characteristic was a contempt for everything distinguished. Nevertheless, they have always had admirers. If their work is not widely collected today, the chief reason may be its unavailability. Since the plates were usually colored, they were more expensive than the black-and-white caricatures of the 1830s and 1840s, and hence sold in much smaller numbers.

The second half of the decade saw the emergence of a different group of observers of the passing scene. These artists used the pen for the most part rather than the crayon, and they made their designs specifically to be colored, often employing mere outlines which depend almost entirely on coloring for their effect. Where this adjunct has been expertly applied, in clear and bright rather than diffused and pastel hues, the resulting plates are as sparkling as they are elegant. Monnier and Lami devoted themselves to depicting contemporary life in this style, and since they also tended to choose higher levels of social life than had their predecessors, the charge of vulgarity can hardly be levelled against them. Grandville and Traviès were unrepentant caricaturists, but the one had a fire and energy which made his work *sui generis*, and the other found a significant focus for his lesser talent in the ineffable Monsieur Mayeux. In consequence the years 1826 to 1830 are the most brilliant period of lithography colored by hand. The albums of this period are much in demand but increasingly difficult to obtain.

REFERENCES Adhémar (1938); Baudelaire; Beraldi; Bouchot; Lemoisne—*Lami*; Marie—*Monnier*.

Carle Vernet

121

Cris de Paris, dessinés d'après nature. Paris, Delpech, [c. 1820–1825]. Lithographic t.p. and 100 hand-colored lithographic plates by Vernet; printed by Delpech. Page size: 13¾ × 10 inches. Bookplate of Michael Sadleir. Contemp. ½ green morocco. Colas 2986.

This celebrated series, prized by the sociologist as well as the historian of costume, has become almost unfindable complete because of an insatiable demand from hotelkeepers seeking wall decorations. In fine contemporary coloring its 100 lithographs are most attractive. The streets of Paris in Vernet's time seem to have been an out-of-doors department store which catered to most needs for goods and services. His itinerants are a sturdy and impassive lot, inured to hardship but not defeated by it. It will be noted that Vernet was content to portray the honest poor; he did not extend his attention to Henry Mayhew's category of "those who will not work." The street entertainer, with his cry of "don't forget the little marionettes" (plate 63), is particularly engaging.

N.º 63.

Carle Vernet

Joueur de Marionnettes.

n'oubliez pas les petites marionnettes.

J. lith. de Delpech

(121) Carle Vernet, *Cris de Paris*

Jean-Henri Marlet (1771–1847)

122

[Cover title:] **Tableaux de Paris.** Paris, Marlet, Martinet, & Emery, [1821–1824]. Printed title and 72 *l.* of text. Illus: 72 hand-colored lithographic plates by Marlet. Inserted is another version of plate 2 by Marlet. Page size: 9⅝ × 12⅝ inches. Bookplate of Michael Sadleir. Contemp. ¾ blue morocco; wrapper of the first *livraison* bound in. Beraldi IX, p. 221.

Marlet was one of the first French painters to turn to lithography. This ambitious album, which is rare in colored form, appeared in twelve parts of six plates each over much the same period as Vernet's *Cris de Paris*. Though Marlet's designs are inferior in draftsmanship to Vernet's, they are far more elaborate in conception. The pastel coloring greatly improves his lithographs, which are otherwise in the pallid grey typical of the period.

It is claimed that the scenes depicted are drawn from "all classes and all conditions," but in fact Marlet directs his attention chiefly to the populace at work and at play: itinerant vendors, street entertainers, beggars, workers, soldiers, and children. His treatment is predominantly realistic, as it is in his occasional excursions into upper-class life, but he sometimes lapses into caricature. Taken together, the plates and the commentary, which is not by Marlet, make the album a significant contribution to social history.

A representative lithograph is "Prostitutes, conducted to the police" (no. 3). The soldiers are carrying out their duty of bringing to the prefecture of police three women who have failed to pay the tax imposed upon them. Characteristically, Marlet makes a little drama of his scene by having the soldiers respond to their charges in different ways. The accompanying text testifies to the exactness with which Marlet has rendered the corner of Paris he has chosen.

✍ William Sams. *Tour of Paris.* London, W. Sams, 1824. Hand-colored etched t.p., 21 *l.* letterpress, and 21 hand-colored aquatint plates. Page size: 9⅞ × 13½ inches. ¾ blue morocco by Root. Abbey *Travel*, 113 (2).

(122) Marlet, *Tableaux de Paris*

The 21 colored aquatints of this album published in London by William Sams were taken without acknowledgement from Marlet's *Tableaux de Paris.* Even the letterpress is a halting and abridged translation. Though the plates lack the vitality and charm of Marlet's lithographs, and their coloring is garish, they remain in demand among collectors of English aquatints.

Louis-Albert Ghislain, Baron de Bacler d'Albe (1762–1824)

123

Promenades pittoresques et lithographiques dans Paris et ses environs . . . Paris, G. Engelmann, 1822. 7 parts, as issued. Lithographic t.p. and 35 [i.e., 36] p. lithographic text. Illus: 43 (of 48) hand-colored lithographic plates heightened with gum arabic, by Bacler d'Albe; plates in parts I and II, and 3 plates in part III printed by Engelmann, the remainder by Villain. Page size: 18½ × 12⅛ inches, uncut. Original wrappers. Beraldi II, p. 84–85.

General Bacler d'Albe made many lithographs of scenery while he was on active duty. His best plates, however, were for his Parisian album. This copy is in the original parts, and it has the uncommon calligraphic text, but it lacks five of the forty-eight colored lithographs (6, 17, 19, 42, and 43). The album is made up of lively scenes of a fresh and sunny city which passes imperceptibly into the countryside. Indeed, there are as many glimpses of Paris's environs as of the city itself. By and large the General is an observant and piquant guide. Concerning the "Boulevard des bains chinois" (no. 47), for example, he calls this survival of *Chinoiserie* in a neoclassic age "a bizarre combination of zig-zags to which the narrow brain of the Pekinese architects gave birth" (p. 35), and points out that the two obelisks, once the sign for a museum of Egyptian curiosities, are made of wood.

(123)   Bacler d'Albe, *Promenades pittoresques* . . .

Jean-Jacques Chalon (1778–1854)

124

[**Twenty-four subjects exhibiting the costume of Paris,**
the incidents taken from nature, designed and drawn
on stone by J. J. Chalon. London, Rodwell and Martin, 1822]. 17 lithographic plates (14 hand-colored),
and 2 duplicates, lacking the lithographic t.p. and 6
plates; printed by C. Hullmandel. Sheet size: 19 ×
13½ inches, uncut. Bookplate of Michael Sadleir. Unbound. Colas 588; Beraldi XII, p. 232.

According to Beraldi (XII, 232) this "very curious
and rare album" appeared as a small quarto in
London. These plates, which are large folio in
size, may represent a French issue of the work,
though the English edition had captions in French.
Jean-Jacques Chalon was a French artist born in
Switzerland who eventually settled in England.
His designs are by no means mere costume plates.
Instead they are animated and faithful studies of
Parisian manners and customs in the years 1820 to

1822. There is hardly a touch of caricature, though
the profiles of his personages have a family likeness
which suggests a domesticated Girodet.

Antoine-Jean-Baptiste Thomas (1791–1834)

125

Un an à Rome et dans ses environs. Recueil de dessins
lithographiés . . . Paris, Firmin Didot, 1823. [2] *l.*, 44
p. Illus: Lithographic t.p. vignette and 68 (of 72) hand-
colored lithographic plates (lacking plates 1, 3, 18,
and 31) by Thomas; printed by Villain. Page size:
16 × 10⅞ inches. Colas 2872; Beraldi XII, p. 1.

This record of a year passed in Rome by the young
French painter Antoine Thomas provides an animated and comprehensive view of the street life of
that city, with emphasis on the way in which Catholicism shaped the existence of the populace.

(125)   Thomas, *Un an à Rome*

Thomas seems to have filled his sketchbooks with these scenes solely because of their picturesqueness; he exhibits no discernible ideological bias. Characteristic is the sequence (nos. 6 to 12) devoted to the eight days of the carnival; a criminal paraded before the people on a donkey, horse races, battles with handfulls of confetti, a masked ball, and so on. On the last night occurred the game of "I moccoletti" (no. 12). Everyone has candles, in the streets, in carriages, and at the windows, and the object is to blow out your neighbor's light and protect your own. As in the *Tableaux de Paris*, the coloring of the plates is soft and harmonious. They occur in various sizes, sometimes with two or three subjects to a page, the smaller designs usually being devoted to costumes. This gifted artist made only one other album of lithographs, *Le rêve* (144).

Victor Adam (1801–1865)

126

[**Un an dans la vie de jeune homme,** histoire véritable en 17 chapitres, écrits par lui-même. Paris, 1824]. 17 hand-colored lithographic plates by Adam; printed by Langlumé. Page size: 13¼ × 10¼ inches. Bookplate of Michael Sadleir. Unbound. Beraldi I, p. 17.

Beraldi (I, 15) assigns between 7000 and 8000 designs to Victor Adam. In many of these he was assisted by his son, Albert. A Parisian by birth, he remained in the capital all his life, but this did not prevent him from drawing negroes, Turks, Chi-

nese, and other peoples all over the world in his Paris studio. He was famous, indeed, as a *faiseur de bonshommes*, that is to say a specialist in adding groups of small figures to the foreground of architectural or landscape drawings by other artists. (See Adhémar [1938], pp. 230–231.) His immense production contains many amusing albums concerning the life of the time such as *Un an dans la vie de jeune homme*. This series is a sort of bourgeois rake's progress. A young man from the country comes to Paris to sample its pleasures. He acquires a new wardrobe; buys a horse; is duped by gamblers; makes a conquest of a pretty lady; exclaims, "Jasmin! she seemed so artless," as he lies recovering from the resulting malady; is imprisoned for debt; writes at last to "the old one," a buxom woman of means; and is accepted by her in the final plate. The series is unusual among the albums of the time in that it tells a consecutive story, and it certainly has more spirit and finish than Adam's usual work.

127

[Cover title:] **Mémorables journées de 1830.** Juillet 27, 28, et 29. Faits historiques recueillis et lithographiés par V. Adam. Paris, Bulla, [etc.] [1830?]. [26] *l.* letterpress text, hand-colored lithographic plate (port.) by Maurin, 26 hand-colored lithographic plates by Adam, and large folding "Plan figuratif des barricades . . ." lithographic plate by Motte printed by Delaporte. Page size: 13¼ × 18½ inches. Bookplate of Michael Sadleir. Contemp. ½ purple morocco; original wrapper bound in.

Scènes de Société.   N.30.

Comptez sur moi, mon cher.

(128)   Pigal, *Recueil de scènes de société*

Comptez sur moi, mon cher.

Pigal, drawing for *Recueil de scènes de société*

Adam's most lasting work is to be found in his albums of pictorial journalism such as this and *Annales de la révolution française* of 1848. He was also a principal collaborator, in his capacity of *faiseur de bonshommes*, in the magnificent folio volume *La translation des cendres*, which records the return of Napoleon's ashes from Saint Helena. The large colored lithographs of *Mémorables journées de 1830* represent the leading episodes of the Revolution of July, including not only the *trois glorieuses* of 27 to 29 July, but also the days before and after. From the inflammatory rhetoric of the accompanying commentary, it would appear that these lithographs were issued in parts not long after the events that they depict. Since Adam draws each scene to the last detail, he must have worked at breakneck speed. Shown is the first encounter between army and aroused citizenry in the Rue Saint-Antoine on 28 July. Having trodden down the bearer of the

tricolor and massacred those who supported him, the royal guard is in turn attacked by workmen concealed in the surrounding houses and forced to retire. Other lithographs devoted to the July Revolution are to be found in Bellangé's *Album patriotique* of 1831, in Raffet's *Album lithographique* of the same year (116), and as separate plates by Charlet.

Edme-Jean Pigal (1798–1873)

128

Recueil de Scènes de société . . . Paris, Martinet & Gihaut, [1822]. T.p. and 50 hand-colored lithographic plates by Pigal; printed by Langlumé. Page size: 14¼ ×10½ inches. Bookplate of Michael Sadleir; binding with arms of the Duc d'Orléans. ½ red morocco by Messier. Colas 2366.

129

Recueil de Scènes populaires . . . Paris, Martinet & Gihaut, [1822]. T.p. and 50 hand-colored lithographic plates by Pigal; printed by Langlumé. Colas 2365. Bound in are 22 further plates from a series of *Proverbes* by Pigal, hand-colored lithographic plates. Page size: 14¼×10½ inches. Bookplate of Michael Sadleir; binding with arms of the Duc d'Orléans. ½ red morocco by Messier.

130

Moeurs Parisiennes . . . Paris, Gihaut frères, [c. 1823]. T.p. and 72 (of 100) hand-colored lithographic plates by Pigal; printed by Langlumé. Page size: 14¼× 10½ inches. Bookplate of Michael Sadleir; binding with arms of the Duc d'Orléans. ½ red morocco by Messier. Colas 2367.

Beraldi makes the painter Pigal the occasion for denouncing the vulgarity of the caricaturists of the 1820s, allowing only that his *Scènes de société* may offer "some information about the costume of the period." The "superlatively vulgar" Pigal, he concludes, was "the Paul de Kock of the print." (x, 276–278.) Surely Baudelaire (p. 995) is nearer the mark in what he writes of this "amusing and kindly" artist. "Pigal's scenes of the people are good. It is not that the originality is very lively, nor even that the design is very comic. Pigal is comical in moderation, but the feeling in his compositions is good and just. These are vulgar truths, but still truths." Pigal does play to the groundlings, and no one would accuse him of excessive delicacy, but he knew his world and could depict it incisively in his lithographs. Consider the economy of "Rely on me, my dear fellow," of *Scènes de société* (no. 30). A nervous suitor, hat in hand and fumbled glove on the floor before him, is approaching a bureaucrat, who gives him his little finger. In the official's other hand is the suitor's letter, which will shortly join many similar appeals in the basket beside him. This study of abjectness and disdain epitomizes the insolence of office.

❧ Edme-Jean Pigal. 13 black chalk, pen-and-ink, and watercolor drawings for: *Moeurs Parisiennes* (nos. 3, 27, 33, 48, 54, and two unidentified subjects), *Scènes de société* (nos. 30, 38), and *Scènes populaires* (nos. 25, 29, 35, and 43). Sheet size: 10½×7⅞ inches.

Even Beraldi admits that Pigal is an "expert lithographer in execution." The drawing for "Rely on me, my dear fellow" shows how little has been lost between it and the print.

(131)   Grandville, *Le dimanche d'un bon bourgeois*

Jean-Ignace-Isidore Gérard, called Grandville

131

[Cover title:] **Le dimanche d'un bon bourgeois**; ou, Les tribulations de la petite propriété. Paris [Langlumé, 1827]. 12 hand-colored lithographic plates by Grandville; printed by Langlumé. Page size: 10×13½ inches, uncut. Bookplate of Michael Sadleir. Orig. wrappers.

The strange genius of Grandville is considered at length in Romantic Engraving below. It is a question here of two of his early lithographic albums. The twelve elaborate studies of a Sunday in the life of a middle-class family in this series are not really caricatures. Though all possible misfortunes descend on this worthy man, his wife, his two children, their nurse, and their dog, Grandville's depiction of their adventures is predominantly realistic. Moreover, his characterization of the various members of the family is admirably sustained throughout the series. The sixth "tribulation," a picnic interrupted by a storm, is representative. One sees how effective a conventional illustrator Grandville might have become, if his career had taken a different course.

132

[Cover title:] **Les métamorphoses du jour** par I. Adolphe Grandville. Paris, Bulla, 1829. [1] *l.* letterpress, 73 hand-colored lithographic plates by Grandville; printed by Langlumé. Page size: 10¾×14½ inches, uncut. ¾ blue morocco by Pouillet, orig. wrappers bound in.

(132) Grandville,
Les métamorphoses du jour

(132) Grandville, *Les métamorphoses du jour*

This famous album, which established Grand-ville's early style of bitter burlesque, has become rare. Indeed, it is known to many of his admirers only through the greatly inferior volume of seventy wood-engraved reproductions published by Havard in 1854. The cover design, a magic lantern display for the instruction of a family group, exemplifies Grandville's method. Vices and follies are to be exposed by giving men and women the heads of beasts. As Achille Comte remarks in his preface, the artist was thereby enabled to encompass "both the living picture of social manners and the satire of institutions and prejudices. Truth can circulate with impunity under the very eyes of the men it attacks."

Lust, gluttony, anger, and the other deadly sins are stigmatized, now with the blow of a hammer, now with the thrust of a stiletto; while the foibles and humors of mankind also receive due attention. Throughout the series Grandville's choice of beast-heads is inspired; and the force of his conceptions and the wit of his captions rarely falter. Occasionally, he produces a design of universal application that calls Goya to mind, as in the bat and owl creatures bewildered by the sunshine of "The light hurts them" (no. 12).

Perhaps his most terrifying plate is "Ménagerie" (no. 67), which shows four prison cells. In the first are complacent commercial offenders, enjoying all the comforts of home; in the second violent criminals, sly or stupid; in the third murderers, one with a countenance of the utmost ferocity; in the fourth, political prisoners, quiet and despondent. Here Grandville has obliquely evaded the government's prevailing suppression of criticism for it is only the last group that evokes sympathy. Grandville turned to direct political satire in his final plates, but the publication of his onslaughts on church ("Famille des scarabées," no. 72) and state ("Une bête féroce," no. 73) was not permitted in France. These plates are present in this copy, but they have a Brussels imprint.

Charles-Joseph Traviès (1804–1859)

&• [Les Mayeux]. An album of 49 hand-colored lithographic plates: nos. 1–37 published by l'Editeur, et

Traviès, *Les Mayeux*

Hautecoeur Martinet; printed by Ratier and his successor, Delanois; repeated nos. 1, 2, 5, 9, 14, 15, 17, 18, 21, 64, and 2 unnumbered plates published by l'Editeur, Charasse, or Aubert; printed by Delaporte, Delanois, Fonrouge, or Langlumé. Page size: 13 1/2 × 10 3/4 inches, uncut. Bookplate of Michael Sadleir. 1/2 purple morocco by Pagnant.

Though he began as a painter, Charles-Joseph Traviès soon became a professional lithographer, modelling himself on Pigal in the 1820s, turning to political subjects for *La caricature* and *Le charivari* in the 1830s, and publishing many albums of caricatures of manners in the 1840s and 1850s. Baudelaire credited him with "a profound feeling for the joys and sorrows of the populace" and wrote appreciatively of his *Scènes bacchiques* (p. 1012). Though few critics have seconded Baudelaire's praise, Traviès has one incontestable claim to fame, his creation, or at any rate his popularization, of Monsieur Mayeux. Champfleury went so far as to argue that the trinity of Daumier's Robert Macaire, Monnier's Joseph Prudhomme, and Traviès' Mayeux personified the bourgeoisie of the July Monarchy. Beraldi (XII, 147) was able to account for some 160 of *Les Mayeux*, as they came to be called, though not all of these were by Traviès. This collection includes numbers 1 to 37 of the series of Hautecoeur Martinet, and eleven published by Aubert, Fonrouge, and others.

Mayeux is a hunchback dwarf with a vast, slack mouth, usually on the grin. He enjoys a certain position in the world and dresses with formality. The scarecrow Mme. Mayeux doesn't count for much, but he is shown in frequent and lascivious pursuit of pretty girls, most of them of doubtful virtue. Ineffably self-important, he sees himself as the Napoleon of private life. Though he figures as the butt of every joke, his self-confidence is never impaired. To say that he is vulgar is totally inadequate. He is so egregiously, so monumentally vulgar as virtually to command laughter. Shown is plate 35 of the Hautecoeur Martinet series, "God's thunder, how I resemble him," certainly the most dignified of his appearances in this collection.

Henry Monnier (1799–1877)

Monnier grew up in the Parisian bourgeois world, where his father was an employee like those he was later to depict with such mastery in his lithographs. A second home was the ancestral property of Parnes, at the juncture of Normandy and the Ile de France. After he finished his education, he served as a notary's clerk and a minor bureaucrat in the Ministry of Justice, where he seems to have been valued chiefly for his handwriting. Balzac's portrait of him as Bixiou in *Les employés* harks back to these years. He then studied in the ateliers of Girodet and later Gros, where he learned lithography and became the friend of Bonington and Lami. His first lithographs, of which the album *Modes et ridicules* of 1825 is representative, are grotesque exaggerations in the manner of Rowlandson that call to mind J.-B. Isabey's *Caricatures de J.J.* (101) and Lami's *Les contretemps* (137).

Between 1825 and 1827 Monnier passed much of his time in London, where he collaborated with Lami in what was to become the *Voyage en Angleterre*. On his return to Paris he embarked on a series of albums in which he recorded the manners and humors of the city with unprecedented profusion. Between 1826 and 1830 he satisfied the insatiable demand for his designs with almost 500 lithographs, nearly all of which were drawn with a pen and colored by hand. For each design he himself colored a master print and carefully supervised its subsequent preparation. An uncolored print by Monnier can seem unsubstantial and trivial, while later impressions, the coloring of which he did not control, are often mere parodies.

Some of the salient titles in his human comedy may be mentioned. There are potpourris like *Récréations du coeur et de l'esprit*, *Paris vivant*, and *Rencontres Parisiennes*. *Macédoine pittoresque*. There are more closely focussed surveys like *Les grisettes*, *Moeurs administratives*, *Galerie théâtrale*, *Boutiques de Paris*, and *Six quartiers de Paris*. There are suites like *Jadis et aujourd'hui* and *Les contrastes*, which take their departure from comparisons in time or of manners. As to illustrations of the work of others, he largely confined himself to the several series which he made for Béranger's poems.

Monnier was a satirist with a difference. His attitude towards his subjects hardly varies. His aim was to set down what he saw with elegance and precision, but with no overt interpretation or judgment. His profound scepticism kept him clear of beliefs and commitments, whether political or literary. Without denying his accuracy—"No one has depicted [the people of our time] more exactly, not even Balzac"—, Gautier accused him of being a stenographic copyist (quoted by Marie, p. 137). Baudelaire found an even more graphic image for Monnier's studied detachment: "It is the coldness of a mirror, the limpidity of a mirror which does

(160)   "Henry Monnier dans *La famille improvisée*" from *La caricature*

not think and which is content to reflect the passers-by" (p. 1008). Yet the graphic realism of his solid and energetic designs is actually neither dry nor cold, and their implied meaning is never far to seek. A volume of selections from his lithographs of Paris during the last years of the Restoration, necessarily in color, would be a revelation to today's amateurs.

We come now to Joseph Prudhomme, Monnier's best-known creation, who figures in his lithographs only in a minor way. He first appeared in a volume of fictional sketches called *Scènes populaires*, which Monnier published in 1830, as an elderly and pompous teacher of handwriting. The "lapidary stupidities" of his conversation soon made him the acknowledged embodiment of middle-class ignorance and prejudice. Indeed, his command of the self-evident statement, the nonsequitur, and the mixed metaphor is unrivalled: "this saber is the most beautiful day of my life"; "take man out of society, you isolate him"; "the ship of state is sailing on a volcano"; "if Bonaparte had remained lieutenant of artillery, he would still be emperor" (Marie, pp. 66–67). When Monnier made his debut as an actor in his own *La famille improvisée* in 1831, he played four roles including Prudhomme. These he recorded in plate 74 of *La caricature*, Prudhomme being the second figure on the left. In time Monnier had sketched his creation so often for friends that he could produce his finished portrait in five minutes.

The rest of Monnier's life can be described as a prolonged anticlimax. His social success was never

in doubt. Everyone granted that he was a droll fellow, and his performances as Prudhomme were an expected part of the private parties he attended. A small, plump, dapper man, he came more and more to resemble his creation as he grew older. His most considerable literary effort was the *Grandeur et décadence de M. Joseph Prudhomme* of 1853, his attempt to sum up the weaknesses and absurdities of the French middle class. Though he pursued an acting career for some time, he never achieved a lasting following, his style being too subtle and demanding for most audiences. He continued to make lithographs during the 1830s, usually with crayon rather than pen, but his vogue was largely over. He also made many drawings for wood-engraved illustrations, most notably for *Les français peints par eux-mêmes* (227) and Balzac's *Oeuvres complètes* (230).

Monnier's later years were passed at Parnes in the comfort of a happy family circle, though he retained an apartment in Paris. His chief occupation was painting, either small original watercolors or elaborately colored and altered versions of his early lithographs. Both are often found with inscriptions to his great friend, the sculptor Pierre-Jules Mène. Balzac's considered judgment of Monnier, which makes some amends for his harsh portrait of him as Bixiou in *Les employés*, may be cited in conclusion: "Henry Monnier speaks to all men strong and discerning enough to see further than others see, to despise these others, not to be bourgeois [themselves], finally he speaks to all those who find something in themselves after disillusion, for he does disenchant" (quoted by Marie, p. 83).

REFERENCES Baudelaire; Beraldi; Bouchot; Champfleury; Marie—*Monnier*.

133

Les grisettes; leurs moeurs, leurs habitudes . . . dessinées d'après nature . . . Paris, Giraldon Bovinet, 1828. Engraved t.p. and 42 hand-colored lithographic plates by Monnier; printed by Bernard. Page size 11½ × 8¼ inches, uncut. Bookplate of Michael Sadleir. Contemp. ½ green morocco. Colas 2130.

This is perhaps the most piquant and original of Monnier's albums. The *grisette*, an impressionable girl of the working class, was virtually his discovery. In the words of his title he "drew after nature,"

(133) *Les grisettes*

(134) *Lithographies d'après les chansons de Béranger*

through these forty-two small lithographs, "their manners, their habits, their good qualities, their mistakes, their weaknesses," and so on. His scenes, which include only two or three figures, typically show these appealing creatures at odds with their followers, but likely to get their way. The inventiveness of his designs and the persuasiveness of his captions are unfailing. In plate 18 a *grisette* admonishes her admirer: "Sir, you are not telling the truth."

134

[Cover title:] **Lithographies d'après les chansons de Béranger** . . . [Paris], Bernard et Delarue, [1828]. 24 hand-colored lithographic plates by Monnier; printed by Bernard. With a duplicate suite of uncolored impressions, later states erasing Bernard's name. Page size: 9½×12 inches, uncut. Orig. wrappers of parts 1 and 3 bound in. Bookplate of Michael Sadleir. ¾ red morocco by René Aussourd.

Béranger was the most frequently illustrated of all authors of the period. Monnier began the tradition with this suite of 1828, and no subsequent artist surpassed him in sympathy and versatility. In "Les hirondelles" (plate 23) a French soldier, held in chains by the Moors, hails the swallows of his native land which have flown south for the winter. This album, which is rare complete, has both uncolored and colored plates. It will be seen how sketchy and incomplete are Monnier's litho-

(134) *Lithographies d'après les chansons de Béranger*

graphs in the former state. Monnier made a second series of forty smaller plates for Béranger's works in 1828 as well as a *suite libre* of twenty plates for his *Chansons érotiques*.

135

Galerie théâtrale. Paris, E. Ardit, [1828]. Lithographic wrapper-title and 24 hand-colored lithographic plates by Monnier; printed by Ardit and Gaugain. Page size: 12 ×9½ inches. Bookplate of Michael Sadleir. Disbound, laid into a wrapper for the *3e livraison*, with the [earlier?] imprint of Gaugain et Ardit.

(136) *Moeurs administratives*

Monnier, Drawing of himself as an old lady, 1874

As a boy Monnier had been fond of fairs and popular entertainments, and in maturity he was fascinated by everything having to do with the stage. In this engaging album he offers an informal view of the theatrical life of his time, ranging from strolling acrobats and sideshows to the ballet and classical tragedy. Only an occasional performance is depicted; for the most part he is content to show actors at the side-scenes and backstage, together with a variety of other people associated with the theatre. Monnier's command of this little world is authoritative, and he presents it with vivacity.

◈► *Galerie théâtrale.* Paris, Gaugain et Ardit, [1828]. 16 hand-colored lithographic plates, 17 duplicate uncolored lithographic plates, and 16 trimmed duplicate plates, these last with the artist's signature, coloring, and reworking. Page size: 14 × 10¾ inches, uncut. Laid into a wrapper with the Gaugain et Ardit imprint, inscribed: "Je certifie que cette épreuve . . . conforme au tirage fait dans mon imprimerie. Paris le 18 juin 1829. E. Ardit."

This remarkable set lacks plates 2 and 3 altogether, but has the rest in colored or uncolored states. Its greatest interest, however, lies in 16 added plates, all but one signed and colored by Monnier himself. The collection was assembled by the musical critic Charles Malherbe (1853–1911), Librarian of the Paris Opera. The inscription "1829 et 1869 à Mène Henry Monnier" on one plate suggests that they all were colored, and in some cases substantially altered by ink and wash, late in Monnier's life. At any rate, he treated them with as much

care as if they had been original watercolors. In "Acrobats," the first plate of the *Galerie théâtrale,* the coloring is far more delicate and harmonious than in the published issue, and by various touches of pen and brush Monnier has individualized the rather featureless figures of the lithograph. It is reproduced after page 154 above.

136

Moeurs administratives, dessinées d'après nature par Henry Monnier, ex-employé au Ministère de la Justice. Paris, Delpech, 1828. Lithographic t.p. and 12 hand-colored lithographic plates by Monnier; printed by Delpech. Page size: 10¼ × 13¾ inches. Bookplate of Michael Sadleir. Disbound.

In this album, "drawn after nature by Henry Monnier, former employee at the Ministry of Justice," the artist shows a typical governmental office hour by hour from eight to four and concludes with four salient scenes outside this time scheme. His principal themes are the inactivity of the staff, their lack of individual character, and their entire submission to superior authority. The curve of supple obsequiousness in terms of which Monnier depicts the office hierarchy "going to compliment a New Excellency" (no. 12) shows how far he was from being a "stenographic copyist" or a "mirror."

৯০ Pen and ink, graphite, and watercolor drawing by Monnier, signed and inscribed: "à Mène, 4 août 74." Sheet size: $8\frac{1}{4} \times 5\frac{3}{4}$ inches.

Monnier, who had few models at Parnes, has drawn himself as an old lady. As in most of his later work, there is little reliance on color, the figure is solidly projected, and attention is concentrated on the face of the subject, here reserved and disdainful. These small drawings of Monnier's last years, which he gave to his friends or sold to dealers for modest sums, are coming to be more and more sought after.

Eugène Lami (1800–1890)

This elegant and brilliant painter devoted much of his time to lithography between 1817 and 1833. The son of an Empire bureaucrat, he grew up in Paris. Beginning in 1815, he studied painting with Horace Vernet and afterwards in the studio of Baron Gros, where Bonington was his friend and instructor in watercolor. To support himself he made lithographs for several albums, including in 1822 a *Collection des uniformes des armées françaises, de 1791 à 1814*, the 100 plates of which are almost entirely his work, though Horace Vernet was his stated collaborator. Other albums followed, among them *Les contretemps*.

Lami paid his first visit to England in 1826, during which he drew the sketches which resulted in his *Souvenirs de Londres*. Under Charles X Anglomania was widespread among the upper classes, and Lami's album was well received. A commission from the London art dealer and publisher Colnaghi, eager for a more ambitious series, brought Lami back to London the following year. He fell in with Henry Monnier, already an expert in things English, and under his guidance comprehensively explored London and the countryside. Indeed, Monnier provided more than a third of the twenty-eight designs which make up Lami's finest album, the *Voyage en Angleterre*. It is here that for the first time Lami struck his distinctive note in lithography. These precise and sparkling plates, which show England in its most attractive aspects,

brought the lithographic recording of the passing scene to an unprecedented level of grace and refinement. Lami's *Tribulations des gens à équipages* of 1827 and *Six quartiers de Paris*, though drawn with less finesse, treat French subjects in the same manner. Their designs center chiefly on carriages, a point which Baudelaire did not forget in "Le peintre de la vie moderne," when he remarked that such vehicles are "marvellously suitable to represent the pomp of dandyism" (p. 1190).

After Lami gained recognition as a painter, he became a frequenter of the fashionable world, which he rendered with sympathy and brio. His chief albums of this kind are the charming *Vie de château*, published in two series in 1828 and 1833, and the *Quadrille de Marie Stuart*. But by this time his career as a lithographer was nearly over. For the rest of his life he was a painter, achieving success after success in his role as "the poet of official dandyism" (Baudelaire, p. 951).

Lami provided designs for two books with steel engravings, Jules Janin's *L'hiver à Paris* and *L'été à Paris* (218, 219). Late in his life, sixty of his watercolors were etched by Adolphe Lalauze as *Illustrations pour les oeuvres de Alfred de Musset* (274), a series much employed as added plates in editions of Musset's works.

REFERENCES Baudelaire; Beraldi; Bouchot; Lemoisne—*Lami*.

(137) Lami, *Les contretemps*

Rowlandson, *Miseries of Human Life*

137

[**Les contretems**. Paris, Gide fils, 1823–1824]. 24 hand-colored lithographic plates by Lami; printed by Villain (19). Page size: 7¾ × 10⅝ inches. Bookplate of Michael Sadleir. Contemp. ¾ green morocco.

This early album of broad caricatures hardly suggests what Lami was to become. Though he took ten of his plates from Rowlandson's *Miseries of Human Life*, he can hardly be accused of plagiarism, since he transposed the English artist's subjects to French settings, in effect making new creations of them. In plate 23 the French officer treading on the gouty toe of his invalid uncle is quite a different figure from the English sea captain of *Misery* no. 11, while the properties beside the two valetudinarians testify to contrasting national habits. Nonetheless, the powerful influence of the English tradition of caricature on French comic artists of the 1820s could not be more clearly demonstrated than by these two albums. Quite as much as Rowlandson's aquatints, Lami's lithographs require color to be effective.

℘ *Miseries of human life*; designed and etched by T. Rowlandson. London, R. Ackermann, 1808. Hand-colored etched t.p. and 50 hand-colored etched plates by Rowlandson and Bunbury. The plates with earlier watermarks (1805–1809) than the Abbey copy. Page size: 7¾ × 10 inches. ¾ blue morocco. Abbey *Life*, 317.

138

[Cover title:] **Souvenirs de Londres**. Paris, Lami Denozan, [etc.], 1826. 12 hand-colored lithographic plates by Lami; printed by Villain. Page size: 10 × 14 inches, uncut. Bookplate of Michael Sadleir. Orig. wrappers.

This album of twelve small lithographs is best regarded as a trial run for the masterly *Voyage en Angleterre*. After a short visit to England in 1826, Lami set down the hasty impressions of a tourist who has glimpsed some of the obvious sights. The besetting fault of the series is crowding too many figures into the picture. Hence, subjects limited in scope, like the cock fight and the boxing match, yield Lami his best results.

Lami and Monnier

139

[Cover title:] **Voyage en Angleterre**. Paris, Firmin Didot et Lami-Denozan, 1829–1830. [4] *l.* letterpress; 28 hand-colored lithographic plates by Lami (17), Monnier (10), and both artists (1); printed by Villain. The final 4 plates in smaller format, with the original wrapper imprint reading: Paris, Gihaut frères. Page size: 16½ × 11¼ inches. Bookplate of Michael Sadleir. ½ red morocco; orig. wrapper bound in. Colas 1748.

Lami's lithographs in this album have a salience and solidity otherwise unmatched in his work, and the bright yet harmonious coloring with which they were completed makes them hardly distinguishable from watercolors. The series also has the interest of showing English life and customs as seen through the fresh eyes of two shrewd foreigners. They emphasize the freedom and well-being of the people, which combine to ensure "order in . . . apparent disorder" (text for no. 20). Coachmen, turnpike keepers, footmen, merchants, farmers, and workmen all behave with ease and confidence. The many glimpses of country and village life exude tranquillity. The social order of which these

men and women are a part is fixed but not oppressive. In "Evening prayer" (no. 17), there is a solidarity about the household at its devotions, even if the family takes its ease on one side of the room, while the servants are huddled together on the other. The culminating plate of the album, in which both artists had a hand, shows Parliament Street in London during the evening rush hour (no. 20). It is a microcosm of the city's "busy scene of crowded life," soldiers drilling at the rear, carriages criss-crossing, and all sorts and conditions of men going their various ways in the foreground.

140

Quadrille de Marie Stuart. [Paris], 1829. Letterpress title (stencil- and hand-colored), and 26 hand-colored lithographic plates by Lami; printed by Fonrouge. Page size: $20\frac{3}{4} \times 14\frac{1}{4}$ inches. Contemp. $\frac{1}{4}$ red morocco. Colas 1747.

The passion for the past manifested by artists and writers in the 1820s occasionally touched the aristocratic world as well. The young Duchesse de Berry, for example, held several historical balls, the best remembered of which was that of 2 March 1829, recalling the arrival of Mary Stuart of Scotland at the Tuileries to wed the future Francis II. Lami's *Quadrille de Marie Stuart* was commissioned by the Duchess as a record of this brilliant event. Of the twenty-six plates, twenty-two are devoted to the sumptuous costumes designed for the occasion. The Duchess herself is shown as Mary Stuart, and the Duc de Chartres as her bridegroom, with other roles being assumed by persons around the court. More interesting still are the remaining lithographs, representing scenes at the ball. That shown depicts the guests ascending the stairway of the Pavillon de Marsan. The fact that this album was given to the principal participants, rather than sold, may help to account for its scarcity.

(140) Lami, *Quadrille de Marie Stuart*

Lithography and Romantic Literature

The coming of Romanticism in French literature coincided with the flowering of lithography in French art. Though David had died in 1826, most critics and artists still saw the world from his neoclassic perspective. Rebellious Romantics found inspiration in the growing familiarity with the remnants of the Middle Ages made possible by Taylor's *Voyages pittoresques* (106–109) and such works of documentation as *Les tournois du roi René*. The record provided by Boulanger and Achille Devéria of the Paris season of Charles Kemble's theatrical troupe in 1827–1828 shows how Shakespeare's plays opened the eyes of Hugo and his fellow Romantics to the deficiencies of the French classical stage. The impact of Delacroix's *Faust*, the high point of Romantic book illustration, was reinforced by his *Hamlet*. Such parodies of *Faust* as Antoine Thomas' *Le rêve* only had the effect of adding to its fame. (It may be mentioned that a subtler parody of the more sedate Romanticism of Lamartine is to be found in the final plate of *Les folies gauloises* (245), Doré's satirical survey of French manners through the ages.) The parallel development of Romantic art and Romantic literature may be examined in detail in several periodicals illustrated chiefly with lithographs, *La silhouette*, *La revue des peintres*, and particularly *L'Artiste*.

REFERENCES Baudelaire; Beraldi; *Bibliothèque Nationale: Delacroix et la gravure romantique*; Bouchot; Calot (1931).

141

Les tournois du roi René d'après le manuscrit et les dessins originaux de la Bibliothèque Royale. Publiés par M.M. Champollion Figeac, pour le texte & les notes explicatives; L. J. J. Dubois, pour les dessins et les planches coloriées; Ch. Motte, lithographe, éditeur de l'ouvrage. Paris, Ch. Motte, Firmin Didot, & L. J. J. Dubois, 1826. 12, 27 p., [1] *l*. Illus: Lithographic title-page (repeating wrapper), frontispiece, section title, head- and tailpiece, and 19 lithographic plates, 11 hand-colored. Page size: 27¼ × 20½ inches, uncut. Orig. wrapper.

This elephant folio is a work of some splendor. It offers what is stated to be the first faithful text of King René's *Traité de la forme et devis d'un tournois*, together with twenty-one plates, eleven of them in color, and two vignettes. Their source is manuscript 8352 in the Bibliothèque du Roi, said to have been composed in Anjou about 1450. The plates begin with meetings of the participants, proceed to the arrival of various groups at the tournament, and conclude with the mock combats themselves. Although the lithographs are unremarkable in design, a vivid sense of their authenticity together with the charm of their lively colors must have made them something of a revelation in 1826. It should be noted that the two figures of the frontispiece are by Delacroix (Delteil, no. 56).

Louis Boulanger and Achille Devéria

142

Souvenirs du théâtre anglais à Paris, dessinés par MM. Devéria et Boulanger. Avec un texte par M. Moreau. [Paris], Gaugain, Lambert et cie., 1827. 72 p. Illus: Wood-engraved t.p. vignette, 13 wood-engraved tailpieces, 15 lithographic plates: 12 hand-colored plates heightened with gum arabic, by Devéria and Boulanger, 1 unsigned plate with lithotint, 1 plate on *chine appliqué* by Bouillet, 1 unsigned plate on *chine appliqué*. Page size: 17 × 11⅞ inches, uncut. Bookplate of Michael Sadleir. Laid into wrappers for parts 3 and 9.

This album records a visit to Paris in 1827–1828 paid by the theatrical company of Charles Kemble. Their repertory included *Hamlet*, represented by three plates, *Othello*, represented by two, *Romeo and Juliet*, represented by five, and Nicholas Rowe's *Jane Shore*, represented by two. There are also portraits of Kemble, and of the two principal actresses, Miss Foote and Miss Smithson, but not of the equally celebrated Edmund Kean and Macready. The performances were in English, which Parisian audiences did not understand, but they were impressed by the energy and ardour of the players. It is significant that the admirers of Kean criticized

(142) Boulanger and Achille Devéria, *Souvenirs du théâtre anglais à Paris*

(143) Goethe, *Faust*

Kemble for not being "sufficiently *outré*" (p. 43). The introduction, though it is judicious in tone, nonetheless predicts a revolution in the French theatre, which is out of touch with the times. It is suggested that, despite the "innumerable faults" of Shakespeare, this "rude genius" may help to bring about such an upheaval (p. 7).

The response of Romantic writers and artists was more enthusiastic. It is crudely summed up in the vignette for the wrapper, which shows the death of Desdemona at Othello's hand, with the legend: "Good ! ! ! " Indeed, the performances of the English company had their influence on Victor Hugo's plays and Delacroix's lithographs for *Faust*. The designs of Boulanger and Devéria emphasize violent action and violent emotion, the very excesses forbidden by the decorous conventions of the French classical theatre. The plate reproduced is from *Othello* (v, i). Roderigo has attacked Cassio at Iago's urging, and has himself been killed by Iago, described in the French text as "Shakespeare's Mephistopheles" (p. 64).

Eugène Delacroix (1798–1863)

The history and character of Delacroix are too well known to require summary. Our concern is with his lithographs, a medium in which his superiority is quite as marked as in his paintings. These belong chiefly to the earlier part of his career; indeed two-thirds of the 131 lithographs listed by Delteil were made before 1830. In these years he was an embattled Romantic, notorious for his "Dante and Virgil," "Massacre at Scio," and other paintings, which attracted the scorn and derision of traditional artists, critics, and amateurs. Yet of all his works, his lithographs for *Faust* offered the sharpest challenge to the conventional canons of art.

As Baudelaire noted (p. 973), Delacroix was an "essentially literary" artist. "Macbeth consulting the witches" of 1825 was his first important lithograph, and he went on to illustrate not only *Faust* and *Hamlet* but Scott's novels (five plates) and Goethe's *Goetz von Berlichingen* (seven plates). Most of his chosen plays and stories were set in the late

Middle Ages, not as they were just beginning to be studied at the École de Chartres, but as his violent and colorful imagination conceived them. These lithographs turned the attention of a generation of French illustrators to subjects drawn from legend and fantasy. Of another important aspect of his work in lithography, his depiction of big cats, "Jeune tigre jouant avec sa mère" from *L'Artiste* (147) offers a prime example.

REFERENCES Baudelaire; Beraldi; *Bibliothèque Nationale: Delacroix et la gravure romantique*; Bouchot; Curtis (1897); Delteil—*Delacroix*; Hofer—*Faust*.

143 JOHANN WOLFGANG VON GOETHE

Faust, tragédie de M. de Goethe, traduite en français par M. Albert Stapfer, ornée d'un portrait de l'auteur, et de dix-sept dessins composés d'après les principales scènes de l'ouvrage et exécutés sur pierre par M. Eugène Delacroix. Paris, Ch. Motte & Sautelet, 1828. [2] *l.*, iv, 148 p. Lithographic illus by Delacroix: Front. and 16 plates, 4 on *chine appliqué*, 1 on *chine rose*; printed by Motte. Page size: 16¼ × 10¾ inches. ¾ red morocco by Champs. Beraldi v, p. 161.

Though Delacroix's lithographs were finally published as illustrations to an edition of *Faust*, his inspiration seems to have come only indirectly from Goethe's tragedy. Remarking that the second part of *Faust*, which had appeared in 1832, was of little literary merit, he had this to say in a letter of 1862 to Philippe Burty about the lithographs which he had drawn for the first part. "You ask me what gave birth to the idea of plates for *Faust*. I recall that I saw about 1821 the designs of *Retsch*, which sufficiently impressed me; but it is above all the performance of a drama with music concerning *Faust* which I saw at London in 1825, that moved me to do something with it. The actor, named Terry, . . . who even came to Paris, where he played, among other parts, that of *King Lear*, was an accomplished, if gross, Mephistopheles, but that did not detract from his agility and his satanic character." (Quoted by Delteil, no. 57.)

Delacroix began his lithographs, which were initially intended for publication as an album by Charles Motte, later in 1825. He intended them to be a manifesto for Romanticism in art, where neoclassic principles still prevailed, much as Victor Hugo's preface to *Cromwell* in 1827 was a manifesto for Romanticism in literature. Since his purpose was "to astonish the middle class" (Bouchot, p. 94), he conceived them as a deliberate act of aggression, and they did indeed arouse resentment as they circulated over the next three years. They were finally published by Sautelet as illustrations to Albert Stapfer's translation of *Faust* in 1828.

The book met with the expected hostile reception. The prevailing style of literary illustration was that exampled in the Desenne's plates for the French classics, small, stiff, formal engravings. Delacroix's large, free, fantastic lithographs could not be readily assimilated. Traditional critics were outraged, and even Delacroix's Romantic allies conceded that he was given to exaggeration. Only gradually did *Faust* begin to be appreciated as the most significant illustrated book of its time.

There was one person, however, who saw its greatness from the first. This was Goethe himself, who had been shown some of Delacroix's lithographs in 1826. He observed to Eckermann on 26 November of that year: "One must acknowledge that this M. Delacroix has a great talent, which in *Faust* has found its true nourishment. The French public reproach him for an excess of savage force, but, actually, here it is perfectly suitable. . . . If I have to agree that M. Delacroix has surpassed the scenes my writing has conjured up in my own imagination, how much more will readers of the book find his compositions full of reality, and passing beyond the imagery which they envision?" (Quoted by Hofer, p. 2, from Goethe's *Gespräche mit Eckermann.*)

Everyone remembers the opening plate of *Faust*, Mephistopheles soaring through the night with the spires of a city below him (p. 15), and there are other masterly compositions such as Mephistopheles in a students' tavern (p. 62), the duel of Faust and Valentine (p. 109), and Margaret in church (p. 112). It must be admitted that there are also plates in which the figures are so out of drawing as to invite ridicule. Yet what really counts is the drive, inventiveness, and sustained harmony of style of the entire series. Delacroix's particular success, of course, was the flamboyant and sardonic Mephistopheles. Over the last 150 years he has become one of the few universally recognized figures of graphic art.

Faust inaugurated a tradition of fantastic medievalism in illustration. Delacroix's whole ap-

(143) Goethe, *Faust*

paratus of melodramatic settings and characters, mannered costumes, and weird accessories, such as the creatures out of Bosch and Bruegel who figure in the large lithograph of the witches' sabbath (p. 123), was drawn upon again and again in the decades that followed. In the early 1830s *L'Artiste* offered many images of this sort in wood engravings after Tony Johannot, lithographs by Boulanger, and etchings by Nanteuil. The tradition reached a second climax in the wood engravings after Doré for Balzac's *Contes drolatiques* (244).

Goethe's judgment has long since prevailed concerning Delacroix's *Faust*. Indeed, even the creators of *livres de peintres* see it as the first link in their own tradition. Few would now deny that it is one of the supreme illustrated books of the world.

Friedrich August Moritz Retzsch (1779–1857)

Retzsch's series of twenty-six **outlines illustrative** of Goethe's tragedy **of Faust**, engraved from the originals by Henry Moses . . . London, Boosey and sons, 1820. [2] *l.*, 60 p. Illus: Front. and 25 plates by Moses after Retzsch. Page size: 12⅞×9⅞ inches. Contemp. red morocco by C. Murton.

This may have been the edition of Retzsch's *Outlines* which Delacroix saw about 1821. A number

of the subjects depicted by Retzsch were selected as well by Delacroix. An example is "Valentine with Faust" (plate 19), in which Delacroix's arrangement of the figures is much the same as Retzsch's. The setting and atmosphere of the two designs, on the other hand, are quite dissimilar, as they remain throughout the series. A glance at the scene from *Othello* in *Souvenirs du théâtre anglais à Paris* will suggest that the added elements have come in part from Delacroix's familiarity with Shakespeare as played on the English stage.

144 ANTOINE-JEAN-BAPTISTE THOMAS

[Cover title:] **Le rêve,** ou Les effets du romantisme sur un jeune surnuméraire à l'Arriéré. Poëme en six chants (avec quelques inversions de rigueur) sorti de la plume d'un anonyme bien connu. Orné de croquis composés et lithographiés par Thomas . . . [Paris], Delpech, 1829. [6] *l.* letterpress text, 6 lithographic plates by Thomas; printed by Delpech. Page size: 13 × 16 inches. Bookplate of Michael Sadleir. ¾ brown cloth, orig. lithographic front wrapper bound in.

In his letter to Burty about *Faust* quoted above, Delacroix goes on to admit "the oddity of its plates which were the object of certain caricatures and placed me more and more as one of the leaders of the *school of the ugly*." The cleverest of these parodies are to be found in *Le rêve, ou les effets du ro-*

(144)   Lithograph by Thomas, *Le rêve*

(145) Shakespeare, *Hamlet*

Delacroix, wash and ink drawing for *Hamlet*

mantisme by Antoine Thomas, whose work we have already encountered in *Un an à Rome* (125). The protagonist of this album is a young clerk, ardently devoted to Romanticism, who has returned to his garret after an evening spent watching a popular melodrama, *Le bourreau d'Amsterdam*, which he finds more amusing than *Faust*, "with its great laughing devil." A nightmare, in which his mistress Melanie and his cat Anatole play their parts, shows him pursued through heaven and earth, now by Mephistopheles, now by the executioner of Amsterdam. After a climax in which the former takes his revenge by disappearing with Melanie after displaying her initial written on the sky (plate 5), he is awakened by the portress with his morning milk. It is explained that the nightmare, "which has been weighing romantically on him during the night," was caused by Anatole sleeping on his chest.

145

Hamlet. Seize sujets dessinés et lithographiés par Eugène Delacroix. Paris, Dusacq, Michel Lévy, & Pagnerre, 1864. [2] *l.* letterpress, 16 lithographic plates by Delacroix on *chine appliqué*; printed by Bertauts. Page size: 21½×14⅛ inches. Wrappers, uncut. Beraldi v, p. 164.

Delacroix made his first lithograph for *Hamlet* in 1828, at about the time that he finished his last for *Faust*. The sixteen included in this series were drawn between 1834 and 1843, five of them in 1834 and 1835, and six in 1843. He published thirteen himself in 1843 with Villain as printer in an edition of eighty copies. After his death all sixteen (including v, xII, and xv as additional plates) appeared in 1864 with Bertauts as printer in an edition of 200 copies.

Delacroix's intimate knowledge of the play is shown in his choice of subjects. He depicts many of the dramatic highlights: Hamlet's encounter with the ghost of his father (II, III), the players' representation of his father's death before Claudius and Gertrude (vI), Ophelia's madness (xII), and the struggle between Hamlet and Laertes in Ophelia's grave (xv). To these he adds several scenes which are the settings for lines that must have appealed strongly to his sardonic turn of mind: "Words, words, words" (IV), "Get thee to a nunnery" (v), "Will you play upon this pipe?" (vII),

and "Alas! poor Yorick" (xIV). Unlike *Faust*, *Hamlet* had Delacroix's unstinted admiration.

As Baudelaire pointed out (p. 898), Delacroix and Shakespeare were linked by their "singular and tenacious melancholy" and their absorption in "human suffering" (p. 898). The blacks and greys of Delacroix's lithographs convey these characteristics more effectively than could any other graphic medium. Having established this somber atmosphere, he avoided scenes such as Hamlet's feigned madness and treated with sobriety such others as the struggle in Ophelia's grave, where he might have approached the extravagance of *Faust*.

Delacroix's *Seize sujets tirés d'Hamlet* is a masterpiece of illustration. His command of every situation, the individuality with which he invests each of his figures, his subtle and developing exploration of the characters, not only of Hamlet, but also of Claudius, Gertrude, and even Polonius, make these plates perhaps the most notable series ever devoted to a Shakespearean play. Yet Delacroix paid a price for his achievement. In this album Romanticism has triumphed and is consolidating its position. One misses the freedom, even the abandon, of his designs for *Faust*.

✎ Pen-and-ink and wash drawing over traces of black chalk by Delacroix for *Hamlet*. The artist's estate stamp in red at lower right. Sheet size: 9¾×6½ inches.

This preliminary drawing for *Hamlet* was not used in Delacroix's lithographs. It illustrates the point in act III, scene ii, marked by the stage direction "Enter one with a recorder." For the player thus mentioned Delacroix substituted Rosencrantz and Guildenstern in the lithograph finally made. He was thus enabled to show Hamlet asking these minions of Claudius the telling question: "Will you play upon this pipe?" Yet one regrets the substitution for this frail and haggard actor, with whom Delacroix no doubt sympathized as a fellow artist, of the two dissembling courtiers, substantial materialists like most persons about the Danish king. In the lithograph, incidentally, the recorder has become a flute and is on an altogether larger scale. The drawing has the red stamp "E.D." which testifies to its having been in Delacroix's estate. It is mounted in the *William Shakespeare* volume of the set of Victor Hugo's *Oeuvres* described in Romantic Engraving below.

(146)   Tony Johannot, lithograph in *La silhouette*

146

La silhouette, journal des caricatures, beaux-arts, dessins, moeurs, théâtres . . . Paris, 29 June 1828 to 2 January 1831. 4 v. in 1. I: [1] *l.*, 104 p. II: [2] *l.*, 104 p. III: [2] *l.*, 104 p. IV: [1] *l.*, 104 p. Illus. by various artists: Wood-engraved t.p. vignette, 61 uncolored, and 45 colored plates: I: 17 uncolored (including 1 on *chine appliqué* and 1 on purple paper), and 9 hand-colored lithographic plates. II: 13 uncolored and 14 hand-colored lithographic plates (including 1 colored plate in 2 states), 1 woodcut vignette. III: 15 uncolored and 12 hand-colored lithographic plates. IV: 16 uncolored and 10 hand-colored lithographic plates. Page size: 10⅜ × 7¾ inches. Perhaps the Descamps-Scrive copy listed by Carteret; bookplate of Michael Sadleir. ½ green morocco by Yseux, orig. wrappers bound in. Carteret III, 563–564.

La silhouette was the first journal an issue of which consisted of two lithographs and a few pages of text, thus showing the way both to *L'Artiste* and *La caricature* (160). Its initial concern was literary, and among other plates in this vein it contains striking representations of Hugo's *Hernani* by Achille Devéria (I, 82) and of Bürger's *Lénore* by Tony Johannot (II, 2). When its emphasis shifted to political caricature, it was censured for a vignette depicting Charles X as a Jesuit. This episode, of which the editors made a good deal, called forth one of Grandville's most fantastic designs (III, 46). He also contributed a series of characteristic animal caricatures. Three plates by Daumier appeared in *La silhouette* (II, 34; IV, 28 and 76). Though the first of these is identified by Delteil as Daumier's earliest lithograph (see below, p. 230), the last, an anticlerical satire on middle-class hypocrisy, is by far the most characteristic. Many of the other leading lithographic artists of the time figure in *La silhouette*, Gerard-Fontallard being the most frequent contributor. A curiosity is Philipon's "La marquise" (I, 14), in which the face of the lady is replaced in some copies by a bit of mirror.

147

L'Artiste. Journal de la littérature et des beaux-arts . . . Paris, [1831–1838]. First series, 15 volumes. Colleast as in Vicaire. Page size: 11 × 8¼ inches. Contemp. ½ red morocco. Vicaire I, 103–106.

Quite as much as *La caricature* (160), the first series of *L'Artiste* is a true *livre de bibliophile*, even though its fifteen large volumes, like *La caricature*'s ten, have usually kept these sets off the shelves of collectors of illustrated books. In its subtitle *L'Artiste* claims both literature and art as its province, and indeed its staple is the regular chronicling of fine arts, music, drama, and books. Each year's Salon is reported in detail, and sometimes Romantic paintings refused admission there are reproduced by lithography. Notable plays and books are reviewed at length. Original stories, short plays, and poetry are occasionally printed. Indeed, the leading events of the Romantic movement are not only described but illustrated. When *Notre-Dame de Paris* is reviewed, there is an accompanying wood engraving after Tony Johannot from the book itself and a lithograph by his brother Alfred (I, 104–106). When Dumas' *Antony* is noticed, Alfred Johannot depicts its sensational last scene: "She resisted me. . . . I killed her!" (I, 184). Several of Balzac's short stories are printed, including "La transaction," in which Colonel Chabert's introduction of himself as "the man who died at Eylau" is shown in a haunting lithograph by Menut Alophe (III, 30). So the chronicle continues throughout these early volumes.

The magazine's surpassing interest, however, resides in the plates that are not illustrations. They are so abundant and significant as to make it for Romantic lithography in general what Taylor's *Voyages pittoresques* (106–109) is for architectural and landscape lithography. Three contributors were virtually staff artists: Menut Alophe with eighty-two lithographs, many after other artists; Léon Noel with fifty-nine, a good number of them portraits, including of Dumas (III, 296) and Hugo (IV, 208); and Gavarni with fifty-five. Gavarni's work, best exampled in "Le champagne" (VII, 24), is more varied and attractive than are the costume plates to which he often devoted himself at this period. Between them Achille and Eugène Devéria were responsible for forty lithographs. Gigoux contributed twenty-five, including fine portraits of Delacroix (IV, 72), Alfred and Tony Johannot (IV, 152), and Vigny (III, 296). Among the other artists represented are Bellangé, Charlet, Dauzats, Decamps, Tony Johannot, Lami, Raffet, and Camille Roqueplan.

The work of three lithographers deserves special attention. Alfred Johannot made a strong impression by a series of somber, sensational, or tragic compositions, two of which have been mentioned. Louis Boulanger drew fourteen dramatic designs, chiefly for the later volumes, including "Chasse infernale" (IX, 192) and scenes from *Faust* (X, 60) and the *Divine Comedy* (X, 96), which upheld the banner of Delacroix against academic art. One sees from these lithographs why Hugo was led to predict for his friend a brilliant career, which in the event he did not quite achieve. Finally, Delacroix himself offered "Jeune tigre jouant avec sa mère" (I, 300), one of his finest plates, which is shown here in the first state with imprint of Delaunois, and "Le jeune Clifford" (VII, 284). The former displays an aspect of his lithographic work admired by critics who find his designs for *Faust* and even *Hamlet* exaggerated and contorted.

Though lithography was the dominant mode in *L'Artiste*, other forms of illustrations were employed as well. Tony Johannot was responsible for seven etchings, including the well-known "Soirée d'artiste" (III, 130), in which Nodier and other Romantic celebrities can be recognized. There are five etchings by Nanteuil, among them "Dina la belle juive" (V, 68) from Petrus Borel's *Champavert*, and "Fuite en Egypte" (V, 264), from his own high renaissance painting of the holy family. The first five volumes also make up a veritable anthology of the wood engravings of the period, for the most part those of Porret after Tony Johannot. Many are from Nodier's *Histoire du roi de Bohême* (179); indeed the episode of the woodcutter and his dog, later to be illustrated by Steinlen (338), is retold by Jules Janin with five illustrations (I, 284–286). Works by Balzac, Hugo, and Vigny, as well as a number of minor writers, are also drawn upon. See Romantic Engraving below.

It is true, unfortunately, that the importance of *L'Artiste* is confined to its first series. Particularly in its early volumes the high hopes of a vigorous artistic movement are everywhere in evidence. During that period the magazine's public was clearly an

(147)   Lithograph by Alfred Johannot in *L'Artiste*

(147)   Lithograph by Louis Boulanger in *L'Artiste*

(147)   Lithograph by Delacroix in *L'Artiste*

elite for which both artists and writers produced their best work. This inspiration gradually faded. The text became pedestrian and the plates commonplace. As Romanticism faltered, so did *L'Artiste*, which finally became merely one more conventional critical journal.

REFERENCES Beraldi; Vicaire.

148

[**La revue des peintres.** Paris, Aubert, 1834–1838]. 4 v. in 2. I: 120 lithographic plates by various artists, including 2 by Daumier (55, 67), and 4 by C. Nanteuil (82, 96, 104, 117). II: 68 p. letterpress; 120 lithographic plates by various artists. Inserted in v. II is a letterpress announcement for the *12ᵉ livraison*. Page size: 11¼ × 8½ inches, uncut. Contemp. red calf; wrappers for parts 1 and 6 inserted.

Each of forty-eight monthly issues of this journal contains five lithographs. There are a few original contributions, but the great majority are copies of contemporary paintings. The Salons of the several years are well represented; indeed, a reasonable awareness of changing fashions in painting may be gathered from these volumes. Beginning with plate 131 there is an accompanying text, usually brief and factual. Daumier is represented by two genre studies: "La bonne grand-mère" (55) and "Le malade" (67). These rare lithographs look forward to his later paintings of common life. The four plates by Nanteuil (82, 96, 104, 117) are less exotic than his contributions to *L'Artiste*, though his characteristic note of strangeness is not entirely absent. Altogether, it is not too much to say that the illustrations for *La revue des peintres* vie in interest with those in *L'Artiste* during the same years.

Sulpice-Guillaume Chevallier, Called Gavarni (1804–1866)

Ever since 1837, when their lithographs began to appear side by side in *Le charivari*, Gavarni and Daumier have been compared and contrasted. Gavarni's renown was greater in his own time, but over the last 100 years he has been far outstripped by Daumier. There can be no quarrel with this judgment, yet if one takes the engravings on wood and metal from his designs into account (see Romantic Engraving) and gives proper emphasis to his underestimated later albums like *Masques et visages*, it becomes evident that he does not rank far below Daumier among French illustrators. Luckily the materials for presenting him are abundant. His letters have survived in some quantity. Edmond and Jules de Goncourt were among his intimates in later life and wrote a major book about him. And there is a full and authoritative biography by Paul-André Lemoisne.

Gavarni was born in Paris, where he was to spend most of his life. His education was mathematical and technical, but he turned to drawing for pocket money, and by the time he was twenty he had published his first lithographic album, *Etrennes de 1825. Recréations diabolico-fantasmagoriques*. In 1824 he went to Bordeaux, where he had a commission to make engravings of a bridge. This came to nothing. Rescued from poverty by "a *bearable* rich man" (Goncourts, p. 30), he discovered his artistic vocation. In 1826, "an old man of 22" (p. 37), he set off with his dog on a tour of the Pyrenees, sketchbook in hand, the chief result of which was a *Lettre de Trilby, chien cosmopolite, à son ami Zamore, chien montagnard*. Indeed, at this time Gavarni was more proficient with words than with pencil and brush. After two years of wandering and contemplation, he returned to the metropolis.

There he began a journal headed "Paris, 1828. Second Epoch," in which he set down his observations of the life around him, declaring that in art

"What remains is to be true." "It is from nature above all that one must paint." (P. 67.) The following year he adopted the name of Gavarni, taken from Gavarnie in the Pyrenees, which he had visited during his travels. As he studied Paris and its people, his drawing, which had been mediocre, attained a degree of grace and elegance. Contributing to *La mode* and *L'Artiste* (147), he soon found himself accepted not only in literary and artistic circles, but in Parisian society as well. The fact that he was a handsome and charming man, something of a dandy in clothes and manner, no doubt eased his way. He became famous for his mistresses. Late in life he told the Goncourts that he had had affairs with 150 women, of whom he had understood none and loved only his wife (*Bibliothèque Nationale: Gavarni*, p. 23).

Etched bookplate by Gavarni for the Goncourt brothers

When two albums of his lithographs appeared in 1830, Balzac praised him as a thinker and observer, remarking that "Gavarni is writing a book without knowing it." That he had literary ambitions is testified by the vast *paperasserie*, described by the Goncourts, which he left behind him at his death. These aspirations came to nothing directly, yet they were fulfilled after a fashion in the legends which add animation and depth to his lithographs. So assured did Gavarni's position seem at the end of 1833 that he began to publish the weekly *Journal des gens du monde* for which he also provided much of the text and illustrations. It failed after twenty numbers, only eighteen of which were issued, leaving him with obligations which were to embarrass him for many years. In 1835 he was arrested for debt and sent to Clichy. Far from being overwhelmed, he saw this experience as a fresh opportunity for observation. Indeed, he made a lithographic series from his memories: *Clichy*, twenty-one lithographs, 1840–1841.

In 1837 Gavarni began his connection with *Le charivari*, which did not conclude until 1848. In all he drew 1054 lithographs for his journal (Armelhault and Bocher, p. 82). Most of these appeared in series, some twenty-five of which extend to ten or more plates, and were afterwards published by Aubert in albums. Perhaps the best of these collections are *Fourberies de femmes en matière de sentiment*, *Les étudiants de Paris*, *Les débardeurs*, and *Les lorettes*; but some of the rest are of hardly inferior interest. Still further series, contributed to periodicals other than *Le charivari*, were also issued as albums. Baudelaire had this part of Gavarni's work particularly in mind when he wrote (p. 1010) that "the true glory and the true mission of Gavarni and Daumier has been to complete Balzac." Certainly the pictures of Parisian society provided by the two artists perfectly complement each other. Daumier's preoccupation was the working middle class with faces and figures heavily marked by life. Gavarni remained for the most part outside the humdrum bourgeois round. He preferred to show "youth at the prow and pleasure at the helm." His pretty girls and sleek young men are bent on enjoyment. They live lives of graceful dissipation, with love intrigues and balls on the one hand, and pawnbrokers' shops and debtors' prisons on the other. Their motto is *carpe diem*, and they rarely think of the day of reckoning.

In 1844 Gavarni married an accomplished musician of great beauty who was studying in Paris. He and his bride installed themselves in an old house with a large garden at Auteuil. Their two sons, Jean and Pierre, were some consolation to

Gavarni for the death of his mother in 1845, an event which deeply affected him. The following year he returned to *Le charivari*, to which he had hardly contributed since 1843. He wished to call the series that ensued *Choses de Paris* but was persuaded instead to employ the general title *Oeuvres nouvelles*. Its major albums were *Carnaval*; *Impressions de ménage, deuxième série*, thirty-nine lithographs, 1846–1847; and *Baliverneries parisiens*, twenty-four lithographs, 1847. As is noted in the account of *Carnaval* below, they mark a further step in his stylistic development. A shorter series entitled *Le chemin de Toulon*, ten lithographs, 1846–1847, should also be mentioned. In these studies of future prisoners he looked almost for the first time at repugnant aspects of life which were later to absorb his attention.

In 1847 Gavarni departed for England, where he passed most of the next three years. Since his work was well known, he had the entrée to London society; indeed he was welcomed at court. Yet he attempted no conquests, remarking that "when an Englishwoman is clothed, she is no longer a woman, she is a cathedral" (Goncourts, p. 287), and he soon forsook the upper world. Moving from Grosvenor Square to Whitechapel and Saint Giles, he found, like Géricault before him (102–105) and Doré after him (251), that the London poor were wonderfully rewarding subjects for an artist.

As time passed, Gavarni became a virtual recluse. This period of self-imposed isolation, study, and meditation worked a profound change in his outlook. He seems to have admitted to himself that he was tired of the empty life of pleasure that he had led and dissatisfied with the triviality of the designs in which he had recorded it. One may attribute to him something of the revulsion which led Browning to write "A Toccata of Galuppi's":

"As for Venice and its people, merely born to bloom and drop,
  Here on earth they bore their fruitage, mirth and folly were the crop.
  What of soul was left, I wonder, when the kissing had to stop?"

"Dust and ashes!" So you creak it, and I want the heart to scold.
  Dear dead women, with such hair, too—what's become of all the gold
  Used to hang and brush their bosom? I feel chilly and grown old.

At any rate, some of the lithographs that Gavarni made in England strike a grim, sardonic note that is new in his work, a note that continued to be dominant after he returned to France in 1851.

Reunited with his family at Auteuil, Gavarni's dispirited mood was soon dissipated. With painting as his passionate distraction, he was soon at work on what was to be his masterpiece in lithography. The immense series called *Masques et visages*, drawn at a rate approaching one plate a day, appeared in *Paris* in 1852–1853. It expresses with unfailing variety and inventiveness his disillusioned, ironic view of the world. Unfortunately this was not what the public wanted from its brilliant and amusing favorite of the 1840s, and the series aroused no enthusiasm.

Gavarni's later life was marked by increasing unhappiness. He could still find enjoyment in the company of friends such as Gautier, the Goncourts, and Sainte-Beuve, but otherwise he shut himself off more and more from society. He found consolation in his mathematical studies, his water-

A *bon à tirer* for *Masques et visages*

Watercolor drawing by Gavarni

colors, and his cherished but sickly older son, Jean. He was living apart from his wife, and after Jean died suddenly in 1857, Gavarni told the Goncourts (p. 383) that "He was my only reason for being." Henceforth there was a touch of irrationality in Gavarni's behavior; indeed he spent ruinous sums in constantly reordering his garden. When *Physionomies parisiennes*; *Par-ci, par-là*; and *D'Après nature* succeeded no better than *Masques et visages*, he was profoundly wounded to find himself virtually without an audience at a time when he was doing his best work. He gave up lithography in 1859. Debt and the expropriation of his beloved garden to clear the way for a railroad made his last years oppressive. When death came in 1866, it may not have been altogether unwelcome.

Gavarni's 2700 plates, most of which were assembled in albums, make him one of the great masters of lithography. This was the judgment, for example, of Degas, who collected more than 2000 of them, including many proofs and early states (Lemoisne, II, 224). The most literary of illustrators, Gavarni had the particular talent of making legend and design into a perfect whole. Indeed, he used to hold back his stones if, as he put it, "they haven't spoken to me" (Goncourts, p. 275). The ingratiating albums of his earlier career have always commanded admiration, and they are sought after today, especially with contemporary coloring. Yet delightful as are the pretty women of these lithographs—the "pale roses" of *Les fleurs du mal*—, engaging as is the society of which they are a part, it is Gavarni's later designs that establish his most convincing claim to greatness. Working "after nature," with no hints of caricature, he offers in some 500 scenes and portraits a picture of life that is consistently powerful and moving. The lithographs of this period need no coloring, which is provided in effect by the blacks, greys, and contrasting whites of the lithographs themselves. Just as Gavarni's watercolors are now ardently pursued, so too will his later lithographs come to be sought after. Since the albums that contain them were published in some quantity (300 copies, it would appear, of *Masques et visages*), they should be available for some time to come.

REFERENCES Armelhault and Bocher; Baudelaire; Beraldi; *Bibliothèque Nationale: Gavarni*; Bouchot; Curtis (1897); the Goncourts—*Gavarni*; Lemoisne—*Gavarni*; Warnod.

Graphite and watercolor drawing by Gavarni touched with china white. Signed in graphite at lower right. Image size: 6⅛×5 inches.

This characteristic watercolor evidently dates from Gavarni's stay in England or afterwards, since it is in his later style as described by the Goncourts (pp. 322–327). It comes from the collection of Paul Gavarni.

149

[**Musée de costumes** dessinées dans les théâtres de Paris, les salons, les bibliothèques, les promenades publiques, etc. Paris, Aubert, 1837–1838]. 117 lithographic plates by Gavarni, including 106 uncolored plates: 54, 77–117, 119, 121–125, 127–158, 160–171, 173–180, 185–187, 279–280, 288; 9 hand-colored: 82, 91, 118, 119, 124, 127, 139, 174, and 175; 2 proofs: 114 (hand-colored, annotated) and 172. Page size: 10½×6⅝ inches. ½ calf.

(149)   Lithograph by Gavarni in *Musée de costumes*

In his early years as an artist Gavarni made many lithographs of costumes and fashions. His most considerable effort in this line is to be found in the *Musée de costumes*. Knowing of the difficulties into which he had been plunged by the failure of his *Journal des gens du monde*, Aubert asked him to contribute to this ongoing series, one aim of which was to portray the leading actors and actresses of the day. Gavarni, whose knowledge of the Parisian theatre was profound, entered into the project with enthusiasm. The plates which he devoted to Montigny, Déjazet, Mlle. Georges and the rest are true likenesses; and the costumes in which he displayed them, most of which he invented himself, are colorful and attractive. The remaining plates are types rather than representations of specific individuals. That shown (no. 114), an early proof touched by the artist, falls in the latter category. Even it is far removed from the puppet or tailor's dummy that one usually associates with costume plates.

150

[**Fourberies de femmes.** Paris, 1837]. 12 hand-colored lithographic plates by Gavarni, heightened with gum arabic; printed by Aubert (1, 2, 9, 12), Caboche (3–8, 10), and Caboche, Grégoire (11).

(bound with)

151

[**Fourberies de femmes en matière de sentiment. 2ᵉ série.** Paris, 1840–1841]. 51 (of 52) hand-colored lithographic plates by Gavarni, heightened with gum arabic; printed by Aubert. Page size: 12⅞×10⅛ inches. Bookplate of Michael Sadleir. Contemp. green morocco. Beraldi VII, p. 51.

After the initial success of *Caricaturana*, Philipon proposed to Gavarni that he draw "Mme. Robert Macaire" for *Le charivari*. He responded with twelve studies of female deception in which he seems to have adopted Vigny's belief that "A woman, more or less, is always Delilah." They made little impression, but three years later Gavarni returned to the theme in a subtler and more amiable way with one of his most searching and amusing series. In no. 37 he offers this exchange: "How did you know, papa, that I loved Mr. Leon?—Because you always talked to me about Mr. Paul." Gavarni's playful mastery of female psychology is not the only attraction of the series. If Daumier could not

(151)   *Fourberies de femmes en matière de sentiment*

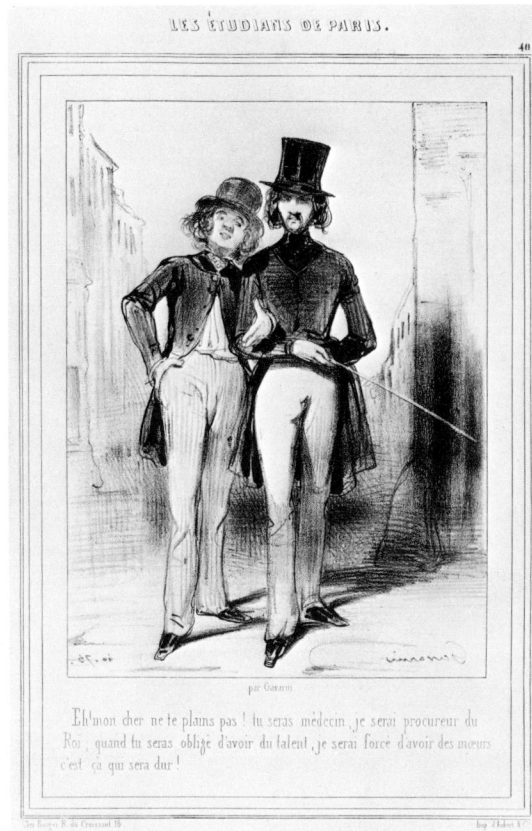

Eh!'mon cher ne te plains pas ! tu seras médecin, je serai procureur du
Roi ; quand tu seras obligé d'avoir du talent, je serai forcé d'avoir des mœurs
c'est ça qui sera dur !

(153)   *Les étudiants de Paris*

draw a pretty woman, as is sometimes alleged, Gavarni at this period could hardly draw an ugly one.

152

[**Les enfans terribles.** Paris, 1838–1842]. 49 hand-colored lithographic plates by Gavarni, heightened with gum arabic; printed by Aubert. Page size: 12⅞ × 10⅛ inches. Bound in the preceding album. Beraldi VII, p. 51.

Gavarni's conception of the *enfant terrible* has passed into a proverb. For all their apparent ingenuousness, his appealing children are preternaturally sharp. They see and hear everything in their little world, and they are infallible in announcing their discoveries where they will cause the most embarrassment. So a little boy asks a visitor: "Sir, who is it that invented gunpowder? . . . since Papa says it isn't you" (no. 10); or a little girl informs a suitor: "Aunt Amelia says that you are very nice; but it's a pity that you are too stupid" (no. 32).

153

[**Les étudians de Paris.** Paris, 1839–1842]. 60 lithographic plates by Gavarni; printed by Aubert. Page size: 13¼ × 9¾ inches. ¾ red morocco by Pagnant. Beraldi VII, p. 51.

This is the first of Gavarni's major series. It concerns students of law and medicine, the flower of French youth, for a few years liberated from the constraints of their bourgeois world. Gavarni knows them intimately, as he does their garret lodgings and chronic lack of money, and he is equally at home with their mistresses, untutored *grisettes* who are loyal and supportive despite their awareness that such liaisons must eventually end. His designs concern the students' distractions rather than their work, which figures only marginally, when a *grisette* expresses wonder at a skeleton or an embryo in a bottle. Occasionally they must think of the proper society from which they came and to which they must return. In no. 40 one student says to another: "Oh! my dear fellow don't complain! you will be a doctor, I'll be public prosecutor; when

LES DÉBARDEURS.

— ..... une douzaine d'huitres et mon cœur
— Ta parole?

(154) *Les débardeurs*

(155) *Les lorettes*

you are obliged to have skill, I'll be forced to behave properly, it's that which will be difficult!"
The success of the series, Lemoisne remarks (I, 84),
owed much to those readers of *Le charivari* who
were enabled by it to relive their own youth.

154

[**Les débardeurs.** Paris, 1840–1842]. 66 hand-colored
lithographic plates by Gavarni, heightened with gum
arabic; printed by Aubert. Page size: 13⅛ × 10⅛
inches. Bookplate of Michael Sadleir. Contemp. ¼
green morocco. Beraldi VII, p. 51.

This is the most considerable of the several series of
lithographs devoted by Gavarni to the balls which
were a passion with him. He was an organizer and
patron of the more elegant, and he found the popular balls at the Opera and elsewhere an attractive
subject for his designs. Théophile Gautier, who believed that at this period Parisian balls had virtually "effaced the former carnival of Venice," called
Gavarni "their depicter and historian." As dan-
cers throw themselves into their round of pleasure,
"a man stands with his back against a pillar; he

watches, he listens, he observes." And the following day on stone "he lends his own wit to all the
masks, perhaps stupid in themselves; he sums up in
a profound word the chit-chat of the foyer; he
translates into a pleasant legend the hoarse excitement of the hall." (Quoted by Lemoisne, I,
120.) In a characteristic design a fantastic young
man offers his masked companion "a dozen oysters
and my heart" for her favors; and she replies, "On
your word?"

155

[**Les lorettes.** Paris, 1841–1843]. 73 (of 79) hand-colored
lithographic plates by Gavarni, numbered 1–18, 25–
79, heightened with gum arabic; printed by Aubert.
Page size: 12⅞ × 9½ inches. Red morocco by Zaehnsdorf. Beraldi VII, p. 51.

This is the most masterly of Gavarni's earlier series. Ladies of the evening of a certain standing
had come to be called *lorettes* because they often
lived in the handsome new buildings of the Rue
Notre Dame de Lorette. No subject could have
been better suited to Gavarni's talents. Indeed,

12.

par Gavarni.

(155) *Les lorettes*

Thomas Vireloque in *Les artistes anciennes et modernes*

(156)   *Carnaval*

Paul de Saint Victor observed (preface to *D'Après nature*, II, 2) that "the lorette is for him what the actress of the Italian Comedy was for Watteau." Gavarni shows them without malice and without indulgence, exactly as they were. The *grisette* of *Les étudiants de Paris* was an ingratiating figure; not so the *lorette*. Love is their business, and they drive hard bargains. They are as luxurious and idle as they are beautiful. Their lives are a tissue of deception and hypocrisy. Among themselves their conversation is cynical to the point of brutality. Their men, usually at least twice their age, also cut a poor figure. At best these gentlemen command a wry irony which derives from their awareness of being dupes. Gavarni presents these brittle and glittering creatures with great deftness. The packed and subtle dialogue of his legends would not be amiss in a novel by Stendhal. It is difficult to select from his remarkable compositions, but one cannot overlook no. 12, in which the backs of a *lorette* and her admirer perfectly express his doubtful reception of her too ingenious story, or no. 27, in which a *lorette* in her bath indulges in

a rare moment of speculative conversation with a friend.

156

[Oeuvres nouvelles de Gavarni. **Carnaval.** Paris, 1846–1847]. 50 lithographic plates by Gavarni, nos. 1–23 and 25 printed on *chine appliqué*; nos. 1–6 printed by Lemercier, nos. 7–50 printed by Aubert. Page size: 12¼×9⅛ inches. ¼ green cloth. Beraldi VII, p. 51.

This is the most substantial and interesting of Gavarni's *Oeuvres nouvelles* of 1846–1847. The change of style to which it bears witness justifies its title of a "new work." Gavarni's compositions have become simpler and more massive; they emphasize the play of light and shade; and they are altogether richer and more velvety in their general aspect. If vestiges of the designer of costumes and fashions remained in his work of the early 1840s, they have now altogether disappeared. "A presentation" (no. 6) is representative of the album as a whole.

⊷ Album of 25 lithographic plates by Gavarni on 24 leaves, chiefly for *Les artistes anciens et modernes*, and *Les artistes contemporains*. 21 of the plates are printed on *chine appliqué*; printed by Bertauts (21) and Lemercier (4). Page size: 15⅛ × 11⅜ inches. From the Beurdeley collection. Green binder's cloth.

This album from the Beurdeley collection includes selected proofs of Gavarni's contributions to Bertauts' two notable lithographic collections, five for *Les artistes contemporains*, eight volumes, 1845–1853, and six for *Les artistes anciens et modernes*, ten volumes, 1848–1862. Particularly revealing with respect to the developing resources of his later style are a superb design in two states of the side-scenes at the Opera (*Les artistes contemporains*, no. 30), a moving study of London poverty (the same, no. 72), and a portrait of Thomas Vireloque (*Les artistes anciens et modernes*, no. 10). These plates in themselves would suffice to demonstrate why critics like Beraldi and Curtis place Gavarni with Géricault, Delacroix, and Daumier among the masters of the lithographic medium.

157

[**Masques et visages.** Paris, 1852–1853]. 329 lithographic plates by Gavarni bound in 3 v.; printed by Lemercier. Beraldi VII, p. 73–75.

(bound with)

[**Le manteau d'Arlequin.** Paris, 1852]. 12 lithographic plates by Gavarni; printed by Lemercier. Page size: 15⅛ × 10¾ inches. Contemp. ¼ purple morocco. Beraldi VII, p. 72–73.

During his years of withdrawal from society Gavarni had been maturing his greatest effort, the immensely long and varied *Masques et visages*. A number of the series that eventually appeared in this work were begun in the late months of 1851, including all of "L'Ecole des pierrots." Gavarni would have nothing further to do with *Le charivari*, but there were abortive beginnings in *L'Illustration* (wood engravings rather than lithographs) and *L'Eclair* (the 12 lithographs of *Le manteau d'Arlequin*). Through the Goncourt brothers, arrangements were finally made with a new literary daily called *Paris*, where between 20 October 1852 and 8 December 1853 280 of Gavarni's lithographs were published. In the ensuing albums forty-nine further lithographs were added for a total of 329.

These appeared in eighteen series divided into units of ten, the more substantial of the series extending to two, three, or even four of these decades.

As his title suggests, Gavarni's preoccupation in *Masques et visages* is the contrast between appearance and reality. Indeed, Lemoisne offers a comparison between Gavarni and La Rochefoucauld, "the brilliant lover of Mme. de Longueville who would one day become the author of the *Maximes*" (II, 114). So in *Masques et visages* youth and beauty have largely disappeared from his scene. He is concerned instead with encroaching age and ugliness. The mordant ironies of Thomas Vireloque expose the imbecility, the egoism, the brutality of a world in which the joyous revelers of *Les débardeurs* have become the sickly and defeated old men of "Les invalides du sentiment."

We may look more closely at three of these series, beginning with "Les anglais chez eux," since it was England which demonstrated to him the misery underlying the plausible surface of society. On the one hand, he shows the lower depths: "Gin" (no. 9), "Misery and her children" (no. 12), and a tramp eyeing with envy the rudimentary costume of a scarecrow (no. 18); on the other, comfortable members of the middle class indifferent to the unhappiness around them. Perhaps of all these plates the most poignant in its implications is no. 16, "A member of a funeral society thinks of the black plumes of his burial."

Thomas Vireloque ("the man speaks") was one of Gavarni's most brilliant inspirations. This philosophical tramp, with his tattered clothes and one-eyed gaze, has his damaging word for every situation. When an orator tells him that "man is the masterpiece of creation," he replies, "And who said that? Man" (no. 9). He remarks about a vacant waif: "He hasn't been educated at all . . . and still he is stupid" (no. 14). Reading newspaper platitudes about "Young Europe," he observes: "a youth of 60 years! and exhausted" (no. 16). Reproduced is the finest of Gavarni's portraits of Vireloque from *Les artistes anciens et modernes* (no. 107).

The communists of this period were called *partageux*. Since pretty ladies shared the wealth of their protectors, Gavarni found the word suitable for them as well. In the series which he devoted to "Les partageuses," the relatively naïve *lorette* of a

Par Gavarni

(157)   *Masques et visages*

(158)   *Par-ci, par-là*

decade earlier has become brazen in her self-assur-
ance. No. 11 offers this exchange between two of
them: "My dear, it is absurd! always the same
song: a woman all to himself."—"Daft! Daft!"
Another such conversation (no. 38) yields the observation: " 'Platonic love.' . . . There's a pose."
In no. 27 a *partageuse* dismisses her noble protector
with the words: "What the devil do you expect
that one should do with your confidence, if not
abuse it?"

Masques et visages, the comprehensive expression
of Gavarni's later view of life, is a neglected masterpiece of nineteenth-century French graphic art.

⊷ Album of prints by Gavarni assembled by Edmond
and Jules de Goncourt, containing their etched bookplate by Gavarni, an engraved portrait, and 16 lithographic plates from *Masques et visages*, including 4 trial
proofs (cut down) and *2 bons à tirer*. Page size: 14⅛ ×
10 inches. ¾ purple morocco by Stroobants.

This album belonged to the Goncourt brothers. It
includes the etched bookplate which Gavarni made
for them, four early proofs, two of them for "Les
partageuses" (nos. 4 and 10), and two final proofs
for "Les invalides du sentiment" on which the publisher has noted his approval of the impression and

the number to be printed. For no. 6, in which an
elderly and dyspeptic diner declares, "My heart
has ruined my stomach," the order is six on China
paper, 300 for album publication, and 3000 for the
periodical *Paris*. See page 218 above.

158

Oeuvres nouvelles de Gavarni. **Par-ci, par-là et Physionomies parisiennes.** 100 sujets. Paris, Aug. Marc, [1857
–1858]. 1 *l.*, 100 lithographic plates (50 in each work)
by Gavarni on *chine appliqué*; printed by Lemercier.
Page size: 16¾ × 11¾ inches. Publisher's ¼ red morocco by Engel. Beraldi VII, p. 51.

Both of these series are continuations of *Masques et
visages*, but their plans differ. The large lithographs
of *Physionomies parisiennes* are devoted to single, full-
length figures, usually of mature years, whose
character, situation in life, or ruling passion is
summed up in Gavarni's legends. Many of the
smaller lithographs of *Par-ci, par-là* are portraits as
well, now seen at three-quarters length, but there
are also a number in which the relationships between pairs of figures are explored. The most striking of these, which shows a lady of a certain age
with a young but by no means artless cavalier,

could serve as the *donnée* of a novel: "Phedra at the Théâtre Français. The debut of Mr. Paul of Three-stars in the role of Hippolytus" (no. 7). The handsome gold-stamped bindings of these volumes were designed by Gavarni himself.

159

D'Après nature par Gavarni, texte par MM. Jules Janin, Paul de Saint-Victor, Edmond Texier, Edmond et Jules de Goncourt . . . Paris, Morizot, [1858?]. 4 v. I: [2] *l.*, 16 p. II: [2] *l.*, 16 p. III: [2] *l.*, 15 p. IV: [2] *l.*, 16 p. Illus: Each volume with wood-engraved t.p. vignette and 10 lithographic plates by Gavarni. Page size: 15¼ × 10⅞ inches. Bookplate of Michael Sadleir. Publisher's polychrome *cartonnage*. Beraldi VII, p. 79–80.

In the title of his last important series Gavarni reiterated his affirmation of thirty years earlier: "it is from nature above all that one must work." The plates are among the most penetrating and compassionate of his career. A woman of the people tells her son with disgust: "You are good for nothing: make yourself an artist" (II, 15). "An orgy" (III, 26) shows an elderly bibliophile avidly searching through the 50 centime box of a Seine bookstall. Finest of all, and a fitting farewell from Gavarni, is a plate in which a pretty girl, who might come from one of his early albums, is assessed from the perspective of his final years: "Much will be forgiven her because she has danced so much"

(159) *D'après nature*

(IV, 40). These four volumes, in their handsome polychrome bindings, reproduced in Appendix I, seem to have been intended as a tribute to the artist. Each has its accompanying essay, that by Edmond and Jules de Goncourt in volume four being a classic of appreciative criticism.

Honoré Daumier (1808–1879)

Daumier is the greatest artist with whom this survey deals. His serious reputation dates from Baudelaire's "Quelques caricaturistes françaises," an essay which went through several reworkings and reached its final form only in 1857. Though Baudelaire declared that Daumier was "one of the most important men, I don't say only of caricature, but even of modern art" (p. 999), his praise had the

effect of fixing Daumier in the public mind as a great caricaturist. For some time there has been a disposition to question this description as too restrictive. Insofar as his paintings and sculpture are concerned, the point may be granted. But in his more than 4000 lithographs, the most significant part of his *oeuvre*, he was a supreme popular entertainer who worked in large part through caricature. To suppress this fundamental fact is to introduce an element of preciosity into the approach to his work which is foreign to the nature of its creator.

For example, Roger Passeron's two enlightening books on Daumier emphasize first, the early states of his lithographs, and second, individual plates, almost always those in which caricature is subordinate, remarkable for their beauty of composition and design. However, as Jean Laran points out, in what is still the most judicious discussion of the subject, "There are so to speak no *states* in the case of Daumier. . . . With rare exceptions, the variants that one remarks are not from his hand and don't relate to the design; they concern the lettering or accessory details." They are important primarily as assurances of early printing. And, though the supreme beauty of these impressions is undeniable, Aubert's first regular printing *sur blanc* (on white paper, without text on the reverse) for album publication was "usually very honorable." (Pp. 16–17.) Only the subsequent impressions in *Le charivari*, on poor paper with the reverse text showing through as a series of broken lines, are distinctly inferior.

In a survey of the illustrated book it is logical to approach Daumier's lithographs historically and as a whole, in terms of the periodicals in which his political plates appeared and the *albums comiques* in which his studies of manners were assembled. Neither need there be any prejudice against the element of caricature in his work. In this way a truer picture of his achievement can be provided than by excluding the great mass of his lithographs which don't altogether meet the rigid criteria of late twentieth-century print collectors.

Daumier was born in Marseilles in 1808. His father, a glazier with poetical aspirations, brought the family to Paris in 1815. Daumier served as a notary's errand boy, but after a time he was allowed to become an artist. Rejecting formal training, he chose instead to walk about Paris and sketch. He learned lithography from a friend and began to draw in the manner of Charlet, as may be seen in his first lithograph, a contribution to *La silhouette* (146). His political caricatures for Aubert and others, which expressed his unwavering liberal and humanitarian convictions, included a plate called "Gargantua." This was the cause of

(146)   Daumier's first caricature in *La silhouette*

his being sentenced to six months in Sainte-Pélagie. Prison life was hard, but Daumier went on drawing, and Charles Philipon recruited him for *La caricature*, with consequences that are described below. It was at this time that Balzac said of him: "That joker there has a bit of Michelangelo under his skin" (quoted by Escholier, p. 24).

When *La caricature* was suppressed in 1835, Daumier perforce shifted his attention to studies of manners in *Le charivari*, though he continued as a contributor to the milder, but still political, *Caricature provisoire*. His chief album of this transitional period was *Caricaturana*. As the title indicates, this history of Robert Macaire was a continuation of *La caricature* in another mode, dealing with private rather than public life. Daumier's change of focus proved fortunate, for outside the political arena, this ferocious republican was a mild, serene, good man. He lived in his atelier on the Ile Saint Louis, after 1846 with his amiable and devoted wife, occupying himself entirely with his art. He wanted to be a painter, but most of his working hours went necessarily to the lithography by which he earned his daily bread. His friends were chiefly other artists, among them Barye, Corot, Daubigny, Delacroix, Diaz, and Meissonier.

(161)   Daumier and Macaire as portrayed in *Caricaturana*

During the years 1837 to 1851, as Passeron has shown in a useful chart and analysis (pp. 120–127), Daumier drew 1711 lithographs, 1108 of which are grouped in series. If "the true glory and the true mission of Gavarni and Daumier has been to complete Balzac," as already noted, Daumier made his contribution largely through these plates, which, at least in the case of the more substantial sequences, were collected by Aubert in albums. For our purposes a stringent selection must be made among these collections, though none is without its claim to attention.

The central panel in his "immense satirical fresco of the French bourgeoisie during the first half of the nineteenth century" (Champfleury, quoted by Beraldi, v, 108) is constituted by four major series: *Les beaux jours de la vie, Moeurs conjugales, Les bons bourgeois*, eighty-two plates, 1847–1849, and *Tout ce qu'on voudra*, seventy plates, 1847–1851. These display the private lives of the middle class generally, as do such shorter albums as *Croquis d'expression*, fifty-three plates, 1838–1839, and *Emotions parisiennes*, fifty-one plates, 1839–1842. Passeron (pp. 127–129) has recently held that *Les bons*

bourgeois is the best of all, on the ground that Daumier made a great advance away from caricature as the 1840s progressed.

Next come the series confined to discrete groups within this immense population. The most esteemed of these, *Les gens de justice*, thirty-nine plates, 1845–1848, was apparently not issued as an album. (This circumstance may account for the relative rarity of its plates, which have long commanded much higher prices than the rest of Daumier's lithographs.) Daumier's animosity towards lawyers is evident throughout his work. They are the subject of some of his finest paintings, but nowhere are they exposed so mercilessly and so comprehensively as in *Les gens de justice*. The play that they make with their robes, their exaggerated courtroom expressions and gestures, their egregious vanity, and their blatant neglect of their clients' interests are presented with restrained anger. Daumier, who believed that women should be womanly, also disliked the rebellious literary ladies of the time, as is to be seen in the self-centered and fanatical figures of *Les bas bleus*. Far more typical in its amiability is *Professeurs et moutards*, thirty-two plates, 1845–1846, where he deals with schoolchildren and their teachers. Finally, there are two albums unique in Daumier's work: *Histoire ancienne*, in which he settled his quarrel with the Greeks and the Romans, and *Les baigneurs*, where he portrayed the naked human form with an unblinking fidelity that opened the eyes of his fellow artists.

Throughout this panorama of the French bourgeoisie Daumier is a caricaturist, indeed a satirist. Yet, like Dickens in his exactly contemporary record of English middle-class life, he is also the poet of these small lives. His attitude is best defined by Baudelaire (p. 1005): "No one like him has known and loved (in the manner of artists) the bourgeois, that last vestige of the Middle Ages, that Gothic ruin whose life is so hard, that type at once so commonplace and so eccentric. Daumier has lived intimately with him, he has spied on him night and day, he has learned the mysteries of his alcove, he has established relations with his wife and children, he knows the form of his nose and the shape of his head, he comprehends the spirit that animates the household from top to bottom."

With the fall of Louis Philippe in 1848 Daumier returned to political caricature. A series of portraits for *Le charivari* called *Les représentans représentés* occupied much of his time in the two following years. During the remainder of his career as a lithographer, however, most of his political plates, as well as most of his studies of manners, appeared in a catchall series called *Actualités*. He offered a vigorous commentary on the rise of Louis Napoleon, sometimes through his Bonapartist adventurer Ratapoil, until censorship was reimposed on domestic political caricature. Then he turned to foreign affairs, where the vicissitudes of European diplomacy, particularly during the Crimean War, offered him many opportunities. In the worst days of the Franco-Prussian War Daumier responded to France's agony with designs, such as those in *Album du siège*, which surpass in grandeur even his great plates for *La caricature*.

Daumier's later years were not the period of penury and obscurity that has sometimes been alleged. He continued to make his living by lithography, despite a three-year break in his employment by *Le charivari*. Indeed, almost 1800 of his more than 4000 lithographs date from after 1851. Painting was his great passion, which he pursued both in Paris and at Valmondois in the valley of the Oise. When incipient blindness ended his career as a lithographer in 1872, he retired to this village, where the sale of his paintings and a pension from the state provided him with a modest living. An exhibition of his work in Paris during 1878, the year before his death, was a success with artists and critics, if not with the public.

No illustrator has ever depended less on words than Daumier. He drew *Les Robert-Macaire* to fit Philipon's legends and *Histoire ancienne* to comment on verses by Albéric Second. Elsewhere he was usually content for staff members of *Le charivari* to provide captions for his designs, vouchsafing the briefest replies to inquiries about his intentions. In making his point by drawing, he relied on memory rather than models. Indeed, when a friend showed him ducks at his request, since he had to include one in a lithograph, he refused a proferred sketchbook with the remark: "you know that I can't draw from nature" (Laran, p. 12). His method, Geoffroy said (quoted by Escholier, p. 122), was to "reflect after nature." To render the images that memory supplied he relied on his comprehensive command of lithography, his ability to render

mass and form, light and shade, in a direct, concentrated way. The artists of his time recognized his mastery. There is a story of Daubigny in Rome stopping before the Moses of Michelangelo to exclaim: "It's a Daumier" (Beraldi, v, 101). What Daubigny and a few others once saw in Daumier is now seen by the whole world.

REFERENCES Baudelaire; Beraldi; *Bibliothèque Nationale: Daumier*; Delteil—*Daumier*; Escholier; Laran; Larkin; *National Gallery of Art: Daumier*; Passeron (1968); Passeron (1979); Vincent.

160

La caricature, journal fondé et dirigé par Ch. Philipon . . . Paris, Aubert, 1830–1835. 10 v. in 6. Collates as in Vicaire. Page size: 13½ × 10¼ inches. Contemp. ¼ red morocco; various wrappers bound in. Vicaire II, 46–81.

Among volumes devoted to pictorial satire, *La caricature* is perhaps the most famous. Despite continuous harassment from its founding until its final suppression, it was unwavering in the ferocity with which it attacked Louis Philippe and his regime. In a "Prospectus et Numéro-Modèle" Charles Philipon explained why the time was ripe for *La caricature*. In France as in England, he argued, caricature had become a power in the land. Indeed, Charlet and Monnier with their designs, like Béranger with his poems, had prepared the way for the Revolution of July. And thanks to the cheapness of lithography, caricature could at last take periodical form. "It was not a laughing audience that was lacking for prints, but prints for a laughing audience." At the price of 46 francs for fifty-two issues, each consisting of two lithographs and four pages of text, *La caricature* would be within the means of the great public.

Though Philipon cast his net widely among the artists of the day, *La caricature* made its mark largely through two artists, Grandville and Daumier. In its early years, indeed until mid-1834, the former was the dominant figure. With the considerable assistance of E. Forest, he typically expressed his powerful animus in large, crowded designs. There is plenty of extravagant invention and bitter wit in these drawings, but only occasionally, as in the relatively spare and forceful "La France livrée

(160) Lithograph by Grandville and E. Forest in *La caricature*

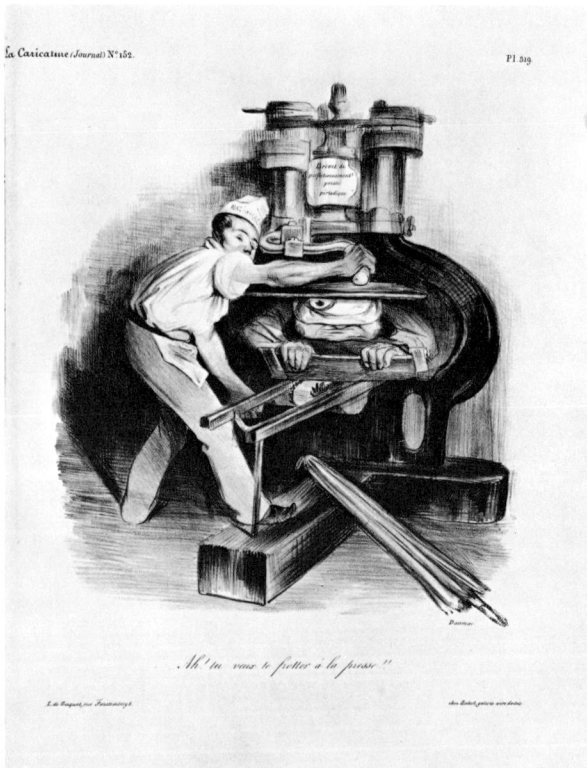

(160) Lithograph by Daumier in *La caricature*

(160) Lithograph by Daumier in *La caricature*

aux corbeaux" (plate 100), did he achieve a memorable simplicity. Otherwise, though Grandville's lithographs admirably served their polemical purpose, his scattershot technique (his most common arrangement is a mere procession) denied him the mastery of composition which marks the inventions of Gillray that in part were his inspiration.

"Gargantua," Daumier's first lithograph intended for *La caricature*, was suppressed, though Philipon did not fail to point out that it could be obtained at Aubert's shop (29 December 1831). As has already been mentioned, it brought Daumier six months in prison. When he did begin to contribute, his designs were for the most part likenesses of July Monarchy politicians, marked by a sculptural solidity and a fidelity of observation not previously achieved in lithography. Enjoined to respect the government, Philipon ironically announced these as "exaggerated portraits" of members of "the not-prostituted chamber, . . . as exact as it is possible to make them at the top of the gallery where the journalists are coffined" (13 June 1833). And as this "monument to contemporary folly" progressed, he came to refer to its subjects more simply and insultingly as *improstituées*. The most impressive of these portraits, and certainly the least exaggerated or "charged," was that of Guizot (17 December 1833), for whom even *La caricature* preserved a modicum of respect.

(160)   Lithograph by Daumier in *La caricature*

Formidable as Daumier's portraits were, however, he made his strongest impression in *La caricature* with the scenes, now symbolic, now realistic, in which he summed up in unforgettable images the oppressive practices of the July Monarchy. Indeed, his weighty and concentrated designs made Grandville's busy inventions seem inconsequential in comparison. Consider, for example, two parallel drawings: plate 92 (15 September 1831), in which Grandville and Forest show the regime grinding the faces of the poor to increase its revenues, and plate 319 (3 October 1833), in which Daumier shows a sturdy workman compressing the countenance of Louis Philippe. In the former, Argout, Talleyrand, and other ministers are hard at their evil work, and the transformation into coin of their victims is properly horrifying. But once its polemical point is made, the image fades. Daumier is equally effective in a topical way. Even in his unfamiliar posture, the Citizen King hardly needs his umbrella to identify him. But Daumier also makes his drawing a general and permanent embodiment of the maxim: "Whoever interferes with the press will perish by the press."

Daumier didn't really come into his own, however, until *La caricature*'s final twelve months. By August of 1834 his great lithographs for *L'Association mensuelle* had made their impression, and he had become the periodical's leading artist. Fifty of his ninety-one drawings for *La caricature* date from this period, and often both plates in an issue were from his hand. Among many masterpieces, a few may be specifically mentioned: "Magot de la Chine" (plate 416), "Celui-là on peut le mettre en liberté" (420), "Baissez le rideau, la farce est jouée" (421), "Le fantôme" (488), "Vous avez la parole, expliquez vous" (490), and "C'était vraiment la peine de nous faire tuer" (524 and last). "The phantom," perhaps the grandest of all, is drawn from a passage in Barthélémy's *Némésis* which tells how the Chamber of Peers will remain haunted as long as those who voted for Marshall Ney's execution continue to sit there. It is shown here in the very rare first state.

La caricature has many kinds of importance, historical as well as artistic, but the amateur of illustrated books will treasure it as the most notable collection of Daumier's political lithographs and hence one of the highpoints of his career.

Though it had a large initial circulation, complete sets in acceptable condition have become very uncommon.

161

[**Caricaturana (Les Robert-Macaire**). Paris, 1836–1838]. 100 hand-colored lithographic plates by Daumier, heightened with gum arabic; printed by Aubert, and Aubert & Junca. Inserted at end is an 8-p. publisher's catalogue by Aubert. Page size: 13¼ × 6¼ inches. Bookplate of Michael Sadleir. Publisher's blue *cartonnage*. Beraldi v, p. 124.

Les Robert-Macaire remains Daumier's best-known series, though its reputation with collectors of prints has declined sharply over the years. Baudelaire chose it, along with *Histoire ancienne*, for specific discussion in his essay on French caricaturists, and Carteret accorded it a place in his bibliography. Its contemporary popularity was immense. As an album it was published by Aubert in an edition of 2500 copies, a far larger number than for any other series. Yet, so persistent was the demand, that 6000 two-volume sets of reduced copies, called *Les cent-et-un Robert-Macaire*, were published in 1839. (Delteil, before no. 354.) The renown of the series seems to have become irksome to Daumier. According to Escholier (p. 88), he remarked: "Why is it that they talk to me all the time about my Robert Macaire? It is perhaps the worst thing I have done."

When politics became a forbidden topic in *Le charivari*, where *Caricaturana* first appeared, Daumier and Philipon turned to social satire. If they could not attack Louis Philippe directly, they could at least show the kind of society that flourished under his gross and venal regime. Taking the flamboyant and florid swindler Macaire from the character that Frédéric Lemaître had created in a hack melodrama called *L'Auberge des adrets*, they showed him and his inseparable companion, the dejected and meager Bertrand, ranging through all kinds of commercial enterprise, in the stock market, in the banks, in the courts, and in dozens of other public settings, never failing to find eager dupes. Macaire is equally persuasive in the encounters of private life, where no situation finds him at a loss for an appropriate flower of sentiment. As *Caricaturana* progresses, Macaire is even

Ch. Ph. inv. H. D. lith.   Chez Aubert gal. vero-dodat   Imp. d'Aubert et C.

Le public, mon cher, le public est stupide..... nous le saignons à blanc, nous le purgeons à mort, il n'est pas content..... il veut du nouveau..... donnons lui en, morbleu, du nouveau! faisons nous homœopates..... il aime les blagues, traitons le par les semblables Similia Similibus (Bertrand) Amen. Tiens, voici une ordonnance qui résume le système! Prendre un tout petit grain de .... de rien du tout .... le couper en dix millions de mollécules .... jeter une .... une seule de ces dixmillionièmes parties dans la rivière .... remuer, remuer, triturer beaucoup .... laisser infuser quelques heures .... puiser un seau de cette eau bienfaisante .... la filtrer .... la couper avec 20 parties d'eau ordinaire et s'en humecter la langue tous les matins à jeun .... Voilà! —Est-ce tout? —Oui .... Ah! diable!! j'oubliais le principal .... Payer la présente ordonnance.

(161) *Caricaturana*

to be found flattering its creator, remarking, as if he had no personal stake in the matter, "Monsieur Daumier, your series of Robert-Macaire is a charming thing! . . . It is the exact portrayal of the rascalities of our time. . . . You don't yet have the cross of honor? . . . It is revolting ! ! " (No. 78.) Though Daumier's designs are superb in themselves, particularly in the variety of supple and telling poses (such as that for no. 70) that he conceives for Macaire and Bertrand, they would be incomplete without the unfailing wit and point of Philipon's captions. It may be suggested that a major reason for the fading appeal of *Caricaturana* has been the neglect of its legends. When they are taken fully into account, as Thackeray does in his essay on "Caricatures and Lithography in France" in *The Paris Sketch Book*, these lithographs remain wonderfully amusing.

Caricaturana is not often encountered in black. Aubert sold many albums colored, and copies issued in black often passed through a colorist's hands at a later date. Of all Daumier's series, however, it suffers least from such additions. Certainly book collectors, with whom it has always been a favorite, have traditionally preferred it in this form.

162

Les cent-et-un Robert-Macaire, composés et dessinés par M. H. Daumier, sur les idées et les légendes de M. Ch. Philipon, réduits et lithographiés par MM. ***; texte par MM. Maurice Alhoy et Louis Huart. Paris, Aubert, 1839. 2 v. I: [3, 100, 2] *l.,* including wood-engraved front. and 100 lithographic plates with letterpress text on versos. II: [3, 102, 2] *l.,* including wood-engraved front. and 102 lithographic plates with letterpress text on versos. 4-p. publisher's catalogue by Aubert bound in. Page size: 11 ×8⅝ inches. Contemp. ½ calf. Carteret III, 187; Beraldi V, p. 124.

These reduced and for the most part reversed copies of Daumier's lithographs, apparently drawn by Menut Alophe, are greatly inferior to the originals. Unlike *Caricaturana,* the series is not often found colored.

163

[**Robert-Macaire.** 2ᵉ série. Paris, 1840–1841]. 20 hand-colored lithographic plates by Daumier, heightened with gum arabic; printed by Aubert. Page size: 13¾ × 10⅛ inches. Bookplate of Michael Sadleir. ½ brown calf. Beraldi V, p. 124.

Macaire remarks in *Caricaturana:* "Fools will never disappear." With this in mind Daumier and Philipon embarked with confidence on a second series of *Robert-Macaire.* The plates are not inferior to those in *Caricaturana,* but the vogue of Macaire and Bertrand had apparently died away. At any rate, of the fifty plates announced (Delteil, no. 866), only twenty appeared.

164

Le musée pour rire, dessins par tous les caricaturistes de Paris; texte par MM. Maurice Alhoy, Louis Huart, et Ch. Philipon . . . Paris, Aubert, 1839–1840. 3 v. I: [2, 100, 2], *l.,* including 50 plates with letterpress on versos: 49 hand-colored lithographs heightened with gum arabic by: anonymous (1), Buchot (5), Daumier (27), Gavarni (14), Pigal (1), and Traviès (1); 1 hand-colored wood engraving after Grandville. II: [2, 100, 2] *l.,* including 50 plates with letterpress on versos: 49 hand-colored lithographs heightened with gum arabic by: Benjamin (4), Bourdet (3), Buchot (17), Daumier (9), Gavarni (15), and Pigal (1); 1 hand-colored wood engraving after Grandville. III: [2, 100, 2] *l.,* including 50 hand-colored lithographic plates heightened with gum arabic, with letterpress text on versos by: Victor Adam (10), Buchot (1), Daumier (9), Gavarni (13), Alophe Menut (2), Platel (2), Plattier (7), Pruche (3), T** (1), and Vernier (2). Page size: 10×7⅝ inches. Bookplate of Michael Sadleir. ¼ green morocco, orig. wrappers bound in. Carteret III, 426–427.

The house of Aubert was ingenious in marketing its products. Its lithographs, as we have seen, were published one by one in periodicals like *Le charivari* and together in *suites* by the same artist without letterpress. Still a third form of publication was in albums made up of lithographs by several artists with accompanying texts. These collections most commonly took the form of volumes with the generic title *Paris comique,* which consisted of twenty colored lithographs accompanied by quite unrelated texts. Aubert remarked that the resulting hodgepodge had "a plan that is easy to follow, for it consists in not having any," and in fact this was indeed a frugal procedure for reusing old texts and already published plates. The interest of the various volumes of *Paris comique* resides entirely in the lithographs they happen to contain. It can be considerable, however, since Daumier and Gavarni are the predominant artists. *Le musée pour rire* represents a more considerable effort on the part of

(165)   *Moeurs conjugales*

Aubert. To accompany 150 lithographs, including forty-five by Daumier (among them twenty-seven from *Croquis d'expression* and eight from *La galerie physionomique*) and forty-two by Gavarni, new commentaries were commissioned on each plate, all except two by Alhoy and Huart. Daumier's lithographs were trimmed slightly, and their captions were relettered. The designs of the other artists were provided with decorative frames. The whole was then published in three handsome volumes, and in copies with expert contemporary coloring like this one, *Le musée pour rire* is among the freshest and most attractive of romantic illustrated books.

165

[**Moeurs conjugales.** Paris, 1839–1842]. 60 lithographic plates by Daumier; printed by Aubert. Page size: 13½ × 10½ inches. Contemp. (publisher's?) ¼ green calf. Beraldi v, p. 125.

These studies of the married condition make up one of Daumier's most characteristic albums. His husbands and wives are not pretty to look at. They are not well matched. They have no great opinion of each other. But they manage to jog along together. Their chief pleasures and irritations de-

rive from their children and their pets. Infidelity, real or imagined, touches their lives, but Daumier, unlike Gavarni, does not make it an overwhelming preoccupation. In the happy family of no. 4, where Daumier has drawn himself as the father, a little boy offers his crude drawings to papa as a birthday gift. Less heartening is the monumental boredom of the couple in "Six months of marriage" (no. 7).

166

[Cover-title:] Plaisirs de l'été . . . [**Les baigneurs**]. Paris, [1840–1842]. Lithographic cover printed in gold and 30 hand-colored lithographic plates by Daumier, heightened with gum arabic; printed by Aubert. Page size: 13¼ × 10 inches. Green cloth. Beraldi v, p. 125.

Among the locales that Daumier frequented to replenish his prodigious visual memory were the cold baths along the Seine. What he saw led to two notable series of lithographs, *Les baigneurs* and *Les baigneuses*, each offered to the public by Aubert under the title of *Les plaisirs de l'été*. Their revelation of "unaccommodated man," the human body as it really is, totally contradicted the idealized representations of both baroque and neoclassical artists. Many found his designs ugly, but they were

(166) *Les baigneurs*

assiduously copied by Delacroix, who once told Daumier: "There is no man whom I esteem and admire more than you" (Escholier, p. 50). In *Les baigneurs* Daumier devotes the majority of his plates to the cold baths, and most of the rest to riverside scenes. Their subjects are less important than the vision of naked humanity that they convey, though mention may be made of no. 13, in which one old friend tells another: "in the water I didn't recognize you; I took you for a lion." Like *Les Robert-Macaire*, *Les baigneurs* no longer enjoys quite the favor with print collectors that it has in the past.

167

[**Histoire ancienne.** Paris, 1841–1842]. 50 lithographic plates by Daumier; printed by Aubert. Inserted at end is an 8-p. catalogue by Aubert. Page size: 12⅞×9⅞ inches. Contemp. purple boards. Beraldi v, p. 126.

This series appeared in *Le charivari* with a magniloquent preface announcing that Daumier would present "the heroic age unveiled," showing the Greeks and Romans as they really were. In his fifty plates he does indeed reduce the ideal figures of antiquity to the level of common humanity by offering undignified and damaging interpretations of familiar moments of legend and history. A *succès de scandale* initially, the series has been a subject of controversy ever since. Even among Daumier's warmest admirers, there are those who find its chief claim to notice in the fact that, like *Les baigneurs*, it contains a good number of his infrequent studies of the nude.

For Baudelaire *Histoire ancienne* was important as "the best paraphrase of the celebrated verse: *Who will deliver us from the Greeks and the Romans?*" Showing Achilles, Ulysses, Telemachus, and the

Chez Bauger, R. du Croissant, 16.   Chez Aubert, Pl. de la Bourse, 29.   Imp. d'Aubert & Cie.

LE BEAU NARCISSE.

Il était jeune et beau, de leurs douces haleines
Les zéphirs caressaient ses contours pleins d'attraits,
Et dans le miroir des fontaines
Il aimait comme nous à contempler ses traits.

Quatrain intime de Mr. Narcisse de Salvandy.

UN TRIOMPHE D'AVOCAT.

Viens contre mon cœur, tu es acquitté!... entre nous, tu méritais bien d'aller aux galères car tu es
un fier gueux.... mais n'importe il est toujours bien doux de sauver ses semblables!.....

(Le voleur fort ému chippe la bourse de son défenseur, histoire d'emporter un souvenir d'estime et d'amitié)

rest as if played by superannuated tragic actors, Daumier offered a "blasphemy" which was "very amusing" and "had its usefulness." It might displease poets like Théodore de Banville, who regarded Helen as others do the Virgin Mary, but those whose respect for Olympus was minimal could only rejoice. (*Oeuvres*, p. 1006.) That the series is funny, after its fashion, can hardly be denied. Once one has seen Helen cocking a snook at Menelaus (no. 1), Socrates dancing the cancan (no. 10), Alcibiades parading with his tailless poodle (no. 19), Narcissus smirking at his image in a pool (no. 23), and Endymion snoring in the moonlight (no. 45), it is not easy to forget these images. Daumier could not have conceived a more vigorous affirmation of his motto: "One must be of one's own time." He returned to the subject in much the same spirit in his wood engravings for Huart's *Ulysse, ou les porcs vengés* of 1852.

(168)   *Les beaux jours de la vie*

168

[**Les beaux jours de la vie.** Paris, 1843–1846]. 90 (of 100) hand-colored lithographic plates by Daumier, heightened with gum arabic; printed by Aubert. Inserted at end is a 16-p. publisher's catalogue by Aubert. Page size: 13⅛×9¾ inches. Bookplate of Michael Sadleir. Contemp. purple cloth. Beraldi v, p. 126.

This sequence of "happy days," only a few of which are quite the reverse, is Daumier's most extensive and ambitious album of the 1840s. Since he has taken his subjects from all aspects of life, it offers a conspectus of his other albums. The designs have a common pattern, large, knee-length figures, rarely more than two or three to a plate, presented with such solidity and animation as to make each "a moment's monument." The small satisfactions and disappointments of the middle class are shown for the most part with benignant sympathy. There is an "amateur of melons" whose delight in finding "the melon of his dreams" is almost seraphic (no. 73). Amidst a rapt audience at the Porte St.-Martin Theater a young man of the people expresses his enthusiasm in forceful if primitive terms (no. 83). Even the legal subjects are comic rather than grim. Indeed, in one of them (no. 42) the client actually gets the better of his lawyer, lifting his purse as "a souvenir of esteem

and friendship." The bourgeois husband and wife beside their portrait at the Salon, thinking themselves admired by an art student, are not disturbed in their complacency by the fact that he is inwardly deriding them. Even the group shown in "A first trip by rail" (no. 90), though their staring or firmly shut eyes reveal their apprehension, in fact has nothing to worry about. As Beraldi remarks, this is a "very important series, in which one finds superb plates" (v, 126).

169

[**Les bas-bleus.** Paris, 1844]. 40 lithographic plates by Daumier; printed by Aubert. Page size: 13×9½ inches. ½ brown calf. Beraldi v, p. 126.

The bluestockings of this series are almost all literary ladies, and Daumier's satire is directed as much against the literary character in general as its feminine manifestations. At the same time, his attitude towards his subjects is consistently severe, and the fact that he made all forty plates in eight months, whereas most of his longer series extended over several years, suggests that they were inspired by deep-seated and well-developed convictions.

(169)   *Les bas bleus*

(170)   *Les baigneuses*

Advocates of women's rights have as little reason to be grateful to Daumier for *Les bas bleus* as Jews have to be grateful to Forain for *Psst...!* (335).

Nevertheless, the album contains some masterly designs. No. 10 displays a lady novelist in a restaurant, the object of the amused glances of male diners, who is indignant because the newspaper she is reading contains no mention of her new story. The library scene of no. 13 places another lady novelist, working up background for her next book from piles of volumes spread around her, between two male readers, one hardly able to contain his rage and the other regarding her askance with alarmed distaste. No. 17 shows a first night at the Odeon, where the male audience is unpleasantly surprised when calls of "author! author!" bring forth a large lady of forbidding aspect. No. 25 depicts a meeting of a female academy at which the president vainly tries to enforce the rule that only five members may speak at the same time. In the final plates Daumier allows his maligned bluestockings to complain about him. How does it happen, asks one of them standing before a poster for *Les bas bleus*, that "the government permits such infamous things to be advertised?" (No. 40.) It is all most unfair and most entertaining.

170

[Cover-title:] Les plaisirs de l'été. [**Les baigneuses**]. Paris, [1847]. Lithographic cover printed in gold and 17 lithographic plates by Daumier; printed by Aubert. Page size: $10 \times 12\frac{7}{8}$ inches. ½ brown morocco. Beraldi V, p. 127.

It was inevitable that Daumier should complement *Les baigneurs* with *Les baigneuses*. One of the plates in the earlier series (no. 11) shows male bathers peering through cracks in a partition at female bathers, and two others (nos. 20 and 21) show the women's baths themselves. Though the subjects in this album are clothed, Daumier's masterly designs allow the viewer to divine the bodies beneath their loose, full costumes. Indeed, his drawings, as in the scene of two women admiring the figure of a third (no. 15), have a three-dimensional solidity that carries one back to the lithographs of *L'Association mensuelle*.

171

Les représentans représentés . . . *1er série*. La constituante. Paris, Bureau du Charivari, [Aubert, 1848–1849]. Lithographic t.p. and 30 (of 50) lithographic plates by Daumier: nos. 1, 2, 8, 10, 11, 13–16, 24, 30, 32, 45, and 50 uncolored, nos. 3, 3, 12, 17–20, 23, 25–29, 34, 35, 37–40, 42–44, and 46–49 hand-colored, heightened with gum arabic; plates 19 and 24 duplicated.

(172) *Les représentans représentés*

(173) Lithograph by Daumier in *Actualités*

172

[**Les représentans représentés** . . . *deuxième série* (Assemblée Législative). Paris, Aubert, 1849–1850]. 29 (of 37) lithographic plates by Daumier: nos. 3, 6, 8, 10, 14, 15, and 18 uncolored; nos. 1, 5, 11–13, 17, 20–22, 24, 25, and 27–37 hand-colored, heightened with gum arabic. Page size: 13⅞ × 10½ inches. Bookplate of Michael Sadleir. Contemp. ¼ purple calf. Beraldi v, p. 130.

Among the consequences of Daumier's resumption of political caricature in 1848 were these portraits of the members of the new legislative assembly. Their disproportionately large heads, a form of exaggeration to which even Daumier's skill can hardly reconcile the viewer, make them greatly inferior to the similar series in *La caricature*. The portrait of Vaulabelle (I, 38), the least "charged" of the series, still pales beside Daumier's earlier study of Guizot. The device works best with Victor Hugo (II, 13), in whose case a vast forehead is not merely arbitrary. Other figures in whom posterity still takes an interest are Proudhon (I, 11) and Tocqueville (II, 5).

173

[**Actualités**. Paris, 1854–1855]. 144 lithographic plates (lacking 11–14, 16–18, 24, and 26, but with 29 and 41 *bis*) by: Daumier (75), Cham (57), and Vernier (12). Page size: 10¼ × 13½ inches. Bookplate of Michael Sadleir. Green cloth. Beraldi v, p. 131–132.

This album may stand as an example of Daumier's political caricatures for *Le charivari* during the 1850s. Many of its lithographs are routine, but from time to time one encounters a memorable image. "The bear restrained" of 18 August 1854 dates from the early months of the Crimean War. Though Russian troops were in Turkey, European opinion prevented open hostilities until the following month. The "imperial stamp" will be noted on the plate.

174

Album du siège par Cham et Daumier. Recueil de caricatures publiées pendant le siège dans Le Charivari. [Paris], Bureau du Charivari, [1870–1871]. Gillotage t.p. and 40 Gillotage plates, 10 by Daumier and 30 by Cham. Bound in is a complete set of t.p. and plates on *papier de chine*. Page size: 12½ × 9½ inches. ¾ red morocco by Hélène Alix, orig. wrappers bound in. Beraldi v, p. 133.

For many of Daumier's admirers his lithographs of 1870–1871 represent the peak of his achievement. They are in his last style, massive, stripped down, direct, which speaks as nothing else could

(174) Gillotage after Daumier in *Album du siège*

for this tragic period in France's history. Particularly to be noted are his bitter reflections on the legend which Charlet, Bellangé, Raffet, and their imitators had helped to create. The desolate battleground of "The empire means peace" (no. 26) offers an ironic commentary on an epigram uttered by Napoleon III in 1852. His "Square Napoléon" (no. 14) displays the gravestones of those for whose death the Emperor has been responsible, beginning with the Boulevard Monmartre in the winter of 1851 and ending with Sedan in 1870. In Cham's "The reverse of the Saint Helena medal" (no. 30), indeed, the country's disaster is attributed specifically to Napoleon Bonaparte as well as to Napoleon III. Daumier's first plate for 1871, showing France "Appalled by her heritage" (no. 17), is bleak indeed, but a later design offers a gleam of hope: "Poor France! . . . The trunk blasted, but the roots hold fast" (no. 33).

It should be mentioned that Cham's contributions to this album, though trivial in comparison with Daumier's monumental compositions, are by no means negligible. He provides the detail that Daumier omitted. The horrors of the bombardment are recorded in his plates, but so too is the black humor of Parisian life during the siege. For example, he shows the population pursuing food in any form—horses, cats, rats, even a large woman regarded with speculation by an impudent boy: "No more meat!—Let's go then!" (no. 20).

The plates included in *Album du siège* were transferred to zinc for engraving by Gillot's process rather than printed directly from Daumier's litho-

(174) Gillotage after Daumier in *Album du siège*

graphic stones. However, in this copy of *Album du siège*, which may be unique, there is a set of proofs of these reproductions on white China paper which are printed in rich blacks not approached by the grey impressions on cream paper of the ordinary edition.

This book has been composed, printed, and bound by
The Stinehour Press and The Meriden Gravure Company.
The design is by Stephen Harvard. The text is set
in Monotype Baskerville, with Bulmer and
Foundry Baskerville for display.